GOD'S WORD
IN OUR
HANDS

THE BIBLE PRESERVED FOR US

JAMES B. WILLIAMS • RANDOLPH SHAYLOR
General Editor   Managing Editor

AMBASSADOR
EMERALD INTERNATIONAL

GREENVILLE, SOUTH CAROLINA • BELFAST, NORTHERN IRELAND
www.emerldhouse.com

God's Word In Our Hands

Ambassador Emerald International
427 Wade Hampton Boulevard
Greenville, S.C. 29609 U.S.A.

and

Ambassador Productions Ltd.
Providence House
Ardenlee Street
Belfast BT6 8QJ, Northern Ireland

www.emeraldhouse.com

Cover design and page layout by A & E Media, Sam Laterza

ISBN 1 889893 87 0

We believe that the Bible teaches that God has providentially preserved His written Word. This preservation exists in the totality of the ancient language manuscripts of that revelation.

We are therefore certain that we possess the very Word of God.

CONTRIBUTORS

Text and Translation Committee

Dr. J. Drew Conley
Pastor, Hampton Park Baptist Church, Greenville, South Carolina

Dr. Paul W. Downey
Pastor, Temple Baptist Church, Athens, Georgia

Dr. Michael Harding
Pastor, First Baptist Church, Troy, Michigan

Rev. John K. Hutcheson, Sr.
Field Representative, Frontline Missions International, Greenville, South Carolina
Former Pastor, Tabernacle Baptist Church, Clayton, Georgia

Dr. Mark Minnick
Pastor, Mount Calvary Baptist Church, Greenville, South Carolina

Dr. Randolph Shaylor
Pastor, Antioch Baptist Church, Riverdale, Georgia

Dr. James B. Williams
Bible Conference Speaker, Former Missionary, Ringgold, Georgia
Chairman of The Text and Translation Committee

Additional Contributors

Rev. Hantz Bernard
Director, Bibles International, Grand Rapids, Michigan

Dr. Daniel K. Davey
Pastor, Colonial Baptist Church, Virginia Beach, Virginia
President, Central Baptist Theological Seminary of Virginia

Dr. Keith E. Gephart
Professor of Bible, International Baptist College, Tempe, Arizona
Former Pastor, Hedstrom Memorial Baptist Church, Cheektowaga, New York

Dr. John C. Mincy
Pastor, Heritage Baptist Church, Antioch, California

Academicians

Dr. Kevin Bauder	Central Baptist Theological Seminary
Dr. David Burggraff	Calvary Baptist Theological Seminary
Dr. Robert Crane	Pillsbury Baptist Bible College
Dr. Sam Horn	Northland Baptist Bible College
Dr. George Houghton	Faith Baptist Bible College and Theological Seminary
Dr. Roland McCune	Detroit Baptist Theological Seminary
Dr. Larry Oats	Maranatha Baptist Bible College
Dr. James D. Price	Temple Baptist Seminary
Dr. Samuel Schnaiter	Bob Jones University
Dr. Mark Sidwell	Bob Jones University

CONTENTS

APPRECIATION

The Text and Translation Committee is very grateful for the positive response we received from our book, *From The Mind Of God To The Mind Of Man*. The book is now in its fourth printing. Many have expressed their appreciation for the practical help and historical information received from the book relative to the translation controversy that has divided Fundamentalists. Interest comes from many who do not consider themselves Fundamentalists yet find the book profitable. Positive response has come from English speaking countries on several continents, and interest in preparation of a similar volume in other languages has come from other lands. We thank our God that our efforts have benefited so many believers.

As editor of GOD'S WORD IN OUR HANDS and chairman of the Text and Translation Committee I express my appreciation to those who have made this volume possible. To each member of the committee I express my thanks for their sacrifices of time, labor, and finances that have been devoted to committee projects for four years. Thanks to their churches, ministries, and families who have graciously sacrificed to allow them to spend so much time away from them. As a committee we must all give thanks to the Metropolitan Baptist Church of Atlanta, Georgia and their pastor, the late, Dr. Robert Cunningham. Pastor and church provided facilities and hosted many meetings of the committee. We especially appreciate the encouragement provided by those who frequently and impatiently asked, "When will the book come out?" I also want to thank Dr. Randolph Shaylor for assisting me in coordinating the work of producing the book. Our publisher, Samuel Lowry, also deserves commendation, not only for encouraging us, but for enduring our delays and missing of schedules.

James B. Williams

THE HEART OF THE STORM
Preface

Douglas R. McLachlan
Pastor, Fourth Baptist Church, Plymouth, Minnesota

Several years ago while I was attending a conference entitled "The Battle For Truth," one of the speakers said "To identify with truth is to place yourself in *the heart of a storm* from which there is no escape until death." Never before has this been more true than it is today. Philip Graham Ryken defines the shape of our post-Christian times by identifying the two key characteristics of what he calls the "new barbarism." *Relativism*, he says, is radical skepticism, the rejection of absolute truth. Accordingly it dismisses the Word of God in favor of the opinions of man. *Narcissism*, on the other hand, is radical individualism or infatuation with the self.[1] Accordingly it displaces the worship of God with the deification of man. The only answer to this relativistic mind-set and this narcissistic heartbeat is the exposition of truth and the exaltation of God. And the only source book for this double answer is the Holy Scriptures, the Word of the living God. There are multiple reasons why Christians celebrate Scripture. The Bible is to be celebrated because it is *sacred* in character, *salvific* in goal, *sterling* in origin and *sanctifying* in function (2 Timothy 3:15-17). At the root of all these celebrated qualities of God's Word is the reality of its sterling origin. This is what Paul had in mind when he said: "All Scripture is given by inspiration of God . . ." (2 Timothy 3:16a).

Paul's word "all" teaches *comprehensiveness*. The Bible in *all of its parts* (plenary inspiration) – Old and New Testaments, miraculous and mundane, Genesis 1-11, Jonah's miraculous experiences and the Chronicler's genealogies – as well as in every word (verbal inspiration) comes from God. Among other things, this means that we are not at liberty to pick and choose, to dissect, to act as judges sitting in judgment of which parts of Scripture are authoritative and essential and which parts are not. We accept Paul's plain and unmistakable affirmation: "All Scripture is given by inspiration of God," and that can only mean Scripture in all of its parts and in every single word as given by God in the *autographa*.

But if Paul's word "all" teaches comprehensiveness, we can be sure that the words "given by inspiration of God" teach *trustworthiness*. Actually the words "given by inspiration," are the translation of one Greek word, *theopneustos*, which would probably best be translated "God-breathed." Greek scholars remind us that "the rabbinical teaching was that the Spirit of God rested on and in the prophets and spoke through them so that their words did not come from themselves, but from the mouth of God and they spoke and wrote in the Holy Spirit. The early church was in entire agreement with this view."[2] And no word affirms that agreement more powerfully or states it more clearly than *theopneustos* as it relates to Scripture's origin. If it is true that Scripture's source can be traced to the inner recesses of God's divine nature and that it was quite literally "breathed out" by Him, then it is equally true that no document on earth is so *trustworthy* as this document.

It is the Apostle Peter who helps us to see how this breathed-out Word was written-down: "Holy men of God spoke as they were moved by the Holy Ghost" (2 Peter 1:21). Peter's word "moved" is *pheromenoi* and it means "to be carried, to be borne along. The word was used of a ship carried along by the wind (Acts 27:15, 17) and the metaphor here is that the prophets raised their sails and the Holy Spirit filled them and carried their craft along in the direction He wished. Men spoke: God spoke."[3] Peter means that the omniscient Spirit supernaturally superintended both the reception and the recording of the divine message by the human authors so that they were preserved from mental and mechanical blunders, errors of the head and errors of the hand. And it must be emphasized that this divine superintendence of human authors is both supernatural and inexplicable – it is a miracle! As such it defies logical or empirical analysis or explanation and must be embraced by faith. The combination of the omniscient divine Spirit and a submissive human servant produced a *theanthropic* Word, the Holy Scriptures. This inscrutable process is perfectly analogous to the incarnation. There, too, the combination of the omnipotent divine Spirit and a submissive human servant [Mary] produced a *theanthropic* Person, the Holy Son of God. The inscripturated Word is infallible; the incarnate Word is impeccable. Both entered the realm of human history in essentially the same way – the miraculous synergism of divine and human elements. To deny the possibility of an infallible Scripture is to dismiss the possibility of an impeccable Savior. Both the written and incarnate Logos owe their flawless entrance into a flawed world through flawed agents to the supernatural superintendence of the Holy Spirit. So without equivocation we are prepared to say that the breathed-out, written-down Word of the living God is absolutely trustworthy.

The authors of this book have decided to take their stand alongside the truth of God's Word. In affirming its inerrancy, infallibility and authority for faith and practice they have placed themselves *in the heart of a storm* from which there is no escape. For their defense and exposition of absolute truth they are to be highly commended. While there may be small nuances of difference on the exegesis of a given text or the statement of a theological conclusion, there is major agreement on the thesis *that God has providentially preserved His written Word.* Under God's providence we have suffered no loss of divine truth. Thus, we can with certainty affirm that we possess God's Word, and with authority, accuracy and clarity proclaim its sacred, salvific and sanctifying message into the teeth of our post-Christian world. Nothing is more needful than that.

"All Scripture is given by inspiration of God, and is profitable for doctrine, for reproof, for correction, for instruction in righteousness: That the man of God may be perfect, thoroughly furnished unto all good works" (2 Timothy 3:16, 17).

---

[1]Philip Graham Ryken, *City On A Hill* (Chicago: Moody Publishers, 2003), p.18.

[2]Fritz Reinecker, & Cleon Rogers, *Linguistic Key To The Greek New Testament* (Grand Rapids: Zondervan Publishing House, 1980), p. 647.

[3]Cleon L. Rogers Jr. & Cleon L. Rogers III, *The New Linguistic and Exegetical Key To The Greek New Testament* (Grand Rapids: Zondervan Publishing House, 1998), p. 584.

FOREWORD

Historically, the Bible has been considered the most precious possession that we could have in our homes and in our churches. When the Pilgrims arrived in America they brought with them the English translation of the Scriptures known as the Geneva Bible and founded their colony upon it. The Bible became the basis for our nation; the principles of liberty and justice that motivated its establishment were derived from the Word of God. References to its content are found upon monuments, public buildings, and in legal documents. If a home could possess only one book, it was the Bible. No other book has so influenced the world, especially the English-speaking world.

That influence was based upon an unshakeable confidence that the Bible is God's revelation to mankind and that the translations in their possession were accurate representations of that revelation. A small minority may have questioned it, but the public at large honored and respected it whether or not they followed its teachings.

It is both sad and tragic that such large numbers of Americans have lost that confidence in the Bible as the inerrant Word of God. That loss of trust is due in part to the modern liberalism and neo-orthodoxy that invaded educational institutions and pulpits at the beginning of the twentieth century. More recently two other factors have contributed to the attitude of doubt: (1) the promotion of scientific investigation has taught people to question and seek empirical proof for everything and (2) a political attitude that rejects absolutes and demands pluralism in all thought, especially religion. With this questioning of God's Word comes loss of respect for and fear of God.

Beginning in the late thirteen hundreds, after centuries of domination by the Latin language and the Latin Bible, the desire for the Bible in the language of the people has produced a growing stream of English translations, some good, some very poor. By most accounts, there are more translations in the English language than any other. The twentieth century witnessed an exploding production of translations and specialized Bibles—some based on honorable motives—some for questionable motives.

The result is the questioning, not only of current translations, but even whether God has preserved His revelation. Christians want to know: Is my Bible really the Word of God? Do I have what God gave to His penmen? Can I really have God's Word in my language?

Some sincere Christians have sought to answer these questions by defending one and only one English translation as the Word of God. Others have freely accepted any work that claims to be a translation of the Bible and have sought one that satisfies their personal preferences.

Against this background and with these questions in view, eleven pastors have sought the advice of conservative theologians and penned these chapters. It is their prayer that their efforts will be used of the Lord to restore confidence in the preservation of God's Word as revealed in the Scriptures.

Special note: All the contributors to this volume wholeheartedly embrace the historic Fundamentals of the Faith. In order to accurately deal with the issues of the Biblical text and its preservation some contributors quote or refer to authors whose positions they cannot fully endorse. They recognize that much of the archeological, textual, and linguistic study that contributes to these important fields has been done by researchers who disagree with some of the positions of the authors and academic advisors of this volume. But where such writers benefit or advance the topic under discussion it may be necessary to recognize and utilize their contributions. The quotation or citation of such authors should not be construed as an endorsement of all their positions.

GOD'S WORD IN OUR HANDS
INTRODUCTION
James B. Williams

From the day of its creation there has been persecution of the body of believers called "the church." We see evidence of it in the last book of the New Testament. John the Apostle, in A. D. 95, was on the Isle of Patmos and gave two reasons for his presence there.

I John, who also am your brother, and companion in tribulation, and in the kingdom and patience of Jesus Christ, was in the isle that is called Patmos **for the word of God** *and* **for the testimony of Jesus Christ**. Revelation 1:9

It may seem strange that he was not there to evangelize the lost and minister to believers but because of persecution by the religious and political opposition to his faithfulness to the Word of God and Jesus Christ. Other apostles had suffered intense persecution. According to traditional church history, Peter had been crucified and Paul beheaded. Now John has been banished from contact with those he might evangelize and disciple. The two reasons John gave for his imprisonment could also be described as the cause of the persecution of Peter and Paul.

1. For the Word of God.

The world system does not accept the Scriptures as from God. The world rejects His standards of morality and the preaching of those standards arouses resentment. The attitudes toward the Bible and Christianity that we encounter in the entertainment and educational world are not new but existed in the Roman world of John's day. Rome considered Caesar a god, but Biblical Christianity proclaims that the God of the Bible is the only true God and Supreme Authority. The absolute standard of right and wrong that He demands is no more pleasing to the post-modern world than it was to Caesar.

2. For the Testimony of Jesus Christ.

Jesus Christ is the exclusive Savior: the only means of forgiveness of sin, regeneration, and eternal and abundant life. He is the unique, only begotten Son of God: God in flesh, provided by grace but rejected by the unconverted.

These two facts have been the cause of persecution by the world throughout history. However, through the centuries there have also been disturbances within the body of believers that have caused serious problems within what is called "the church." Many of these problems have arisen because of differences of interpretation of some Scripture. The Reformation that began with Luther in Germany during the 16th century brought fervent preaching of salvation by grace through faith. It spread like a flame, but soon bitter controversies over theological interpretations arose between both the reformers and their followers. Too soon the focus on the souls of lost men was forgotten. The vision was gone and so was God's blessing.

The present controversy over the preservation of the Scriptures and the King James Version is unfortunate. It unnecessarily detracts from the main purpose for the church's existence and has developed an unchristian spirit among many believers. The positive response that we have received from our book, *From The Mind Of God To The Mind Of Man,* confirms the need for clear practical help and historical information on textual and preservation issues. The first book purposely avoided a detailed discussion of preservation because the focus was on the translation and King James Only controversy which has divided Fundamentalists. We sought to give Christians confidence in the Word of God as opposed to confidence in one translation. Soon questions began to arise about what historic Fundamentalists believe about the preservation of the Scriptures and more importantly about what the Scriptures actually teach about the matter. The theologian and academician may consult the theological journals and doctoral dissertations but very little has been available to the average pastor or layman. Most of what has been available has focused on the defense of a personal belief or a particular English translation.

The members of the committee realize that there are many important questions in the controversy. We hope that our present work, *God's Word in Our Hands,* will provide some answers that will benefit God's people.

As in our previous book we do not disparage the King James Version of the Bible. In fact we want to encourage people to use it or another trustworthy translation on a daily basis. We agree with Charles Haddon Spurgeon when he explains, " .... we are fully assured that our old English version of the Scriptures is sufficient for the plain man for all purposes of life, salvation, and goodness." There is a vast difference between saying, "We only use the King James Version," and saying, "The King James Version is the only Bible that should be used in the English language." (Some have gone even farther and promoted translation of the King James into other languages.) Don't forget, there were English Bibles before the King James Version that were the Word of God, and there are some good English translations since the King James Version that are the Word of God.

Someone has indicated that there are nearly 100 new translations of the Bible into English. The number grows almost every year. Some are beneficial but others cause us to wonder why time and paper were wasted in printing them. On the other hand, conservative English translations are clear in their presentation of the revelation from God: His declaration of Himself, His plan of salvation, His instruction for Christian living, and His prophetic plan.

Problems arise when we make any translation the exclusive revelation from God. It prompts questions about how and where the Word of God is perpetuated. Those questions are important because we are dealing with God's revelation. Reaching some conclusions about how God transmitted his Word to other generations and to other parts of the world is an import goal. There are varied opinions among true believers. Our desire is that the information in this book will be helpful. The authors of these chapters touch on important topics such as these:

1. What happened to the autographs [the original manuscripts]? God, in His wisdom, has kept this information secret.

2. Were the copyists, who copied these originals, inspired? Were those copies inspired?

3. If the copies were inspired and inerrant, why is it that no two of the 5000 plus New Testament manuscripts now in hand are in perfect agreement?

4. Why do those who study manuscripts classify them into families? Can we confidently know which best reflect the original manuscripts?

5. Since there is so little significant variance in the known manuscripts, why do some believers reject some manuscripts and consider others to be the sole representatives of the originals?

The debate about Greek texts has produced an embarrassing amount of misinformation. The fury of the storm focuses upon the Westcott and Hort Greek New Testament text and the manuscript evidence that underlies it. Even though the manuscripts those men used were among the latest to be discovered, they identified them as the earliest copied texts. Early criticism of Westcott and Hort focused on the manuscripts but eventually criticism moved from the texts to personal attacks on these men and their doctrinal positions. Three commentaries by Westcott have been misrepresented or misinterpreted by some who hold extreme KJV only views. Some very vocal members of this group appear willing to circulate any information that seems to support their views regardless of how questionable that information may be. This led one pastor to call me and express how incensed he was over the misinformation that was being published about the Westcott commentaries. He was disturbed because he had meticulously read them, and—other than the Anglican views of Westcott—he did not find them laced with teaching that would be contrary to Fundamentalism.

An important question that needs addressing is whether or not the King James Version is as inerrant as the original autographs. Care must be exercised in its consideration because we may allow sentiment and emotion to enter into the decision. The King James Version has long held an honored and trusted position among Bible believers. We are confident that the King James Version does not promote false doctrine. Spurgeon had this to say about this question, "I do not hesitate to say that I believe that there is no mistake whatever in the original Holy Scriptures from beginning to end. There may be, and there are, mistakes of translation; for translators are not inspired; but even the historical facts are correct."[1]

Another question that is raised concerns the fact that some passages in the Gospel of John, the Gospel of Mark, the Epistle of I John, and Revelation do not appear in some of the newer translations. Does that mean these translations are to be rejected? Was there a conspiracy by the translators of the newer versions to present a corrupted Bible? The translators of some of the most popular translations are reputed to be good, godly, and scholarly believers who would not purposely corrupt the Bible. Their reasons for not including those passages rest on the study of manuscripts and texts. Among Bible believers there is unanimous agreement about the overwhelming majority of passages.

Unfortunately, some of the strongest contenders in the controversy over the method of translation do not realize that a word by word translation from one language to another is impossible, particularly if it is a document such as the Bible. Words within a language have different meanings according to the way they are used. For example, I can think of six different ways that the English word "scratch" is used, each with a different meaning. Added to that translation problem is the fact that all languages are rich with idioms. If I had a husky throat and voice, in English I might say, "I have a frog in my throat;" in French I might say, "I have a cat in my throat;" while in Mexico, I might say, "I have a chicken in my throat." In Bariba, the language of an African tribe that I evangelized, I might say, "I have a lizard in my throat."

When translating Scripture into the Bariba language of West Africa I consulted several English translations, two French translations, several Greek texts and Africans who used Yoruba and Housa Bibles. Someone suggested that the King James Version, alone, would have been sufficient. Impossible! Any translation which is based on the KJV alone must be carefully compared with the original languages. Using seventeenth century English as a sole basis for translation into a modern language, especially one in which no Bible previously existed, would produce questionable results. No reputable philologist would ever attempt this procedure.

Once a tribal language of West Africa was reduced to writing some Bible translation began. The best of care was taken. African informants were employed. There was a constant revising of the translations. Years later, when the Bible was completed, the people of the tribe told the missionaries that the first translations were considered the white man telling them, in their African language, what God had said. But now, with the improved translation, they felt that God was speaking to them in their language just as they would say it.

It is interesting to note that when the King James Version was translated and first published it was not readily accepted by all believers. The Puritans, in particular, questioned it. Puritans and others objected to the way certain words were translated (or not translated). Those who came to America and formed the Plymouth colony used the Geneva Bible. It was years before the King James Version supplanted the Geneva and Bishops' Bibles. Although there were those who had strong convictions about the matter, they did not convey the mean spiritedness and use the vitriolic language so often present today in discussions of translations.

The ecclesiastical words such as "church" had been translated more accurately in the Geneva Bible but were adopted in the King James to satisfy some Anglican high-church men. The Greek βαπτιζω, "to immerse," was not translated but was transliterated "baptize." This protected the practice of sprinkling by the Anglican Church. The Greek word "ekklesia," εκκλησια, was translated by the word "church" rather than the more accurate "assembly."

The same slow acceptance was true with the currently used French Bible, the *Louis Segond Version*, a translation into the common French language. When it was first published there were those who opposed it. It took years for it to supplant the older version which used out-dated French. Healing of the division in the present controversy over the English Bible may be slow in coming, but it is necessary that it come. Christian tolerance must be exercised by all parties. Vitriolic language must be abandoned.

The late Dr. James Singleton, in his paper *Whetstone* [September 2000 issue], had an article, "Rules of the Road," which gave some wise observations that apply in this controversy;

1. We will not transfer our preferences into convictions, and ostracize those within the pale of Biblical Fundamentalism who do not agree with us.

2. We realize that unity and separation are both Biblical mandates and must be held in fine tension.

3. We will deal with personalities only as needed to illustrate a position, preferring instead to analyze the position itself.

4. We believe that a battle can never be truly won if it is unfairly fought.

5. We believe that Christian brothers who hold a different point of view should be dealt with differently than those who are involved in apostasy.

6. We believe that Biblical Fundamentalism must be militant, but militancy must be practiced in Christian grace.

The fact that thousands of believers carry a recent translation to church on Sundays does not make them heretics, nor are churches that use one of these versions in their worship and their Bible teaching necessarily apostate. Fundamental doctrines can be taught from any of the these versions. No doctrine of the Christian faith is really corrupted by use of these translations. Should some prefer the King James Version, that is their prerogative. If some prefer one of the other conservative versions, that is their privilege.

Most believers would prefer harmony and unity among Fundamentalists. This needless division over translations can be healed. But it will take the proper application of God's Word.

Consider 1 Corinthians 16:14, *Let all your things be done with charity.* The word "charity" translates αγαπη, but there is no one word in English that conveys the meaning of "agape" love. It is quite different from human love. It is better described negatively. "Agape love" means there is the absence of jealousy, envy, bitterness, and vitriolic speaking, both to and about others.

Note how it is explained in 1 John 4:19, *We love him because he first loved us.* He loves us because of Who and What He is not because of who and what we are. That is "subjective love." Human love is activated by something seen in the object loved. When we exercise Christian love we do so because of who and what we are and not because of who and what the loved ones are. This is the kind of love that will bring healing in this controversy.

Earlier we mentioned the necessity of translating the Scriptures into other languages in a way that they will be best understood. Let me illustrate from my experience as a missionary putting the Scriptures into a previously unwritten language.

One of the first verses of Scripture we translated into the Bariba language was John 14:6. We had a problem with the word "way." The Baribas told us the only way to translate it understandably was with their word for "path." They said in Bariba, "When we get saved, we enter the Jesus [Yesu] path." They would testify of themselves, "I am in the Yesu path."

Another very interesting phrase was their way of describing a good Christian. They said, "He has both feet in the Yesu path." A "not so good Christian" was said to have "only one foot in the Yesu path." A good translation must be true to God's revelation, but it must be understood by the readers.

As you read these chapters you will note that there is some overlapping of content as well as variety in style of the chapters. This results from several facts: the authors wrote with a great degree of independence; the recognition that some chapters may be read independently of others; and each of the authors has his personal opinions about secondary details. Nevertheless, the authors are united in the statement on preservation presented in the book and have sought to advance that view. The very nature of the subject matter of the various chapters demands some difference in style and content. Some topics demand a more theological and exegetical expression while others are best approached in a less formal manner. In presenting what we believe is the Biblical view of preservation, the committee has sought to maintain a conciliatory tone. Belief in the inspiration of the Scriptures is fundamental to the Christian faith. That is essential, but we believe that good men can disagree on non-essentials without being disagreeable.

It is our hope that this book will lead you to the conclusion that God has, indeed, preserved His Word even though He has not revealed the specific details of how this is done. God's "words" are preserved in the manuscripts. Therefore, the Christian faith is not at stake when believers study the existing Biblical manuscripts in an effort to determine exactly what God has said, or consult the Biblical languages and various translations in an effort to express God's Word understandably. We may have differing opinions about the best translation to use and still be sound in the faith and brotherly in spirit. The Christian faith is not threatened when someone uses one of the conservative newer translations.

---

[1]Charles H. Spurgeon. "Bible Tried and Proved" Sermon no. 2089, *Metropolitan Tabernacle Pulpit,* vol. 35, year 1889, C. H. Spurgeon Collection (Albany, Oregon: Ages Electronic Software), p. 329.

WE HAVE THE WORD OF GOD

A STATEMENT OF THE PRESERVATION OF GOD'S WRITTEN WORD

Randolph Shaylor

We believe that the Bible teaches that God has providentially preserved His written Word. This preservation exists in the totality of the ancient language manuscripts of that revelation. We are therefore certain that we possess the very Word of God.

The historic statements of faith have attempted to concisely state what the Scriptures teach on important doctrinal matters. In the same vein, this statement is an attempt to verbalize the position held by Bible believers. Some might phrase it somewhat differently, but we believe that careful attention to this wording will reveal that we believe, by faith and by evidence, that we have the Word of God. This position is founded upon and is a necessary corollary to the Biblical doctrine of inspiration called plenary verbal inspiration.

"We"—*We* specifically refers to the contributors of this publication. Nevertheless, this volume sets forth evidence that this is the position held by Bible believers throughout church history, especially those orthodox evangelical believers who have been called "Fundamentalists." This is evidenced in the historic statements of faith, the preaching, and the writings of Bible believing Christians. More importantly, this historic position is based on the statements and implications of the Holy Scriptures.

"Believe"—Faith is the foundation of Biblical Christianity. The existence of God is received by faith (Hebrews 11:6). Salvation is dependent upon faith in the redemptive work of Jesus Christ. That faith is grounded in the Word of God. Prior to the completion of the canon of Scripture, this involved both the spoken Word of God and the written Word of God. With the completion of the canon true faith rests upon the written Word of God. This necessitates the transmission of His revelation from its inerrant, directly inspired, written form to all successive ages and its translation into the various languages of men.

"Bible"— The *Bible* refers to the sixty-six books recognized by Protestants as given by inspiration. These specific books can be traced to their appearance in canon lists dating from the earliest centuries of the Christian era. Witness to their content is found in the manuscripts of the Scriptures themselves and confirmed by ancient translations, quotations in ancient lectionaries, and by the writings of those early church leaders called the church fathers.

"Teaches"—By *teaches* we mean the specific statements and clear implications of the actual words of Scripture. The Bible speaks truth in all its statements but that which is intended for application we call teaching or "doctrine." We believe that we must be guided by the historical-grammatical understanding of the statements given in the Biblical language texts.

"**God**"—By *God* we mean that eternal, omnipotent, omniscient Being who has revealed His eternal existence in the Trinity of Father, Son, and Holy Spirit. This God is the author of all revealed truth. Through the agency of the Holy Spirit He has delivered this truth to us in written form by means of that inspiration which produced inerrant original copies.

"**Providentially**"—The *providence* of God is His sovereign guidance of the affairs of history utilizing the natural laws which He has created and His leading the minds of men to accomplish His intended purpose. It is contrasted with direct supernatural intervention as seen in miracles and in the unique superintendence that He used in "breathing out" His written Word. In His miraculous intervention God sets aside the natural course of events and directly causes an event to happen. On the other hand, in providence God works in an unseen manner through the normal course of events to accomplish His plan.

"**Preserved**"—God moved (bore along) "holy men of old" enabling them to convey His message to human beings. Expression of an inerrant message demanded the inerrant words that He inspired (*breathed out*). Those inerrant words were entrusted to men for transmission to others. They were spoken, written, and copied with care through the ages. Without the supernatural element present in the "breathing out" of the autographs, the frailty of the human instruments of this transmission allowed variations in these transmitted copies. In His providence, God has enabled His children to compare copies and their variations in order to arrive at an accurate representation of the original inscripturation. God's Word has not passed away but has been transmitted in a manner that preserves the truth that He gave in a form that is consistent with the original writings.

"**Written word**"—God has not chosen to preserve every Word which He has spoken by audible voice through His prophets. He has chosen to convey the message of His person, purpose, glory, and works in written form. It is this written Word that has been transmitted to us and needs translation and application in the affairs of His creation.

"**Ancient manuscripts**"—By *ancient manuscripts* we refer to those thousands of Scripture portions handwritten in the languages of the autographa[1] (Hebrew, Aramaic, and Greek) before the advent of printing. For this reason, although translations dating to the early centuries of the Christian era provide additional witness to the text, manuscripts are its most valuable confirmation. These range from mere fragments of a verse to almost complete Bibles. Often overlooked in the textual discussion is the fact that these manuscripts were once people's Bibles (or portions thereof). They depended upon these Bibles, just as we do ours, in order to learn of saving faith in Christ and how to serve Him.

"**Confident**"—*Confidence* is produced, not by subjective feelings or mystical experience, but by objective examination of the evidence of the Biblical writings and the witness of the Holy Spirit confirming that evidence.

"**We possess the very Word of God**."—When the ancient manuscripts are carefully compared and collated into a reliable text, we believe that it is still the Word of God, retaining the quality of inspiration and inerrancy to the degree that it accurately represents the autographs. That text can be translated into the multiple languages of men so that the readers can, with confidence, believe that by those translations we have "God's Word in our hands." This Word is the basis of our faith, the assurance of our salvation, the guide for our lives, and our hope for the eternal blessings of our Savior and Lord.

---

[1]*autographa* - the original inspired manuscripts of the Bible books written in the author's own hand or that of his amanuensis (secretary).

THE HERITAGE OF Ał ORTHODOXY

John K. Hutcheson, Sr.

In the twenty-first century when one hears the term "fundamentalist, tends to associate it right away with Islamic terrorists and right-wing crack pots. The term has its roots in American Christianity—not Islam—and conservative Christians who committed themselves to the classical doctrines of historic Christianity wore it with honor. Unfortunately the word fundamentalist has been hijacked in the last quarter century and has been misapplied to designate the radical adherents of any religion. Hence, the media uses the name fundamentalists to refer to extremist Muslims who are bent on terrorizing the enemies of Islam by means of a *jihad*. Yet, we must be historically accurate and theologically honest if we are to examine the doctrines and practices of authentic Fundamentalists in American Christianity.

A study of the movement named Fundamentalism—stretching over nearly a century and a half—is fascinating indeed. Such a study is marked by uncommon men who stood for truth in an age when it became popular and expedient to bow to the prevailing winds of scholarship in liberal institutions of higher learning that were attacking the supernatural revelation of God to man, the Bible. Those theological liberals, originally known as modernists, focused on re-interpreting and adapting the Bible to the prevailing thought of the modern age. Orthodox believers in various denominations, on the other hand, shared a common commitment to and conviction regarding the Bible's inspiration, inerrancy and authority as the very Word of the living God.

While the name Fundamentalist is less than one hundred years old, the early standard bearers were confident that they stood in a rich heritage of classical orthodoxy. That a noted theological liberal from Harvard University should acknowledge this fact during the early years of the Fundamentalist movement is noteworthy indeed. Kirsopp Lake characterized Fundamentalism as follows:

> represent[ing] an unwavering attachment to the great traditional doctrines of Christianity…. But it is a mistake …to suppose that Fundamentalism is a new and strange form of thought. It is nothing of the kind…. The Fundamentalist may be wrong; I think that he is. But it is we who have departed from the tradition, not he, and I am sorry for the fate of anyone who tries to argue with a Fundamentalist on the basis of authority.The Bible and the *corpus theologicum* of the Church is on the Fundamentalist side.[1]

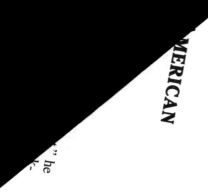

, Edward J. Carnell, who was a
ller Theological Seminary in the
entalism when he stated that their
blical Christianity were incompat-
vement preserved the faith once for
entalists were the faithful guardians
, in contrast to the liberals who had
a belief system built on rationalism,

of both dedicated intellect and fervent
scholars, preachers and soulwinners,
rs and educators who trained men for
the ministry.   their calling to preach the Word, to
declare sound doctrine, and   l the faith once delivered to the saints.
And contend for the faith they did, both by positively stating the historic
Christian doctrines and by negatively attacking the modernists whose rationalistic doctrines reduced the Bible to a mere human book. These conservative believers were battle-scarred veterans who paid their dues in the fight, in
order to preserve the faith from the withering attacks by apostates in mainline
denominations.

Bible-believing Christians today owe these men our undying gratitude for
the price they paid to be faithful to the Word of God. That price included the
rejection that they experienced from fellow ministers who chose to compromise on obedience to Scripture. Yet, it has become fashionable in some circles in our generation to cast aspersion on those giants of the faith by claiming that they were misguided or untaught in their position on the inspiration
and preservation of the Word of God. Jasper James Ray claimed that "even
Dr. C. I. Scofield was 'brainwashed'…." because of the position that he took
in the marginal notes of the reference Bible that bears his name.[3] With harsh,
vitriolic language, Peter Ruckman repeatedly vilifies godly soulwinners and
Greek scholars, like R. A. Torrey and A. T. Robertson, who did not accept his
King James Version Only position.[4]

It is an injustice to accuse any of those men of introducing or passing along
liberal techniques for studying the original text of the Scriptures. With their
commitment to the full inspiration and authority of God's revelation, they
were the last people on earth who would dilute orthodox Christianity by introducing any form of liberalism into it. Some today—with a new bias against
textual criticism—are attempting to accuse these Godly believers of injecting
what they disparagingly call "the leaven of textual criticism" into the
Fundamentalist movement. This is unconscionable.

Any objective study of the heritage of American orthodoxy will demonstrate that they had committed themselves to a balanced position on the transmission of the Word of God into the English language. Their position—that God's Word was preserved in multiple faithful translations—was consistent with both the claims of Scripture, and with their forefathers in church history, including the early English translators and even the King James translators themselves. Every believer should make a point to read "The Translators to the Reader," the original preface of the 1611 King James Version written by the translators themselves to explain their translation principles. Unfortunately, that preface no longer appears in most of our contemporary printings of the King James Version, and we are the poorer for it. Notice their perspective:

> Now to the latter [our unscrupulous brethren] we answer, that we do
> not deny, nay, we affirm and avow, that the very meanest[5] translation
> of the Bible in English set forth by men of our profession ... con-
> taineth the word of God, nay, is the word of God:[6]

By 1611, there were at least seven English translations of the Bible available to Christians for reading and studying. The King James translators contended that the poorest of those translations—which differed from each other in their wording—was the very Word of God. Does it strike you as odd that the King James translators themselves did not believe that their new version was the only inspired Word of God? In other words, the King James translators themselves did not hold to a King James Only position.

Therefore, those orthodox believers in America, following in that heritage, did not limit themselves solely to the King James Version as the only acceptable translation for Bible-believers to read and from which to preach. It has been falsely alleged that the early Fundamentalists used only the *Textus Receptus* and the King James Bible. The reader can judge for himself whether those godly warriors for the faith held to a KJVO position, or whether they cited and quoted from other conservative translations with great freedom.

In fact, a salient question needs to be answered. Who crowned the King James Version as the only Bible an obedient Christian can use? It will become obvious from this study that it was not the early conservative Christians who did so, because we will see that they used a variety of orthodox versions in their writing and preaching.

This study will by necessity be largely historical in scope, highlighting numerous names and dates in order to show the substantial heritage enjoyed by Bible-believing Christians for a balanced position on the preservation of the Bible in the English language. Much of this chapter will consist of

3

quotations from our predecessors so that the reader can see their doctrinal position stated in their own words.

Some of the names of these Bible-believing forefathers may be unfamiliar to many of today's readers. That is most unfortunate because it means we have lost a sense of our historical roots. Many preachers are completely unaware of their rich spiritual heritage. Not only do they not know who these spiritual warriors were, they do not realize that the position they themselves are taking on the Bible today is—in many cases—one hundred and eighty degrees from their forefathers.

HISTORICAL FRAMEWORK

As theological liberalism began to creep into American denominations in the nineteenth century, coupled with a loss of the expectation for the "blessed hope" of the second coming of Christ among the Lord's people, faithful, conservative pastors from various denominations became burdened to see a revival of preaching on the great doctrines of the faith.

Ahlstrom explains that "several historians, in fact, would virtually <u>define</u> Fundamentalism as the creation of an interdenominational group of evangelical ministers, predominately Presbyterian and Baptist, who after 1876 convened a series of annual meetings for Bible study, and who later organized two widely publicized Prophecy Conferences."[7] (emphasis author's)

In 1920, as Marsden states, these conservative evangelicals became known as Fundamentalists.[8] Curtis Lee Laws first used the term to describe Bible-believers who stood for the core doctrines of historic Christianity as delineated in the series of essay booklets known as *The Fundamentals.*[9]

Keep in mind that the English translation, which was in use at this juncture in history, was the King James Bible. The orthodox Christians in the nineteenth century used that greatly revered translation which had been handed down to them. Since its appearance in 1611, the King James Version had gained prominence as the primary English translation and had been blessed of God over the previous two hundred fifty years.

Then, in the last part of the nineteenth century came a major revision of the King James Version, known as the English Revised Version (abbreviated RV) that was published in Great Britain.[10] It was based on the textual findings of the older Greek manuscripts that were incorporated into the texts of Tregelles, Tischendorf, and Westcott and Hort. "When the complete Revised Version appeared in 1885, it was received with great enthusiasm. Over three million copies sold in the first year of its publication."[11] This new translation was used by godly British pastors like G. Campbell Morgan and C. H. Spurgeon.

As we look back to that time in history, the questions before us are these: What was the attitude of the early American Fundamentalists towards this new translation? Did they condemn it or embrace it? Were they exclusively committed to one English translation, namely the King James Version, because of its longevity and because of its underlying traditional text? Did they believe in the inspiration of the original texts written by the prophets and the apostles, or did they believe in inspired translations?

This historical overview of the Fundamentalists' views on the Bible will survey the men whose ministries existed primarily before the publication of the special twelve-volume set, known as *The Fundamentals: A Testimony to the Truth,* from 1910-15. Then we will survey *The Fundamentals* set itself, and finally we will cite several of the later Fundamentalists of the twentieth century.

EARLY FUNDAMENTALISTS

James H. Brookes
While the name Fundamentalist was not used until the 1920s, the roots of the movement trace back into the latter half of the nineteenth century. A godly Presbyterian pastor from St. Louis, James H. Brookes, was instrumental in the leadership of those annual "Believers' Meetings for Bible Study" that began in the 1860s. A substantial part of Brookes' legacy to Fundamentalism was his discipling of an attorney who was converted and later became a pastor and writer, Cyrus I. Scofield.

It was at the 1878 Niagara Bible Conference that Pastor Brookes assisted in the composition of a doctrinal statement that became famous as a benchmark of orthodoxy and was adopted by both churches and Bible colleges as their own. The official title of the fourteen-point statement was "The Fundamentals of the Faith as Expressed in the Articles of Belief of the Niagara Bible Conference." This creed is very significant in that it came down solidly for the position that perfect inspiration applied only to the words found in the original manuscripts, and not across the board to all future translations. Practically, inspiration extends to translations insofar as the translations are faithful to the original text. Article I stated,

> ...and that His Divine inspiration is not in different degrees, but extends equally and fully to all parts of these writings, historical, poetical, doctrinal, and prophetical, and to the smallest word, and inflection of a word, provided such a word is found in the original mss.: 2 Timothy 3:16,17; 2 Peter 1:21; I Cor. 2:13; Mk. 12:26, 36; 13:11; Acts 1:16, 2:4.[12]

5

Bible-believing Christians in the nineteenth century did not believe in inspired translations, which would therefore render the translations flawless. Their doctrinal position, based on the claims of the Word of God, was that inspiration only applied to the original manuscripts (*autographa*). God has subsequently providentially preserved His Word through the many copies and manuscripts that have come down to us in time. Yet, there is no promise in Scripture that says God would miraculously protect every copyist and every translator and every printer from unconsciously introducing human errors into the text.

Even the first printing of the 1611 edition of the King James Version contained numerous printing and textual errors that had to be corrected in subsequent printings. A 1631 edition of the KJV accidentally left the word "not" out of the seventh commandment in Exodus 20:14, and thus became known as the "Wicked Bible." Someone might quickly reply that the errors were corrected in the next editions, and therefore that is not a valid issue. The doctrine of the providential preservation of the Bible does not apply to the work of copyists and printers.

These conservative believers understood this fact, and they sought to find the most accurate renderings of the original text in the English translations that were available. So, when the English Revised Version of 1881 was published, men like Brookes used it when they found that it more clearly rendered the meaning of the original text. In his *An Outline of the Books of the Bible*, published sometime after that Niagara Conference and before his death in 1897, Brookes quoted from the Revised Version, "The first epistle of Peter is addressed to believing Jews, touchingly called 'the strangers,' or as the Revised Version has it, the 'sojourners of the Dispersion,' scattered through Asia Minor."[13]

Significantly, later in the same book while discussing the coming apostasy, he quoted from even another version, Young's Translation.[14] There are those today who are claiming that multiple translations of the Bible are evidence of apostasy. Yet, James H. Brookes, whose orthodox credentials are beyond question, had no problem quoting from other translations, including the 1881 Revised Version that has been attacked in some circles for being the work of Westcott and Hort. It certainly gives one cause to wonder why anyone would dare to say that a man like James H. Brookes was wrong in his position on the preserved Word of God.

B. H. Carroll

A converted infidel who possessed a keen mind and extraordinary debating skills, Benajah Harvey Carroll stood as a Titan among early Southern Baptist preachers and scholars. Carroll served as pastor of the First Baptist Church of Waco, Texas, for nearly thirty years from 1870-99. He was instrumental in the founding of Southwestern Baptist Theological Seminary in 1908 and served as its first president until he died in 1914.

Carroll was the author of some forty books, including a 13-volume commentary set on the entire Bible, *An Interpretation of the Bible.* One of his colleagues, J. B. Cranfill, praised him "as the most commanding figure that has ever marched through the history of American ecclesiasticism...."[15]

In the last part of the nineteenth century, as German rationalism was attempting to make headway into Southern Baptist academic circles, Carroll was one of three key Baptist professors who taught and wrote vigorously in the defense of the inspiration and inerrancy of the Scriptures. Along with his colleagues, John L. Dagg and James P. Boyce, Carroll taught many young preachers the orthodox doctrine regarding the divinely inspired Word of God. In terms of the extent of inspiration, all three of them taught that the original manuscripts alone possessed inerrancy.[16] Furthermore, throughout his commentary Carroll repeatedly vilified higher criticism, evolutionary concepts, and preachers who raised doubts about the Word of God.[17]

In *Inspiration of the Bible,* published some years after his death, Carroll made it clear that inspiration did not apply solely to the King James Bible, nor was that version the only one to be used by Bible-believing Christians.

> Let me say further that only the original text of the books of the Bible is inspired, not the copy or the translation.... A version is a translation. We have the American Standard Version, or translation, the King James Version and the Septuagint in Greek ... and hundreds of other versions.... Versions, or translations, are not inspired; if they were, all of them would be just alike; but the original manuscript was inspired. [18]

Carroll very carefully laid out the implications of the biblical doctrine of inspiration and preservation for his readers. He was explicit in teaching that the King James Version is not the standard by which all versions are measured, but rather the original texts are.

> We do not try to make a new standard, but try to get back to the original text as nearly as possible, and in that way instead of the deviations increasing as the years roll by, the variations are diminishing. There are less now than there used to be, and if we were to make another translation, say forty years hence, that translation would be nearer the original than *the American Standard translation, which we are now using*, and of course very much nearer than the King James translation.[19] (emphasis mine)

A common question raised by some is why God has not left us with a perfect translation that would never need revision and why the work of textual scholars is necessary. Carroll addressed that question when he wrote:

> God's leaving this kind of labor to be performed by man has had a tremendous effect in bringing about a study of the Bible that would never have been undertaken if to every nation there had been handed down, in God's own handwriting, a text of the Bible in their own language. If it had been handed down as a solid book from the skies it would not have brought about that reverence for the Bible, that attention to its study that has been accorded it. It would not have called forth that wholesome effect, with sacrifices of toil and money. It would not have engaged the study of so many devout scholars.[20]

If Bible-believing Baptists today understood and accepted the historical doctrinal position on the Bible espoused by B. H. Carroll, much of the King James Version Only controversy would be non-existent.

Cyrus I. Scofield

The Bible of the Fundamentalist movement for the major part of the twentieth century was the *Scofield Reference Bible*, first published in 1909 and edited by Cyrus I. Scofield, a Congregationalist pastor. With its emphasis on the premillennial return of Christ and its distinctions between Israel and the Church, the *Scofield Reference Bible* helped many pastors and laypeople to become serious about personal Bible study. This popular study Bible, with its center column references and extensive footnotes, was to twentieth century believers what the Geneva Bible with its references and footnotes was to the Puritans of the sixteenth and seventeenth centuries.

Scofield's editorial comments in the reference Bible that bears his name—loved by Fundamentalists for several generations—include his observations in the center column reference concerning verses that were not part of the original inspired texts, but were added later by scribes. He did not hesitate to point out where the older fourth century Greek manuscripts differed from the Textus Receptus. Note the following samplings.

At Matthew 17:21 regarding prayer and fasting Scofield's notation for letter "i" reads, "The two best MSS. omit v. 21."[21]

At Mark 11:26 regarding forgiving others, Scofield's note for letter "i," reads, "Verse 26 is omitted from the best MSS."[22] What is astounding—yet not as widely known—is that the King James translators *themselves* put the same marginal note about the lack of legitimacy for verse 26 in their original 1611 edition of the King James Bible. If it was wrong for Scofield to "raise

8

doubts about the Word of God," then it was also wrong for the King James translators to do so as well.

At Acts 8:37 where the Ethiopian eunuch makes his confessional agreement with the person of Jesus Christ, Scofield writes in his center column notation at letter "*h*," "The best authorities omit v. 37."[23]

Who were the "best authorities" and "the two best MSS" to which Scofield referred on a number of occasions? They were the older fourth century Greek manuscripts, copied much closer to the writing of the New Testament documents, and are called *Sinaiticus* and *Vaticanus*, which later Fundamentalists like W. B. Riley and John R. Rice praised. Those two manuscripts were not available to the King James translators in 1611. Scofield's study notes more closely reflected the renderings of both the English Revised Version and the American Standard Version, rather than slavishly following the readings of the King James Version.

One final quotation from the Scofield Bible merits our attention. Notice his comment at I John 5:7, a passage about which there has been some question since the time of Erasmus. Erasmus had originally omitted it from his first edition of the TR because he had no Greek manuscript evidence for it. Then, he bowed to pressure from the Catholic Church to include verse 7 in his third edition. It is the verse concerning "three that bear record in heaven." Scofield writes at center note "*o*,"—"It is *generally agreed* that v. 7 has no real authority, and has been inserted."[24] (emphasis mine) Scofield was not merely rendering his own personal opinion on the matter. Rather, since he wrote that statement in 1909, he was reflecting the overall consensus of the orthodox position of his day. Their commitment was to search for the most accurate readings of God's Word, rather than holding to a tradition of using only one Greek text or only one English translation. In other words, there was no King James Only movement in 1909.

Furthermore, the scholarly *The Criswell Study Bible,* published in 1979, followed the same position as the *Scofield Reference Bible* concerning I John 1:7. "This verse is not found in the most ancient Greek manuscripts. The almost total lack of manuscript support suggests that these words were written by a later hand during the Christological controversies which raged after 300 A.D."[25]

Interestingly enough, in Scofield's popular *Rightly Dividing the Word of Truth,* published thirteen years before his study Bible, he cited the English Revised Version (abbreviated R. V.) in both his Scriptural references and in actual verse quotations. "'The great tribulation'... is terminated by the glorious appearing of our Lord (Matt. 24:21,22; Rev. 7:14, R.V.; 2 Thess. 2:3-9,

9

R.V.)."[26] Nor was he hesitant to quote an entire verse from the Revised Version.   "Verily, verily, I say unto you, He that heareth my word, and believeth him that sent me, hath eternal life, and cometh not into judgment, but hath passed out of death into life (John 5:24, R.V.)."[27] Since the historic goal has been to communicate God's Word so that any layman can understand it, Scofield selected the Revised Version's clearer rendering of Philippians 3:20-21 which uses "our citizenship is in heaven," instead of the KJV's "our conversation," that was archaic even in 1881.[28]

For Scofield to be considered as one of the "founding fathers" of Fundamentalism and his Reference Bible to be held in such high esteem, it is difficult to understand how some believers today so strongly reject Scofield's balanced views on the preservation of the Scriptures in multiple English translations.

James M. Gray

Another leading light among early Fundamentalists, James M. Gray, was both a scholar and an educator. His contributions included sitting on the editorial board of the *Scofield Reference Bible*, as well as training several generations of preachers and missionaries at Moody Bible Institute, where he served as dean and as president until 1934. In *Bible Problems Explained*, published in 1913, Gray argues,

> Of course, when we speak of verbal inspiration we refer to the original autographs of the Scriptures as they came from the sacred writers, and not any translation of them. It is the province of Biblical criticism by an examination of the various translations, versions, and other data to get at the exact text of the original; and so thoroughly and satisfactorily has this been done that a good authority declares that so far as the New Testament is concerned, we have in nine hundred and ninety-nine cases out of every thousand the very words of the original autographs.[29]

Instead of holding textual criticism up for scorn and ridicule by calling it a practice of liberals and Bible-criticizers, Gray rightly acknowledged the proper place for Biblical, textual criticism to determine from the many manuscripts what the wording of the original was in the disputed places. Nor did Gray think that he had "a lost Bible" that needed to be rediscovered. He simply recognized Biblical criticism was a necessary field of study to use the tools God has given us to deal with the tough questions about the text, just as Erasmus did with the handful of manuscripts he possessed in reconstructing his Greek text in 1517. Gray went on to state that the work of Biblical, textual criticism has been so effective that the believer can have great confidence that he holds the very Word of God in his hands!

Reuben A. Torrey

The dean of the Fundamentalist movement was the Presbyterian scholar-evangelist Reuben A. Torrey who died in 1928. Torrey was graduated from Yale University and Divinity School, and he used his scholarship to defend the Scriptures with unsurpassed passion and insight. Furthermore, Torrey "continued his theological studies in Germany, doing graduate studies at the University of Leipzig and the University of Erlanger," as noted approvingly by popular pastor/evangelist Tom Malone in his *Forward* to a reprint of Torrey's *How to Work for Christ.*[30] Torrey's thorough background in the original languages stands as salient reproof to those today who allege that the early Fundamentalists were unaware of textual issues, or else that they lacked the skills to assess the true text of Scripture. Observe Torrey's own testimony as quoted by the outstanding pulpiteer, R. G. Lee, in a sermon on the doctrine of Hell:

> I claim to be a scholarly preacher. I have a right to so claim. I have taken two degrees, specializing in Greek in one of the most highly esteemed universities of America. I have also studied at two German universities. I have read the Bible in three languages every day of my life for many years. I have studied a large share of what has been written on different sides of the question in English and in German. I have written between thirty and forty different books which have been translated, I am told, into more languages than the books of any other living man. I say this simply to show that I have a right to call myself a scholarly preacher.[31]

Torrey's unique contribution to Fundamentalism was that he was no ivory tower scholar. Combining the mind of an educator with the zeal of a soulwinning evangelist, Torrey was well known for his evangelistic crusades in Australia, New Zealand, India, and Great Britain, in which more than 100,000 people publicly professed Christ as Savior. He also preached in Japan and China before assuming the pastorate of the Moody Memorial Church.

While in Chicago he also filled the role of Superintendent of Moody Bible Institute, where he trained preachers and missionaries to preach the Gospel. In 1908 he headed to the West Coast where he helped plant the Church of the Open Door. He also served as the dean of the Bible Institute of Los Angeles (BIOLA). A prolific writer, Torrey was the author of many books on Bible study, prayer, and evangelism, some of which have been used as textbooks in Bible colleges. He was an ardent defender of the inspiration and inerrancy of the Word of God.

One of the hallmarks of his ministry was that of serving as a co-editor of *The Fundamentals,* the definitive collection of essays that set forth a defense of orthodox Christian doctrine. Torrey contributed three chapters to the series on the topics of the bodily resurrection of Christ, the ministry of the Holy Spirit, and the place of prayer in evangelism.

What was this knowledgeable dean of Fundamentalism's position concerning which Bible Fundamentalists should use? Read what he wrote in *Is the Bible the Inerrant Word of God?*

> By the Bible I do not mean any particular English version of the Scriptures, the Authorized Version [1611], the English Revision [1881], or the American Standard Revision [1901] or any other Version, but the Scriptures as originally given. And we can now tell with substantial accuracy how the Scriptures, as originally given, read. Furthermore, any of these versions mentioned are a substantially accurate rendition of the Hebrew and Aramaic of the original Old Testament manuscripts, and of the Greek of the original New Testament manuscripts, and to that extent they are 'the Holy Scriptures,' the Bible.[32]

Notice that Torrey called all three versions mentioned—the AV, the RV and the ASV—"the Holy Scriptures."

As Torrey outlined the study methods for pastors and Bible teachers to use in their preparation to teach the Scriptures, one step in the process that he listed was, "Note any important changes in R.V. from A.V."[33] Obviously, he advocated using the most up-to-date reading of the text in order to "rightly divide the Word of Truth." He certainly did not view any changes from the KJV to the newer RV as "correcting the Bible."

On what degree of certainty for the text of Scripture did Torrey advocate, as one who staked his life's ministry and the Gospel proclamation to multiplied thousands? Here is what he wrote in 1918 in *The Fundamental Doctrines of the Christian Faith:*

> There are, it is true, many variations in the many manuscripts we possess, thousands of variations, but by a careful study of these very variations, we are able to find with marvelous accuracy what the original manuscripts said. A very large share of the variations are of no value whatever, as is evident from a comparison of different manuscripts that they are mistakes of a transcriber.... When all the variations of any significance have been reduced to the minimum to which it is possible to reduce them by a careful study of manuscripts, there is not one single variation left that affects any doctrine held by the evangelical churches, and the Scriptures as we have them today translated into our English language, either in the A.V. or R.V., are to all practical intents and purposes the inerrant Word of God.[34]

This dean of the early Fundamentalist movement insisted the manuscript variations do not affect any basic doctrine of our faith, and that a believer can trust either the Authorized Version or the English Revised Version as the Word of the living God.

John Roach Straton

New York City—home to the apostate Union Theological Seminary and the infidelity of the liberal Baptist preacher, Harry Emerson Fosdick—was greatly in need of a strong voice for biblical Christianity to stand without apology for God's revealed truth. In His providence, God raised up such a fearless man, John Roach Straton, pastor of the Calvary Baptist Church from 1918 to 1929. However, his ministry was not limited to his pulpit in New York City. He also stood shoulder to shoulder with W. B. Riley in the early 1920s against the trends of apostasy within the Northern Baptist Convention.

Committed to engaging cultural issues with the absolute truth of the Bible, Straton's ministry was regularly discussed in newspaper articles in *The New York Times*. He also interacted with the noted liberal ministers in his city in public debates on the great classic doctrines of Christianity.

Thankfully, his presentations reveal where Straton, as an early militant Fundamentalist, stood on the Bible's preservation. In his debate with Unitarian pastor, Dr. Charles Francis Potter, concerning the authority of the Bible, Straton explained that the orthodox position concerning inspiration was that it applied to the original manuscripts, and that God had not prevented copyists' errors from entering the text.

> Those of us who hold to the infallibility of the Bible believe that the original manuscripts were absolutely accurate. No man would question the possibility of minor errors through copyists slipping in, however, and as I said in my opening speech, it seems evident that God may even have permitted some such difficulties to enter, ...[35]

William J. Erdman

Another Presbyterian scholar, William J. Erdman, was an early Fundamentalist whose name showed up frequently as a Bible Conference speaker and author. His life spanned some eighty-nine years until 1923, and he served as one of the consulting editors of the *Scofield Reference Bible*. He too was a contributor to *The Fundamentals* with a chapter entitled, "The Holy Spirit and the Sons of God."

His ministry spanned the era in which the English Revised Version was published, and he had no qualms about quoting from it. In *The Parousia of*

Christ: A Period of Time, that was evidently published before his death, Erdman stated in the preface, "The renderings of the Revised Version have been frequently used."[36] Apparently, he harbored no doubts that the English Revised Version is equally the Word of God as is the King James Version. In fact, he believed it to be clearer in communicating God's message to the reader.

A. T. Robertson

Perhaps the greatest Greek scholar that America has ever seen was the warm-hearted Southern Baptist professor, Archibald Thomas Robertson. His Greek grammar of over 1,000 pages is unsurpassed in its field.

In the heyday of the Fundamentalist Bible Conference movement, Robertson was a frequent speaker, testifying to the fact that he did not fit the mold of a dry seminary lecturer, though he taught at the Southern Baptist Theological Seminary in Louisville, Kentucky, for forty-six years until his death in 1934.

Nor did he hesitate to speak out publicly against fellow Baptist A. H. Strong (author of a widely used systematic theology) who, very disturbingly, drifted into liberal views concerning the inspiration of the Scriptures and also pan-theism.[37]

Robertson powerfully defended the inerrancy of the original manuscripts which came from the breath of God to man, while acknowledging that there are "discrepancies and inconsistencies" in the multitudes of copies which have come down to us. Both extremes of the spectrum, theological liberals and King James Version Only advocates, have attacked this view as being implausible, since none of the originals remain today for examination. Robertson maintained, however, that this doctrine is very compatible with the plan of God in creation. God's original creation was perfect, but was subse-quently tainted by man. Robertson stated, "It is in accord with God's deal-ings in his world when he gave a revelation to make it free from error.... Hence, I boldly maintain that the analogy of nature is in favor of the inerrancy of God's original Scriptures."[38]

In his widely-used multi-volume set, *Word Pictures in the New Testament*, Robertson used the English Revised Version of 1881 as his basic text, not the King James Version, believing that the R.V. more closely reflected the origi-nal Greek and Hebrew. "The words of the Canterbury Version [RV] will be used, sometimes with my own rendering added, and the transliterated Greek put in parenthesis.... The text of Westcott and Hort will be used though not slavishly."[39]

14

The Set Known as *The Fundamentals*

In this study on the transmission and preservation of the Word of God, we have been tracing the historical roots of orthodox Christianity and observing what the early Fundamentalists believed and wrote on this critical subject. *The Fundamentals: A Testimony to the Truth* is the major reference point to which we now go, because it is the most complete representation of the doctrinal position of the Fundamentalist movement. Unfortunately, at the beginning of the twenty-first century that set of volumes has been largely collecting dust on the shelves of the pastors who even possess such a set. In many cases it would seem that conservative pastors do not own a set themselves, and they are therefore totally unaware of the views of their forefathers.

Some may say that we are not supposed to appeal to man for what we believe, but rather we go back directly to the Scriptures. The problem with that claim is that it ignores the wisdom that the Holy Spirit has given to godly men of previous generations, and it ignores the fact that all spiritual insight does not reside in our contemporary age. Furthermore, for those who are going to claim the name Fundamentalist, it is incumbent on them to make sure that they are standing on the same basic theological foundation regarding the Word of God as the founders of their movement, rather than on a totally opposite foundation.

At the beginning of the twentieth century, with the inroads of modernism reaching beyond the theological seminaries to the pulpits and into the pew, the need was great to provide a written defense of the faith on the layman's level. In fact, it was the generosity of two committed laymen, Lyman and Milton Stewart of Los Angeles, who provided the funds to undertake such an ambitious project. They "created a $250,000 fund in order that 'every pastor, evangelist, minister, theological professor, theological student, Sunday school superintendent, YMCA and YWCA secretary in the English speaking world' might be given twelve substantial booklets in which the theological issues of the day would be addressed."[40]

The first executive secretary selected to oversee this project was A. C. Dixon, until he moved to England. He was then succeeded by Louis Meyer, and then by R. A. Torrey who saw the project to completion. The chapters in these booklets were written by well-known orthodox pastors and scholars from various denominations in America and Britain. These were men who used various English translations of the Bible, and they fellowshipped together around the cardinal doctrines of classical Christianity.

The set originally consisted of twelve paperbacks containing over eighty essays, and they were distributed freely to more than 300,000 ministers and missionaries around the globe. Later, the paperbacks were combined into a compact four-volume set, which every pastor should possess and read with profit. The articles are timeless, and they comprise a real treasure of material for study and for preaching. The content is not only doctrinal in scope, but also practical in terms of studies on prayer, soulwinning, missions, evolution, cults and finances, in addition to including personal testimonies of the impact of the Word of God unleashed in people's lives.

Though there were differences of interpretation among the writers regarding denominational distinctives, eschatological views, and dispensationalism, the contributors were united in their defense of the authority and inerrancy of the Bible. They believed that God had authoritatively spoken in the written revelation known as the Bible, and that He had preserved His Word over the centuries for their benefit. They accepted the fact of the preservation of God's Word without dissension over the method of preservation that the Holy Spirit used.

The entire first volume of nineteen articles is devoted to refuting the liberal views of higher criticism that portrayed the Bible as a human book. Individual articles defended many of the specific areas of Scripture that were under attack in their day, such as the Pentateuch and the books of Isaiah and Daniel.

The very first essay in Volume One is "The History of Higher Criticism" by Canon Dyson Hague, a pastor from London, Ontario, and lecturer at Wycliffe College in Toronto. This early Fundamentalist makes a clear distinction between higher criticism of the Bible, which became synonymous with German rationalism and unbelief, and lower criticism or textual criticism. Far from condemning the latter field of study, Hague stated,

> One of the most important branches of theology is called the science of Biblical criticism, which has for its object the study of the history and contents, and origins and purposes, of the various books of the Bible. In the early stages of the science Biblical criticism was devoted to the two great branches, the Lower, and the Higher. The Lower Criticism was employed to designate the study of the text of the Scripture, and included the investigation of the manuscripts, and the different readings in the various versions and codices and manuscripts in order that we may be sure we have the original words as they were written by the Divinely inspired authors.[41]

Notice also that Hague explained that the purpose of textual criticism is so "that we may be sure we have the original words as they were written." His words reflect confidence and certainty, not doubt and mistrust in the Word of God!

As we peruse the rest of the essays in Volume One, we find the notation "R.V." in the Scripture quotations cited on a number of occasions. These early Fundamentalists welcomed the English Revised Version for the clarity that it added to understanding the Scriptures.

Then we come to Chapter Eight, "The Tabernacle in the Wilderness: Did It Exist?" by David Heagle of Ewing College. Dr. Heagle makes this very telling comment:

> And, finally, as perhaps the crowning feature of this array of evidence for genuineness of the text under consideration, it can be affirmed that, for English readers at least, there exists one authority, easy to be consulted, which would seem to put beyond all reasonable doubt the genuineness of this text [I Samuel 2:22]. That authority is our Revised English Version of the Scriptures—a literary work that in point of scholarship and general reliability stands perhaps second to none produced in recent years.[42]

It is most interesting that he did not make his appeal, to settle the disputed wording, to the King James Version.

Volume Two begins with two essays outlining the doctrine of the verbal inspiration of the Bible. The first one is by James M. Gray of Moody Bible Institute whom we have cited earlier in this study. His contribution is "The Inspiration of the Bible—Definition, Extent and Proof," and his Fundamentalist definition of inspiration included this statement:

> Let it be stated further in this definitional connection, that the *record for whose inspiration we contend is the original record*—the autographs or parchments of Moses, David, Daniel, Matthew, Paul or Peter, as the case may be, and not any particular translation or translations of them whatever. There is no translation absolutely without error, nor could there be, considering the infirmities of human copyists, unless God were pleased to perform a perpetual miracle to secure it.[43] (emphasis author's)

Gray did not believe that the preservation of the Bible involved a direct "perpetual miracle" by God, but rather that preservation is a *providential* act of God by which He worked through man's efforts to make sure that His Word has still survived for us. Gray further defended the paradox of inerrant autographs and the flawed manuscripts with an analogy to the person of Christ. Remember that A. T. Robertson defended the same paradox using the analogy of creation. Listen to Gray:

> Some ...would argue speciously that to insist on the inerrancy of a parchment no living being has ever seen is an academic question

merely, and without value. But do they not fail to see that the character and perfection of the Godhead are involved in that inerrancy?... Is it not with the written Word as with the incarnate Word? Is Jesus Christ to be regarded as imperfect because His character has never been perfectly reproduced before us? Can He be the incarnate Word unless He were absolutely without sin? And by the same token, can the scriptures be the written Word unless they were inerrant?[44]

Gray, as a non-Presbyterian, concluded his chapter with a quotation from an 1893 creedal statement by the General Assembly of the Presbyterian Church in America, which he commended "for depth as well as breadth of learning, [and] for wealth of spiritual experience":

> THE BIBLE AS WE NOW HAVE IT, IN ITS VARIOUS TRANSLA-
> TIONS AND REVISIONS, WHEN FREED FROM ALL ERRORS
> AND MISTAKES OF TRANSLATORS, COPYISTS, AND PRINT-
> ERS, (IS) THE VERY WORD OF GOD, AND CONSEQUENTLY
> WHOLLY WITHOUT ERROR (upper case in the original).[45]

The second chapter in Volume Two, written by the Methodist evangelist, L. W. Munhall, is simply entitled, "Inspiration." Significantly, in the fourth paragraph of this essay, Munhall repeats the same 1893 Presbyterian creedal statement that Gray had just cited in the previous chapter. That doctrinal statement is very significant as the accurate representation of historic Fundamentalism in that it appears twice in the *The Fundamentals* and is quoted by men of different denominations.

Munhall's masterful chapter, with text after text cited to demonstrate the entirety of Scripture's support for the doctrine of verbal inspiration, draws to a conclusion with this admission:

> That there are difficulties, I well enough know. But many difficulties have disappeared as a result of patient, reverent, scholarly research; and without doubt others will soon go the same way. So, while I bid the scholars and reverent critics God-speed in their noble work, with the late learned Bishop Ryle I say: 'Give me the plenary verbal theory with all its difficulties, rather than the doubt. I accept the difficulties, and humbly wait for their solution; but while I wait I am standing on a rock.'[46]

What a testimony of a balanced position on the Bible: simple faith to trust God's Word as the rock on which we stand, coupled with approval for the scholarly work of "reverent critics" who endeavor to present us with the clearest texts and translations! It takes a humble honesty to acknowledge that, yes, there are difficulties with some of the wording of the text, instead of blithely acting as if we have a perfect translation in spite of the evidence to the contrary.

The Fundamentals are the presentation of the doctrinal underpinnings of the Fundamentalist movement. These essays lay out the biblical teaching on the inspiration and preservation of the Holy Scriptures for God's people. They quoted from the American Standard Version of 1901 more frequently than any other translation. It was as a result of these books that the conservative, Bible-believing men of God gained the title "Fundamentalists." Those today who claim that same title must make sure that they are faithfully carrying the same torch for the faith once delivered to the saints, and not a distorted substitute.

LATER FUNDAMENTALISTS

William Bell Riley

An outstanding defender of the faith among the Northern Baptists was William Bell Riley who lived from 1861 to 1947 and was pastor of the First Baptist Church of Minneapolis for 46 years. His ministry spanned the early struggles of the Fundamentalists to its establishment as a stable movement, and he was outspoken in fighting the battles against the theological liberals of his day. Riley was an esteemed pulpiteer, a writer, and an educator. He set forth his position on the foundational doctrine of the Word of God in a book published ten years before he died, called *My Bible: An Apologetic.*

In one of the chapters titled, "The Meaning of Modernism," he addressed the issue of the Bible's unique preservation. Under the heading "The Conservation of the Canon Is Extended to the Text," Riley explained how he marveled at

> the painstaking task to which these copyists were subjected; and yet so wonderful was their expert work that the scholarship of the ages has stood astounded at the result; and scholars of no less note than Westcott and Hort have been able to affirm that not one word in a thousand, in the New Testament, was the product of a mistake![47]

It is obvious that Riley was not a critic of Westcott and Hort's textual work. On the contrary, in addition to praising their scholarship, he accepted their conclusions on the overwhelming confidence we have in the reliability of the New Testament text, which underlies our English translations.

Further addressing the Old Testament side of the issue, Riley continued, "The Septuagint has been criticized by some as clumsy and inaccurate, but it is doubtless the Version with which Christ Himself was familiar and from which He brought His quotations; and it has been basal for all translations to date." [48] Even though the Septuagint differs from the Hebrew Masoretic text in places, Riley recognized that our Lord had no problems quoting from the Septuagint Old Testament—a translation, not an original—and that Christ Himself was not on a crusade to stick with only one Bible.

Another point worth noting was this statement of Riley's: "This original translation [of the Bible] does not exist, but three world-famed copies—The Vatican, the Sinaitic, and The Alexandrian Manuscripts—are prized possessions."[49]

Richard V. Clearwaters

A more recent leader in the separatist Baptist movement in the North was Richard V. Clearwaters, pastor for 42 years of Fourth Baptist Church in Minneapolis. He, like Riley his contemporary, was a soulwinning preacher with a lengthy pastorate. His strong leadership was instrumental in guiding the Minnesota Baptist Association to break ties with the Northern Baptist Convention. Later it became necessary under his direction to sever relationships with the Conservative Baptist Association because of its compromise.

Dr. Clearwaters was the first president of Pillsbury Baptist Bible College, as well as the founder of the Central Baptist Theological Seminary in 1956.

In *The Great Conservative Baptist Compromise,* Clearwaters made statements that apparently were delivered in the 1960s regarding the translation controversy:

> Honesty compels us to cite the 1901 American Revised as the best English Version of the original languages which places us in a position 290 years ahead of those who are still weighing the King James of 1611 for demerits.... [50]

Clearwaters went on further to declare where the Fundamentalist Baptist movement in the North stood on the translation issue in his day:

> We know of no Fundamentalists ... that claim the King James as the best English translation. Those in the main stream of Fundamentalism all claim the American Revised of 1901 as the best English translation.[51]

Noel Smith

A brilliant and colorful preacher and author, Noel Smith received his theological training under A. T. Robertson at Southern Baptist Seminary in the 1930s. After serving as pastor of several Southern Baptist churches, Smith worked for a brief time with J. Frank Norris of Fort Worth.[52] In 1950, Smith joined with William Dowell and G. B. Vick in the formation of the Baptist Bible Fellowship. He became professor of Bible at the newly formed Baptist Bible College in Springfield, Missouri, where he trained young men for the ministry.

When *The Baptist Bible Tribune* was also established in 1950, Smith served as its first editor until he passed away in 1974. His quick mind was evidenced by his insightful editorials that analyzed the trends of his day, and he fearlessly defended the Fundamentalist position on the inspiration and preservation of the Word of God.

In a December 13, 1968, review that Smith wrote for the *Tribune* concerning a book that espoused a weak view of divine inspiration, notice what he had to say about the translation issue:

> The King James, the English Revised, and the American Standard versions remain the great authoritative translations of the Hebrew Old Testament and the Greek New Testament into English. As to the King James Version. Any number of English words in that version should have been corrected long ago....

> And there are mistranslations in the King James.... [I]n the 16th verse [of Romans 8] what do we have? 'The Spirit ITSELF beareth witness with our spirit, that we are the children of God.'

> How can you refer to any personality, not to mention the Third Person of the Trinity, as 'it'? It is unpardonable. It is obscene. More than half a hundred years ago the English Revised and American Standard versions made all the corrections in the cases I have mentioned, and more ....

> Why should the King James men speak of the Holy Spirit as 'it.' I don't know, except that all translations and revisions have been made by human beings....

> You don't have to follow the fanatics. You have the King James Version, the American Standard Version, the New Scofield Reference Bible. You don't have to discard your King James. You have all three.... You can keep on using your King James Version, as I do. But you should have the American Standard Version, if you are a real Bible student and an authentic and accurate expositor of the Word of God. [53]

John R. Rice

One of the most well known of Fundamentalist preachers and authors of the twentieth century was the Baptist evangelist John R. Rice. He has been described by his biographer, Robert L. Sumner, as "the twentieth century's mightiest pen." His appeal to grassroots pastors and laymen began with his weekly paper, *The Sword of the Lord,* in the 1930s and expanded through city-wide evangelistic crusades in the 1940s.

As an author, he is credited with writing nearly 200 books and pamphlets, until his death in 1980. He was noted for his emphasis on revival, evangelism, personal holiness, and contending for the faith. Rice condemned the compromise and apostasy that existed in the major denominational colleges and seminaries, in addition to exposing the dangers of ecumenical evangelism.

By means of *The Sword,* his pamphlets and his books, Rice strongly opposed liberal translations and paraphrases produced by scholars with a low view of divine inspiration. He named the *Revised Standard Version,* the *New English Bible,* the *Living Bible,* and *Good News for Modern Man*, as being unacceptable for the Lord's people and as dilutions of the Word of God. No one could call John R. Rice weak in contending for the Word of God!

Let's examine Rice's writings during the last twenty years of his life as he confronted the growing KJV Only controversy in the 1960s and 70s. Rice frequently quoted from the American Standard Version of 1901 in *The Sword* and in his books, stating as early as 1962 that the "American Standard Version, translated in 1901, is perhaps the most accurate of all versions... It takes advantage of the three great manuscripts—the Sinaiticus, the Vatican, and the Alexandrian manuscripts—which were not available when the King James Version was translated."[54] In taking this position, he was well aware that he stood on the shoulders of the early Fundamentalist leaders. He wrote in *The Sword* that "many of the best Bible teachers, including Dr. R. A. Torrey, and others more recent, have regarded it [ASV] as the most accurate of all translations."[55] Nor did he hesitate to commend other good translations:

> I think the Williams Translation of the New Testament is generally accurate and good, better perhaps than other one-man translations of the New Testament. It gives very careful attention to the tenses of the Greek verbs and is especially helpful on some difficult passages.[56]

A year before the end of his lengthy ministry, Rice stated, "I have probably done more to promote the King James Bible than anyone else in America in many years."[57] Yet, he did not shrink from addressing translational weaknesses in the King James Version. He cited Revelation 22:14 in the KJV, which states that the ones who have the right to eat of the tree of life and to enter the gates of the heavenly city are "they that do his commandments," thus implying a works salvation for entrance into Heaven. With a desire to be consistent with the rest of Scriptural teaching on the doctrine of salvation by grace alone, Rice commented unequivocally,

> In that, the translation is not correct, and that is not really what the Greek says in the original manuscript.... In that case if Erasmus, who selected and collected the Greek Received Text, had it that way he was mistaken and the translators were mistaken. I think the correct translation is, 'Blessed are they that wash their robes,[58] that they may have right to the tree of life, and may enter in by the gates into the city,' as it is given in the American Standard Version.[59]

He raised a thought-provoking question along with its answer:

> Where in the Bible does God guarantee that any translator of the Bible, anyone who copies the Bible, anyone who preaches the Bible, or anyone who teaches the Bible, will be infallibly correct? There is no such Scripture. *The doctrine of the infallibility of the translation in the King James is not a Bible doctrine*; it is a manmade scheme by some partly ignorant and some partly influenced by bad motives.[60] (emphasis mine)

Another of his responses to a letter that he received on the subject and reprinted in *The Sword* two years before he died was entitled, "We Prefer K.J. Version But Flaws in All Translations."[61] He addressed the KJV translation in Acts 12:4 in which the English word "Easter" was used, and called it "a mistake." He said the Anglican translators used "Easter" in keeping with their liturgical calendar, when the Greek word is actually "Passover."

Rice articulated his position clearly, in keeping with his Fundamentalist heritage: "God never promised that He would always have in every language a translation that is letter-perfect. Since the Bible doesn't teach that, nobody else ought teach it."[62]

Rice's overall position on Bible translations is best explained in this statement:

> Well, there are many, many translations. The differences in the translations are so minor, so insignificant, that we can be sure not a single doctrine, not a single statement of fact, not a single command or exhortation, has been missed in our translations. And where the Word of God is not perfectly translated in one instance, it is corrected in another translation. And if the Word of God is not perfectly portrayed in one translation, it is portrayed, surely, in the winnowed sum of

them all... Have copyists passed on to us any major errors so that in any particular matter we miss the Word of God? There is abundant evidence that they have not. Do the various translations differ materially on any doctrine, any fact of history, any Christian duty, on the plan of salvation, or the Person of Christ, or any comfort or instruction? No, they do not! God has preserved His Scriptures.[63]

Dr. Rice's successor as editor of *The Sword*, Curtis Hutson, also followed in Rice's non-KJV Only footsteps. Along with other independent Baptists like A. V. Henderson, pastor of Temple Baptist Church in Detroit, Hutson served on the North American Review Committee for the New King James Version.[64]

One final aspect of Rice's Fundamentalist position must be examined here. Rice also took to task—as being unscriptural—the carnal spirit and attitudes displayed by the KJVO advocates.

He referred to the writings of an unnamed Englishman whom he said was "very vigorous in denying God could have used others [texts] in translation. In this matter he is not scholarly and his attitude and railing is unchristian."[65]

He posed a penetrating question that gets to the heart of this matter:

> Why cannot fans and extremists about the King James Version be good Christians also? It is a sad thing that those in some heresy often err greatly in matters of righteousness also. They write mean letters; they make slanderous charges; they ignorantly jump to conclusions about people; they have suspicions and innuendoes. No, if a man is a good enough Christian to be right on the matter of inspiration, he ought to be a good enough Christian to control his tongue.[66]

In *I Am a Fundamentalist*, Rice included a chapter entitled, "Be a Fundamentalist BUT NOT A NUT!" (emphasis his). Along with listing a number of imbalanced positions to which Fundamentalists tend to gravitate, Rice warned that when a person contends

> that Origen and Westcott and Hort and others all united to pervert the Scriptures and go against the Bible and God and that all are modernists or hypocrites or ignorant who do not agree that the King James Version—even the translation—is inspired perfectly, then we know that that arrogant attitude, that calling of good men by bad names, shows... [they] cannot be trusted in doctrine.[67]

CONCLUSION

Where has our study of the writings of the Fundamentalists brought us? It has brought us full circle back to the answer to a question posed at the beginning. Who crowned the King James Version as the exclusive translation for use by Bible-believing Christians who desire to be faithful to the Scriptures? It most obviously was not the pioneer orthodox leaders in America who espoused clear and strong views in favor of God's Word preserved in multiple English translations.

We would be hard-pressed to find a single KJV Only adherent among them. It has been alleged that there have always been Fundamentalists who have criticized the King James Version. The fact of the matter is that most—if not all—of the conservative American forbearers were committed to and recommended various English translations of the Bible.

Let's summarize the historical survey that we have examined. R. A. Torrey's credentials as a soulwinner are unimpeachable. Why do you think that some would have us believe today that real soulwinners use only the King James Version? Torrey called other conservative translations besides the KJV the "Word of God." Yet, there are some Christians today who contend that only the King James Version is the "Word of God," and they condemn other conservative English translations, as well as any Christians who quote from those translations.

Consequently, if a pastor uses the New King James Version, for example, as his basic text in his writings or in the pulpit, he is opening himself up to criticism. Keep in mind that when critics condemn the New King James Version, *they are attacking the Word of God.* Though the NKJV differs from the KJV by updating the wording of the English text, it is just as much the Word of God as the Geneva Bible was the Word of God fifty-one years prior to the King James Bible. How far we have drifted as a movement away from the historic position on the Bible advocated by the orthodox leaders of the past!

It has only been in recent years that a new generation of self-professed Fundamentalists have trumpeted a new "King James Only" orthodoxy, making the assertion that their position is the true biblical position. A man may be a committed Christian and have a strong conviction for using the *Textus Receptus* and the King James Version. However, when a person crosses the line of orthodoxy to demand that the TR and the KJV be the only text and the only translation that define a biblical Christian, he is guilty of distorting history as well as of making unbiblical claims. By espousing a new brand of Fundamentalism that is unfaithful to its biblical roots, he has slipped from historic Christian doctrine.

It has further been alleged that Bible-believing Christians cannot have fellowship together unless they are committed to the "right Bible," namely the King James Version. We are told that if believers fellowship together—while differing on the best underlying textual tradition or the best English translation, they are guilty of compromise. However, that was not true of the early conservative believers who worked and fellowshipped together around the Biblical doctrine of the inerrancy of the original manuscripts, while using the English Revised Version, the American Standard Version and the King James Version. It is very grievous to realize that those early giants of the faith would not be welcomed to preach in the pulpits of some today. Why? Because those giants did not always use the "right Bible," as some refer to the KJV.

What about the issue of textual criticism? Is it a man-made procedure based on an evolutionary scheme of thought, as some are alleging today? James M. Gray commended the field of textual criticism for aiding in our understanding of the words that God originally gave. Remember, Gray at Moody Bible Institute trained hundreds of missionaries who laid the foundation of the Gospel in China before Communism took over. Yet, some today are telling us that Gray's position was infected by "leaven" and that the use of textual criticism in Biblical studies is wrong because it allegedly comes from a lack of faith in trusting God to preserve His Word in the *Textus Receptus*. Such teaching is diametrically opposed to the doctrinal position as presented in *The Fundamentals.* Those who attack textual criticism are taking a non-fundamentalist position and are attempting to rewrite the history of Fundamentalism.

Remember how the early conservative leaders cited the English Revised Version as the authority for settling disputed passages in the English translations? Dr. David Heagle, who contributed the chapter on the Tabernacle to *The Fundamentals,* claimed that the Revised Version was "perhaps second to none" of the recent translations in his day in terms of scholarship and reliability. He believed, as did his orthodox brethren, that God's Word is preserved in the multiple conservative English translations, and that more recent translations are often more accurate—as well as clearer in understanding—for the reader. Furthermore, Fundamentalist leaders like B. H. Carroll, A. T. Robertson, R. V. Clearwaters, and John R. Rice all believed that either the English Revised Version or the American Standard Version was a more accurate English translation than the King James Version.

As late as the 1960s Fundamentalist leaders such as R. V. Clearwaters contended that the King James Version is not the best English translation. It follows then that the KJV Only movement is indeed of recent origin, and not the historic, orthodox position on the Bible.

26

Echoing the same position was Noel Smith, who as a godly editor did not hesitate to point out the translational weaknesses in the King James Version, especially where it reflects in a negative doctrinal fashion on the personality of the Holy Spirit. However, Smith was not anti-King James Version. He was simply candid concerning the fact that all translations have problems, including the beloved King James Version. Furthermore, he urged Bible students and expositors to be well-equipped with other modern, conservative English translations. He was a staunch Fundamentalist in the Baptist Bible Fellowship, but he was not in the King James Only camp.

Nor should John R. Rice's statements be forgotten. He repudiated translations with a liberal theological bias, as well as inaccurate paraphrases. Yet he was quick to encourage God's people to read and study the Word in an up-to-date, conservative, translation. He said that those who hold to the inerrancy of the King James translation are not following "Bible doctrine," but rather "a manmade scheme." If he was right in 1979, then he is still right today. I think most readers would agree that Rice's words need a fresh circulation today among those who claim to follow his soulwinning heritage.

The pioneers of the movement argued for the inerrancy of the autographs alone, as Scripture breathed out by God. Yet, God providentially did not allow the autographs to remain in existence, and theological liberals delight in attacking this fact. It is noteworthy that Gray, as well as Robertson, were answering the criticisms of those liberals who vilified the position that the autographs alone were inerrant. Unfortunately, those same criticisms against the autographs are being recycled in our generation by some Fundamentalists who advocate the inerrancy of a particular English translation. By causing doubt about the nature of the inerrant autographs, they are unwittingly joining ranks with the very liberals that the early orthodox scholars were fighting.

Is it not interesting that these fourth century Greek manuscripts, which have been vociferously attacked by proponents of the King James Only movement, were highly regarded by these defenders of the Faith? It is puzzling that some today claim that a "valiant-for-the-truth" warrior against liberalism like W. B. Riley was misinformed, or outright wrong, in his position on the Bible because he praised those early Greek manuscripts.

Let us be absolutely certain regarding the historical record. The men who fought the battles for the Bible in the last century and earned the name Fundamentalist did not elevate the text and translation issue to either a fundamental doctrine of the faith or a test of fellowship. Keep in mind that the reason they did not do so was not because they lacked either the faith or the scholarship to do so. Perhaps the two most prominent Fundamentalist scholars with great skills in the Greek language were R. A. Torrey and A. T.

Robertson. Both of those giants of the faith were committed to the preserved Word of God in the eclectic Greek text and in multiple conservative translations. To suggest today that there were "few if any [of the early Fundamentalists who] had researched the critical text," is to overlook these gifted men who used their reverent language skills to deal with the text issue in their preaching and writings.[68]

Nor did the early Fundamentalists even debate the providential methods of preservation used by God, as some in our day have done. They were fighting on the proper battlefield against theological liberals over the inerrancy of the Scriptures, while some today are sidetracked from the proper battlefield and have busied themselves fighting their brethren over a particular translation. As the secular culture around us wonders if there is a God who has spoken, some of our brethren are preoccupied with trying to prove that God has spoken—but only in King James English.

Are we trying to move the Lord's people away from the time-honored King James Version? Not at all. The King James Version will continue to be the translation of choice for many believers. However, God's people (including the great number with limited educational backgrounds) must be free—with a clear conscience and in the rich heritage of historic Christian doctrine—to use any conservative English Bible in the pew and in the pulpit, in order to hear the Holy Spirit communicate His truth to them with words in understandable, everyday English.

Have we forgotten that this was the goal of the martyred William Tyndale— a readable translation that even an uneducated plowboy could understand? Tyndale did not try to keep the Bible in an elevated English style so that it would *sound* like the Word of God. His interest was only in an accurate translation that commoners could read and comprehend.

Have we forgotten the prized Biblical doctrines of the priesthood of the believer and the autonomy of the local church? Individual believers and individual churches should be free to make decisions about using conservative English translations without censure from their brethren.

What have we learned from this historical overview?

1. The history of American Fundamentalism demonstrates a uniform commitment to various conservative English translations, not to King James Onlyism.

2. Early Fundamentalists argued for the biblical doctrine of inspired autographs, and rejected the idea of inspired translations.

3. A number of notable Fundamentalists believed that several of the contemporary translations were more accurate renderings of the Greek text than the King James Version.

4. The scholarly Fundamentalists praised the contributions of lower textual criticism and of the fourth century Greek manuscripts.

5. Early Fundamentalists fought the battles against liberalism over the inerrancy of the Bible, instead of fighting fellow Fundamentalists over the King James Version.

The issue before us is this: Will we be faithful to our biblical heritage concerning the preserved Word of God, or will we replace that heritage with an emotionally based, manmade tradition—now masquerading as a major doctrine—that binds the Lord's people to a translation they have great difficulty in understanding? Will we stand where the orthodox Christian leaders of the past stood on the preserved Word of God, or will we exchange their balanced position for the more recent, non-orthodox, King James Only view? While we reject liberal translations and inaccurate paraphrases of Scripture, we must stand where our forefathers stood, with great confidence that we hold God's Word in our hands in the various conservative English translations available to us in our day.

AMERICAN FUNDAMENTALISM	
Proponents of God's Word Preserved in the **Totality of Manuscripts and in Conservative English Translations**	Proponents of God's Word Preserved in **Only One Greek Text (TR) and in the King James Version**
James H. Brookes	J. J. Ray
B. H. Carroll	David Otis Fuller
C. I. Scofield	Edward F. Hills
James M. Gray	Peter Ruckman
R. A. Torrey	D. A. Waite
L. W. Munhall	Gail A. Riplinger
William B. Erdman	
A. T. Robertson	
John Roach Straton	

AMERICAN FUNDAMENTALISM (CONT.)	
Proponents of God's Word Preserved in the **Totality of Manuscripts and in Conservative English Translations**	Proponents of God's Word Preserved in **Only One Greek Text (TR) and in the King James Version**
A. T. Pierson	
W. B. Riley	
Richard V. Clearwaters	
Noel Smith	
John R. Rice	

Though Ray and Fuller identified themselves as Fundamentalists they relied extensively on the writings of Seventh Day Adventist Benjamin Wilkinson, even to the point of plagiarizing his works. Ray and Fuller provided the foundation from which others drew, and thus introduced spurious views on the Bible into American Fundamentalism.

More recent proponents of the KJV Only position have written on the subject by depending heavily on the authors listed above. These include Samuel Gipp, Jack Moorman, David Cloud, William Grady, and David Sorenson. Also a non-Fundamentalist writer, Lutheran scholar Theodore Letis, argues for the superiority of the TR based on the authority of the institutional church, calling it the "ecclesiastical text." His view is similar to the Catholic view that holds that the Roman Catholic Church gave the Bible to the Church, and then conferred inspiration upon it by papal authority.

---

[1]Kirsopp Lake, *The Religion of Yesterday and To-morrow* (Boston: Houghton Mifflin, 1925), pp. 61-62.

[2]Edward J. Carnell, *The Case for Orthodox Theology* (London: Marshall, Morgan, and Scott, 1959, rpt. 1961), p. 113.

[3]Jasper James Ray, *God Only Wrote One Bible* (Junction City, OR: The Eye Opener Publishers, 1955, 1976), p. 105.

[4]Peter S. Ruckman, *The "Errors" in the King James Bible* (Pensacola, FL: Bible Baptist Bookstore, 1980), pp. 13, 31, 53, 458.

[5]In 1611 the word meant "poor in quality," not "average" as it does today. A similar usage of the word in that era was this: "The cyder (the meanest of which

will serve the purpose) is first to be drawn off fine. (1766)" *The Oxford English Dictionary* (Oxford: Clarendon Press, 1989, second edition), IX, 518.

[6]"The Translators to the Reader" in *The Holy Bible, 1611 Reprint Edition, King James Version* (Nashville: Thomas Nelson Publishers, 1990).

[7]Sydney E. Ahlstrom, *A Religious History of the American People* (New Haven, CT: Yale University Press, 1972), p. 808.

[8]George Marsden, *Understanding Fundamentalism and Evangelicalism* (Grand Rapids: Wm. B. Eerdmans Publishing Company, 1991), p. 3.

[9]The publication was the July 1, 1920, issue of the *Watchman-Examiner.* Unfortunately, the term *Fundamentalist* has been distorted in a pejorative way in our day to refer to extremists of all varieties.

[10]The English Revised Version (also referred to as the Canterbury Version) is not to be confused with the National Council of Churches' Revised Standard Version (1948-52), which minimizes the doctrine of the Virgin Birth of Christ in Isaiah 7:14.

[11]Philip W. Comfort, "History of the English Bible" in *The Origin of the Bible* (Wheaton, IL: Tyndale House Publishers, 1992), p. 272.

[12]David O. Beale, *In Pursuit of Purity: American Fundamentalism Since 1850* (Greenville, SC: Unusual Publications, 1986), pp. 375-76.

[13]James H. Brookes, *An Outline of the Books of the Bible* (New York: Fleming H. Revell, n.d.), p. 156.

[14]Ibid., p. 160.

[15]L. Russ Bush and Tom J. Nettles, *Baptists and the Bible: Revised and Expanded* (Nashville: Broadman and Holman, 1999), p. 280.

[16]Paul A. Basden, ed., *Has Our Theology Changed? Southern Baptist Thought Since 1845* (Nashville: Broadman and Holman, 1994), p. 25.

[17]Ibid., p. 33.

[18]B. H. Carroll, *Inspiration of the Bible* (New York: Fleming H. Revell Company, 1930), pp. 26, 52.

[19]Ibid., p. 109.

[20]Ibid., p. 110.

[21]*The Scofield Reference Bible*, C. I. Scofield, ed. (New York: Oxford University Press, 1909), p. 1023.

[22]Ibid., p. 1061.

[23]Ibid., p. 1160.

[24]Ibid., p. 1325.

[25]W.A. Criswell, Ph.D., ed. *The Criswell Study Bible* (Nashville: Thomas Nelson Publishers, 1979), p.1467.

[26]C. I. Scofield, *Rightly Dividing the Word of Truth* (Westwood, NJ: Fleming H. Revell Co., 1896), p. 32.

[27]Ibid., p. 59.

[28]Ibid., p. 9.

[29]James M. Gray, *Bible Problems Explained* (Chicago: Moody Press, 1913, 1941), p. 11.

[30]R. A. Torrey, *How to Work for Christ* (Old Tappan, NJ: Fleming H. Revell Company, 1901) rpt. Christian Book Gallery, n.d., p. i.

[31]Quoted in R. G. Lee, *Bread from Bellevue Oven* (Murfreesboro, TN: Sword of the Lord Publishers, 1947), pp. 53-54.

[32]R. A. Torrey, *Is the Bible the Inerrant Word of God?* (New York: George H. Doran Company, 1922), pp. 14-15.

[33]Torrey, *How to Work for Christ,* p. 351.

[34]R. A. Torrey, *The Fundamental Doctrines of the Christian Faith* (New York: Fleming H. Revell Company, 1918), pp. 36-37.

[35]John Roach Straton, *The Famous New York Fundamentalist-Modernist Debates: The Orthodox Side* (New York: George H. Doran Company, 1924, 1925), p. 45.

[36]William J. Erdman, *The Parousia of Christ: A Period of Time* (Chicago: Gospel Publishing Company, n.d.), p. 5.

[37]James Oliver Buswell, *A Systematic Theology of the Christian Religion* (Grand Rapids: Zondervan Publishing House, 1963), II, p. 97.

[38]Bush and Nettles, p. 272.

[39]A. T. Robertson, "Preface," *Word Pictures in the New Testament* (Nashville: Broadman Press, 1930), pp. viii-ix.

[40]Ahlstrom, p. 815.

[41]Dyson Hague, "The History of Higher Criticism" in *The Fundamentals* (Los Angeles: The Bible Institute of Los Angeles, 1917; reprinted by Baker Book House Company, 1998), I, p. 9.

[42]David Heagle, "The Tabernacle in the Wilderness: Did It Exist?" in *The Fundamentals,* I, p. 171.

[43]James M. Gray, "The Inspiration of the Bible" in *The Fundamentals*, II, pp. 12-13.

[44]Ibid., p. 13.

[45]Ibid., p. 43.

[46]L. W. Munhall, "Inspiration" in *The Fundamentals,* II, p. 59.

[47]W. B. Riley, *My Bible: An Apologetic* (Grand Rapids: William B. Erdmans Publishing Company, 1937), pp. 21-22.

[48]Ibid., pp. 22-23.

[49]Ibid., p. 23.

[50]Richard V. Clearwaters, *The Great Conservative Baptist Compromise* (Minneapolis: Central Seminary Press, n.d.), p. 192.

[51]Ibid., p. 199.

[52]Doug Kutilek, *J. Frank Norris and His Heirs: The Bible Translation Controversy* (Pasadena, TX: Pilgrim Publications, 1999), pp. 64-65.

[53]Noel Smith, "Translations of Our English Bible" in *The Baptist Bible Tribune,* December 13, 1968, pp. 6-7.

[54]John R. Rice, *Dr. Rice, Here Is My Question* (Wheaton: Sword of the Lord, 1962), p. 59.

[55]John R. Rice, "Why Divide God's People Over Greek Manuscripts?" in *The Sword of the Lord* (Murfreesboro, TN: Sword of the Lord Publishers), December 15, 1972, p. 5.

[56]Rice, *Dr. Rice, Here Is My Question,* pp. 59-60.

[57]Rice, "Some Questions for King James Fans" in *The Sword of the Lord,* March 30, 1979.

[58]Interestingly, the late Jack Hyles, who served on Rice's *Sword of the Lord* board for many years and was once thought to be Rice's successor, agreed with both Rice and the Nestle/Aland Text on this verse in his sermon series on Revelation: " 'DO HIS COMMANDMENTS' should be translated, 'wash their robes.' The only way that you may have a right to the tree of life is to wash your robes." *Let's Study the Revelation* (Murfreesboro, TN: Sword of the Lord Foundation, 1967), pp. 116-117.

[59]Rice, "Some Questions for King James Fans" in *The Sword of the Lord,* March 30, 1979. (The New American Standard Version also reflects this reading of "wash their robes.")

[60]Ibid.

[61]Rice, "We Prefer K. J. Version But Flaws in All Translations" in *The Sword of the Lord,* June 9, 1978.

[62]Ibid.

[63]John R. Rice, *Our God-Breathed Book, the Bible* (Murfreesboro, TN: Sword of the Lord Publishers, 1969), p. 355.

[64]Arthur L. Farstad, *The New King James Version in the Great Tradition* (Nashville: Thomas Nelson Publishers, 1989; second edition, 1993), pp. 153-54.

[65]Rice, "We Prefer K. J. Version But Flaws in All Translations" in *The Sword of the Lord,* June 9, 1978.

[66]Rice, "Some Questions for King James Fans" in *The Sword of the Lord,* March 30, 1979.

[67]John R. Rice, *I Am a Fundamentalist* (Murfreesboro, TN: Sword of the Lord Publishers, 1976), p. 74.

[68]David H. Sorenson, *Touch Not the Unclean Thing: The Bible Translation Controversy and the Principle of Separation* (Duluth, MN: Northstar Baptist Ministries, 2001), p. 217.

BIBLIOGRAPHY

Ahlstrom, Sydney E. *A Religious History of the American People.* New Haven, CT: Yale University Press, 1972.

Basden, Paul A. ed. *Has Our Theology Changed? Southern Baptist Thought Since 1845.* Nashville: Broadman and Holman Publishers, 1994.

Beacham, Roy E. and Kevin T. Bauder. eds. *One Bible Only? Examining Exclusive Claims for the King James Bible.* Grand Rapids: Kregel Publications, 2001.

Beale, David. *In Pursuit of Purity: American Fundamentalism Since 1850.* Greenville, SC: Unusual Publications, 1986.

Brookes, James H. *An Outline of the Books of the Bible.* New York: Fleming H. Revell Company, n.d.

Bush, L. Russ and Tom J. Nettles. *Baptists and the Bible: Revised and Expanded.* Nashville: Broadman and Holman Publishers, 1999.

Buswell, Jr., James Oliver. *A Systematic Theology of the Christian Religion.* Grand Rapids: Zondervan Publishing House, 1963. 2 volumes.

Carnell, Edward J. *The Case for Orthodox Theology.* London: Marshall, Morgan, and Scott, 1959, rpt. 1961.

Carroll, B. H. *Inspiration of the Bible.* New York: Fleming H. Revell Company, 1930.

Clearwaters, Richard V. *The Great Conservative Baptist Compromise.* Minneapolis: Central Seminary Press, n.d.

Comfort, Philip W. *The Origin of the Bible.* Wheaton, IL.: Tyndale House Publishers, 1992.

Criswell, W. A. *The Criswell Study Bible.* Nashville: Thomas Nelson Publishers, 1979.

Dixon, A. C. *Present Day Life and Religion.* Chicago: The Bible Institute Colportage Association, 1906.

Erdman, Charles R. *The Return of Christ.* New York: George H. Doran Company, 1922.

Erdman, William J. *The Parousia of Christ: A Period of Time.* Chicago: Gospel Publishing House, n.d.

Farstad, Arthur L. *The New King James Version in the Great Tradition.* Nashville: Thomas Nelson Publishers, 1989; second edition, 1993.

Gray, James M. *Bible Problems Explained.* Chicago: Moody Press, 1913, 1941.

The Holy Bible, Containing The Authorized Edition of the New Testament, A.D.1611, and The Revised Version of A.D. 1881. Philadelphia: A. J. Holman and Company, 1888.

Hyles, Jack. *Let's Study the Revelation.* Murfreesboro, TN.: Sword of the Lord Publishers, 1967.

Kutilek, Doug. *J. Frank Norris and His Heirs: The Bible Translation Controversy.* Pasadena, TX: Pilgrim Publications, 1999.

Lee, Robert G. *Bread from Bellevue Oven.* Murfreesboro, TN: Sword of the Lord Publishers, 1947.

Lefever, Alan J. *Fighting the Good Fight: The Life and Work of Benajah Harvey Carroll.* Austin: Eakin Press, 1994.

Marsden, George. *Understanding Fundamentalism and Evangelicalism.* Grand Rapids: Wm. B. Eerdmans, 1991.

The Oxford English Dictionary. Second Edition. Oxford: Clarendon Press, 1989. 20 vols.

Ray, Jasper James. *God Only Wrote One Bible.* Junction City, OR: The Eye Opener Publishers, 1955, 1976.

Rice, John R. *Dr. Rice, Here is My Question.* Wheaton, IL.: Sword of the Lord, 1962.

_____. *I Am a Fundamentalist.* Murfreesboro, TN: Sword of the Lord Publishers, 1975.

_____. *Our God-Breathed Book—The Bible.* Murfreesboro, TN: Sword of the Lord Publishers, 1969.

_____. "Some Questions for King James Fans" in *The Sword of the Lord.* Murfreesboro, TN: Sword of the Lord Publishers. March 30, 1979.

_____. "We Prefer K.J. Version But Flaws in All Translations" in *The Sword of the Lord.* Murfreesboro, TN: Sword of the Lord Publishers. June 9, 1978.

_____. "Why Divide God's People Over Greek Manuscripts?" in *The Sword of the Lord.* Murfreesboro, TN.: Sword of the Lord Publishers. December 15, 1972.

Riley, William B. *My Bible: An Apologetic.* Grand Rapids: Wm. B. Eerdmans, 1937.

Robertson, Archibald Thomas. *Word Pictures in the New Testament.* Nashville: Broadman Press, 1930. 6 vols.

Ruckman, Peter S. *The "Errors" in the King James Bible.* Pensacola, FL: Bible Baptist Bookstore, 1980.

Scofield, C. I. *Rightly Dividing the Word of Truth.* Westwood, NJ: Fleming H. Revell Company, 1896.

_____. *The Scofield Reference Bible.* New York: Oxford University Press, 1909.

Smith, Noel. "Translations of Our English Bible," in *Baptist Bible Tribune.* Springfield, MO: *Baptist Bible Tribune.* December 13, 1968.

Sorenson, David H. *Touch Not the Unclean Thing: The Bible Translation Controversy and the Principle of Separation.* Duluth, MN: Northstar Baptist Ministries, 2001.

Straton, John Roach. *The Famous New York Fundamentalist-Modernist Debates: The Orthodox Side.* New York: George H. Doran Company, 1924, 1925.

Sumner, Robert L. *Man Sent from God.* Murfreesboro, TN: Sword of the Lord Foundation, 1959, rev. 1981.

Torrey, Reuben A. *The Fundamental Doctrines of the Christian Faith.* New York: Fleming H. Revell Company, 1918.

Torrey, Reuben A., A. C. Dixon, et. al. *The Fundamentals: A Testimony to the Truth.* 1917. Reprint, Grand Rapids: Baker Books, 1998. 4 volumes.

_____. *How to Work for Christ.* Old Tappan, NJ: Fleming H. Revell Company. 1901. Reprint, St. John, IN: Christian Book Gallery, n. d.

_____. *Is the Bible the Inerrant Word of God?* New York: George H. Doran Company, 1922.

_____. *You and Your Bible: An Anthology of R. A. Torrey.* Westwood, NJ: Fleming H. Revell Company, 1958.

THE VOICE OF THE PREACHERS

J. Drew Conley

> *"I am a creature of a day, passing through life as an arrow through the air. I am a spirit come from God and returning to God, just hovering over the great gulf, till, a few moments hence, I am no more seen; I drop into an unchangeable eternity. I want to know one thing–the way to heaven, how to land safe on that happy shore. God himself has condescended to teach me the way. For this very end he came from heaven He ha[s] written it down in a book. O give me that book! At any price, give me the book of God! I have it. Here is knowledge enough for me. Let me be homo unius libri ('a man of one book'). Here then I am, far from the busy ways of men. I sit down alone. Only God is here. In his presence I open, I read his book–for this end, to find the way to heaven."* [1]

These words of John Wesley capture the deep love for the Holy Scriptures that has always characterized healthy Christianity. John and his brother Charles, whom we best remember for his powerful hymns, were divinely empowered "sons of thunder" during the Evangelical Awakening in England, along with other mighty evangelists such as George Whitefield. To trace the awesome work of God over the centuries through men such as these provides wonderful encouragement to believers today. Such an historical perspective also gives us valuable insight into the challenges we face. Most of our conflicts now have been battled through before. Many of the modern distortions of God's Word turn out to be little more than old heresies revived. And a large share of our difficulties reveal themselves to be the result of having left the old paths, well-worn by the saints of God.

Some portray the current translation controversy as a battle between those who believe God has preserved His Word and those who don't. But that is not where the disagreement is. Over the last century we have certainly seen the kind of flagrant disregard for the Bible that would discount its preservation, but those on both sides of today's translation debate strongly believe that God has preserved His Word. Without the Scriptures we have no divinely reliable, objective truth in which to anchor true Christianity. No Bible—no doctrine; no doctrine—no Christian faith. Nor is this divide over whether we should avoid bad translations or whether there can be a superior one.

The question is whether godly, informed men can legitimately differ on what manuscript readings and translations are best. Some good men believe that certain manuscript readings reflect a corrupt tradition. Can other men reach a different conclusion from the same evidence and still be "good men"? Some are avowing today that anyone who accepts non-majority text readings, or non-TR readings, or translations other than the King James, has departed from the faith. They argue that because some good men strongly hold to a particular family of texts or to a specific translation, anyone that disagrees with them could not possibly be good.

Translations of God's Word have been around for a long time, and over the centuries God's men have not been silent about how we are to view them. What have men, recognized for their faithful devotion to the Scriptures, known for their godly example, and remembered for their powerful, Spirit-anointed ministries had to say on this subject? What did they believe? Is the preservation of God's Word limited to only one translation, or to only certain groups of manuscripts? Is the rejection of all other translations and manuscripts a valid test of whether we are upholding historic Biblical Christianity? To answer these questions and others, I invite you to come with me on a historical survey of the great preachers of the past to discover what they taught about the translation of God's Word.

AMBROSE (A.D. 340-397)

Trained as a lawyer, Ambrose became an eloquent spokesman of God's Word as bishop of Milan. He is best remembered as the preacher under whom Augustine was converted. He preached in Latin from a Latin Bible because Latin was the language people spoke. But the following statement reveals that he relied on the Greek texts to test the accuracy of the Latin translations: "But if any one disputes because of the variations of the Latin codices [plural for *codex*, a manuscript stitched together in book form], some of which heretics have falsified, let him look at the Greek codices, and observe that it is there written."[2]

Note that there already existed variations among the translations of God's Word, some of which variations reflected heresy, but all of which were to be tested by the copies of God's Word in the original language.

AUGUSTINE (A.D. 354-430)

Considered the greatest of the Latin church fathers, Augustine was a powerful preacher and excellent writer whose Biblical teaching has been used by God to help stir revivals and great spiritual awakenings through the centuries. Although the Romanists claim him, he ministered in the days before Rome's great departure from Biblical Christianity, and his teaching largely reflects the great truths recovered by Protestants at the end of the dark ages.[3] His preaching was strongly doctrinal, and his works such as *The City of God* and *Confessions* are still read by believers today.

Augustine reiterates that the reliability of a translation is its adherence to the original language text, encouraging men preparing for the ministry to familiarize themselves with Greek and Hebrew: "Men who speak the Latin tongue, of whom are those I have undertaken to instruct, need two other languages for the knowledge of the Scripture, Hebrew and Greek, that they may have recourse to the original texts if the endless diversity of the Latin translators throw them into doubt."[4]

He advocates comparing translations to aid one's understanding of God's Word: "When now the meaning of the two translators is compared, a more likely sense of the words suggests itself." But he notes the necessity of checking the text in the original language: "Now which of these is the literal translation cannot be ascertained without reference to the text in the original tongue."[5]

Furthermore, Augustine insists that the preacher of God's Word is duty bound in his public teaching to make corrections to the translation whenever it does not rightly reflect the original language. "And very often a translator, to whom the meaning is not well known, is deceived by an ambiguity in the original language, and puts upon the passage a construction that is wholly alien to the sense of the writer. . . . Now translations such as this are not obscure, but false; and there is a wide difference between the two things. For we must learn not to interpret, but to correct texts of this sort."[6]

Augustine believed that gaining a true understanding of God's Word demands that we study either from the Scriptures in their original languages or from very literal translations that keep as close to the original as possible. "We must either endeavor to get a knowledge of those languages from which the Scriptures are translated into Latin, or we must get hold of the translations of those who keep rather close to the letter of the original, not because these are sufficient, but because we may use them to correct the freedom or the error of others, who in their translations have chosen to follow the sense quite as much as the words."[7]

In keeping with what he taught others, Augustine makes frequent correction of the Latin text by means of the Greek New Testament. Because he did not consider his understanding of Hebrew to be adequate, he corrected the Latin Old Testament passages by using the Septuagint, the Greek translation of the Old Testament.[8]

For about 1,000 years the Roman Catholic church dominated Christendom. Jerome's Latin Vulgate was the standard translation. Designed to make the Scriptures available to the common man (hence its name Vulgate, from the old meaning of *vulgar*–common), Jerome's translation of the Bible nonetheless receded from the populace over the course of time. Latin became the language of scholar and priest but not of the average man. Recovery of the languages and culture of the ancient world not only spawned the Renaissance but also created renewed interest in studying God's Word in the ancient languages and in turn a desire to translate the Bible into language everybody could understand.

But even during the dark period of medieval Christianity there shine devout men committed to the Scriptures and burdened for translation work: men like the Venerable Bede, John Wycliffe, and Girolamo Savonarola. Like the faithful men before and after them, they believed in the crucial importance of making the Scriptures understandable to the common people. The men familiar with Hebrew and Greek were careful to consult the original language texts to check the accuracy of their teaching and of the translations available to them.

BEDE (A.D.673-735)

The Venerable Bede, known as the father of English history, was, according to Philip Schaff, "the most learned man of his times."[9] He was a skilled Bible teacher, whose last great work was to finish a translation of the Gospel of John the very day he died. Of Bede's Bible expositions, Schaff remarks: "He wrote either on the whole or a part of the Pentateuch, Samuel, Kings, Ezra, Nehemiah, Proverbs, Ecclesiastes, Canticles, Isaiah, Jeremiah, Daniel, the Twelve Minor Prophets, Tobit [in the Apocrypha], Matthew, Mark, Luke, John, Catholic Epistles and the Apocalypse. His comments are of course made upon the Latin Bible, but his scholarship comes out in the frequent correction and emendation of the Latin text by reference to the original. . . . Throughout he shows himself a careful textual student."[10]

Important to note is not only the burden of Bede to get the Scriptures into the language of his people, but also his care to consult the original languages in order to explain the Scriptures accurately. This approach had been largely neglected since the days of Jerome, and what had resulted was allegorical and mystical interpretations, and hence, gross distortion of the Bible's true teachings.[11]

JOHN WYCLIFFE (C. 1328-1384)

Called the Morning Star of the Reformation, John Wycliffe was not only preacher and a scholar, but a beloved holy man. It is very possible that his contemporary, Geoffrey Chaucer, refers to Wycliffe in *The Canterbury Tales*, for Chaucer's description of the "parson" fits Wycliffe:

> *In a small town, a good man and a poor;*
> *But rich he was in holy thought and work.*
> *Also he was a learned man, a clerk,*
> *Seeking Christ's gospel faithfully to preach;*
> *Most piously his people would he teach.*
> *Benign and wondrous diligent was he,*
> *And very patient in adversity.*
>
> . . .
>
> *Going on foot, his staff within his hand–*
> *Example that his sheep could understand–*
> *Namely, that first he wrought [practiced] and after taught.*
>
> *These words from holy gospel he had brought. . . .*
> *No better priest doth anywhere reside.*
> *He had not thirst for pomp or reverence,*
> *Nor bore too sensitive a conscience,*
> *But taught Christ's and his twelve apostles' creed,*
> *And first in living of it took the lead.*

Although Wycliffe knew neither Hebrew nor Greek, he was first to give the English people the entire Bible in their own language. He believed the Bible belonged to both clergy and laity alike and that it was the sole rule of faith and practice. His massive 1,000 page work, the *Truth of Scripture* (*De veritate Scripturae*, published in 1387-88) lays out his convictions on this and other subjects. "Logic," he argues, "changes very frequently, yea, every twenty years, but the Scriptures are yea, yea and nay, nay. They never change. They stand to eternity" (I.54). He dismissed false methods of interpretation in favor of the literal method. Schaff records that Wycliffe believed that "to withhold the Scripture from the laity is the fundamental sin . . . . Christen men and women, olde and young, shulden study fast in the New Testament, and no simple man of wit shulde be aferde unmeasurably to study in the text of holy Writ."[12]

Schaff concludes: "The call to honor the Scriptures as the Word of God and to study and diligently obey them, runs through Wyclif's writings like a scarlet thread. Without knowing it, he departed diametrically from Augustine when he declared that the Scriptures do not depend for their authority upon the judgment of the Church, but upon Christ."[13] Wycliffe would also be at odds with those today who argue that church authority establishes the value of a manuscript family or a translation.

GIROLAMO SAVONAROLA (1452-1498)

Very likely the most extraordinary preacher of righteousness Italy ever produced, Savonarola preached strong Biblical sermons to bring about, in his words, "'the regeneration of the Church, taking the Scriptures as my sole guide.'"[14] Schaff describes his sermons as "flashes of lightning and reverberations of thunder," striking against the prevalent loose living of clergy and laity alike.[15] Although he remained in the Catholic Church, his strong denunciation of the evils he found there created many enemies. He eventually died a martyr's death by papal decree, but not without leaving the impress of Biblical repentance and reform in a land dominated by ecclesiastical tradition. What makes this unusual prophet of God pertinent to our study is his attention to studying the Scriptures in a day when even many of the clergy were ignorant of them. In the town of his ministry, Florence, Italy, two copies of his Bibles have survived, with his handwritten notes written between the lines, in the margin, and on added pages. He advocated studying the Scriptures in the original languages, and left, among other writings, expositions of Psalm 32 and Psalm 51, which Martin Luther later published with high commendation.[16]

MARTIN LUTHER (1483-1546)

Great German preacher, hymn writer, and translator who served the Lord as the foremost leader of the Reformation, Martin Luther had an impact on persons high and low throughout Europe. His preaching was strongly scriptural, doctrinal, and practical. His burden to put the Scriptures into the language of the common man shows in the following excerpt from a letter he wrote to George Spalatin on March 30, 1522:

> I have not only translated the Gospel of St. John in my Patmos, but the whole of the New Testament, and Philip and I are now busy correcting it, and with God's help, it will be a splendid work. Meantime we need your help, to find out proper words, therefore be ready to supply us with the common terms for some things we require, but not those used at Court, for this book is to be written in the simplest language that all may understand it.[17]

WILLIAM TYNDALE (C. 1492-1536)

The "father of the English Bible," Tyndale's burden to get the Bible into the everyday language of the people had to do with his concern for their spiritual survival. Unless they could clearly understand the Scripture they were hearing or reading, they could not discern whether or not they were being taught heresy or God's truth:

"I perceived how that it was impossible to establish the lay-people in any truth, except the scripture were plainly laid before their eyes in their mother tongue, that they might see the process, order, and meaning of the text. For else, whatsoever truth is taught them, these enemies of all truth quench it again, partly . . . with apparent reasons of sophistry and traditions of their own making, founded without ground of scripture; and partly in juggling with the text, expounding it in such sense as is impossible to gather of the text, if thou see the process, order and meaning thereof."[18] In other words, the less familiar people are with the language of the Bible, the more susceptible they are to false teaching.

Tyndale's translation work demonstrated that the best deliverance and protection from error is an accurate translation of God's Word in the everyday language of the common man. Tyndale literally gave his life to bring the Bible to the English-speaking world, but getting the Scriptures to the common Englishman spawned revival and eventually delivered England from the darkness of Romanist error.

HUGH LATIMER (1485-1555)

Once an ardent foe of the gospel doctrines of Luther and Tyndale, Hugh Latimer became a powerful advocate for the gospel after he was converted through the faithful witness of a fellow graduate at Cambridge. His forceful preaching earned him the description, "father of the English pulpit." It also brought him to a martyr's stake by the command of bloody Mary Tudor. Who can forget his words to Bishop Ridley the day he died for his Lord: "Master Ridley, play the man. We shall this day light such a candle, by God's grace, in England, as I trust shall never be put out."

Since it was the availability of the Scriptures that had sparked the spread of the gospel at Cambridge, Latimer's fierce loyalty to the Bible is not hard to understand. He defended Tyndale's translation as worthy of reverence by virtue of its being a translation of God's Word. In a letter he wrote to Hubbardine, he rebukes the Romanist's opposition to translation of the Bible into simple language as in fact an attack on God's Word itself, amounting to blasphemy:

> But you will say, that you condemn not the scripture, but Tyndal's [sic] translation. Therein ye show yourself contrary to your words; for ye have condemned it in all other common tongues, wherein they be approved in other countries. So that it is plain, that it is the scripture, and not the translation, that ye bark against, calling it *new learning*. And this much for the first lie.

> As for the two other, [they] be soon confuted, that it is not the truth, nor of God, but lies and of the devil. O Jesu, mercy! That ever such blasphemy against the Holy Ghost should proceed out of a Christian man's mouth! Is it not one to say, that the doctrine of Christ is lies, and cometh of the devil, and that Christ is a liar, and the devil?[19]

Latimer's words underscore the relationship between translations of God's Word and God's very words. Albeit for reasons other than those of 16th-century Catholicism, demonizing various Bible translations has become common once again. When debates over the quality of a Bible translation descend into vilifying that translation, they risk crossing the line into blaspheming God's Word—insofar as that translation conveys the words of the original.

MILES COVERDALE (1488-1568)

A Church of England clergyman who served as bishop of Exeter, Coverdale assisted William Tyndale in his translation work and was first to publish a printed English translation of the entire Bible (1535). His work eventually served in large part as the basis of the revision we know today as the King James Version. In his "Prologue to the Bible: Miles Coverdale unto the Christian Reader," Coverdale addresses the importance of multiple translations of God's Word:

> Whereas some men think now that many translations make division in the faith and in the people of God, that is not so; for it was never better with the congregation of God, than when every church almost had the Bible of a sundry translation [that is, a translation that varied some from other translations]. Among the Greeks, had not Origen a special translation? Had not Vulgarius one peculiar, and likewise Chrysostom? Beside the seventy interpreters, is there not the translation of Aquila, of Theodotion, Symmachus, and of sundry others? Again, among the Latin men, thou findest that every one almost used a special and sundry translation; for insomuch as every bishop had the knowledge of the tongues, he gave his diligence to have the Bible of his own translation. The doctors, as Ireneus, Cyprian, Tertullian, St.

Jerome, St. Augustine, Hilary, and St. Ambrose, upon divers [various] places of the scripture, read not the text all alike.[20]

Coverdale argues that having a number of translations does not promote the evil of disunity and doctrinal error as some contend [in his day, the Roman Catholic bishops]:

Seeing then that his diligent exercise of translating doth so much good and edifieth in other languages, why should it do evil in ours? Doubtless, like as all nations in the diversity of speeches may know one God in the unity of faith, and be one in love, even so may divers translations understand one another, and that in the chief articles and ground of our most blessed faith, though they use sundry words.

Further, Coverdale reveals that his work is not to be regarded as a repudiation of earlier translations, for which he expresses gratitude:

I took the more upon me to set forth this special translation; not as a checker, not as a reprover or despiser of other men's translations, for among many, was yet I have found none without occasion of great thanksgiving unto God, but lowly and faithfully have I followed mine interpreters, and that under correction.[21]

With characteristic humility, Coverdale pleads for a charitable response wherever his translation could have been better. In so doing he conveys the limitations under which every translator labors:

Though I have failed any where, as there is no man but he misseth in some thing, Christian love shall construe all to the best, without any perverse judgment. There is no man living that can see all things, neither hath God given any man to know every thing. One seeth more clearly than another, one hath more understanding than another, one can utter a thing better than another, but no man ought to envy or despise another. . . . If thou hast knowledge therefore to judge where any fault is made, I doubt not but thou wilt help to amend it, if love be joined with thy knowledge.[22]

THE KING JAMES TRANSLATORS (1611)
(Church of England clergy)

These men of stature that worked together to produce the King James Version have long been revered for the wonderful contribution they made to generations of English speakers. When they published the first edition of the King James in 1611, they included a thorough defense of their work that outlines the history and major principles of translating the Bible. The tenets they put forth in that preface still hold today among those who labor responsibly in this crucial calling.

Sadly, many subsequent publications of the Authorized Version leave out the preface, to the detriment of God's people. Some Bibles are including "The Translators to the Reader" once again, and the American Bible Society has published the preface in a booklet that includes a facsimile of the original pages, a transcription of the text in modern typeface, and then a translation that uses modern English. It would do well for those who deeply love the King James to read what the men who produced it believed.

The great reverence the King James translators had for God's Word barred them from demonizing the other eight English translations of God's Word available in their day, despite their imperfections: "We do not deny, nay, we affirm and avow, that the very meanest translation of the Bible in English set forth by men of our profession . . . containeth the word of God, nay, is the word of God. . . . No cause therefore why the word translated should be denied to be the word, or forbidden to be current, notwithstanding that some imperfections and blemishes may be noted in the setting forth of it."[23]

The following points summarize the principles put forth in the original preface to the King James Version:

1. Expectation of strong opposition to their work (p. 29)

2. Affirmation that the Word of God is perfect and necessary to salvation (pp. 31-32)

3. Necessity of translation to gain the divinely-ordained benefit of the Scriptures (pp. 33-34)

4. Need for new translations and revised translations (pp. 34-42)

5. Crucial importance of translating into the common language

6. Answers to objections to adding another revision/translation:

   a. New translation work is not a condemnation of earlier translations, but a continuation of the same good work (pp. 44-45).

   b. Former translations can be improved and those who did the work before would applaud efforts to do so. Such work improves the good and affirms the best (p. 46).

   c. The poorer quality translations of God's Word are still God's Word (not a blanket endorsement of purposeful distortions) despite faults in the translation (See quotation above; p. 47).

d. Translations should not be disregarded or maligned simply because heretics did them (pp. 48-49).

7. Intention to make a principal good (better) translation from previous good translations (p. 54)

8. Comparison with the original languages the test of accuracy (pp. 55-56)

9. The importance of alternative readings (placed in the margin) to the reading in the main body of text, the fact that these alternatives do not negate any doctrine, and the liberty to disagree on which reading is best (pp. 57-58)

10. The validity of variety of English word choice in translating the same Hebrew or Greek words (pp. 59–61)

11. Reiteration that the "very vulgar" (that is, very common persons) should be able to understand the Bible (p. 62)

12. Urgent appeal to heed the Scriptures (p. 62)

As will become increasingly clear from the teaching of other great preachers of God's Word, what the King James translators present in their preface is solidly in line with the position of God's people throughout the history of Biblical Christianity.

JOHN OWEN (1616-1683)

Puritan congregationalist pastor and vice-chancellor of Oxford University in England, John Owen is known for his precise exposition of the Scriptures. His theological works fill twenty-four volumes. Owen clearly explains what translations of God's Word are and warns against the abuse of them. First, Owen underscores that translations are the Word of God insofar as they accurately convey the meaning of the original: "Translations contain the word of God, and are the word of God, perfectly or imperfectly, according as they express the words, sense, and meaning of those originals." This truth leads to a pointed application: "To advance any, all translations concurring, into an equality with the originals, . . . –much more to propose and use them as means of castigating, amending, altering any thing in them, gathering various lections [variations] by them, is to set up an altar of our own by the altar of God, and to make equal the wisdom, care, skill and diligence of men, with the wisdom, care, and providence of God himself."[24] In other words, Owen teaches that elevating any translation to equal status with the original, or worse, maintaining loyalty to it over the original, amounts to idolatry.

RICHARD BAXTER (1615-1691)

Truly a pastor of pastors, puritan Richard Baxter is best known for the phenomenal transformation his ministry brought to the town of Kidderminster. Baxter was a master of bridging the gap between theoretical knowledge of the truth and practical living of it. His works on pastoral ministry are highly profitable to ministers today. In his massive volume on practical Christian living, *A Christian Directory*, he mentions among other errors, one mistake some make regarding the preservation of God's Word: "Those give too much (in bulk, but too little in virtue) to the Scripture . . . that say that God hath so preserved the Scripture, as that there are no various readings and doubtful texts thereupon, and that no written or printed copies have been corrupted. . . . All these err in over-doing."[25] In other words, the doctrine of the inspiration and preservation of God's Word does not guarantee that we can eliminate every question about which reading of some texts is best. This reality holds true even if we limit ourselves to one family of manuscripts or one Greek text because no two manuscripts are exactly alike in every single detail.

BENJAMIN KEACH (1640-1704)

A non-conformist and one of the earliest Baptists, Benjamin Keach suffered being fined, pilloried, and imprisoned for his beliefs. He nonetheless enjoyed a prolific ministry first as an evangelist and then as a pastor of the church Charles Spurgeon would one day serve. He wrote a number of works, among them a catechism for teaching children the truths in the London Baptist Confession of 1647 (*The Child's Instructor*, 1664) and *Expositions of the Parables in the Bible* (1671). Keach was also the first to introduce hymn singing into Baptist congregations. A number of his written works deal with Scriptural worship and the place of music in it.

What Keach taught about translations maintains the course of thought we've found thus far: that the test of a translation is how well it conveys the words of the original and that while translations vary in quality when they are so judged, even the poorer ones are still spiritually profitable.

"Now though some translations may exceed others in Propriety, and significant rendering of the Originals; yet they generally (even the most imperfect that we know of) express and hold forth so much the Mind, Will, and Counsel of God, as is sufficient . . . to acquaint a Man with the Mysteries of Salvation, to work in him a true Faith, and bring him to live godly, righteously, and soberly in this World, and to Salvation in the next."[26]

GEORGE WHITEFIELD (1714-1770)

Powerful evangelist during the First Great Awakening, Whitefield had profound impact on both England and America. J. C. Ryle says of him:

> The crowning excellence of Whitefield's teaching was that he just spoke of men, things, and doctrines, in the way that the Bible speaks of them. God, Christ, and the Spirit,–sin, justification, conversion, and sanctification,–impenitent sinners the most miserable of people, –believing saints the most privileged of people, –the world a vain and empty thing,–heaven the only rest for an immortal soul,–the devil a tremendous and ever-watchful foe,–holiness the only true happiness,–hell a real and certain portion of the unconverted; –these were the kind of things which filled Whitefield's mind, and formed the staple of his ministry.[27]

In the course of his preaching, it was not uncommon for Whitefield to clarify and to correct a translated word with the meaning of the original. The dominant translation of Whitefield's day was the King James Version, but his preaching reveals that he did not consider it beyond improvement. Preaching on John 16:8, he refers to the original language text in order to correct the translation: "The word, which we translate reprove, ought to be rendered convince; and in the original it implies a conviction by way of argumentation, and coming with a power upon the mind equal to a demonstration."[28]

JONATHAN EDWARDS (1703-1758)

An extraordinary servant of God as pastor, theologian, and educator, Jonathan Edwards is among the greatest American preachers ever. Most of us were introduced to Edwards as school children when we were assigned to read "Sinners in the Hands of an Angry God." His genius, his zealous love for God, his precision and power in presenting Biblical truth, his experiences of revival during the Great Awakening–these make Edwards a man to be studied even today. Martyn Lloyd-Jones says of him: "No man is more relevant to the present conditions of Christianity than Jonathan Edwards. . . . He was a mighty theologian and a great evangelist at the same time. . . . If you want to know anything about true revival, Edwards is the man to consult. My advice is, Read Jonathan Edwards. Go back to something solid and deep and real."[29]

As did the careful expositors before him, Edwards determines the accuracy of the translation by means of the original. Consider his comments on Genesis 10: "And whereas it is said, Genesis 10:11,12 in our translation, 'Out of this land went forth Ashur, and built Nineveh, and the city of Rehoboth, and Colah, and Resen, between Nineveh and Calab, the same is a great city.' It might have been rendered as agreeably to the original, and much more agreeably to the preceding verses, and the drift of the historian, 'Out of that land he went forth into Ashur, and built Nineveh etc.'"[30]

Edwards does the same thing with Isaiah 40:15: "'He taketh up the isles as a very little thing.' A very fine remark, and a solid correction of the common translation, is here made by that learned, sagacious, and devout expositor, Vitringa. He observes that the common translation is neither answerable to the import of the original, nor consonant to the structure of the discourse."[31] In both these cases, the translation Edwards is correcting is the King James, and he clearly feels no reluctance in doing so. The issue for Jonathan Edwards is accuracy of meaning–and that is determined by the text in the original language.

JOHN WESLEY (1703-1791)

The Wesley brothers have left an indelible mark on the history of Christianity, even if the denomination they founded has in large measure drifted from the kind of Biblical teaching they championed. Both John and Charles were preachers at the center of the Evangelical Awakening. We still sing hymns that Charles wrote, and we still benefit from the effect the Wesleys' ministry had on America during its foundational years. John Wesley loved the Scriptures. He was "a man of one book," as he himself put it, but not a man of one *translation*. He used the King James and revered it, but he did not confine himself to the King James alone.

John Wesley's letters reveal that he carefully studied various New Testament translations in comparison with the original language: "I have myself closely and carefully examined every part of it [Christianity], every verse of the New Testament, in the original, as well as in our own and other translations."[32] We learn further that in his preaching he would correct the Authorized Version to reflect better the reading in the Greek and Hebrew manuscripts: "No marvel that such 'love is not provoked.' . . . Let it be observed, the word *easily*, strangely inserted in the translation, is not in the original. St. Paul's words are absolute."[33]

John's letters and journal entries make intriguing references to the Wesley brothers' work on a new translation of the New Testament and of the Psalms:

> "Wed. 27.–My brother came down from London, and we spent several days together, in comparing the translation of the Evangelists with the original."[34] Another entry—"Wednesday, 12. I began reading over the Greek Testament and the Notes, with my brother and several others; carefully comparing the translation with the original, and cor-

recting or enlarging the notes as we saw occasion."[35] And another—"Wednesday, 14. I preached in the evening in the old Temple Church, on Psalm 74:12. In the old translation [the KJV] it runs, 'The help that is done upon the earth, God doeth it himself.' A glorious and important truth! In the new [Wesley's own translation], 'Working salvation in the midst of the earth.' What a wonderful emendation! Many such emendations there are in this translation: One would think King James had made them himself."[36]

F. F. Bruce sheds light on the new translation to which Wesley often refers: "In 1768 John Wesley issued a revised edition of the A.V., with notes 'for plain, unlettered men who understand only their Mother Tongue.' This revision was based on careful study of the Greek original; there were some 12,000 alterations in all, but none of them, the reader is assured, for altering's sake. The English text is divided into sense-paragraphs, 'a little circumstance which makes many passages more intelligible to the Reader.'"[37]

In John Wesley's introduction to his update of the King James New Testament, observe his high regard for the Authorized Version and at the same time his use of the original Greek to improve it—sometimes from manuscript readings the King James translators did not use: "I design, first, to set down the text itself, for the most part, in the common English translation [the KJV], which is in general (so far as I can judge) abundantly the best I have seen. Yet I do not say, it is incapable of being brought, in several places, nearer to the original. Neither will I affirm that the Greek copies from which this translation was made are always the most correct. And therefore I shall take the liberty, as occasion may require, to make here and there a small alteration."[38] In another place he expresses both his care in not altering too much and at the same time the significance of what he did change: "In this edition the translation is brought as near as possible to the original; yet the alterations are few and seemingly small; but they may be of considerable importance."[39]

Samuel Davies (1723-1761)

Powerful evangelist and pastor during the First Great Awakening and successor to Jonathan Edwards as President of the College of New Jersey (now Princeton). He led the way in establishing new churches and supplying them with ministers, and was considered one of the greatest American evangelists of the 18th century. Martyn Lloyd-Jones goes so far as to call Davies "the most eloquent preacher the American continent has produced."

In an evangelistic defense of Biblical Christianity, he comments, "It is matter of astonishment as well as conviction, that all the various copies and translations of the Scriptures in different nations and libraries are substantially the same, and differ only in matters of small moment; so that from the worst copy of [or?] translation in the world, one might easily learn the substance of Christianity."[40] Just as in Davies' day, there are those today that dismiss the Bible because they are under the mistaken impression that the ancient manuscripts of it are too diverse and thus too corrupted to be trusted. Well-meaning believers must be careful not to exaggerate the significance of the variations in manuscript readings not only because doing so misrepresents the truth, but also because it undermines belief in the integrity of the Scriptures.

JOHN GILL (1697-1771)

Baptist pastor in London for over fifty years in the church eventually led by Spurgeon, John Gill is still recognized for his doctrinal precision. Of the doctrine of inspiration, he writes:

> This is to be understood of the Scriptures, as in the original languages in which they were written, and not of translations; unless it could be thought, that the translators of the Bible into the several languages of the nations into which it has been translated, were under divine inspiration also in translating, and were directed of God in the use of words they have rendered the original by; but this is not reasonable to suppose.

He argues that translations must be judged and corrected by the Bible text in its original languages:

> To the Bible, in its original languages, is every translation to be brought, and judged, and to be corrected and amended; and if this was not the case, we should have no certain and infallible rule to go by; for it must be either all the translations together, or some one of them; not all of them, because they agree not in all things: not one; for then the contest would be between one nation and another which it should be . . . : so the papists, they plead for their vulgate Latin version; which has been decreed authentic by the council of Trent; though it abounds with innumerable errors and mistakes; nay, so far do they carry this affair, that they even assert that the Scriptures, in their originals, ought to submit to, and be corrected by their version; which is absurd and ridiculous.

Gill is aware that these truths may unsettle some, so he adds these words of comfort:

Let not now any be uneasy in their minds about translations on this account, because they are not upon an equality with the original text . . . ; for . . . he [God] has taken care, in his providence to raise up men capable of such a performance . . . ; for whenever a set of men have been engaged in this work, as were in our nation, men well skilled in the languages, and partakers of the grace of God; of sound principles, and of integrity and faithfulness, having the fear of God before their eyes; they have never failed of producing a translation worthy of acceptance; and in which, though they have mistook some words and phrases, and erred in some lesser and lighter matters; yet not so as to affect any momentous article of faith or practice; and therefore such translations as ours may be regarded as the rule of faith.[41]

JOHN NEWTON (1725-1807)

Former sea captain and slave trader, English pastor John Newton is unforgettable for his masterful hymns like "Amazing Grace," "How Sweet the Name of Jesus Sounds," and "Glorious Things of Thee Are Spoken." He served the Lord sixteen years in Olney, Bucks and then twenty-seven years at St. Mary, Woolnoth, London. His ministry was both practical and powerful, with much focus on Christ. Newton testified, "It will not be a burden to me at the hour of death that I have thought too highly of Jesus, expected too much from Him myself, or labored too much in commending and setting Him forth to others."[42]

Newton's preaching shows that although he had the highest regard for the English version of his day (the King James), he considered it important at times to change certain expressions to make them more clear. He also affirms the practice of using the original language as the test of accuracy:

It would be improper to propose an alteration, though a slight one, in the reading of a text, without bearing my testimony to the great value of our English version, which I believe, in point of simplicity, strength, and fidelity, is not likely to be excelled by a new translation of the *whole* Scripture. But there are, undoubtedly, particular passages, where a small change in the expression might render the sense clearer, and be equally answerable to the original Hebrew or Greek.[43]

ANDREW FULLER (1754-1815)

English Baptist pastor Andrew Fuller helped to found the Baptist Foreign Missionary Society, which sent William Carey to India. He also served as its first secretary. Fuller was known for his expository preaching and solid doctrinal content. His instruction on the relationship between translation and text provides helpful insight and is in line with the historic view:

> Allowing all due honour to the English translation of the Bible, it must be granted to be a human performance, and, as such, subject to imperfection. Where any passage appears to be mistranslated, it is doubtless proper for those who are well acquainted with the original languages to point it out, and to offer, according to the best of their judgment, the true meaning of the Holy Spirit. Criticisms of this kind, made with modesty and judgment, and not in consequence of a preconceived system, are worthy of encouragement.[44]

WILLIAM CAREY (1761-1834)

Called "the Wycliffe of the East," William Carey considered translation work among the highest priorities in mission work. Translating from the original languages, he labored to make the Scriptures available to the people of India in their vernacular, thus providing the missionaries with a powerful tool for evangelism. He completed his translation of the New Testament into Bengali in 1801, and the translation of the Old Testament by 1809. Knowing that all translations fall short of perfection, he recognized the faults of his own translation work. Consequently, he kept striving to improve his Bengali translation of the Bible, publishing eight editions of the New Testament and five of the Old during his lifetime. Carey helped translate the Bible into Ooriya, Marathi, Hinki, Assamese, Sanskrit, as well, along with portions of the Bible into some twenty-nine other languages.[45]

ADONIRAM JUDSON (1788-1850)

Judson worked hard to translate twenty-five to thirty verses a day in order to put the Bible into the Burmese language. He chose the more laborious task of translating directly from the Hebrew and Greek, rather than from the King James English. He believed strongly that a translation of a translation would lose too much of the original meaning.[46] He finally completed the great undertaking in 1834. In his words of gratitude to God on that occasion, he gives insight into the sacred, but imperfect nature of Bible translating: "'Imploring his aid in future efforts to remove the errors and imperfections which necessarily cleave to the work, I have commended it to his mercy and grace; I have dedicated it to his glory. May he make his own inspired word, now complete in the Burman tongue, the grand instrument of filling all Burmah with songs of praise to our Great God and Savior Jesus Christ.'"[47]

J. C. RYLE (1816-1900)

Author of more than 100 pamphlets and books on doctrinal and practical subjects, J. C. Ryle is unsurpassed when it comes to compelling exposition of the Scriptures. His *Expository Thoughts on the Gospels* are marked by pointed simplicity and theological integrity that prove invaluable to preaching from the Gospels today. His emphasis on practical godliness combined with his precise handling of the Scriptures make him a voice to be heeded when it comes to authentic Christianity.

Ryle's comments on Bible translations are significant for at least two reasons: first is the careful integrity that characterizes his writings; second is that the span of his ministry covers the period when Westcott and Hort published their Greek text and when the English Revised Version was released. Ryle states, "I lay no claim to the inspiration of every word in the various versions and translations of God's Word. So far as those translations and versions are faithfully and correctly done, so far they are of equal authority with the original Hebrew and Greek. We have reason to thank God that many of the translations are, in the main, faithful and accurate."[48] He says further, "We have no right to expect infallibility in transcribers and copyists, before the invention of printing. But there is not a single doctrine in Scripture which would be affected or altered if all the various readings were allowed, and all the disputed or doubtful words were omitted."[49]

Ryle's position is in line with historic Christian doctrine, but it flatly contradicts the teaching that makes a translation of full equal authority with the original. It also serves to correct the misguided though often sincere exaggeration of the impact manuscript differences have on Bible doctrine.

F. H. A. SCRIVENER (1813-1891)

A member of committee of the English Revised Version, Scrivener consistently favored Textus Receptus readings over those of Westcott and Hort and was one of the most respected critics of their text. He produced his own Greek New Testament based on the Textus Receptus. Later he integrated the Codex Sinaiticus into his Greek text.

Scrivener's comments on the relationship between the King James Version of the New Testament and its underlying Greek text help set the boundaries of what we can rightly claim even for an English Version we may consider best: "Beza's fifth and last text of 1598 was more likely than any other to be in the hands of King James's revisers, and to be accepted by them as the best standard within their reach. It is moreover found on comparison to agree more closely with the Authorised Version than any other Greek text. . . . There are, however many places in which the Authorised Version is at variance with Beza's text [Scrivener lists all 190 instances in the Appendix.]; chiefly because it retains language inherited from Tyndale or his successors, which had been founded on the text of other Greek editions. . . . in some places the Authorised Version corresponds but loosely with any form of the Greek original, while it exactly follows the Latin Vulgate."[50]

ROBERT DABNEY (1820-1898)

Respected Presbyterian theologian and pastor who served as Stonewall Jackson's Chief of Staff, Dabney staunchly criticized the work of Westcott and Hort and the English Revised Version of 1881. But his opposition does not mean he believed the Textus Receptus could not be improved in some cases to get closer to the original writings of the apostles: (1881) "No one claims for the Textus Receptus, or common Greek text of the New Testament, any sacred right, as though it represented the ipsissima verba, [Latin for "the very words"] written by the inspired men in every case. . . . It is therefore not asserted to be above emendation."[51]

CHARLES HADDON SPURGEON (1834-1892)

There could hardly be a better known pastor than "the prince of preachers." Spurgeon's ministry enjoyed the marks of revival throughout his over forty years of preaching, with conversions every week and a congregation that grew to over 6,000. Spurgeon was a workhorse, full of zeal for Christ and love for people. He established orphanages, founded churches, wrote books and articles, and trained men for the ministry. At great personal cost he fought to counteract the "downgrade" of the Baptist Union as it began to accommodate doctrinal error within its ranks. There is no question about either the orthodoxy or the productivity of this extraordinary man of God.

Because Spurgeon was pastoring before, during, and after the time the English Revised Version was produced, his treatment of the preservation and translation of the Scriptures is especially instructive. His published sermons show that his consistent practice was to correct the English translation to reflect better the reading of the text in the original language. He often referred his congregation to the marginal readings in both the King James and the English Revised versions. Once the English Revised Version came out, he immediately made use of it, at times taking his text from the new translation. His high esteem for the Authorized Version remained intact, however, and he considered the old translation generally superior to the new. Nonetheless, he would choose the wording of the English Revised over that of the King James whenever he considered it an improvement. And he did so in the majority of his sermons from 1881 onward. Spurgeon made too many references to Bible translation to include them all, but the following examples from his published sermons will give you an overview of his approach.

Correction Of The English Translation
To Conform To The Text In The Original Language

"Joy Born at Bethlehem," Luke 2:10-12, preached December 24, 1871: "After the angel had said 'to you,' he went on to say, 'it shall be *to all people.*' But our translation is not accurate, the Greek is, 'it shall be to all *the* people.' This refers most assuredly to the Jewish nation; there can be no question about that; if any one looks at the original, he will not find so large and wide an expression as that given by our translators. It should be rendered 'to all *the* people."[52]

"Joy in a Reconciled God," Romans 5:11, preached April 7, 1872: "The word 'atonement' is a very improper translation here. It is the only case in which our translators have used the word at all in the New Testament, and it is very unfortunate that they should have used it in the wrong place, because the word is as plainly as possible 'reconciliation.'"[53]

"By All Means Save Some," 1 Corinthians 9:22, preached April 26, 1874: "What a very wonderful address that was which Paul delivered to the council of philosophers upon Mars' Hill. It is most courteous throughout, and it is a pity that our translation somewhat destroys that quality, for it is eminently conspicuous in the original. The apostle began by saying, 'Ye men of Athens, I perceive that ye are on all points very God-fearing.' He did not say, 'Too superstitious,' as our version has it, that would have needlessly provoked them at the outset."[54]

Correction of the Translation
Because of the Change of Language Over Time

"The Paraclete," John 14:16, preached October 6, 1872: "The 'Holy Ghost,' but the name is now an erroneous one. The word 'ghost' was the same as 'spirit' in years gone by, when the present translation of the Bible was made, but it does not popularly signify 'spirit' now; superstition has degraded the word from its elevated meaning, and it might be as well perhaps if the word were dropped altogether and we confined ourselves to the more accurate word, 'Holy Spirit.'"[55]

"The Bible Tried and Proved," Psalm 12:6, preached May 5, 1889: On: "The commandments of the Lord are just and right. We have occasionally heard opponents carp at certain coarse expressions used in our translation of

59

the Old Testament; but the coarseness of translators is not to be set to the account of the Holy Spirit, but to the fact that the force of the English language has changed, and modes of expression which were current at one period become too gross for another."[56]

"A Stanza of Deliverance," Exodus 12:35-36, preached July 31, 1890: "It was a very unfortunate mistake of our translators when they rendered the original by the word 'borrowed,' for it is not the correct word. Our Revised Version has it more accurately, 'And the children of Israel did according to the word of Moses; and they asked of the Egyptians jewels of silver and jewels of gold, and raiment: and the Lord gave the people favor in the sight of the Egyptians, so that they let them have what they asked.'"[57]

Importance of the Text in the Original

"Heart-Disease Curable," Isaiah 61:1, preached June 19, 1881: "Concerning the fact of difference between the Revised and the Authorized Versions, I would say that no Baptist should ever fear any honest attempt to produce the correct text, and an accurate interpretation of the Old and New Testaments. For many years Baptists have insisted upon it that we ought to have the Word of God translated in the best possible manner, whether it would confirm certain religious opinions and practices, or work against them. All we want is the exact mind of the Spirit. . . . By the best and most honest scholarship that can be found we desire that the common version may be purged of every blunder of transcribers, or addition of human ignorance, or human knowledge, that so that word of God may come to us as it came from his own hand."[58]

"Our Lord's Prayer for His People's Sanctification," John 17:17, preached March 7, 1886: "You cannot change Holy Scripture. You may arrive more and more accurately at the original text; but for all practical purposes the text we have is correct enough, and our old Authorized Version is a sound one."[59]

"The Bible Tried and Proved," Psalm 12:6, preached May 5, 1889: "It is also a book pure in the sense of truth, being without admixture of error. I do not hesitate to say that I believe that there is no mistake whatever in the original Holy Scriptures from beginning to end. There may be, and there are, mistakes of translation; for translators are not inspired; but even the historical facts are correct. Doubt has been cast upon them here and there, and at times with great show of reason—doubt which it has been impossible to meet for a season; but only give space enough, and search enough, and the stones buried in the earth cry out to confirm each letter of Scriptures. Old Manuscripts, coins, and inscriptions, are on the side of the Book and against it there are nothing but theories."[60]

Advantageous use of Another Translation
of a Particular Text, Such as in a Marginal Reading

"The Hand of God in the History of Man," Job 7:1, preached October 10, 1875: "But we must consider the other translation of our text. It is generally given in the margin of the Bibles. 'Is there not an appointed *warfare* to the man upon earth?' which teaches us that *God has appointed life to be a warfare.*"[61]

"Farm Laborers," 1 Corinthians 3:6-9, preached June 5, 1881: "We shall first remark that the church is God's farm: 'Ye are God's husbandry.' In the margin of the revised version we read 'Ye are God's tilled ground,' and that is the very expression for me."[62]

Spurgeon,"The Holy Road," Isaiah 35:8, August 1, 1886, No. 1912, MTP 32, 531: "You can look at the margin of your Revised Old Testaments, or indeed in the margins of the old Bibles, will find that this clause may be read thus:–'He shall be with them:' that is, God shall be with them."[63]

"Prodigal Love for the Prodigal Son," Luke 15:20, preached March 29, 1891: "In the Revised Version, if you will kindly look at the margin, you will find that the text there reads, 'and kissed him much.' This a very good translation of the Greek, which might bear the meaning, 'Kissed him earnestly,' or 'Kissed him eagerly,' or 'Kissed him often.' I prefer to have it in very plain language, and therefore adopt the marginal reading of the Revised Version, 'Kissed him much,' as the text of my sermon, the subject of which will be, the overflowing love of God toward the returning sinner."[64]

Preference for the Older Manuscript Readings

"Free Grace a Motive for Free Giving," 2 Thessalonians 2:16-17, preached June 13, 1880 (Note that Spurgeon preached this sermon the year before the Revised Version of the New Testament came out.): "Read–'Stablish you in every good word and work.' Certain of the oldest manuscripts run 'in every good work and word,' and I suppose in our new translation [the Revised Version] we shall have it so, and very properly too. In this case work is probably first, and word next."[65]

"'And We Are': A Jewel from the Revised Version," 1 John 3:1, preached July 19, 1885: "That the addition ["and we are'] is correct I have not the slightest doubt. Those authorities upon which we depend–those manuscripts which are best worthy of notice–have these words; and they are to be found in the Vulgate, the Alexandrian, and several other versions. They ought never to have dropped out. In the judgment of the most learned, and those best to be relied on, these are veritable words of inspiration."[66]

"In Christ No Condemnation," Romans 8:1, preached August 29, 1886: "'Who walk not after the flesh, but after the Spirit.' You who have the Revised New Testament will kindly look at it. Do you see this sentence there? To your surprise it is omitted, and very rightly so. The most learned men assure us that it is no part of the original text. . . . The oldest copies are without it, the versions do not sustain it, and the fathers who quoted abundance of Scripture do not quote this sentence."[67]

"Heart-Disease Curable," Isaiah 61:1, preached June 19, 1881: "I confess that it looks a grievous thing to part with words which we thought were part and parcel of Luke; but as they are not in the oldest copies, and must be given up, we will make capital out of their omission."[68]

Continued High Regard for the King James Version

It would be a major mistake to think that because Spurgeon made corrections to the translation and referred to translations other than the King James, that he was an enemy of the Authorized Version trying to belittle it. On the contrary, it is clear from his sermons that he has the utmost reverence for the King James Version, calling it "the grand old Bible of our fathers."[69] He just understood the limitations of even the best of translations.

"Love's Medicines and Miracles," Isaiah 38:17, preached January 21, 1877: "Before, however, I divided my text, I ought to have given you another translation of it. Not that I would readily find fault with our version at any time, for it is, as a rule, marvelously correct and singularly forcible, and I am afraid when the new translation of the Bible [referring to the English Revised Version] comes out it will be better to light our fires with it than to give up the old version, which is so dear to us and so interwoven into all our religious life. *I trust our grandfather's Bible will maintain its hold on the mind of the English public against all comers, for it is so simple and yet so sublime, so homely and yet so heavenly in style.* The translation which I shall now submit to you is, however, more exactly literal according to the Hebrew: 'Behold, to peace my bitter bitterness'; or, 'Marah, Marah,' 'and thou hast loved my soul from the pit of destruction, because thou hast cast all my sins behind thy back.'" [Italics mine][70]

"The Blood of the Testament," Hebrews 9:20, preached November 14, 1880: "Upon the whole, our translation is as nearly perfect as we can look for a human work to be. I do not know what the new translation will turn out to be, but the good men must have risen up very early, and they must have sat up very late if they have produced a version which will surpass that which has for so long been used among us. . . . Our translators were not inspired, but they were marvelously guided and directed when they made this version."[71]

"Our Sanctuary," Jeremiah 17:12-14, preached June 15, 1884: "It seems to me that the translators of the Authorised Version have given us the true meaning of the original, as I think they generally do. The men are not yet born will give us a better rendering either of the Old or the New Testament than is to be found in our old English Bibles, and it is my belief that they never will be born. These men wrote a marvelously pure English, and really translated the Bible into our mother tongue, being helped of God not only to see the meaning, but to write it in words which are understood of the people. . . . You may place every confidence in your grandmother's Bible; whatever small improvements the translation may require, it is in the main so good that its rivals have had but short lives, while it retains all its primitive power."[72]

"Our Own Dear Shepherd," John 10:14-15, preached November 20, 1885: "'I am the good Shepherd; and I know mine own, and mine own know me, even as the Father knoweth me, and I know the Father; and I lay down my life for the sheep.' This reading I have given you is that of the Revised Version. For that Revised Version I have but little care as a general rule, holding it to be by no means an improvement upon our common Authorized Version. It is a useful thing to have it for private reference, but I trust it will never be regarded as the standard English translation of the New Testament. The Revised Version of the Old Testament is so excellent, that I am half afraid it may carry the Revised New Testament upon its shoulders into general use. . . . Returning to our subject, I believe that, on this occasion, the Revised Version is true to the original. We will therefore follow it in this instance, and we shall find that it makes most delightful and instructive sense."[73]

Use of the Revised Version When He Considered it More Accurate

"Heart-Disease Curable," Isaiah 61:1, preached June 19, 1881: "I intended to have preached from these words in Luke 4:18, but when I looked at the Revised Version and found that the words were not there at all I was somewhat startled. I began to ask whether the omission was a correct one or not; and, without making pretense to scholarship, I feel convinced that the revisers are acting honestly in leaving it out. It was not in the original manuscript of Luke."[74]

"The True Gospel No Hidden Gospel," 2 Corinthians 4:3-4, preached June 4, 1882: "I think in this case the Revised New Testament gives a better translation than does the Authorized Version, and I will therefore read it: 'But and if our gospel is veiled, it is veiled in them that are perishing: in whom the God of this world hath blinded the minds of the unbelieving, that the light of the gospel of the glory of Christ, who is the image of God, should not dawn upon them.' Paul had been speaking of Moses with the veil over his face, and we lose the track of his thought if we use the word 'hid' instead of 'veiled.'"[75]

"The First Recorded Words of Jesus," Luke 2:48-49, preached June 25, 1882: "Here I am obliged to amend our version, and I am certain that the correction is itself correct. I am all the more strengthened in this opinion because the Revised Version endorses the emendation. This is how they read it: 'Wist ye not that I must be in my Father's house?'"[76]

"'And We Are': A Jewel from the Revised Version," 1 John 3:1, preached July 19, 1885: "A genuine fragment of inspired Scripture has been dropped by our older translators, and it is too precious to be lost. . . . The half lost portion of our text is restored to us in the Revised Version. Never did a translation of the New Testament fail more completely than this Revised Version has done as a book for general reading: but as an assistant to the student it deserves honorable mention, despite its faults. It exhibits here and there special beauties, and has, no doubt, in certain places brought into notice words of sacred Scripture which had fallen out: we have a notable instance in my present text [1 John 3:1]."[77]

"Immanuel–The Light of Life," Isaiah 9:1-2, preached September 14, 1890: After reading his text in the Authorized Version, he goes on to say "As in this case the Revised Version is much to be preferred, we will now read it: 'But there shall be no gloom to her that was in anguish. In the former time he brought into contempt the land of Zebulun and the land of Naphtali, but in the latter time hath he made it glorious, by the way of the sea, beyond Jordan, Galilee of the nations. The people that walked in darkness have seen a great light: they that dwelt in the land of the shadow of death, upon them hath the light shined.'–Isaiah 9:1, 2." Verse 1 of the Authorized reads: "Nevertheless the dimness shall not be such as was in her vexation, when at the first he highly afflicted the land of Zebulun and the land of Naphtali, and afterward did more grievously afflict her by the way of the sea, beyond Jordan, in Galilee of the nations."[78]

This avalanche of evidence from Spurgeon's sermons demonstrates his position on Bible translations to be firmly in line with the historic orthodox view we have observed so far. Furthermore, it refutes the notion that he was somehow unaware of the issues involved. These quotations have been drawn from Spurgeon's preaching, that for which he is best known. What is not as well known is that the prince of preachers actually edited a book on the English Bible published in 1859, early in his ministry. We will finish out our survey of Spurgeon's translation views with an excerpt from his preface to that book:

The cant [pious drivel-ed.] and fudge [senseless filler-ed.] which cries out against the least alteration of the old version of our forefathers, as if it were positive profanity, are nothing to me. I love God's Word better than I love King James pedantic wisdom and foolish kingcraft.

We want God's own book pure and unaltered. It is out [of] firm belief that the present version is so good that it will abundantly repay for revision. If it were utterly base, we would cry, "Away with it"; but because it is to a great degree faithful, and never contrary to sound doctrine, we desire to see it yet further purified till it shall be as near perfection as a human translation of the Divine Book can possibly be brought. Do I love my friend any the less because I desire to brush away the dust which has accumulated upon his time-honoured portrait? No; it is because I love him, that I desire a correct likeness of him; and it is because I think that likeness a good one, that I desire to have every spot removed from it. And it is because I love the most Holy Word of God that I plead for a faithful translation; and from my very love to the English version, because in the main it is so, I desire for it that its blemishes should be removed, and its faults corrected.

It is an arduous labour to persuade men this, although in the light of common sense the matter is plain enough. But there is a kind of Popery in our midst which makes us cling fast to our errors, and hinders the growth of thorough reformation; otherwise the Church would just ask the question, "Is the King James' Bible the nearest approach to the original?" The answer would be, "No; it is exceedingly good, but it has many glaring faults." And the command would at once go forth, –"Then ye that have learning amend these errors; for at any cost, the Church must have the pure Word of God.[79]

JOHN WILLIAM BURGON (1813-1888)

A Church of England clergyman, Burgon vehemently criticized the English Revised Version of 1881, decrying the work and textual methods of Westcott and Hort as inferior. He was not opposed to the idea of revising the Authorized Version, but to the strategies employed to do so.[80] First, he considered it "a serious breach of Church order" to include Baptists, Methodists, Presbyterians, Congregationalists, and Independents in the revision project. These he considered divisive sects that undercut exposing "the sinfulness of Schism."[81] What troubled him the most, however, was the weight given to a handful of early codices over against other ancient manuscripts, early translations, and textual readings quoted by the early church fathers. He argues that *old* does not necessarily mean *good*. Just as many heresies arose very early in church history, so inferior manuscripts appeared very early, as well. He believed that the manuscripts revered most by Westcott and Hort and hence, by the English Revised Version translation committee, included many "fabricated readings which the Church has long since refused to acknowledge, or else rejected with abhorrence."[82]

Although many modern opponents of Westcott and Hort have maintained many of Burgon's arguments both in content and style, many have departed from his view that the Received Text is not perfect, a view consistent with what we have found thus far in this historical survey: "Once for all, we request it may be clearly understood that we do not, by any means, claim perfection for the Received Text. We entertain no extravagant notions on this subject. Again and again we shall have occasion to point out (e.g. at pg. 107) that the Textus Receptus needs correction."[83]

Again, he writes: "I am not defending the 'Textus Receptus'; I am simply stating the fact of its existence. That it is without authority to bind, nay, that it calls for skillful revision in every part, is freely admitted. . . . I do not believe it to be absolutely identical with the true Traditional Text."[84]

ALEXANDER MACLAREN (1826-1910)

Outstanding Baptist pastor in Manchester, England, Alexander Maclaren is considered "the prince of expository preachers." The multi-volume set of his sermons, *Expositions of the Holy Scriptures*, still serves as a valuable resource for preachers today who value the combination of keen scholarship and pastoral concern. A diligent student of God's Word, Maclaren read the Hebrew and Greek text daily throughout his forty-five years of pastoral ministry. His handling of text and translation issues proves to be similar to what we have found with other careful preachers of God's Word, as illustrated by the following translation comments he makes in a sermon on Matthew 25:8, "Our lamps are gone out":

> This is one of the many cases in which the Revised Version, by accuracy of rendering the tense of a verb, gives a much more striking as well as correct reproduction of the original than the Authorised Version does. The former reads, 'going out,' instead of 'gone out,' a rendering which the Old Version has, unfortunately, relegated to the margin. It is clearly to be preferred, not only because it more correctly represents the Greek, but because it sets before us a more solemn and impressive picture of the precise time at which the terrible discovery was made by the foolish five.[85]

A. T. PIERSON (1873-1911)

Successor to C. H. Spurgeon, Pierson was a powerful preacher and prolific writer with a keen interest in missions and revival. He participated in the Northfield Conferences and often spoke at the Moody Bible Institute. He authored more than thirty-five books, including *George Mueller of Bristol*, and served as consulting editor for *The Scofield Reference Bible*. His remarks on Bible manuscripts and translations concur with the historic orthodox position:

> Inspiration is affirmed, of course, only of the original documents, now no longer extant. Many mistakes may have been made by copyists, and some interpolations by officious scribes and translators are fallible. It is the part of reverent criticism to seek, by careful examination and comparison of all existing documents, to detect errors and restore as far as possible the Scriptures in their original purity.[86]

Pierson's biography recounts an incident in which Pierson answered what comes up from time to time as an objection to the standard orthodox position he held on the Scriptures:

> One evening he remarked that no one claimed verbal inspiration for the English Bible–although that was remarkably accurate–but only for the text of the original writings. "Then," exclaimed a gentleman rising in the front seat, "if we cannot read the original we might as well have no inspired Bible at all." "Well," replied the lecturer quickly, "my daughter, who is a missionary in Japan recently sent me a photograph of her child whom I have never seen. No doubt it is not a perfect likeness. Do you suppose that I said, as I looked upon it, that is not the original and therefore I might as well have no grandchild at all?"[87]

D. L. MOODY (1837-1899)

A powerful evangelist used by God in both America and in England, Dwight L. Moody started schools in Northfield, Massachusetts, for training poor children and founded Moody Bible Institute. With simple forceful sermons, he sought to reach the heart of the common man. Singer-songwriter Ira Sankey accompanied Moody on many of his evangelistic tours. Although Moody would not classify himself as a scholar, he nonetheless made good use of more than one translation, including marginal readings. His instructions on how to study the Bible include the following remark: "I also find it helpful to mark. . . . Variations of the Revised Version: thus Romans 8,26 reads– 'the

Spirit Himself' in the R.V, not 'itself.' Note also marginal readings like Mark 6,19, 'an inward grudge' instead of 'a quarrel.'"[88]

F. B. MEYER (1847-1929)

British Baptist pastor and international Bible conference speaker, F. B. Meyer is known for his biographical sermons and strong devotional emphasis. He was close friend of D. L. Moody and a regular participant in the Northfield Bible Conference. Charles Spurgeon said of F. B. Meyer, "Meyer preaches as a man who has seen God face to face."[89] Writing about taking notes in our Bibles Meyer advises, "After a while, we shall begin to make references for ourselves; and then we may use a copy of the Revised Bible; that we may not only be able to read God's Word in the most approved English rendering, which is an immense advantage; but that we may also be able to fill up the empty margins with the notes of parallel passages."[90]

C. H. MACKINTOSH (1820-1896)

A faithful Plymouth Brethren pastor active in the 1859 revival in Ireland, Mackintosh displays his great skill as a solid Bible expositor in his *Notes on the Pentateuch*, as well as other expositions, and his gospel zeal in a number of solid evangelistic tracts. Charles Spurgeon held his work in high regard. His honest scholarship is evident in his comments on the nature of manuscript copies: "We could not say how much we prize the labors of those learned men who have consecrated their energies to the work of clearing the sacred text of the various errors and corruptions, which, from age to age, had crept into it, through the carelessness or infirmity of copyists."[91]

G. CAMPBELL MORGAN (1863-1945)

British Congregationalist pastor, educator, and author of over sixty volumes of commentaries and devotional writings, G. Campbell Morgan has been called "the prince of Bible expositors." He pastored Westminster Chapel in London and took part in the Northfield Bible Conference lectures with D. L. Moody. Combining thoughtful exegesis with devotional fire, his sermons and commentaries provide significant help to many Bible preachers and teachers today.

Morgan's life and ministry span the time when many new translations came on the scene, so his perspective on them is instructive to those that love God's Word as he did. In a 1923 letter Morgan writes, "You ask me which is the best translation of the New Testament. I do not hesitate to say that it is the

American Revision [American Standard Version, 1901]. Of course, the English Revision is very fine, but the American Committee have gone a little further sometimes, and, on the whole, I consider it, as I have said, the best. Then again, I most emphatically say that the best translation into modern English I have known is Weymouth's."[92]

In 1935 he writes, "We must remember that all these translations are from translations, and we have no translation which can be considered absolutely final and authoritative. Personally I think you are wise in your study of the Word in referring to any or all of them, whether those better known (Authorized or Revised), or such as Weymouth's, for instance, to which you refer."[93]

W. E. VINE (1873-1949)

A classical scholar, skilled expositor, and acute theologian, W. E. Vine authored a number of books, perhaps the best known of which is his *Vine's Expository Dictionary of Old and New Testament Words.* His comments on the significance of the differences between manuscripts is encouraging, and expresses, once again, the view that we have found to be standard among the great preachers of the past: "The importance of most of the variations in the manuscript readings has been greatly exaggerated. . . . There is no doctrine in Scripture which would be affected if all the various readings were allowed or if all the disputed words, or those about which there is any doubt, were omitted."[94]

Clearly not a man ignorant of the issues involved in the translation debate, he nonetheless preferred the English Revised Version: "Among English versions he gave his exclusive preference to the Revised Version, which remains to this day the best translation for the accurate student of the English Bible."[95]

H. A. IRONSIDE (1876-1951)

Bible expositor who authored of over sixty volumes, H. A. Ironside pastored Moody Memorial Church. He has been called "the Apostle of Fundamentalism," whose commentaries still serve the Bible study needs of many today. He, too, addresses the text and translation issue:

> As to Bible translations, the most generally used is the Authorized Version, sometimes called the King James Version, because it was authorized for use in churches in England by King James I. Nearly three hundred years later the American Standard Version was produced, and it is in some respects to be preferred to the older version,

69

though it has never gained the favor of people generally that was expected. The differences are not very important, but are based upon some older texts which were not in evidence when the Authorized Version was being translated.[96]

CONCLUSION

What emerges from the published works of these recognized preachers of God's Word is clear agreement on many facets of the preservation and translation of the Scriptures. We find in their preaching a great reverence for God's Word and a settled belief in its preservation. At the same time, these godly men voice their understanding that no translation is perfect. They hold, therefore, to the legitimacy and value of other possible translations of any given text, such as those given in the marginal readings. They all demonstrate in their preaching that they believe that the original text is the standard of whether the translation is accurate. Some reveal a preference for the older manuscripts as nearer the original wording. Those that used the Authorized Version show a love for it because of its clarity, accuracy, and proven value. But they still maintained the legitimacy and value of other translations of the whole OT or NT–in some cases a preference for other than the Authorized Version.

Furthermore, these stalwart defenders of God's Word and the Christian faith agree that a translation should be in clear language that the common layman can easily understand that the translation should be as accurate as possible. They consequently exercise the freedom to amend the translation for sake of clarity, for sake of closer adherence to the original language, or on the basis of what they consider better manuscript support. Finally, consistent with these commonly held principles regarding the place and use of Bible translation, many of them consider it proper to study and even to preach from more than one translation.

Whether one agrees with the consensus or not, the position of these servants of the Lord is clear. None of these men would claim personal infallibility, but they knew what it was to contend for the faith and for many of them, to suffer greatly for doing so. Most of them are known for the extraordinary blessing of God upon their ministries. But none of them held the exclusivist views on Bible translation that some today demand to be a test of orthodoxy–not even those few that are often quoted to advance this new teaching.

From the testimony and example of these past leaders of the flock of God, it should be clear that a believer ought to be free to use the Bible version he believes best meets the established criteria for reliable translation of God's

Word. He may have come to believe that the MT or the TR or the KJV are better than other choices. But when his brother in the Lord reaches a different conclusion, that brother should also have the freedom to use what he believes is the best manuscript reading or translation. History demonstrates that this is no new license within Bible Christianity. As this chapter has shown, great preachers of the past have clearly exercised this liberty, and such a brother will find he is in the good company of many giants of the faith. Making adherence to one manuscript tradition or to one translation *a test of orthodoxy* has never been a tenet of truly Biblical Christianity. And it does not deserve that place today. [97]

So what do we make of the current debate? In general, this, that even godly men–and *godly* men are first to admit it–are not perfect in their judgments. Godly men have differed on which manuscript readings and translations they prefer. Human judgment is always subject to human frailty and to human sin. In addressing the problem of divisions among God's people, John Owen writes: "It is granted that they may fall into divisions, and schisms, and mutual exasperations among themselves, through the remainders of darkness in their minds and the infirmity of the flesh, Romans 14:3; and in such cases mutual judgings and despisings are apt to ensue, and that to the prejudice and great disadvantage of that common faith which they do profess."[98]

John Owen continues: "But so far as their divisions and differences are unto them unavoidable, the remedy of further evils proceeding from them is plainly and frequently expressed in the Scripture. It is love, meekness, forbearance, bowels of compassion with those other graces of the Spirit wherein our conformity unto Christ doth consist, with a true understanding and the due valuation of the 'unity of faith,' and the common hope of believers, which are the ways prescribed unto us for the prevention of those evils which, without them, our unavoidable differences will occasion."[99]

It is easy for our flesh to take advantage of our zeal. Evil speaking or malicious talk leveled against other believers–however tempted any of us may be to engage in it–is of the flesh, not of the Holy Spirit. When true Christians speak so, they "do not know what spirit they are of." They are joining with the accuser of the brethren. They are, in the words of G. Campbell Morgan, "fighting the battles of heaven with the spirit of hell."

Let us cease from the hurtfulness of demonizing those that are genuine, devout, Bible-loving believers, merely for not holding a view that *only some* believers have held. Let us guard against misrepresenting what those differing from us hold. Let truth prevail. Let love rule. To do otherwise is contrary to the Bible *in every version.*

Let us not boast that we are defending what we refuse to obey.

71

[1]*Works*, Vol. 5, *First Series of Sermons*, 1-39 (1872 ed.; rpt. Grand Rapids: Zondervan, n.d.), p. 3.

[2]Schaff, ed. *Nicene and Post-Nicene Fathers*, Series 2, Vol. 10, in *The Master Christian Library*, Version 6 (Albany, OR: AGES Software, 1998), p. 267, point 46.

[3]Those that read through Augustine's works will find that in some cases his teaching reflects the religious theories of his times, not the doctrines of the Word–such as his advocating prayers for the dead: "On the Care to Be Had for the Dead [De Cura Pro Mortuis]," translated by H. Browne; *Nicene and Post-Nicene Fathers*, Series 1, Vol. 3, edited by Philip Schaff, in *The Master Christian Library*, Version 6 (Albany, OR: AGES Software, 1998), pp. 972-995.

[4]Book 2, Chapter 11: "Knowledge of Languages, Especially of Greek and Hebrew, Necessary to Remove Ignorance or Signs," in *On Christian Doctrine*, in *The Nicene and Post-Nicene Fathers, First Series*, Vol. 2, 1127:16.

[5]Book 2, Chapter 12: "A Diversity of Interpretations is useful. Errors arising from Ambiguous Words," in *On Christian Doctrine*, in *The Nicene and Post-Nicene Fathers,* First Series, Vol. 2, 1128:17. In his "How the Meaning of Unknown Words and Idioms is to be Discovered," Augustine observes: "In this matter, too, the great number of the translators proves a very great assistance, if they are examined and discussed with a careful comparison of their texts."1132, Chapter 14.

[6]1129, Chapter 13: "How Faulty Interpretations Can be Emended," p. 18.

[7]1129-30, Chapter 13: "How Faulty Interpretations Can be Emended," p. 19.

[8]Augustine's reluctance with Hebrew may explain in part why he held a unusual view of the Septuagint (often denoted by the Roman numerals LXX). He believed the legend that the LXX had been produced under the direct guidance of the Holy Spirit. In those places where the seventy translators differ from the Hebrew text, he believed that they were getting at the "spiritual sense," even if it were different from the literal sense. In a number of letters, Augustine takes Jerome to task for introducing changes to the Latin text in Jerome's Vulgate on the basis of the Hebrew Old Testament rather than the Greek LXX. *(On Christian Doctrine*, Book 2, Chapters 15 and 43. See also Letter 71 from Augustine to Jerome, in Volume 1.)

[9]*History of the Christian Church. Volume 4: Mediaeval Christianity* (Charles Scribner's Sons, 1910; rpt. Grand Rapids: Eerdmans, 1987), p. 671.

[10]Ibid, p. 674.

[11]Ibid, p. 613.

[12]Schaff, Volume 6: *The Middle Ages*, pp. 338-342.

[13]Ibid, pp. 345-46.

[14]Ibid, p. 689.

[15]Ibid, p. 687.

[16]Ibid, pp. 685-86, 710-11.

[17]*The Letters of Martin Luther*, in *The Reformation History Library*, Version 2.0 (Albany, OR: AGES Software, 1998), p. 134.

[18]William Tyndale, *Doctrinal Treatises*, in *The Reformation History Library*, Version 2.0 (Albany, OR: AGES Software, 1998), p. 13.

[19]*Sermons and Remains of Hugh Latimer*, in *The Reformation History Library*, Version 2.0 (Albany, OR: AGES Software, 1998), p. 295.

[20]*Writings of John Fox, Bale, and Coverdale*, in *The Reformation History Library*, Version 2.0 (Albany, OR: AGES Software, 1998), pp. 466-67.

[21]*Writings of John Fox, Bale, and Coverdale*, p. 468.

[22]*Writings of John Fox, Bale, and Coverdale*, p. 468.

[23]*The Translators to the Reader: The Original Preface of the King James Version of 1611 Revisited*, edited by Erroll F. Rhodes and Liana Lupas (New York: American Bible Society, 1997).

[24]*Of the Integrity and Purity of the Hebrew and Greek Text of the Scripture*, in *Works*, Vol. XVI (London and Edinburgh: Johnstone and Hunter, 1853), p. 357.

[25]*A Christian Directory* (Rpt. Morgan, Pennsylvania: Soli Deo Gloria Publications, 1996), p. 725.

[26]*Tropologia: A Key to Open Scripture Metaphors to which are prefixed Arguments to prove the Divine Authority of the Holy Bible* (Printed by John Richardson and John Darby for Enoch Prosser, 1681), p. xxi.

[27]*George Whitefield: Sermons*, Vol. 1 (New Ipswich, NH: Pietan Publications, 1991), back cover.

[28]"The Holy Spirit Convincing the World of Sin, Righteousness, and Judgment," Sermon 40, in *George Whitefield, 59 Sermons*, in *The Master Christian Library*, Version 6 (Albany, OR: AGES Software, 1998), p. 552.

[29]*The Puritan Experiment in the New World*. (The Westminster Conference Papers, 1976), pp. 103ff.

[30]Jonathan Edwards, *Notes on the Bible: The Pentateuch Written by Moses*, in *Works*, Vol. 6, in *The Master Christian Library*, Version 6 (Albany, OR: AGES Software, 1998), p. 816.

[31]Jonathan Edwards, *Works*, Vol. 6, pp. 1002-3.

[32]Wesley, "A Letter to the Reverend Mr. Downes, Rector of St. Michael's, Wood-Street; Occasioned by His Late Tract, Entitled, 'Methodism Examined and Exposed,'" in *Works*, Vol. 9, p. 115.

[33]Wesley, Sermon 22: "Upon Our Lord's Sermon on the Mount," in *Works*, Vol. 5, p. 340.

[34]John Wesley, *Works*, Vol. 2, p. 353.

[35]John Wesley, *Works*, Vol. 2, p. 583.

[36]John Wesley, *Works*, Vol. 4, p. 335.

[37] F.F. Bruce, *History of the Bible in English*. 3rd edition (New York: Oxford, 1978), pp. 129-30.

[38]Wesley, *Notes on the Whole Biblethe New Testament*, in *Works*, Vol. 14, p. 341.

[39]Wesley, *Works*, Vol. 14, p. 420.

[40]"Of the Christian Religion," in *Sermons of the Rev. Samuel Davies*, Vol. 1 (Rpt. Morgan, PN: Soli Deo Gloria, 1993), p. 105.

[41]*A Complete Body of Divinity: Or, a System of Evangelical Truths* (London: Mathews & Leigh, 1839; The Baptist Standard Bearer reprint, 1984), pp. 13-14.

[42]*The Works of John Newton* (Rpt. Edinburgh: Banner of Truth, 1988), flyleaf.

[43]John Newton, "Salvation Published from the Mountains," from Isaiah 50:9, Sermon VI, Vol. 4 of *The Works of John Newton* (Rpt. Edinburgh: Banner of Truth, 1988), p. 68.

[44]*Works*, Vol. 3 (Philadelphia: American Baptist Publication Society, 1845), p. 810.

[45]Timothy George, *Faithful Witness: The Life and Mission of William Carey* (Birmingham, AL: New Hope, 1991), pp. 137-143.

[46]Courtney Anderson, *To the Golden Shore: The Life of Adoniram Judson* (Boston: Little, Brown, and Company, 1956), p. 409.

[47]Anderson, p. 411.

[48]*Old Paths* (Cambridge: J. Clarke, 1972), p. 20.

[49]Ibid, p. 29.

[50]*The Parallel New Testament: Greek and English* (Cambridge University Press, 1882; rpt., 1908), pp. xxiv-xxv.

[51]"The Revised Version of the New Testament," in *Discussions: Evangelical and Theological*, Vol. 1 (London: Banner of Truth, 1967), p. 398.

[52]*Metropolitan Tabernacle Pulpit*, Volume 17, No. 1026, in *The C. H. Spurgeon Collection*, Version 1.0 (Albany, OR: AGES Software, 1998), p. 891.

[53]Ibid, Volume 18, No. 1045, p. 259.

[54]Ibid, Volume 20, No. 1170, p. 308.

[55]Ibid, Volume 18, No. 1074, p. 693.

[56]Ibid, Volume 35, No. 2084, p. 328.

[57]Ibid, Volume 38, No. 2241, p. 70. Note: In this case the King James Translators were using an older usage of *borrow*, which included the meaning, "to ask."

[58]Ibid, Volume 27, No. 1604, p. 439.

[59]Ibid, Volume 32, No. 1890, p. 200.

[60]Ibid, Volume 35, No. 2084, p. 329.

[61]Ibid, Volume 21, No. 1258, p. 712.

[62]Ibid, Volume 27, No. 1602, p. 407.

[63]Ibid, Volume 32, No. 1912, p. 531.

[64]Ibid, Volume 37, No. 2236, p. 823.

[65]Ibid, Volume 26, No. 1542, p. 442.

[66]Ibid, Volume 32, No. 1934, p. 853.

[67]Ibid, Volume 32, No. 1917, p. 606.

[68]Ibid, Volume 27, No. 1604, p. 439

[69]"Consolation from Resurrection," preached September 30 AM, 1888 in *Metropolitan Tabernacle Pulpit*, Volume 34, No. 2046, p. 695. Some today charge that acknowledging any limitations of the KJV constitutes disdain for it and rises from an effort to destroy it. Simply not true. The fact is that all translations–even the very best of them–have limitations, and there are times the careful expositor must note them. Not to do so elevates one translation of God's Word above God's Word itself, in that eventually the *traditional* way of communicating a text can become more important than what the underlying text actually says. One has but to look at the Roman Catholic exaltation of the Vulgate during the Reformation to see the terrible havoc such a policy can produce. On the other hand, honestly acknowledging limited imperfections in a translation does not remove its value as a translation of God's Word.

[70]*Metropolitan Tabernacle Pulpit*, Volume 23, No. 1337, p. 94.

[71]Ibid, Volume 26, No. 1527, pp. 808-809.

[72]Ibid, Volume 30, No. 1786, p. 435.

[73]Ibid, Volume 32, No. 1877, pp. 2-3.

[74]Ibid, Volume 27, No. 1604, p. 437.

[75]Ibid, Volume 28, No. 1663, p. 393.

[76]Ibid, Volume 28, No. 1666, p. 444.

[77]Ibid, Volume 32, No. 1934, p. 852.

[78]Ibid, Volume 36, No. 2163, p. 622.

[79]H. C. Conant, *The English Bible*, ed. C. H. Spurgeon (London: Arthur Hall, Virtue; Trubner, 1859), pp. xi-xxi.

[80]*The Revision Revised* (1883; rpt. Paradise, PN: Conservative Classics, 1978).

[81]Ibid, *pp.* 6-7, 504-505.

[82]Ibid, p. vii.

[83]Ibid, p. 21.

[84]*The Traditional Text of the Holy Gospels* (London: G. Bell, 1896), *pp.* 13,15.

[85]*Expositions of Holy Scripture,* Vol. 7 (rpt. Grand Rapids: Baker, n.d.), p. 181.

[86]*Knowing the Scriptures* (Grand Rapids: Zondervan, 1910), p. 21.

[87]Delavan Leonard Pierson, *Arthur T. Pierson: A Biography* (Chicago: Revell, 1912), p. 284.

[88]*Pleasure and Profit in Bible Study* (Chicago: Revell, 1895), p. 104.

[89]A. Chester Mann, *F. B. Meyer: Preacher, Teacher, Man of God* (London: George Allen & Unwin, 1929), p. 165.

[90]*Steps into the Blessed Life* (Philadelphia: Henry Altemus, 1895), p. 294.

[91]"The Bible, Its Sufficiency and Supremacy," *Miscellaneous Writings of CHM* (New York: Loizeaux, 1898; rpt. 1955), p. 5.

[92] *This Was His Faith,* edited by Jill Morgan (Westwood, NJ: Revell, 1952), p. 22.

[93]Ibid, p. 21.

[94]*The Divine Inspiration of the Bible* (London: Pickering and Ingles, 1923), pp. 27,28.

[95]F.F. Bruce, "W.E. Vine: The Theologian," in *W.E. Vine: His Life and Ministry,* edited by Percy O. Ruoff (London: Oliphants, 1951), p. 73.

[96]*What's The Answer* (Grand Rapids: Zondervan, 1944), p. 1213.

[97]By contrast, Romanism does make such decrees. In the Preface to the Challoner revision (1749-1752) of the Douay-Rheims appear the following assertions regarding the Latin Vulgate and the Douay-Rheims translated from it: citing the Council

of Trent, "'Moreover, the same Holy Council . . . ordains and declares that the old Latin Vulgate Edition, which, in use for so many hundred years, has been approved by the Church, be in public lectures, disputations, sermons and expositions held as authentic, and that no one dare or presume under any pretext whatsoever to reject it.' (Fourth Session, April 8, 1546). . . . "The Latin Vulgate 'is not onely better then al other Latin translations, but then the Greeke text itselfe, in those places where they disagree.' (Preface to the Rheims New Testament, 1582). They state that the Vulgate is 'more pure then the Hebrew or Greke now extant' and that 'the same Latin hath bene farre better conserved from corruptions.' (Preface to the Douay Old Testament, 1609)." *The Holy Bible: Douay Rheims Version*, revised by Richard Challoner. Rockford, Illinois: Tan Books and Publishers, 1989.

[98]John Owen, "A Discourse Concerning Evangelical Love, Church Peace, and Unity," in Vol. XV of *The Works of John Owen* (Edinburgh: Banner of Truth, rpt.1965), p. 80.

[99]Ibid.

BIBLIOGRAPHY

Anderson, Courtney. *To the Golden Shore: The Life of Adoniram Judson.* Boston: Little, Brown, and Company, 1956.

Augustine. *On Christian Doctrine,* in *The Nicene and Post-Nicene Fathers,* First Series. Vol. 2. *The Master Christian Library,* Version 6. Albany, Oregon: AGES Software, 1998.

Baxter, Richard. *A Christian Directory.* Rpt. Morgan, Pennsylvania: Soli Deo Gloria Publications, 1996.

Bruce, F. F. *History of the Bible in English.* 3rd Ed. New York: Oxford, 1978.

Bruce, F. F. "W. E. Vine: The Theologian," in *W. E. Vine: His Life and Ministry.* edited by Percy O. Ruoff. London: Oliphants, 1951.

Burgon, John William. *The Revision Revised.* 1883. Rpt. Paradise, Pennsylvania: Conservative Classics, 1978.

Burgon, John William. *The Traditional Text of the Holy Gospels.* London: G. Bell, 1896.

Conant, H. C. *The English Bible: History of the Translation of the Holy Scriptures into the English Tongue.* Ed. C. H. Spurgeon. London: Arthur Hall, Virtue, & Co.; Trubner & Co., 1859.

Dabney, Robert L. "The Revised Version of the New Testament," in *Discussions: Evangelical and Theological.* Vol. 1. London: Banner of Truth, 1967.

Davies, Samuel. *Sermons of Samuel Davies.* Vol. 1. Rpt. Morgan, Pennsylvania: Soli Deo Gloria, 1993.

Edwards, Jonathan. *Notes on the Bible: The Pentateuch Written by Moses,* in *Works,* Vol. 6, in *The Master Christian Library,* Version 6. Albany, OR: AGES Software, 1998.

Fuller, Andrew. *Works.* Vol. 3. Philadelphia: American Baptist Publication Society, 1845.

George, Timothy. *Faithful Witness: The Life and Mission of William Carey.* Birmingham, Alabama: New Hope, 1991.

Gill, John. *A Complete Body of Divinity: Or a System of Evangelical Truths.* London: Mathews and Leigh, 1839. Rpt. The Baptist Standard Bearer, 1984.

Grudem, Wayne A. *The First Epistle of Peter*. Grand Rapids: Eerdmans, 1988, reprint 2002.

Ironside, H. A. *What's the Answer*. Grand Rapids: Zondervan, 1944.

Keach, Benjamin. *Tropologia: A Key to Open Scripture Metaphors to which are prefixed Arguments to prove the Divine Authority of the Holy Bible*. n. p.: John Richardson and John Darby for Enoch Prosser, 1681.

Kistemaker, Simon J. *Exposition of James, Episltes of John, Peter, and Jude*. Grand Rapids: Baker, 1996.

Lloyd-Jones, D. Martyn. "John Owen on Schism" in *The Puritans: Their Origins and Their Successors*. Edinburgh: Banner of Truth, 1987. Rpt. 1996.

Lloyd-Jones, D. Martyn. *The Puritan Experiment in the New World*. Westminster Conference Papers, 1976.

Luther, Martin. *The Letters of Martin Luther*, in *The Reformation History Library*. Version 2.0. Albany, OR: AGES Software, 1998.

Mackintosh, C. H. "The Bible, Its Sufficiency and Supremacy." *Miscellaneous Writings of CHM*. New York: Loizeaux Brothers, 1898. Rpt. 1955.

Maclaren, Alexander. *Expositions of the Holy Scripture*. Vol. 7. Rpt. Grand Rapids: Baker, n.d.

Mann, A. Chester. *F. B. Meyer: Preacher, Teacher, Man of God*. London: George Allen & Unwin, 1929.

Meyer, F. B. *Steps into the Blessed Life*. Philadelphia: Henry Altemus, 1895.

Michaels, J. Ramsey. *Word Biblical Commentary:1 Peter*. Waco: Word Books, 1988.

Moody, D. L. *Pleasure and Profit in Bible Study*. Chicago: Revell, 1895.

Morgan, Jill, ed. *This Was His Faith*. Westwood, New Jersey: Revell, 1952.

Newton, John. *The Works of John Newton*. 6 Volumes. Rpt. Edinburgh: Banner of Truth, 1988.

Owen, John. "Of the Integrity and Purity of the Hebrew and Greek Text of the Scripture," in Vol. XVI of *The Works of John Owen, D. D*. London and Edinburgh: Johnstone and Hunter, 1853.

——————. "A Discourse Concerning Evangelical Love, Church Peace, and Unity," in Vol.XV of *The Works of John Owen*. ed. William H. Goold, Rpt. Ediburgh: Banner of Truth, 1965.

Pierson, A. T. *Knowing the Scriptures*. Grand Rapids: Zondervan, 1910.

Pierson, Delavan Leonard. *Arthur T. Pierson: A Biography*. Chicago: Revell, 1912.

Rhodes, Erroll F. And Liana Lupas, eds. *The Translators to the Reader: The Original Preface of the King James Version of 1611 Revisited*. New York: American Bible Society, 1997.

Ryle, J. C. *Old Paths*. Cambridge: J. Clarke, 1972.

Schaff, Philip. *History of the Christian Church*. 8 Volumes. Charles Scribner's Sons, 1910. Rpt. Grand Rapids: Eerdmans, 1987.

Schaff, Philip, ed. *Nicene and Post-Nicene Fathers*. Series 2, Vol. 10, in *The Master Christian Library*, Version 6. Albany, OR: AGES Software, 1998.

Scrivener, F. H. A. *The Parallel New Testament: Greek and English*. Cambridge: University Press, 1882. Rpt. 1908.

Selwyn, Edward Gordon. *The First Epistle of St. Peter*, London: Macmillan. 1947

Sermons and Remains of Hugh Latimer, in *The Reformation History Library*. Version 2.0. Albany, OR: AGES Software, 1998.

Spurgeon. Charles Haddon. *Metropolitan Tabernacle Pulpit* in *The C. H. Spurgeon Collection*. Version 1.0. Albany, OR: AGES Software, 1998.

The Holy Bible: Douay Rheims Version. Revised by Richard Challoner. Rockford, Illinois: Tan Books and Publishers, 1989.

Tyndale, William. *Doctrinal Treatises*, in *The Reformation History Library*. Version 2.0. Albany, OR: AGES Software, 1998.

Vine, W. E. *The Divine Inspiration of the Bible*. London: Pickering and Ingles, 1923.

Wesley, John. *First Series of Sermons, 1-39*, Vol. 5 of *Works*. 1872 ed. Rpt. Grand Zondervan, n.d.

Wesley, John. *The Works of John Wesley*, in *The Master Christian Library*, Version 6. Albany, OR: AGES Software, 1998.

Whitefield, George. *George Whitefield, 59 Sermons*, in *The Master Christian Library*, Version 6. Albany, OR: AGES Software, 1998.

Whitefield, George. *George Whitefield: Sermons*. Vol. 1. New Ipswich, NH: Pietan Publications, 1991.

Writings of John Fox, Bale, and Coverdale, in *The Reformation History Library*. Version 2.0. Albany, Or: AGES Software, 1998.

WHAT THE BIBLE REALLY SAYS ABOUT ITS PRESERVATION

By the Editorial Committee

We have reviewed the sermons and writings of preachers and theologians and searched the doctrinal statements of churches and councils. Far more important is what the Scriptures themselves reveal about their preservation. It is vital that Bible believers consider carefully what the Scriptures actually say and not read into them more than God has revealed. To gain a proper understanding of any Biblical passage care must be exercised to consider the contextual setting and the language that God has used to give His revelation.

Using this approach, various members of the Editorial Committee (Text and Translation Committee) have contributed sections. That is, exegetical analyses of various passages prominent in the preservation discussion have been prepared by different individuals. Since it is our intention that each writer be allowed to speak in his own words and to explain given passages in his own way, little effort has been made to harmonize the methods of presentation in the various sections. As a result, the reader may find this chapter to be a bit uneven stylistically, may see occasional redundancies, and might even notice subtle distinctions between the perspectives of different parts of the chapter. However, this chapter does present the harmonious view of the committee that, while proper exegesis of various passages does not support supernatural preservation, the Bible does teach providential preservation of the Word of God.

THE BIBLE'S PRESUPPOSITION OF ITS OWN PRESERVATION

When one examines what the Bible commands of believers, it becomes apparent that there is implicit teaching regarding the preservation of the Word of God. Obviously, as believers we could not carry out obedience to these commands if God had not preserved His Word for future generations. The Scriptures give repeated assurances that there was an ongoing process of the preservation of the Word of God in written form.

In the Pentateuch the LORD instructed the Israelites on the verge of crossing into the Promised Land to "write them [these words which I command thee this day] on the doorposts of thy house and on thy gates" (Deuteronomy 6:9). In terms of the Jewish theocracy, God instructed future kings of Israel through Moses to "write him a copy of this law in a book" (Deuteronomy 17:18). Then to Joshua the Lord mandated that he should meditate on the book of the law day and night for the express purpose of obeying "all that is written therein" (Joshua 1:8).

During the time of the prophets, the LORD stressed, through Isaiah, the responsibility of the Israelites to determine who the true and false prophets were. This process was to be carried out by comparing their statements to the written Word. "To the law and to the testimony: if they speak not according to this word, there is no light in them" (Isaiah 8:20).

Nearly one thousand years after the LORD's commands to Israel through Moses, the Jewish people returned to Canaan from the Babylonian captivity. During the revival at the Water Gate, Ezra the priest and the other Levites read to the assembled congregation a copy of "the book of the law of Moses" which had been preserved through those seventy years of captivity. Great conviction resulted from the expositional preaching as the people understood how to bring their lives into conformity to God's written Word (Nehemiah 8:1-18).

In the first century A.D., the Lord Jesus Christ pointed the Pharisees back to the written Old Testament Scriptures when He said, "Search the Scriptures; for in them ye think ye have eternal life, and these are they which testify of me" (John 5:37).

In the early days of the history of the church, as the gospel spread throughout the Mediterranean world, the God-fearing Jews in Berea were commended for their study of the Old Testament Scriptures which had been preserved and taken with them in the Dispersion. They were deemed "more noble than those in Thessalonica, in that they received the word with all readiness of mind, and searched the Scriptures daily, whether those things were so" (Acts 17:11).

Under the inspiration of the Holy Spirit, James, the first pastor of the church at Jerusalem, urged believers to "be doers of the word, and not hearers only," in order to avoid spiritual self-deception (James 1:22-23).

During the apostolic era, the Apostle Paul repudiated those who would "handle the word of God deceitfully (2 Corinthians 4:2)," and the Apostle Peter indicated that there were "unlearned and unstable" men who "wrest ... the other scriptures, unto their own destruction" (2 Peter 3:16).

In his inspired letter to the church at Colossae, Paul instructed the believers there to forward their letter from him to the church at Laodicea for their reading (Colossians 4:16). The public reading of the Scriptures was apparently a regular practice in the early church in that Paul told Timothy to give himself to "reading" of the Scriptures (1 Timothy 4:13).

Timothy was further instructed by the Apostle Paul to "preach the Word" that he had been taught from his earliest years (2 Timothy 4:2; 3:15). He was particularly to give himself diligently the study of God's written Word in his preaching and teaching so that he could carefully "cut it straight" by interpreting it according to the Holy Spirit's original intent (2 Timothy 2:15). Timothy's ministry was to be so Word-saturated that he was to "consent to wholesome words, even the words of Jesus Christ" (1 Timothy 6:3). Both Timothy and Titus were challenged by Paul to "hold fast the form of sound words," and they were to be "holding fast the faithful word," that they had been taught by Paul (2 Timothy 1:13; Titus 1:9).

Finally, it was on account of the preserved Word of God, which were considered illegal writings, that the Apostle John was charged by the Roman Empire and imprisoned on the island of Patmos (Revelation 1:9).

Memorizing, reading, studying, and preaching God's Word necessitates the preservation of His written Word. The passages surveyed above contain the implicit assurance that this is what God has done. He has preserved His Word for His people. The question then arises, "How has God preserved His Word?"

Many passages of Scripture are often cited as demanding supernatural preservation of every word of Scripture in a particular extant text or lineage of texts—even in a particular translation. Careful exegesis of these texts leads to the conclusion that they are often misunderstood and/or misapplied. We have selected those most frequently cited and provided detailed exegesis and exposition. From the time of the Reformation biblical Christians have believed that the grammatical-historical method of interpretation leads to proper understanding of God's Word. Only by consistently applying this method can the true meaning of Scripture be ascertained.

SCRIPTURE PASSAGES OFTEN USED IN SUPPORT OF PRESERVATION

The Words of the Psalmist

The book of Psalms, especially Psalm 119, is rich in teaching about the Word of God. In our effort to strengthen confidence in the Scriptures, we must be careful to understand and apply the statements as actually written. Accurate translation into any language attempts to covey what was expressed in the source language. Since the Psalms were written in Hebrew and in the form of poetry it is imperative that we understand the grammatical relationships between the words and the contextual settings that are used by God to communicate His truth. Careful exegesis and exposition of passages often cited in relation to the preservation of God's Word will clarify what the Bible actually teaches.

Psalm 12:6-7

Psalm 12:6-7—*"The words of the LORD are pure words: as silver tried in a furnace of earth, purified seven times. Thou shalt keep them, O LORD, thou shalt preserve them from this generation forever."*

This is one of the most frequently cited passages in the text debate. Benjamin G. Wilkinson appears to be the earliest to use this passage in defense of the King James Bible. In his *Our Authorized Bible Vindicated*, he writes:

Inspiration declares that this revelation has been under the special protection of Him who has all power in heaven and in earth. 'The words of the Lord are pure words,' says the Psalmist, 'as silver tried in a furnace of earth, purified seven times. Thou shalt keep them, O Lord, thou shalt preserve every one of them [margin] from this generation for ever' (Ps. 12:6, 7).[1]

Others, like Jasper James Ray (*God Only Wrote One Bible*, 1955) and David Otis Fuller, have popularized Wilkinson's interpretation. More recent writers, like Jeffrey Khoo, continue this trend. Khoo writes, "God has indeed promised that His Holy Scriptures would not only be presented in all its purity to the Church then, but also to the Church now (Ps. 12:6-7)."[2] Later in the same essay, Khoo concludes, "We therefore find Ps. 12:6-7 teaching us that God will preserve His Word as a whole (plenary preservation), and His Word in its parts (verbal preservation.)."[3]

However, the verses as they appear above have been divorced from their context. To get a clear picture of their meaning we'll need to look at the entire Psalm.

The Twelfth Psalm is a prayer for help. David is crying out to God because "the godly man ceaseth; for the faithful fail from among the children of men" (v. 1). In verses two through four, he goes on to voice his fear that the wicked would prevail over the righteous. Then in verse five, God speaks: "For the oppression of the poor, for the sighing of the needy, now will I arise, saith the LORD; I will set him in safety from him that puffeth at him."[4]

David then speaks again saying, "The words of the LORD are pure words: as silver tried in a furnace of earth, purified seven times." Recently, some have interpreted the simile comparing the purity of the words of the LORD to refined silver as a prophetic statement on the production of the English Bible. Their theory is that the "furnace of earth" is the crucible of persecution that heroes and martyrs faced in the process of transmitting the text and producing an English translation. They trace it through various stages, always finding seven, but not necessarily agreeing among themselves on what constituted the seven stages. Some advocates of this theory end the sevenfold purification process with the production of the King James Bible in 1611. Others count differently and arrive at the 1769 Blayney revision of the King James, which is the revision currently in use.

In contrast to such misinterpretation, J. A. Alexander expresses the historic, orthodox, and exegetically accurate understanding of what the Psalmist is saying.

> The Psalmist does not use the term commonly translated words, but one derived from the verb to say, with obvious allusion to the use of the verb in the preceding verse. What Jehovah there says, the promises there given, are here declared to be true without any mixture of mistake or falsehood. This is expressed by the favourite figure of pure metallic ore. The idea of extreme or perfect purity is conveyed by the idiomatic phrase, purified seven times, i.e. repeatedly, or sevenfold, i.e. completely.[5]

Verse six is a clear statement of David's confidence in the truthfulness, purity, and trustworthiness of God's words—He would protect the righteous from the wicked. David could count on this promise to be true. A. F. Kirkpatrick says that this verse states "a general truth with direct application to the promise of the preceding verse. In Jehovah's words there is no dross of flattery or insincerity or falsehood. Unlike the words of men, they are wholly to be relied on."[6]

It seems obvious that this verse should not be interpreted prophetically, as if God's words would need to undergo a sevenfold refinement on earth to finally be purified. Just as clearly, the passage has nothing to do with English text history. But if it is not the text that is being preserved, what (or who) is God promising to protect?

Significantly, the KJV 1611 includes a marginal reading in verse seven noting that the second occurrence of the word "them" actually reads "him" in the Hebrew. That notation identifies the Hebrew pronoun to be masculine in gender and singular in number. This word is the object of the verb "shalt preserve." The fact that "words" in verse six is feminine indicates that this pronoun cannot have "words" as its antecedent. That which is preserved must also be masculine. The grammar of the passage indicates that the references to "keeping" and "preserving" are to God's promise to guard and protect the righteous (masculine gender) so the wicked will not ultimately prevail. David expresses his confidence in God by reiterating God's promise, "thou shalt keep them [i.e. guard the righteous], O LORD, thou shalt preserve them [i.e. protect the righteous] from this generation [the workers of iniquity] forever." Kirkpatrick says that verses seven and eight are a "concluding expression of confidence in Jehovah's protection, which is sorely needed when wickedness prevails unchecked."[7] Keil and Delitzsch explain the passage as follows:

> [T]he announcement of Jahve is followed by its echo in the heart of the seer: the words of Jahve are pure words, i.e. intended, and to be fulfilled, absolutely as they run without any admixture whatever of untruthfulness....The suffix em...refers to the miserable and poor; the suffix ennu...refers back to the man who yearns for deliverance mentioned in the divine utterance....The "preserving for ever" is so constant, that neither now nor at any future time will they succumb to this generation. That oppression shall not become a thorough depression, the trial shall not exceed their power of endurance.[8]

Other commentators have expressed a similar understanding of this passage. Matthew Henry says,

> This intimates that, as long as the world stands, there will be a generation of proud and wicked men in it, more or less, who will threaten by their wretched arts to ruin religion....But let God alone to maintain his own interest and to preserve his own people. He will keep them from this generation.[9]

William S. Plumer states,

> The persons referred to by the pronouns of this verse [v. 7] are those mentioned in verse 5. These pronouns, because they designate the same persons, are properly both given in the plural, them, though in the Hebrew the latter is singular, him. But Hammond thinks them refers to the words of the Lord mentioned in the preceding verse, and him to the just man, and so he would read, Thou, O Lord, shalt keep, or perform, those words; thou shalt preserve the just man from this generation forever....For him, Edwards has each one of them; Chaldee: Thou wilt preserve just (men), thou wilt guard them. The Septuagint, Vulgate, Ethiopic, Arabic and Fry have us instead of them.[10]

Plumer has indicated that even if the first "them" is thought to apply to the words, as Hammond suggested, the singular masculine form of the second "them" ("him") must refer to the victims of the wicked. Kirkpatrick does not accept Hammond's reading, and concurs with Plumer, saying,

> Them refers to the poor and needy of verse 5; him in the second line singles out each one of the victims of persecution as the object of divine care....But possibly we should follow the LXX and read us, instead of them and him, or at any rate in place of him.[11]

Concerning the phrase "this generation," Kirkpatrick adds, "As the men of one age are commonly distinguished by special characteristics, generation acquires an ethical significance, and denotes kind, class in good or bad sense."[12] Plumer makes the same point, saying, "By this generation is meant this sort of men, viz., those described in vv. 2, 3, 4....The wicked shall not have power either to corrupt and debauch, or to destroy and exterminate the saints."[13]

H. C. Leupold summarizes the passage:

> Since God may be rightly described in reference to His words as just indicated [in verse 6], the Psalmist draws proper conclusions with regard to the situation in which he and other godly men like him find themselves. Addressing God in prayer, he expresses the confidence that God will keep His watchful eye on those that have suffered oppression ("Thou wilt regard") and will go farther in that He will keep His protecting hand over them. The Psalm here takes on a note of the more personal feelings in that the writer includes himself ("Thou wilt guard us"). This protection is offered in the face of this wicked class of oppressors above described (in the sense the word "generation" is here used), and this protection of God will be exercised for all time to come.[14]

Classic, orthodox commentators uniformly say that in this Psalm God's promises to "keep" and "preserve" are applied to men, not words.[15] John P. Lange applies this passage as saying, "God watches over His people and protects those who sigh after Him."[16] W. Graham Scroggie says, "No matter to what extent evil prevails, the righteous may always reckon on the keeping power of God."[17] David did not say that every word of God would remain in the hands of every generation. Rather, he asserted that everything God says can be counted on to be true, with specific reference to God's promise to protect the righteous.

Even some proponents of supernatural preservation in a particular text or textual lineage recognize that this passage does not support that position. Thomas Cassidy, an active member of the Dean Burgon Society,[18] states,

> God's preservation of His word is not in question, but the interpretation of the above verse is often a bit twisted by those with an axe to grind from either side.

> It is clear from the Hebrew grammar that the "them" of verse 7 is the "godly" and "faithful" of verse one. But what must be understood from this verse is that we know God will preserve His people because He has given His word on it, and His word can never fail to come to pass.[19]

Similarly Charles Surrett, who has published one of the more irenic books advocating the primacy of the Byzantine text writes,

> One passage that has been improperly used by some preservationists in defense of their position is Ps. 12:6-7....Some have relied upon these verses as the principle "proof-text" of the preservation of Scripture. However, such usage is not justified by the Hebrew language this passage translates. The noun rendered "words" in verse six is a *feminine* Hebrew noun, while the pronoun "them" in verse seven is a *masculine* pronominal suffix. Evidently, the assertion is that God will "keep" and "preserve" the "godly" and the "faithful," who are referred to in verse one.[20]

Psalm 119:89

Psalm 119:89—"For ever, O LORD, thy word is settled in heaven."

Some contemporary writers see this as teaching the eternal durability of the *written* word—the text of the Bible. But is that really what this verse says? In the context of this Psalm, the Psalmist actually points to the contrast between the principle of change and decay that operates on *all that exists in the world*, and the fact that God's Word is *not* subject to change. Since texts exist as a part of this material world, it seems more legitimate to conclude that this verse implies that texts, too, will show signs of decay and disruption.

This verse (89) introduces the twelfth section of Psalm 119. The theme of this section is God's preserving providence over all that He has made. The section begins by acknowledging the eternal stability of God's word in heaven (or, the heavens). The Hebrew word translated "word" (Heb. *dabar*—see discussion under Isaiah 40:7-8) is a general designation for God's communication, whether spoken or written, although the vast majority of its uses have direct application to the spoken, not the written word. For instance, in Genesis 18:14, "Is any thing [*dabar*] too hard for God?" the reference is to God's ability to keep His verbal promise to cause Sarah to conceive in her old age. Other random examples are found in Numbers 22, "I will bring you word [*dabar*] again" (v. 8); "the word [*dabar*] which I shall say unto thee" (v. 20); "The word [*dabar*] that I shall speak unto thee" (v. 35); and "the word [*dabar*] that God putteth in my mouth" (v. 38).

After acknowledging the eternal nature of God's word, the Psalmist then affirms the faithfulness of God to all generations on the basis of His perpetual maintenance of the heavens and earth "according to thine ordinances [commands, decrees, verdicts]" (vv. 90-91; cf. Heb. 11:3). The psalm proceeds to make personal application to God's preserving power in the Psalmist's own life (vv. 92-95). The section then concludes with the Psalmist's assertion, "I have seen an end of all perfection: *but* thy commandment *is* exceeding broad" (v. 96). Plumer says of the first clause of this verse that "All merely earthly things are by their very nature vain, unsatisfactory, and through our depravity, delusory, v. 96. All human attainments are shallow, all human enjoyments transitory, all human virtue marred."[21] Of the second clause, he says that God's commandments are "comprehensive, including actions, words, thoughts and emotions; the matter, manner and motive of all that man can do, or say, or think."[22]

Charles Spurgeon writes,

> Jehovah's word is not fickle nor uncertain; it is settled, determined, fixed, sure, immovable....God's purposes, promises, and precepts are all settled in his own mind, and none of them shall be disturbed.[23]

John Calvin says,

> [A]s there is reason to fear that the minds of the godly would hang in uncertainty if they rested the proof of God's truth upon the state of the world, in which such manifold disorders prevail; by placing God's truth in the heavens, he allots to it a habitation subject to no changes....Our salvation, as if it had been said, being shut up in God's word, is not subject to change, as all earthly things are, but is anchored in a safe and peaceful haven.[24]

To say that the Word of God is "settled (*natsav*) in heaven" is not identical with saying it is "protected by heaven," no matter how much one might wish that were what the Psalmist had said. Spiros Zodhiates provides the following explanation of the word translated "settled":

Natsav; to be set up, be stationed, station oneself, stand; to be firm....The main idea of this verb can best be seen in Ex. 7:15 where God ordered Moses to station himself by the edge of the Nile to meet Pharaoh. In another place, Moses was to "present" himself before God on Mount Sinai (Ex. 34:2). God is described as "standing in the congregation" (Ps. 82:1) for administering justice.[25]

Plumer cites the Syriac reading, "Thou art for ever, O Lord, and thy word continues in heaven." He then defines *natsav* as *"is settled, stands, stands still, is set, is established."*

There is some disagreement among conservative scholars on the identification of the place where God's word is settled—is it in "heaven," or "the heavens"? Taking essentially the same position as Spurgeon (above), Plumer treats the phrase "in heaven" as a reference to that which is commonly called the "third heaven"—the eternal abode of God. He says,

> Where God himself is; where his throne is built upon his truth; whence all causes derive their efficiency; whence all his servants receive their commands; "beyond the reach of all disturbing causes."...All holy Scripture is found in the foundation of God's throne.[26]

Leupold, however, translates the verse as "Forever, O Lord, Thy Word stands fast in the heavens." The implication is that he believes the reference is to the "second heaven"—essentially the atmosphere and beyond, including the abode of the celestial bodies. He says,

> The writer begins [this section of the Psalm] by considering the work of God's creation (vv. 89-91). The heavens themselves have an enduring quality. It is as though the author were saying that in those eternal heavens the Word, which proceeds from the eternal Lord of the heavens, has its abiding resting place and will, like them, endure forever.[27]

Essentially, Leupold is saying that the created universe was "settled" by God's command—His word established the heavens and is verifiably trustworthy by virtue of the fact that His creation is a *cosmos*, not a *chaos*.

Whether we conclude that the Psalm refers to the second or the third heaven, the Psalmist has asserted the *immutability of God's truth.* Still, he has not actually said anything about the *durability of the text* of Scripture, unless it is to imply that since texts exist in the material world they are subject to the same principle of decay that affects all creation since Adam sinned. "The world has been created by the word of God, and by His word it shall be prepared for His kingdom—Everything changes, but not God and His word."[28]

A few years ago I had to replace the Bible I carry into my pulpit. The binding of my old Bible had broken, and several of the leaves had come loose and some had been lost. Similarly, the wife of a friend and fellow pastor recently purchased a new copy of the original Scofield Reference Bible, but when she looked up *this Psalm* (119), she found that *it had been omitted*. An entire section of her Bible had been left out by the printer/binder, so she was left with a Bible that did not contain this very verse which is often taken to promise that no verse of Scripture could ever be missing. How ironic!

Even the best of Bibles wear out and are subject to human weakness in their production. Should I accuse God of infidelity because I've lost a few pages from my Bible, or should my friend's wife despair of knowing what God said because a section of the Psalms was missing from hers? Of course not. But it would be just as absurd for either of us to argue vehemently that we believe "by faith" that these Bibles are complete and all others have "additions," despite the fact that by comparing our Bibles with others we can easily discover how ours came to have specific omissions. It is much more appropriate for us to respond like the Psalmist—rejoicing because God's Word is not altered by the affects of time and space on anything He has made. He is on His throne. His creation is maintained by His ordinances. His Word is established in heaven (or, the heavens).

Psalm 119:152

> Psalm 119:152—"Concerning thy testimonies, I have known of old that thou hast founded them forever."

In this verse, the Psalmist is expressing his absolute confidence in the promises of God because they are "founded" upon His eternal nature and integrity. This becomes clear as the context of the passage is considered.

This verse comes at the conclusion of the nineteenth section of Psalm 119. The theme of this section of the Psalm is a cry for deliverance coupled with confidence in God's promises. At the beginning of the section, the Psalmist begs God to hear him, and promises to obey His statutes/testimonies as God gives him grace in answer to his prayer (vv. 145-146). In verse 147 the intensity of his prayer increases, since *shava*, "to cry out, to shout" (v. 147) is a stronger word than *qara*, "to call out to someone" (vv. 145, 146), and since he now claims to be up before dawn ("preventing the dawning," v. 147) and during the night ("prevent the night watches," v. 148). At the same time, the Psalmist expresses increasing confidence in God's word in which he hopes and on which he meditates. He then throws himself on the mercy of God that he might be heard "according to thy lovingkindness," and he asks that God "quicken me according to thy judgment" (or "revive me according to Thy will," v. 149). The cause of the Psalmist's distress is implied in verse 150: "They draw nigh that follow after mischief: they are far from thy law." That is, those plotting malicious mischief against him were drawing near to the Psalmist, but they were far from God. Still, the writer is confident that the Lord is also near him and God's commandments are trustworthy and reliable (v. 151). God would surely save him, because He had said that He would, and everything He says is truth. The section closes with an affirmation of the Psalmist's absolute confidence in God's promises, despite the evil intent of his enemies, because God's testimonies have been "founded...for ever" (v. 152).

The word translated "founded" (*yasad*) means "to be established or set up." While some assume that this is a promise of God's continual maintenance of His Word on earth, there is nothing in the word *yasad* that implies a continuing relationship. It communicates a *fixed condition of stability*, not a *perpetual activity of sustenance*. Perhaps its most significant usage is in the Messianic prophecy of Isaiah 28:16—"Behold I lay in Zion for a foundation a stone..." Peter applies this verse to Christ Jesus in 1 Peter 2:4-8, as does Paul in Romans 9:32-33. God told Isaiah that He had established this "foundation" centuries before Christ's incarnation, and Peter and Paul tell us that Christ remains this "foundation" forever. This "founding" was established by God's decree.

Psalm 119:152 says the same thing about God's Word—it is established by God's decree. Commenting on this verse, Plumer says, "God's word cannot change because God cannot change....God's testimonies are true, eternal, unchangeable, indispensable, irrevocable."[29] Charles Spurgeon cites George Horne, saying,

> This portion of our Psalm endeth with the triumph of faith over all dangers and temptation. "*Concerning thy testimonies*," the revelation of thy will, thy counsels for the salvation of thy servants, "*I have known of old*," by faith, and by my own experience, as well as that of others, "*that thou hast founded them for ever*"; they are unalterable and everlasting as the attributes of their great Author, and can never fail those who rely upon them, in time or in eternity.[30]

Albert Barnes writes,

> Every Command of God is in fact a testimony of his as to what is right; every promise is a testimony of his own purpose in regard to mankind....They were laid in eternity past; they will continue in the

eternity to come. They are based on eternal principles of right; they will never be changed.[31]

Kirkpatrick says of this verse,

> Men may affirm or act as if they believed that God's laws are absolute: but from the study of those laws themselves, the Psalmist has long ago learnt their eternal validity; and his deeply rooted convictions cannot be shaken by the contempt or the threats of his enemies.[32]

Leupold describes this verse as closing this section of the psalm on a note of "a spirit of strong assurance" that what the Psalmist "knows about the value of the Lord's testimonies is a truth that has long been his conviction, that God's words are 'founded forever.' They are the immutable factors in the changing situations of life."[33]

Essentially, the Psalmist has here asserted that God's promises are perpetually reliable. In the context of this section of the psalm, he is saying enemies that would ensnare him or lead him astray (v. 150) would be unable to do so because of the promise that "God's order of salvation, or His appointments that relate thereto"[34] could not be overthrown by the Psalmist's enemies.

> [T]hey go forth purposing this, but God's law is altogether self-verifying truth. And the poet has long ago gained the knowledge from it that it does not aim at merely temporary recompense. The sophisms of the apostates cannot therefore lead him astray.[35]

> God's word cannot change because God cannot change....God's testimonies are true, eternal, unchangeable, indispensable, irrevocable. The saints rejoice and are glad, for they *know* by a long experience how sure every word of God is.[36]

The word "testimonies" (or *witness*) has to do with God's revelation to men, so this verse has stronger implications for the *text* of Scripture than does Psalm 119:89. Still, there is no promise here that neither human weakness nor evil intent will be capable of adulterating any specific copy of the written revelation of God. The Psalmist has stopped well short of saying what many seem to think he should have said. He does *not* say that God will superintend the maintenance of His testimonies, protecting them from all possibility of variation in transcription and translation. This promise should be understood to apply to God's eternal intentions as expressed in the revealed Word of God in general, not to the written words of any particular manuscript or translation. The Psalmist has said his salvation is sure and unshakable because it is based on the immutable promises of God.

It is imperative that any effort to validate our confidence in the preservation of the Scriptures be based on sound exegetical and hermeneutical principles. Verses that exalt the Word of God must not be interpreted in isolation from their contexts. Their interpretation must be consistent with the grammar, syntax, and word meanings of the language used by the inspired penman in that specific context. Good intentions are not accomplished by misuse of "proof texts," when those texts are misunderstood or misapplied. It must be remembered that even those passages that do support our doctrine of preservation apply only to the Sacred Writings as originally given, not to the words of a particular translation. Attempts to apply them to translations make one guilty of "wrestling" the Scriptures about which Peter warned (1 Peter 3:16).

THE WORDS OF THE PROPHET ISAIAH

The Old Testament Prophets were conscious that they were speaking for God: *Hear the word of the LORD* (Isaiah 1:10). *The word of the LORD came to me* (Jeremiah 1:4). *The word of the LORD came expressly unto Ezekiel* (Ezekiel 1:3). *The word of the LORD that came unto Hosea* (Hosea 1:1). *Now the word of the LORD came unto Jonah* (Jonah 1:1). Almost identical words are found in Micah 1:1; Zephaniah 1:1; Haggai 1:1; and Zechariah 1:1. Malachi 1:1 records *The burden of the word of the LORD to Israel by Malachi*. There is no question that the words they penned were the words of God. The question we must answer is, "Did these prophets teach that the words they wrote would be supernaturally preserved in a particular manuscript or translation?" A passage often cited is found in Isaiah.

Isaiah 40:8 b

The grass withereth, the flower fadeth: but the word of our God shall stand for ever.

Contextual Meaning of Isaiah 40:1-11

The political and military contests among the nations were understood by the surrounding Gentile nations as contests among the gods of these nations. The question that would be raised with the Babylonian exile was whether the gods of Babylon had, in effect, defeated the God of Israel. The thought would have been that Judah's God was superior to the Assyrian gods, since Assyria failed to capture Jerusalem in Isaiah 36 and 37, but apparently not to the Babylonian gods. In these chapters (Isaiah 40 ff.), Isaiah establishes several irrefutable facts. The first is that Babylon, like Assyria, was an instrument in the hand of Judah's God to punish His wayward people for violations of the covenant. The second is that once Babylon's role was completed, God would overthrow Babylon just as he had done with Assyria, demonstrating His power and sovereignty. The third is that Judah's God would *eventually restore* His people to their land, *precisely as he had promised* in His covenants with Abraham and David.

Even though Judah had been sinfully rebellious and unfaithful to her covenant, God had not abandoned His people. He would chasten Judah with exile, but he would also restore Judah in *fulfillment* of His promises. In the first section of chapter 40, Isaiah offers a prophecy of comfort and hope, involving several messengers described as "voices" (40:1-11). It begins with the voice of the Lord, announcing the impending termination of Judah's punishment (vv. 1-2). This is followed by the voice of a royal legate or emissary, calling on the nation to prepare for the Lord's coming to deliver His people (vv. 3-5). Next, an unidentified voice directs the prophet to declare the frailty of sinful humanity in contrast to the *faithfulness of God's promises* (vv. 6-8). Finally, the inhabitants of Jerusalem are directed to announce throughout Judea the coming of the Lord and the regathering of His people to their land (vv. 9-11).

The fulfillment of this chapter can be confusing. The initial verses of this passage could be addressing the Jews in exile in Babylon, the Jews under Roman domination during the first advent of Christ, or the Jews in the Tribulation. Taken at face value, the activity depicted in these verses appears to describe the ultimate or eschatological deliverance. In particular, verses 3-5 and 9-11 indicate that, in conjunction with this deliverance, the Lord himself would be involved, personally leading His people and ruling over them. Having said this does not suggest that these verses have no significance for the Jews in Babylon or for the Jews under Roman domination in the first century. The fact that verses 3-5 are cited in the NT and applied to John the Baptist argues to the contrary (cf. Matt. 3:3; Mk. 1:3; Lk. 3:4-6; Jn. 1:25). However, the significance of this passage for these other contexts is one of application, not fulfillment. What Isaiah says here concerning God's delivering the Jews at the end of the Tribulation may also be applied in principle to the nearer contexts. Just as He would deliver the eschatological exiles, so He would intervene and deliver the historical exiles, and in fact, all who would trust in Him.

Exposition of Isaiah 40:8
*. . . but the **word** of our God shall **stand** for ever.*

An understanding of two key terms "word" and "stand" in Isaiah 40:8 is essential for a proper interpretation of the passage. The most common term in the Old Testament for "word" is the Hebrew term *dabar* (דבר).[37] In the New Testament the most frequent term for "word" is the Greek expression *logos* ("reason," "discourse," "speech"), but also frequently the term *rhema* is used. *Rhema* is often viewed as a specific "word" itself; *logos* is a "word" with reference generally to that which is in the speaker's mind. Some of the chief applications of "word" are as follows.

We have the word of *Yahweh* described as (1) the revelation to a patriarch, prophet, or writer of Scripture as *spoken forth or written* by that person (Gen. 15:1; Ex. 20:1; Nu. 22:38; Ex. 4:30; 34:1; 2 Ki. 7:1; Isa. 1:10, etc.). (2) "Word" is often a commandment, sometimes equivalent to "the Law" (Ex. 32:28; Num. 20:24; Deut. 6:6; Psa. 105:8; 119:11, 17; Isa. 66:2, etc.). (3) Sometimes this term is used as a promise and ground of hope (Psa. 119:25, 28, 38; 130:5) or (4) as a personal designation of one's thoughts and identity (Jn. 1:1). *Logos* in Greek-Jewish philosophy meant both reason or thought and its utterance. The eternal *Logos* is incarnated in Jesus Christ (John 1:14; 1 John 1:1, 2; Rev. 19:13, "His name is called, The Word of God"). (7) The term "word"is also used as a designation of the Gospel of Christ (Mt. 13:19; Mk. 2:2; Acts 4:4, 29, 31, etc.). In John's Gospel Jesus frequently speaks of His *"word" and "works"* as containing the divine revelation and requirements which men are asked to believe in, cherish, and obey (John 5:24; 6:63, 68; John 4:41).

The verb *qûm* (קוּם) is the second key term in Isaiah 40:8, and it appears in many and varied contexts. *Qûm* (קוּם) has a basic meaning to arise, stand up, or stand. In the Qal stem it can mean *stand, maintain, be established, confirmed, endure, be fixed, be valid, be proven,* or *be fulfilled.* Brown, Driver, and Briggs list קוּם in Isaiah 40:8 under the meaning *"fulfilled"* along with Isaiah 46:10 and Jeremiah 44:28.[38] Etymologically, קוּם denotes rising up from a prostrate position (Josh. 3:16). More importantly, however, this term also carries a legal usage whereby it connotes the *validity of one's testimony* in a trial (Deut. 19:15). A related usage is the sense of the valid transfer of property (Gen. 23:17). God reflects on this legal sense of the verb in His statements that *His word shall stand* (Num. 23:19; Isa. 40:8; etc.). This usage often occurs in contexts referring to covenants, and especially the divine covenant. God announces his covenant to men (Gen. 9:11), and asserts that He will see that it is *accomplished* (Gen. 17:19). In our present context, *qûm* (קוּם) means that ultimately all of man's promises will *fall,* but God's covenant will *stand* by being permanently fulfilled or accomplished (Isa. 28:18; 40:8).

Conclusion

In Isaiah 40:7 Isaiah states that the transience of humanity cannot survive any conflict with God. The grass dries up and the flowers wither. In the middle east, a hot dry wind can turn the countryside from green to brown in a matter of days. So God is able to subdue man with His breath. Great powers are as transient as the wild flowers. They are no more to be feared than a blade of grass. The nations cannot prevent God from delivering His own; neither are the people of God able to save themselves. Salvation is from God alone.

In verse 8, Isaiah repeats the point he made in the previous verse and drives it home with a powerful statement. The Spirit that breathes out judgment for all human pride is the same Spirit who speaks the eternal word of life over all withered and faded human hopes. Whatever may lie ahead for the Israelites, they may know that <u>God's word of promise will not fail them</u>. Isaiah brings to the forefront the characteristics of human transitoriness and weakness in order to more sharply contrast man's fallibility with the unfailing and enduring quality of the word of God. By referring to the word of God the prophet means every word that proceeds out of the mouth of God, not simply those which have been inscripturated in the Bible (cf. Deut. 8:3; Matt. 4:4). In the present passage the emphasis falls upon the vivid contrast between the absolute fulfillment of God's promise and the transitory character of human flesh. In verse 9 God tells Israel, "Be not afraid." Zion need not fear that God's word will fail. "When God speaks, His word expresses the truth; and that truth cannot be annulled or changed."[39]

Harmonization with 1 Peter 1:23-25

For you have been born again not of perishable seed, but of imperishable [seed] through the living and abiding word of God (1 Pet. 1:23 [author's translation]).

Peter begins verse 23 with a causal participle which refers to regeneration and all that results from it. The apostle Peter borrows an agricultural metaphor by referring to "seed" that does not bear spiritual fruit. He then uses the strongest adversative in Greek (*alla*) to point to the true means of our regeneration—the imperishable seed (the same word as "perishable" with the *alpha* primitive). "Seed" is provided by ellipsis. The living and abiding word of God refers to the Gospel message in this context (v. 25). The word of God is able to make alive as the instrument through which the Holy Spirit imparts life. It also continues to operate in the life of the redeemed by effectively producing love for the brethren (2 Thess. 2:11).

For all men are like grass and all their glory like the flower of the grass - the grass dries up and the flower falls, but the word of the Lord abides forever, and this is the word which was preached to you (1 Pet 1:24-25 [author's translation]).

Verses 24-25 support verse 23. The word of God continues to equip and enable the believer. In order to demonstrate that such is the case, Peter cites

Isaiah 40:6-8. This citation follows the Septuagint translation with some minor variations rather than quoting directly from the Hebrew text. Peter is drawing a comparison of similarity between man and grass. All "flesh" represents mankind, and man's "glory" refers to all the achievements man can do apart from the operation of the grace of God. Mankind and grass are both frail and fleeting. Humankind and its achievements are transitory. Peter's use of Isaiah 40:6-8 is consistent with the context of the Isaiah passage. In Isaiah the grass refers to the nation of Israel in exile because of its covenantal disobedience and subsequent chastisement. Isaiah encourages the nation by reminding her that God's word promises forgiveness of sin through the future coming of their Messiah. Both in 1 Peter and Isaiah the perishing of people is contrasted with the surety and reliability of God's promises. God's word will never fall or fail but will *accomplish* what God has designed for it to accomplish. Peter uses the Greek word *rhema* rather than *logos* in verse 25, because he is quoting from the Septuagint. Here, *rhema* is equivalent to *logos* in verse 23. Peter is simply using the terms synonymously and interchangeably. God's word continues in its authority and power to accomplish God's will in the life of the redeemed. Peter identifies the specific word in view as the Gospel preached to the readers. It is this Gospel by which they have been born again and which continually equips them for obedience and service. 1 Peter 1:23-25 does not directly address the preservation of God's word, but rather its power to accomplish God's sanctifying purpose in the lives of those who have received the Lord Jesus Christ through repentant faith. On the other hand, both Isaiah 40:6-8 and 1 Peter 1:23-25 *indirectly* teach the preservation of God's word. We must have the word of God, if we are to continue in the word of God. This is a necessary corollary.

THE WORDS OF OUR LORD HIMSELF

Our Lord frequently cited or referred to Old Testament passages, as the basis for His teaching. Bible-believing Christians depend on the testimony of Christ—because of His Person and character—to validate the authorship and authenticity of disputed OT writings (e.g. Moses, Daniel, Jonah). In the same fashion we believe that His statements regarding the preservation of the Scriptures are the final court of appeals. He always affirmed the authority and perpetuity of God's Word given in what we call the Old Testament even though his quotations are not often identical to that which has come down to us in the Masoretic text.

Matthew 5:18

Matthew 5:18—For verily I say unto you, Till heaven and earth pass, one jot or one tittle shall in no wise pass from the law, till all be fulfilled.

Question: Is our Lord here guaranteeing the preservation of all the written words of Scripture?

The answer to this question emerges through identifying (1) the exact relations existing between the verse's propositions, (2) the precise meaning of its terms. It takes patience to work through these, but apart from such careful exegesis there can be no certain answer to the issue at hand. So, let's take the time and trouble to exposit our way carefully through this oft misunderstood text.

The Relationships between the Propositions

This saying consists of three clauses.

(1) *till heaven and earth pass*
(2) *one jot or one tittle shall in no wise pass from the law*
(3) *till all be fulfilled*

The second of these is grammatically related to the first and third by an identical combination of particles (εως combined with αν).

one jot or one tittle shall in no wise pass from the law. . .
till (εως αν)   *heaven and earth pass* εως
till (εως αν)   *all be fulfilled*

This combination of particles (εως αν) is the standard temporal conjunction employed with subjunctive verbs to mark the *terminus ad quem*[40] of activities or events—that is, their termination point. In this case, then, the termination point of the event in question (the passing of the jots and tittles) is identified by two temporal clauses: (1) *heaven and earth passing*, (2) *all being fulfilled*.

There are now two questions which must be answered concerning this event, one having to do with its subjects (*one jot or one tittle*), and the second having to do with its activity (*shall pass*). To begin with the verb, what meaning does it have in our Lord's mind?

The Meaning of the Verb

This verb (παρερχομαι; 31 occ. NT) is a compound of the common root ερχομαι, meaning to "come" or "go," and the prefixed preposition παρα. Sometimes this preposition is left untranslated so that παρερχομαι is rendered quite simply, "pass." At other times, however, the preposition is made explicit by translations such as "over" (*pass **over** judgment and the love of God*; Lk. 11:42), or "by" (*passing **by** Mysia*; Acts 16:8), or "away" (*this cup may not pass **away***; Mtt. 26:42).

101

Of these, the translation "pass **away**" is that employed for the "ending" of something, its "disappearing," or its "ceasing to exist." Thus we read that *the flower of the grass shall **pass away*** (Jam. 1:10), that is, it shall cease to exist. It shall disappear. Similarly, *the first heaven and the first earth were **passed away*** (Rev. 21:1), that is, they had come to an end. They had ceased to exist.

Now in Matthew 5:18 παρερχομαι occurs twice, once with "heaven and earth" as its subjects and once with "one jot or one tittle" as its subjects. Both times the King James translators have rendered the verb "pass."

> *Till heaven and earth **pass**, one jot or one tittle shall in no wise **pass** from the law. . . .*

This translation, however, is inconsistent with their work in every other case where the subjects of παρερχομαι are heaven or earth. Thus, in the Olivet Discourse, they translate, *heaven and earth shall **pass away*** (Mt. 24:35; Mk. 13:31; Lk. 21:33). In II Peter 3:10 they translate, *the heavens shall **pass away***, and, as already noted in the paragraph above, in Revelation 21:1 they translate, *the first heaven and the first earth were **passed away***. Thus, in every case but Matthew 5:18, when the subjects are heaven or earth, the King James translators consistently rendered παρερχομαι, "pass away."

The NASV, on the other hand, reads "pass away" in every case, including Matthew 5:18.

> *. . . until heaven and earth **pass away*** (Mtt. 5:18)
> *Heaven and earth will **pass away*** (Mtt. 24:35)
> *Heaven and earth will **pass away*** (Mk. 13:31)
> *Heaven and earth will **pass away*** (Lk. 21:33)
> *. . . the heavens will **pass away*** (II Pet. 3:10)
> *. . . the first heaven and the first earth **passed away*** (Rev. 21:1)

Since the subjects of all of these statements are the same, and the natural understanding of what is predicated of these subjects is the same (that they will come to an end/cease to exist), the NASB consistency appears to be correct.

How, then, should παρερχομαι be translated in the second clause of the verse where "one jot or one tittle" are its subjects? Consider the three clauses again.

(1) Till (εως αν) heaven and earth **παρελθη**
(2) one jot or one tittle ου μη **παρελθη** from the law
(3) till (εως αν) all be fulfilled.

What is apparent, not only to the eye, but also to the ear upon hearing the saying, is that the first two clauses are related to one another in not just one way, but in two. The first is through the temporal connection which we have already considered (one jot or one tittle shall in no wise pass till ($εως$ $αν$) heaven and earth pass away). But the second relationship is the one indicated by the obvious grammatical symmetry between the two clauses.

Note that each clause is composed of two subjects and one verb. Note also that though the subjects of the clauses are different, their verb is identical, creating grammatical symmetry.

This symmetry would be termed *comparative parallelism* if there were no other grammatical elements present. That is, the two sets of subjects would have a point of comparison between them—they both παρερχομαι.[41] In this case, however, there is one additional element in the second clause, the emphatic negation, ου μη (*in no wise*). This element creates a different kind of parallelism. Now we have, not comparative, but *contrasting parallelism.*[42] What happens to the one set of subjects will not happen to the other.

What is it that will happen to the first set of subjects? They will *pass away.* What is it then, by way of contrast, that will not happen to the second set of subjects? That which happens to the first two. It is only consistent, therefore, to translate the second occurrence of the verb just as the first has been. The second set of subjects, the jots and tittles, will not *pass away.* They will not cease to exist or disappear—that is, until ($εως$ $αν$) heaven and earth do and all the law is fulfilled.[43] This brings us to the question of what our Lord meant by "jots and tittles."

Jots and Tittles

The word "jot" (ιωτα) occurs only here in the NT. "It is evidently the Greek equivalent of the Aramaic *yod* which, in the original form of the saying, represented the smallest letter of the alphabet" (BAGD). The word "tittle" (κεραια), occurring only here and in Luke 16:17, is literally a "horn," and refers to a "projection" or "hook as part of a letter" (BAGD). It was the identifying stroke that distinguished one letter from another, just as only a small diagonal line distinguishes a "P" from an "R" or only an extra hump indicates an "m" rather than an "n" in the English alphabet.[44]

Our Lord's referring to these minutia of the written law has been regarded generally by conservatives as the most explicit possible confirmation that He viewed the Old Testament to be verbally inspired and therefore inerrant. John Murray writes,

It would be impossible to think of any expression that would bespeak the thought of the meticulous more adequately than precisely this one used here by our Lord. In respect of the meticulous, our English expression "one letter or syllable" is scarcely equivalent. Could anything establish more conclusively the meticulous accuracy, validity and truth of the law than the language to which Jesus here attaches his own unique formula of asseveration? . . . The indissolubility of the law extends to its every jot and tittle. Such indissolubility could not be predicated of it if it were in any detail fallible, for if fallible it would some day come to nought. . . . Nothing could be plainer than this, that in the smallest details he regards the law as incapable of being made void and that in the smallest details it is taken up by him, and finds, in his fulfillment of it, its permanent embodiment and validity. By the most stringent necessity there is but one conclusion, namely, that the law is infallible and inerrant.[45]

Similarly, R. Laird Harris concludes,

Thus in Matthew 5:18 Christ is clearly referring to the sacred writings of the Jews as a unit and a well-defined sacred unit, too. But He says very positively that this Book is perfect to the smallest detail. It is not merely verbal inspiration that He teaches here, but inspiration of the very letters![46]

Occasionally this view has been disputed on the grounds that Jesus was speaking hyperbolically, that is, that for emphasis' sake He was purposely exaggerating. David Hubbard, a non-inerrantist, writes that much of the language in the Sermon on the Mount is hyperbolic and refers to this verse as an example.[47]

But even were Hubbard a theological conservative, there would yet remain at least two objections to his view. The first, most obvious, is that there is no proving it.[48] But the second, more serious, is that it undercuts the primary point which our Lord is most solemnly making.

Our Lord's Primary Point

Although our Lord's statement (1) indicates His belief in the inspiration of even the minutia of the written law, and (2) predicts the events which will trigger their ultimate passing out of existence, neither of these is actually His primary point. In other words, His first intent is not to teach something about inspiration. Nor is it to reveal the exact time when the written law will cease to exist. His first intent is to make the point that all the law will be fulfilled.

What makes this point so very important? It is so due to the tendency of his hearers to misconstrue His mission: *Think not that I am come to destroy the law or the prophets*, he cautions. But apparently this is the very thing they were thinking. He asserts therefore that His mission is not annulment but fulfillment. And in order to make this point in the most emphatic possible terms, He indicates beyond any possibility of further misunderstanding His own position on the smallest pen strokes of the law. What is that position? It is that that they will not pass away or cease to exist.

To make this point emphatically He employs the double negative, ου μη, used "for making categorical and emphatic denials."[49] In addition He modifies both "jot" and "tittle" with its own numeral, "one." *One jot or one tittle by no means shall pass away. . . .*[50] And finally, he prefaces the entire statement with a solemn "amen," an adverb He employed numerous times at the beginning of particularly emphatic assertions. It can scarcely be conceived how our Lord could have guaranteed preservation of the written words of the law any more specifically or dogmatically.

A further fact confirming that our Lord was speaking in literal rather than figurative terms is the position that his hearers themselves held regarding the preservation of the written law. Hyperbole, by definition, is exaggeration for the sake, not of deception, but of emphasis. In other words, it is an *understood* and therefore *mutually acceptable* exaggeration.

In this case, however, Christ's hearers held a dogmatically literal view of the permanent preservation of the very minutia of the written law. His statement, if hyperbolic, would never have been reassuring to them. Their painfully conscientious labors to preserve, in every manuscript, every letter of the Old Testament scriptures is legendary. According to later Jewish tradition, "if all men in the world were gathered together to abolish the least letter in the Law, they would not succeed."[51]

> Not a letter could be removed from the Law—a saying illustrated by this curious conceit, that the Yod which was taken by God out of the name of Sarah (Sarai), was added to that of Hoshea, making him Joshua (Jehoshua). Similarly, the guilt of changing those little hooks (tittles) which make the distinction between such Hebrew letters as ד and ר, ה and ח, ב and כ, is declared so great, that, if such were done, the world would be destroyed.[52]

Therefore, had Christ said anything less than what He did, His whole credibility would have collapsed in their view. If He had not affirmed the permanency of even the smallest letters and the smallest distinguishing strokes between those letters, they would have concluded that their suspicions were right after all. He was attempting to do away with part of the law.

Now, obviously, the Lord did not say what He did simply to accommodate an erroneous view. He was not speaking tongue-in-cheek in order to get past their prejudice. His use of the solemn affirmation, *amen*, precludes any such possibility. To the contrary, He was speaking in the most literal terms and doing so deliberately to an audience questioning the whole authority of His person and mission because of its suspicion that He was setting aside certain parts of the law as if they had never come from God. Nothing could be further from the truth, our Lord assures them. Think of heaven and earth. They seem so permanent. So indissoluble. But they will pass away.

By contrast, think of the smallest strokes of the law. They seem so fragile. So vulnerable to omission or substitution. But they will not pass away. They will remain throughout all of history. . . *until* all of heaven and all of earth and all that in them is passes out of existence.

The Bottom Line

Returning now to the question, "Is our Lord here guaranteeing the preservation of all the written words of Scripture?" the answer is an emphatic "yes." Although, as has been shown, preservation is not His *main* point, it is nevertheless *the* point He chooses to contribute to the way in which He makes that main point (that all the Law would be fulfilled). What He does not do, however, is give even so much as a hint as to *how* or *where* preservation will take place. Answers to these questions are simply beyond the scope of what is revealed in this passage. The conclusion one must reach is that this passage does not teach that those words are preserved in one particular manuscript or lineage of manuscripts alone. Neither does this passage guarantee that all the words will be always available at all times.

THE WORDS OF THE APOSTLES

The apostles believed that the writings of their Bible (Old Testament) were the Word of God. They declared its inspiration and authority. They also believed that certain writings of other apostles had the authority of inspiration. They believed that they, too, were writing God's truth. If we are to have the Biblical view of inspiration and transmission of the Scriptures, we must determine precisely what the apostolic epistles teach on this important matter.

1 Peter 1:22-25

1 Peter 1:22-25—"Seeing ye have purified your souls in obeying the truth through the Spirit unto unfeigned love of the brethren, see that ye love one another with a pure heart fervently: 23 Being born again, not of corruptible seed, but of incorruptible, by the word of God, which liveth and abideth for ever. 24 For all flesh is as grass, and all the glory of man as the flower of grass. The grass withereth, and the flower thereof falleth away: 25 But the word of the Lord endureth for ever. And this is the word which by the gospel is preached unto you."

The insight 1 Peter 1:23-25 provides into the nature of God's Word has made it an oft-cited passage in the text and translation debate. As with any Scriptural passage, understanding these important verses demands attention to their context. Peter's description of the Word is not mere academic theology. It is vitally practical and had everything to do with the gospel and the transformation being born again produces.

Let's look more closely at how Peter lays out this teaching. Doing so will help us benefit from the main thrust of these verses and at the same time clarify what they reveal about God's Word. Verse 22 gives us the central command that Peter's discussion of the Word supports: "Seeing ye have purified your souls in obeying the truth through the Spirit unto unfeigned love of the brethren, see that ye love one another with a pure heart fervently." Loving others in this self-sacrificing way from the heart with unmixed motives and with strenuous intensity is not the way the natural man behaves. So you'll note that this agape love is preceded by what makes it possible. The persons Peter addresses have "purified their souls in obeying the truth."[53] In faith they have yielded themselves to the truth of the Gospel. Some see "obeying the truth" as descriptive of saving faith at the point of one's conversion. Thus the purification is that initial cleansing we receive upon coming in faith to Christ. Others believe Peter is referring to the sanctification stage of salvation. According to this interpretation, "obeying the truth" is that active obedience to God that true faith produces in a believer (cf. 2 Cor. 7:1; Jas. 4:8; 1 John 3:3)."[54]

Either interpretation we take, "purifying your souls in obedience to the truth" leads to "unfeigned (unhypocritical) love of the brethren." Our word *philadelphia* is a direct transliteration of the word translated "love of the brethren." It refers to the warm, tight-knit affection that family members have for one another. When we are truly born again (v. 23), we are born into God's family. We posses the same spiritual genes, if you will, that every other genuine Christian possesses. Affectionate family love for one another naturally rises from that reality. That's why Peter can say that this love is "unfeigned." Our English word "unhypocritical" comes directly from this word. No pretense. No masks. This brotherly love expresses what we really are and how we really feel toward those who like us have been born from above.[55] Verse 22 commands us to forge from this *philadelphia* a strenuous self-sacrificing agape love. This command is Peter's first specific application of the general command to be holy, found in verses 13-21.[56] Fervent love for other believers marks a person as having been genuinely transformed at the core of his identity—born again. God empowers such love, and God commands it. So those that practice it show their living connection to God.[57]

None of this progress in holiness is possible apart from the life-giving work of God. We must be born again. We must become "partakers of the divine nature" (2 Peter 1:4). We must be made spiritually alive by the Holy Spirit of God. Verse 23 explains how this regeneration happens. And that is where Peter's teaching on the nature of God's Word comes in: "Being born again, not of corruptible seed, but of incorruptible, by the word of God, which liveth and abideth for ever." "Incorruptible" means imperishable, immortal, not subject to decay. "Seed" (*spora*) can refer to the activity of sowing or to the seed itself. The seed of life out of which (*ek*) our new life springs is not subject to decay or death. All natural human life obviously is. But this life we have received from God will never succumb to death, for it is the life of the eternal, incorruptible Spirit of God.[58]

Peter has already stressed in verses 18-19 that holy living should result from the fact that we "were not redeemed with corruptible things," but "with the precious blood of Christ." Corruption and death belong together. If we have been ransomed by the Christ who is "without spot or blemish," if we have been born again by incorruptible seed of the immortal God not corruptible seed of mere human beings, it stands to reason that our everyday lives will display that reality. Some interpreters take *seed* as an agricultural metaphor, but in context it more likely refers to *divine seed* versus *human seed*.[59] Either way, the main thrust of the passage is clear.[60] What instrument does God use to produce this life in us? The Word of God. We are born again *out of* (*ek*) the incorruptible seed of Divine life *through* or *by means of* (*dia*) the Word of God.[61] Because other Bible passages do use *seed* as a metaphor for the Word of God, some interpreters understand this verse to do so, as well. But the context and prepositions used in 1 Peter 1:23 lead to the conclusion that the incorruptible seed in this passage refers to Divine Spiritual life, whereas the Word of God is *the instrument* God uses to implant the seed of incorruptible spiritual life. Even if we take *seed* to refer here to the Word, the word is incorruptible and life-giving precisely because it is the Word *of God*.

Peter's further description of the Word of God sheds light on why the Spirit uses it as the instrument of infusing Divine life: it "liveth and abideth forever." The Word of God is full of life and as such, is life-giving in its effect. The writer of Hebrews expresses a similar thought in Hebrews 4:12—"For the word of God is quick (alive), and powerful, and sharper than any two-edged sword, piercing even to the dividing asunder of soul and spirit, and of the joints and marrow, and is a discerner of the thoughts and intents of the heart."[62]

Furthermore, the Word will never become obsolete or ineffective. It "abides" or remains. In contrast, human life and all its most exalted achievements wither like the grass and fall off like wilted flowers. That is what Isaiah 40:6-8 teaches, from which Old Testament passage Peter draws in 1 Peter 1:24-25 to back his claims: "For all flesh (all mankind in its natural state) is as grass, and all the glory of man as the flower of grass. The grass withereth, and the flower thereof falleth away: but the word of the Lord endureth for ever."

What is particularly enlightening is that Peter identifies the Word of God not only with the Old Testament passage he cites, but as in fact the very gospel he and the other apostles have been preaching: "And this is the word which by the gospel is preached unto you." Peter is not out of line to do so. The very next verse in the Isaiah passage (Isaiah 40:9) reads: "O Zion, that bringest *good tidings* [good news, that is, the gospel], get thee up into the high mountain; O Jerusalem, that bringest *good tidings* [italics mine], lift up thy voice with strength; lift it up, be not afraid; say unto the cities of Judah, Behold your God!"

Although Peter uses *logos* to refer to God's Word in verse 23, in this verse he uses the word *rhema*. The words are synonyms, and he may be using the terms in free variation. It is, however, appropriate that he uses *rhema* to refer to the gospel preached. In its most precise sense, *rhema* refers to a specific message preached, rather than to the written word in general. Peter's teaching on the nature of the Word of God includes not only God's written revelation as such, but also the oral preaching of the gospel, whether written down yet or not.

Now what does the imperishable, life-giving quality of God's Word have to do with the main command to love one another intensely? Chiefly this: if you have truly been born again by the Holy Spirit through the imperishable and life-giving Word, the intrinsic incorruptible nature of God and His Word will unfailingly produce in you love for the brethren. And as those who received divine life, we are to see to it that we nurture this *philadelphia* family affection into an intense and lasting *agape* love. Peter's instruction here identifies this self-sacrificing love as the first mark of true experiential holiness. As such, it is to be aggressively cultivated by all those who have purified their souls in obeying the truth.

Anyone who claims to be defending God's Word must first pay attention to what it really teaches. Thankfully, we can say on the authority of this passage that nothing is able to negate the abiding power of God's Word to bring life by the Spirit to those dead in sin. But 1 Peter 1:22-25 emphatically does not teach that God's written revelation could never be copied down wrong by someone, or that an absolutely perfect copy would be produced. Nor does the passage envision the coming of a perfect translation distinct from all other inferior ones. Peter is not even addressing these issues. Those that use these verses to teach such doctrine twist both the purpose and the meaning of the very Scriptures they are trying to defend. 2 Peter 3:16 warns that "wresting" [torturing, twisting] the Scriptures leads to destruction. It is very serious business.

Furthermore, using a twisted interpretation of this text to spew hatred and slander against brethren who love the Lord and His Word directly disobeys and thus obliterates the whole point of the passage. Such behavior amounts to making void the Word of God for the sake of human tradition (Mark 7:13). It promotes unholiness, which is the fruit of false teaching. Reliable teachers of God's Word, in contrast, not only submit their beliefs and teaching to what the Word actually says; but they also submit their lives to its authority.

SUMMARY AND CONCLUSION

In this chapter we have dealt with an aspect of bibliology that has only recently been subjected to theological inquiry: "What does the Bible teach about its own preservation?" We must allow the Scriptures to say what they mean and to mean what they say.

As we have shown, the Bible's statements and commands often require its availability. In much the way a radio broadcaster addresses his audience with the assumption that they are listening, the Bible addresses the reader with the assumption that he actually has God's Word before him. However, we have also shown that the key passages cited by those who insist that the Bible demands its perfect preservation in a *single* manuscript or translation simply do not support the claims of this position.[63]

The Bible does teach that God's Word is absolutely reliable and eternally durable—the entire physical universe will come to its God-appointed end to be reconstituted in the eternal state as the New Heaven and the New Earth, and still God's Word will stand. But these passages do *not* teach that all

110

copyists and translators, or any individual ones, will be supernaturally guided and protected from all possibility of miscopying or mistranslating a single word or letter of the inspired original.

Can we be confident that we know what God has said? Absolutely! While it can be demonstrated that no two ancient manuscripts (Bibles) are identical, and each one has its own transcription problems (spelling errors; words crossed out, skipped, or inserted), manuscripts which have large portions of Scripture are essentially the same, and small fragments help confirm this agreement. For reasons He has not revealed, God has chosen to preserve His Word, not in a single document, but in the totality of original language man-uscripts and ancient translations.

It is troubling that so many who set out to defend the Scriptures end up lift-ing verses out of context and even grossly distorting their meaning in an attempt to prove God has promised us a perfect English translation. *The fact that they believe they need to defend the Scriptures at all actually negates their position.* If God's Word is supernaturally protected, what can be accom-plished by emotion based proclamations? Has the hand of God waxed so weak that suddenly His Word is threatened with demise without their aid? These misguided "defenders" are guilty of the very misuse of Scripture which Peter condemned. Speaking of the intentional twisting of the words of the Apostle Paul, Peter said, "They that are unlearned and unstable wrest [liter-ally, *torture*], as they do also the other Scriptures, unto their own destruction" (2 Peter 3:16). When men and women resort to mishandling God's Word in order to defend their position on the text, they should take another look at both their bibliology and their hermeneutics.

---

[1]Benjamin G. Wilkinson, *Our Authorized Bible Vindicated*, 1930, as cited by David Otis Fuller, *Which Bible?*, (Grand Rapids: Institute for Biblical Textual Studies, 1970), p. 313. In his introduction to this 143 page reprint of Wilkinson's work, Fuller praises Wilkinson as "a scholar of the first rank with a thorough knowledge of the subjects about which he wrote" (p. 174) without identifying him as a Seventh Day Adventist. Further, we must not overlook the irony of Wilkinson's having used a *marginal reading* in his effort to prove the *word-for-word perfection* of the King James Bible.

[2]Jeffrey Khoo, *Reviews of the Book From the Mind of God to the Mind of Man*, (Pensacola, FL: Pensacola Theological Seminary, 2001), p. 13. This is a reprint of his book review that first appeared in *The Burning Bush Theological Journal*, Mar. 2000 (for Calvary Bible Presbyterian churches), Singapore.

[3]Khoo, p. 48.

[4]At "puffeth at him," the KJV 1611 supplies an alternate reading: "or, *would ensnare him.*" The translators of the KJV admitted their uncertainty of the best reading at this point. The incontrovertible fact of alternate marginal readings in the KJV 1611 within the context of a verse many have claimed as a proof text for supernatural preservation of the Scriptures in the KJV is quite ironic.

[5]J. A. Alexander, *The Psalms Translated and Explained*, Vol. 1, (New York: Baker and Scrivener, 1850), p. 95.

[6]A. F. Kirkpatrick, *The Book of Psalms*, (London, Cambridge University Press, 1939), p. 62.

[7]Kirkpatrick, p. 63.

[8]C. F. Keil and Franz Delitzsch, *Commentaries on the Old Testament*, Psalms, Vol. 1 (Grand Rapids: Eerdmans, 1968, 1971), pp.196-197.

[9]Matthew Henry, *Commentary on the Whole Bible*, Vol 3, (Peabody, MA: Hendrickson Publishers, 1991 reprint edition), p. 229.

[10]William S. Plumer, *Studies in the Book of Psalms*, (Philadelphia: J. B. Lippincott & Co., 1867), p. 178.

[11]Kirkpatrick, p. 63.

[12]Kirkpatrick, p. 63.

[13]Plumer, p. 178.

[14]H.D. Leupold, *Exposition of The Psalms*, (Grand Rapids: Baker Book House, 1959), p. 133.

[15]As previously noted, there are rare exceptions that would apply the first "them" to the words, but these still insist that the emphasis of the Psalm is God's promise to preserve His people.

[16]John Peter Lange, *Commentary on the Holy Scriptures: Psalms*, (Grand Rapids: Zondervan Publishing House, no date [preface by Philip Schaff dated September 23, 1872), p. 108.

[17]W. Graham Scroggie, *The Psalms,* Vol. 1. (London: Pickering & Inglis Lmt., 1948 rev. ed.), p. 92.

[18]The Dean Burgon Society is committed to promotion of the King James Version as the only acceptable translation and to the texts underlying it as the only pre-served texts. cf. http://www.deanburgonsociety.org

[19]Thomas Cassidy. Internet discussion, BaptistBoard (http://www.BaptistBoard.com) September 05, 2000. Thomas Cassidy, a strong proponent of the TR and KJV, pastor of First Baptist Church of Spring Valley, CA and president of San Diego Baptist Seminary, was educated at Central Baptist

Theological Seminary, is a speaker and writer for the Dean Burgon Society and is author of a number of booklets and articles including *Textual Criticism Fact and Fiction.*

[20]Charles L. Surrett, *Which Greek Text? The Debate Among Fundamentalists*, (Kings Mountain, NC: Surrett Family Publications, 1999), pp. 50-51.

[21]Plumer, p. 1061.

[22]Plumer, p. 1060.

[23]Charles Spurgeon, *The Treasury of David*, Vol. 3, (Peabody, MA: Hendrickson Publishers, 1988 reprint), p. 315.

[24]John Calvin, *Commentary on the Psalms*, Vol. 2, in *The Master Christian Library*, Version 8, (Rio, WI: AGES Software, Inc., 2000), p. 558.

[25]Spiros Zodhiates, *The Hebrew-Greek Key Study Bible*, (AMG Publishers, 1991), p. 1638.

[26]Plumer, p. 1059.

[27]Leupold, p. 842.

[28]Lange, p. 598.

[29]Plumer, p. 1082.

[30]George Horne, cited by Charles Spurgeon, *The Treasury of David*, Vol. 3, (Peabody, MA: Hendrickson Publishers, no date), p. 411.

[31]Albert Barnes, *Notes on the Bible*, Vol. 5, in *The Master Christian Library*, Version 8, (Rio, WI: AGES Software, Inc., 2000), pp. 1852-1853.

[32]Kirkpatrick, p. 729.

[33]Leupold, p. 855.

[34]Keil and Delitzsch, Psalms Vol. III, p. 261.

[35]Keil and Delitzsch, Psalms Vol. III, p. 261.

[36]Plumer, p. 1082.

[37]The verb דָּבַר (dabar) means to speak, declare, converse, command, promise, warn, threaten, sing, etc. The noun דָּבָר (dabar) can be in reference to a word, speaking, speech, thing, anything, everything, nothing, matter, act, event, history, account, cause, or reason. These two words occur more than 2500 times in the OT, the noun more than 1400 times and the verb more than 1100 times. In the KJV the verb דָּבַר is translated by nearly thirty different words and the noun form is translated by more than eighty-five words. Some of these are synonyms, but many are not. All have some sense of thought process or communication. The noun ranges

from any matter to the most dynamic expression of the word of God. The Qal occurrences of the verb in Hebrew commonly designate one who speaks something of abiding relevance. In this regard, the most important declaration in the use of דבר is that God has spoken (about 400 times), and what God said will be *accomplished* (1 Ki 6:12; Jer 36:22; Isa 55:11). The noun form basically means what God said or says. For example, the ten commandments are actually called the "ten words" (Ex 34:28; Deut 4:13; 10:4). In 2 Chronicles 33:18 "acts," "words," "speak" and "book" are all derived from דבר . [Harris, R. Laird, Gleason L. Archer, Bruce K. Waltke. *Theological Word Book of the Old Testament* (Chicago: Moody Press, 1980) דָּבַר, pp. 178-180].

[38]Brown, Francis, S. R Driver, and Charles A. Briggs. *A Hebrew and English Lexicon of the Old Testament.* (Oxford: Clarendon, 1907), 1955.

[39]Edward J. Young, *The Book of Isaiah*, vol. 3 (Grand Rapids: Eerdmans, 1977), pp. 33-35.

[40]*Thayer's Greek-English Lexicon of the New Testament. Terminus ad quem* refers to "the end point of a chronological era or the latest date for an event" (*A Student's Dictionary for Biblical and Theological Studies*, by F. B. Huey, Jr. and Bruce Corley).

[41]Comparisons occur when two or more objects (or activities) have a point or points of similarity between them.

[42]Contrasts occur when two or more objects have a point or points of dissimilarity between them.

[43]"Ἑως. . . w. the aor. subj. and (as the rule calls for) αν. . . denote that the commencement of an event is dependent on circumstances" (BAGD, p. 334). BAGD then references Matthew 5:18 as an example of this rule. The "event" which will commence, in this case, is the passing away of the jots and tittles of the law. The "circumstances" upon which this event are dependent are denoted to be (1) heaven and earth's passing, and (2) all the law's being fulfilled. As J. C. Lambert points out, "The jots and tittles, be it observed *are* to pass away when the Law is fulfilled" ("Tittle," *Dictionary of Christ and the Gospels*, James Hastings, ed., II, 733). Our Lord's statement that "Heaven and earth shall pass away, but my words shall not pass away" (Mtt. 24:35; Mk. 13:31; Lk. 21:33) is no contradiction to the future passing away of the jots and tittles of the written Word, inasmuch as our Lord was in the Olivet Discourse referring to His spoken words. Most of these were never inscripturated. But they have not, and will not, cease to exist in the senses that all which He said is settled fact, truth incapable of alteration, effective contradiction, or destruction.

[44]"The 'jot' (KJV) has become "the smallest letter" (NIV): this is almost certainly correct, for it refers to the letter י (*yod*), the smallest letter of the Hebrew alphabet.

The 'tittle' (*keraia*) has been variously interpreted: it is the Hebrew letter ו (*waw*) . . . or the small stroke that distinguishes several pairs of Hebrew letters . . . or a purely ornamental stroke, a 'crown'. . . or it forms a hendiadys with 'jot,' referring to the smallest part of the smallest letter (*Matthew* by D. A. Carson, in *The Expositor's Bible Commentary* (vol. 8, p. 145)). Since tittles distinguish one letter from another it must be remembered that those distinctions were present in all forms of Hebrew orthography (style of writing).

[45]John Murray, "The Attestation of Scripture." In *The Infaillible Word: A Symposium*. Edited by N. B. Stonehouse and Paul Wooley (Philadelphia: Presbyterian and Reformed Publishing Company, 1946),pp. 22, 23.

[46]R. Laird Harris. *Inspiration and Canonicity of the Bible* (Grand Rapid: Zondervan Publishing House, 1957), p. 46. Similar views are expressed by James M. Gray ("The Inspiration of the Bible," *The Fundamentals*, II, 32-33), Henry Clarence Thiessen (*Introductory Lectures in Systematic Theology*, p. 111), the *Criswell Study Bible,* the *MacArthur Study Bible*, Charles Ryrie (*Basic Theology*, pp. 88-89), James Montgomery Boice (*Foundations of the Christian Faith*, pp. 43-44), Paul Feinberg ("The Meaning of Inerrancy," in *Inerrancy*, ed. by Norman Geisler p. 284), Robert P. Lightner (*Evangelical Theology*, p. 30), and many others.

[47]"The Current Tensions: Is There a Way Out?" in *Biblical Authority*, Jack Rogers, ed., pp. 172-173.

[48]Paul Feinberg dismisses Hubbard simply on this basis, writing, "Hubbard must bear the burden of proof that the passage in question is hyperbole. I see no such proof" ("The Meaning of Inerrancy," *Inerrancy*, Norman L. Geisler, ed., p. 284).

[49]*A Manual Grammar of the Greek New Testament*, H. E. Dana and Julius R. Mantey, p. 267.

[50]"Bengel says that there are 66,420 yodhs in the Hebrew Scriptures. Just one of such a number would not seem to be important, but even that will not pass away, Jesus says" (*The Gospel According to Matthew,* Leon Morris, p. 109).

[51]Alfred Edersheim, *The Life and Times of Jesus the Messiah*, II, 537. The fact that Edersheim is quoting rabbinical tradition later than the time of Christ is not sufficient reason for dismissing its legitimate relevance for assessing the Jewish viewpoint in New Testament times. The positions codified by rabbis long after those times had their roots in oral traditions centuries older.

[52]Ibid, pp. 537-538.

[53]I. Howard Marshall offers the following distinction: "The verb 'purify' (Gk hagnizo) must be distinguished from the verb 'sanctify' (Gk hagioazo) . . . though it properly belongs to the same realm of ideas. Whereas 'holy' refers more to the

status of the people of God, 'purify' refers to the actual cleansing which they must undergo." *1 Peter* (Downers Grove: InterVarsity, 1991), p. 58.

[54]"'In your obedience to the truth' indicates the sphere in which that purification becomes operative. . . . It is an obedience that springs from hearing in faith." D. Edmund Hiebert, *First Peter* (Chicago: Moody, 1984), p. 101.

[55]J. Howard Masterman, as quoted by Hiebert, 102.

[56]E. H. Plumptre gives insight into the connection *agape* love has with holiness: "The purity implied is prominently . . . freedom from sensual lust, but includes within its range freedom from all forms of selfishness." *The General Epistles of St. Peter and St. Jude* (Cambridge: University Press, 1889), p. 104.

[57]H. A. Ironside comments: "The Word of God has been brought home to their souls in the convicting and convincing energy of the Holy Spirit, thus producing a new life and nature, the characteristic feature of which is love—the love of God shed abroad in our hearts, as Paul tells us, by the Holy Spirit who is given unto us (Rom. 5:5)." *Expository Notes on the Epistles of James and Peter*. New York: Loizeaux Brothers, 1947), p. 22.

[58]"Corruptible seed brings forth flesh unto death; the incorruptible seed of the Word brings forth life everlasting." R. C. H. Lenski, *The Interpretation of the Epistles of St. Peter, St. John and St. Jude* (Columbus, Ohio: Lutheran Book Concern, 1938), p. 74.

[59]"Peter may have used seed in the sense of 'plant seed.' . . . . But in the context, the picture of the new birth more naturally implies the father's seed out of which the new life springs (cf. John 1:13; James 1:18; 1 John 3:9)" (Hiebert, p. 104).

[60]In his ancient commentary on 1 Peter, Didymus the Blind explains: "There is a first birth, in the descent of Adam, which is mortal and therefore corruptible, but there is also a later birth which comes from the Spirit and the ever-living Word of God." Gerald, Bray, ed. *James, 1-2 Peter, 1-3 John, Jude*, Volume XI of *Ancient Christian Commentary on Scripture* (Downers Grove: InterVarsity, 2000), p. 80.

[61]"'Out of' *ek*, states the source of spiritual life and names the seed; *dia* adds the thought that this seed is the means for our being begotten" (Lenski, 74). "Scripture is clear that new birth is by means of the Word, which the Spirit of God brings to bear upon the heart and conscience. Apart from this there is no divine life" (Ironside, p. 23).

[62]"It is grammatically possible to connect those two epithets with *God* and render 'through means of the word of a Living and Abiding God.' . . . . It is better to relate *living* and *abiding* to *word* (*logou*) and to understand those participles to specify the nature of the means (*word*) used in regeneration. Emphasis on the lasting quality of the regenerating Word is appropriate to the argument. It compliments the following

quotation in the text, which places the emphasis upon the abiding nature, not of God, but of the word of God. . . . .The original order closely connects *living* with *word* and then adds that the Word is God's and has the further characteristic of being abiding—literally, 'through a word living, God's, and abiding'" (Hiebert, p. 105).

[63]Obviously there are dozens of other passages cited by various advocates of the King James Only position that we have not addressed. Space would not permit a thorough exegesis of all of them. Such an exhaustive treatment would require an independent volume on the subject. We have addressed those passages that appear most frequently in their arguments and that those writers have generally treated as foundational for their position.

BIBLIOGRAPHY

Alexander, J. A. The Psalms Translated and Explained, Vol. 1.New York: Baker and Scrivener, 1850.

Bauer, Walter, William F. Arndt, F. William Gingrich, Fredrick W. Danker. *A Greek-English Lexicon of the New Testament and Other Early Christian Literature.* Chicago: The University of Chicago Press, 2000.

Barclay, William. *The Letters of James and Peter.* Philadelphia: Westminster, 1976 rev. ed.

Barnes, Albert. *Notes on the Old Testament: Explanatory and Practical*, Vol. 5. Grand Rapids: Baker, 1983

Boice, James Montgomery. *Foundations of the Christian Faith.* Downers Grove, IL: Inter-Varsity Press, 1978.

Bray, Gerald, ed. *James, 1-2 Peter, 1-3 John, Jude*, Volume XI of *Ancient Christian Commentary on Scripture.* Downers Grove: InterVarsity Press, 2000.

Brown, Francis, S. R Driver, and Charles A. Briggs. *A Hebrew and English Lexicon of the Old Testament.* Oxford: Clarendon, 1907, 1955.

Calvin, John. *Commentary on the Psalms*, Vol. 2, in *The Master Christian Library*, Version 8. Rio, WI: AGES Software, Inc., 2000.

Carson, D. A. " Matthew," *The Expositor's Bible Commentary,* Frank E. Gaebelein, ed. Grand Rapids: Zondervan Publishing House, 1979.

Criswell, W. A., ed. *The Criswell Study Bible.* Nashville: Thomas Nelson, 1979.

Dana. H. E and Julius R. Mantey. *A Manual Grammar of the Greek New Testament.* New York: Macmillan, 1927, 1955.

Davids, Peter H. *The First Epistle of Peter.* Grand Rapids: Eerdmans, 1990.

Edersheim, Alfred, III. *The Life and Times of Jesus the Messiah*, Grand Rapids: Eerdmans, 1953.

Feinberg, Paul."The Meaning of Inerrancy," *Inerrancy*, ed. by Norman Geisler. Grand Rapids: Zondervan, 1979.

Gaebelein, Frank E. *The Expositor's Bible Commentary*, Grand Rapids: Zondervan Publishing House, 1979.

118

Gray, James M. "The Inspiration of the Bible." *The Fundamentals*, Vol. 2. Edited by R.A. Torrey. 1917 rpt. Grand Rapids: Baker Book House, 1998.

Grudem, Wayne A. *The First Epistle of Peter*. Grand Rapids: Eerdmans, 1988, reprint 2002.

Harris, R. Laird, Gleason L. Archer, Bruce K. Waltke. *Theological Word Book of the Old Testament*. Chicago: Moody Press, 1980.

_____, *Inspiration and Canonicity of the Bible*. Grand Rapids: Zondervan Publishing House, 1957

Henry, Matthew, *Commentary on the Whole Bible*, Vol. 3. Peabody, MA: Hendrickson Publishers, 1991 reprint edition.

Hiebert, D. Edmond. *First Peter*. Chicago: Moody, 1984.

Horne, George, cited by Charles Spurgeon, *The Treasury of David*, Vol. 3. Peabody, MA: Hendrickson Publishers, no date.

Hubbard. David A. "The Current Tensions: Is There a Way Out?" in *Biblical Authority*, Jack Rogers, ed. Alexander, J. A. *The Psalms Translated and Explained*, Vol. 1.New York: Baker and Scrivener, 1850.

Ironside, H. A. *Expository Notes on the Epistles of James and Peter*. New York: Loizeaux Brothers, 1947.

Keil, C. F. and F. Delitzsch. *Commentaries on the Old Testament, Psalms*, Vol. 1. Grand Rapids: Eerdmans, 1968.

Khoo, Jeffrey. *Reviews of the Book From the Mind of God to the Mind of Man*. Pensacola, FL: Pensacola Theological Seminary, 2001.

Kirkpatrick, A. F., *The Book of Psalms*, London, Cambridge University Press, 1939.

Kistemaker, Simon J. *Exposition of James, Episltes of John, Peter, and Jude*. Grand Rapids: Baker, 1996.

Kittel, Gerhard, ed., Geoffrey W. Bromiley, trans. *Theological Dictionary of the New Testament*. Grand Rapids: Erdmans, 1964.

Lambert, J. C. "Tittle," *A Dictionary of Christ and the Gospels*, James Hastings, ed. Charles Scribner's Sons, New York, 1907/08.

Lange, John Peter, *Commentary on the Holy Scriptures: Psalms*. Grand Rapids: Zondervan Publishing House, no date.

Lenski, C. H. *The Interpretation of the Epistles of St. Peter, St. John and St. Jude*. Columbus, Ohio: Lutheran Book Concern, 1938.

Leupold, H.D. *Exposition of The Psalms* Grand Rapids: Baker Book House, 1959.

Lightner, Robert P. *Evangelical Theology*. Grand Rapids: Baker, 1990.

MacArthur, John. *MacArthur Study Bible*. Nashville: Thomas Nelson, 1997.

Michaels, J. Ramsey. *Word Biblical Commentary: 1 Peter*. Waco: Word Books, 1988.

Moritz, Fred. *Contending for the Faith*. Greenville, SC: Bob Jones University Press, 2000.

Morris, Leon. *The Gospel According to Matthew*. Grand Rapids: Erdmans, 1992.

Murray, John. "The Attestation of Scripture." In *The Infallible Word: A Symposium*. Edited by N. B. Stonehouse and Paul Wooley. Philadelphia: Presbyterian and Reformed Publishing Company, 1946.

Plumer, William S. *Studies in the Book of Psalms*. Philadelphia: J. B. Lippincott and Company, 1867.

Plumptre, E. H. *Expository Notes on the Epistles of James and Peter*. New York: Loizeaux Brothers, 1947.

Rogers, Jack. *Biblical Authority*. Waco, TX: Word Books, 1977.

Ryrie, Charles. *Basic Theology*. Wheaton, IL: Victor Books, 1986.

Scroggie, W. Graham, *The Psalms,* Vol. 1. London: Pickering & Inglis Limited, 1948 rev. ed.

Selwyn, Edward Gordon. *The First Epistle of St. Peter*. London: Macmillan, 1947.

Spurgeon, Charles. *The Treasury of David*, vol. 3. Peabody, MA: Hendrickson Publishers, 1988 reprint.

Thiessen, Henry Clarence. *Introductory Lectures in Systematic Theology*. Grand Rapids: Eerdmans, 1977.

Wilkinson, Benjamin G. *Our Authorized Bible Vindicated*, 1930, as cited by David Otis Fuller, *Which Bible?*. Grand Rapids: Institute for Biblical Textual Studies, 1970.

Young, Edward J. *The Book of Isaiah*, vol. 3. Grand Rapids: Eerdmans, 1977.

Zodhiates, Spiros. *The Hebrew-Greek Key Study Bible*, Chattanoonga, TN: AMG Publishers, 1991.

PRESERVATION OF THE COPIES

By John C. Mincy

There are over 3,000 preserved copies of various portions of the Hebrew Old Testament and over 5,000 preserved copies of portions of the New Testament. These copies are scattered all over the world in libraries, museums, monasteries, and private collections. It is impossible to trace the history of many of these documents, but there is enough information to get a good picture of how God has providentially preserved His words. This chapter will attempt to trace the historical trail of some of these and address the issue of the preservation of the copies of the original manuscripts. We are trying to answer several questions in this essay: Where were the major extant (those known to exist) manuscripts found? How old are they estimated to be? How were they found? How did they get where they were found? From where did they originate (provenance)? The answers to these questions will give us a good idea of what means God used to preserve His words down to the present hour.

Before we get into the details it might help to discuss what kinds of materials the existing manuscripts of the Bible are written on. The oldest copies are written on papyrus, a kind of paper made from the sliced and glued pieces of the papyrus plant which was plentiful in Egypt, but also available in Syria, Babylon, and other swampy places. To produce a long document, papyrus sheets were joined together into long rolls or scrolls. Later they were put together much like our books today. Such a "book" was called a codex (plural is codices), and Christians first popularized the codex as a medium for literature. "The remains of Christian manuscripts from the 2d and 3d centuries are predominately in codex form, and items of Christian 'scriptural' literature are almost exclusively in codex form, while the remains of non-Christian manuscripts from this period are by large majority in traditional roll form."[1] Parchment or vellum was also a material used for writing. It was made from the skins of sheep, goats, cows, or even deer. Parchment was also made into scrolls and codices. Manuscripts are often dated by the kind of papyrus, parchment, ink, binding, text divisions, order of books, or handwriting used.

OLD TESTAMENT COPIES
It is clear that the Old Testament itself demanded that many copies of God's words would be made. Deuteronomy 17:18 reads, "Also it shall be, when he sits on the throne of his kingdom, that he shall write for himself a copy of this

law in a book, from *the one* before the priests, the Levites." Moses is requiring the kings of the future to have a copy of this law (Book of Deuteronomy maybe) copied from the one in the Tabernacle or Temple. Joshua 8:32 reveals that on Mount Ebal Joshua wrote a copy of the "law of Moses" as all the people observed. In 2 Kings 11:12 King Josiah was presented with a copy of the "testimony," probably referring to a copy of God's covenant with His people. The most interesting reference to copies comes from the time of Josiah. Josiah, the King of Judah, gave orders for the house of the LORD to be repaired. During the repair, a copy of the Law of Moses was discovered.

> 14 Now when they brought out the money that was brought into the house of the LORD, Hilkiah the priest found the Book of the Law of the LORD *given* by Moses. 15 Then Hilkiah answered and said to Shaphan the scribe, "I have found the Book of the Law in the house of the LORD." And Hilkiah gave the book to Shaphan. 16 So Shaphan carried the book to the king, bringing the king word, saying, "All that was committed to your servants they are doing. 17 "And they have gathered the money that was found in the house of the LORD, and have delivered it into the hand of the overseers and the workmen." 18 Then Shaphan the scribe told the king, saying, "Hilkiah the priest has given me a book." And Shaphan read it before the king. 19 Thus it happened, when the king heard the words of the Law, that he tore his clothes. 20 Then the king commanded Hilkiah, Ahikam the son of Shaphan, Abdon the son of Micah, Shaphan the scribe, and Asaiah a servant of the king, saying, 21 "Go, inquire of the LORD for me, and for those who are left in Israel and Judah, concerning the words of the book that is found; for great *is* the wrath of the LORD that is poured out on us, because our fathers have not kept the word of the LORD, to do according to all that is written in this book" (NKJ 2 Chron. 34:14-21).

The indication here is that the written Word of God had been lost for some time, probably during the reign of wicked Manasseh. God's promises for the preservation of His words do not apparently necessitate the availability of that written Word at every moment in history. It is therefore possible for a portion of His words to be unavailable at a point in time, only to be found later.

Certainly the Lord is able to use direct or indirect ways to preserve His words for us. His restoration of the Ten Commandments (Exodus 34) and the scroll of Jeremiah (Jeremiah 36) are examples of how He directly and miraculously replaced the "lost" words. God can use supernatural means to preserve His words, but there is no evidence to demonstrate that He is using anything other than acts of providence to preserve His words for us today.

MASORETIC TEXT

The Masoretic Text of the Old Testament is the basis of our Old Testament today. The name comes from "editors" who produced and safe-guarded the OT manuscripts for many years (c. A.D. 500-1000). These editors or Masoretes treated the documents "with the greatest imaginable reverence, and devised a complicated system of safeguards against scribal slips. They counted, for example, the number of times each letter of the alphabet occurs in each book; they pointed out the middle letter of the Pentateuch and the middle letter of the whole Hebrew Bible, and made even more detailed calculations than these."[2] The Masoretic Text comes to us through the influence of the ben Asher family of the ninth and tenth centuries A.D., although there are still manuscript witnesses to the ben Naphtali tradition, a "competing" text tradition in the same centuries, which indicates that there were variations in the Masoretic tradition.

Ellis R. Brotzman has written a very helpful, simple, and practical book, *Old Testament Textual Criticism*, for the Christian who wants to know more about how we got the Hebrew Old Testament text of the Bible. Brotzman lists the following as important Masoretic manuscripts: Aleppo Codex, Leningrad Codex, British Museum 4445, Cairo Codex, Sassoon 507, Sassoon 1053, and the Petersburg Codex (also known as the Babylonian Codex of the Prophets).[3]

The story of the ancient Aleppo Codex is a good example of the providential hand of God in preserving witness to the text of the OT. A. A. MacRae writes:

> The colophon [a note of explanation in a manuscript] of this MS [manuscript] stated that Aaron ben Asher (the son of Moshe ben Asher), who died about A.D. 940, added the vowels and Masora [notes added by the Masoretes] to this MS. It is written on parchment in three columns. At first it was in Jerusalem, then for a time in Cairo, and later it was taken to Aleppo [a city in Syria]. It is generally considered to be the MS designated by Moses Maimonides [famous Jewish philosopher, A.D. 1135-1204] as the codex that he regarded as most reliable.[4]

What happened at Aleppo is interesting. MacRae continues:

> In 1948 the Sephardic [Spanish Jews] synagogue in Aleppo was raided by a local mob and burned, and for a number of years it was

feared that the MS had also been destroyed. However, Izhak Ben-Zvi, president of the state of Israel, refused to give up hope that it might have been saved. For a long time he kept trying to find the place where it might be hidden, and often discussed with Sephardic leaders ways and means by which the 'discovery' of the venerable MS might be brought about, and its transfer to safety in Jerusalem assured. At last his efforts succeeded, and in 1960 he was able to announce to the world that the codex had been found and brought to the Heb. University at Jerusalem. Unfortunately it had suffered much at the hands of the rioters; before 1948 it had been complete; now about a fourth of it was missing, including nine-tenths of the Pentateuch.[5]

The Cairo Codex of the Prophets has a colorful history as well. Again, MacRae writes:

> This MS, dated in A.D. 895, contains the entire second division of the Hebrew Bible. It was written and pointed by Mose ben Asher, the next to the last of the famous Ben Asher family. The MS was presented to the Qaraite [or Karaite, strict Jewish sect] community in Jerusalem, but was seized by the Crusaders in 1099. Later it was returned to the Jews, and came into possession of the Qaraite community in Cairo. It is written in three columns, with Tiberian vowels and accents.[6]

The Leningrad Codex is the world's oldest complete manuscript of the Hebrew Bible. It is housed in the Russian National Library in St. Petersburg (formerly Leningrad). "It also has all the Hebrew Masoretic textual and marginal notations characteristic of this scribal tradition. These notations are invaluable today, for they represent the medieval technical apparatus needed to reconstruct the history of textual transmission. They and the vowel and accent pointings added to the consonantal text follow the tradition of the Masoretes, in particular, the school of Masoretic scholars centered in Tiberias near the Sea of Galilee." [7] As stated in the first colophon (explanatory note) of the Codex, it originated in the city of Cairo. "Shemu'el ben-Ya`akob copied it from authoritative manuscripts prepared by Aaron ben-Moshe ben-Asher himself. . . . We know nothing further of the wanderings of the Leningrad Codex until the notation in its colophon citing the bill of sale presumably in Damascus in 1489. The trail vanishes until Abraham Firkovich [see below] turned up with it in the 1840s, although we do not know precisely when he acquired the manuscript, how much he paid for it, or even where he found it."[8]

According to Brotzman the Leningrad is close to the ben Asher tradition, but not as close as the Aleppo, "the differences having to do with certain vowel letters and the use of the *metheg* [a small vertical line indicating a secondary word accent]."[9]

There have been numerous manuscript hunters through the years who have been responsible for "recovering" many of the manuscripts which now reside safely in the museums of the world. Abraham Firkovich was one of the most famous. He was a Karaite leader and successful businessman in Poland, Crimea, and throughout the southwestern regions of Russia. He journeyed to Jerusalem, Constantinople, and throughout the Middle East ransacking old synagogues and their store rooms (genizah or geniza) in search of manuscripts. "Over the course of his travels he managed to assemble the largest collection of Hebrew manuscripts now [1998] existing in the world. These manuscripts comprise the two Firkovich Collections in the Russian National Library (Saltykov-Shchedrin) in St. Petersburg."[10] Hershel Shanks estimates that there are over 2,500 Hebrew manuscripts in Russia.

Most translations of the OT since 1937 have been translated from a text based on the Leningrad Manuscript. Previous translations were based on the 1524-25 Bomberg edition prepared by Jacob ben Chayyim, a Hebrew Christian. Both are forms of the Masoretic text, and the differences between the two are minute. The Masoretic text has had no rivals since the twelfth century (and probably no serious rival since the first century and the influence of Rabbi Aqiba, A.D. 55-137) and has been accurately copied and preserved in the many synagogues and scriptoriums around the world.

OTHER HEBREW MANUSCRIPTS

There are over three thousand other Hebrew manuscripts (ranging from tiny pieces to large sections) to consider as witnesses to the Old Testament Hebrew text. They most often represent a text that is very similar and very often identical to the Masoretic. Such texts would be the Dead Sea Scrolls (Qumran), the Cairo Genizah finds, fragments at Masada (A.D. 66-73), the texts of Wadi Murabba`at (A.D. 135), the Erfurt Codices, the Aberdeen Codex, and the Nash Papyri.

The discovery of the Cairo Genizah is yet another unusual event that demonstrates that the Lord has left things here and there perhaps to help us understand the history and preservation of the Bible better. Most synagogues had store rooms for well-used, damaged, or deficient documents. These rooms were called genizahs. Items would be stored in the genizah until there was a convenient time to dispose of them. Saint Michael's Church occupied a building in Cairo until A.D. 882 at which time it became a Jewish synagogue. This synagogue's genizah had apparently been walled up and forgotten. For hundreds of years its precious documents were preserved in the dry Egyptian climate until the building was refurbished in the late 1800's. When first discovered many of the documents were simply buried until the caretakers realized that people and universities were willing to pay good money for the documents. Several collectors had removed unnumbered pieces from the genizah before Solomon Schechter was sent from Cambridge to make a thorough investigation, the result of which garnered over 100,000 fragments, including Biblical texts. It is estimated now that there are approximately 200,000 texts (not all Biblical) that have come out of the Cairo Genizah, the main value of which is to further trace the development of the Masoretic text. Most of the fragments are in the Cambridge University Library. Others are in the Bodleian Library in Oxford, the Russian Public Library in St. Petersburg, the Jewish Seminary Library in New York, and a few additional places.

We must bring the study of God's preservation of Old Testament copies to a close and move on to the New Testament documents, but before we do there is one other fascinating discovery that must be mentioned, the Dead Sea Scrolls. The exciting story of how the Scrolls were found has been told many times with many "variants." Hershel Shanks, one of the leaders in getting the Scrolls published, tells it this way:

> The first of the Dead Sea Scrolls was found in 1947 by some Bedouin shepherds. While they were searching for lost sheep, one of these young boys took a stone and tossed it into a cave. That cave later became very famous as Cave 1, because when he tossed the stone into the cave, the boy heard a cracking sound. What he actually heard was the sound of a pottery vessel being broken. The next day the shepherds examined the cave where the pottery vessel had been broken and they found some scrolls in there. They did not know what they were. They were members of the Ta'amireh tribe of Bedouin and they took their find to Bethlehem.

> Eventually the scrolls found their way into the hands of a cobbler nicknamed Kando, who also dealt in antiquities in the back of his shop. Kando has become very famous. He died only in the last couple of years. Eventually he had a fine souvenir and antiquities shop in Jerusalem. It is still there in the lobby of St. George's Hotel. At that time, however, Kando was not very knowledgeable and his connections were not so great, but he started finding ways to sell the scrolls.

This was just before the state of Israel was proclaimed. By the time the fragments got to scholars at the American School of Oriental Research in Jerusalem and to professors at Hebrew University, it was early 1948. There were the usual questions about whether the scrolls were fakes and, if not, what the date of the documents was. The great American archaeologist William F. Albright saw a fragment and recognized it as genuine and about 2,000 years old; he telegraphed his view back to Jerusalem. Others in Jerusalem claimed that they had recognized this even earlier.

The story of the negotiations and the acquisition of these early scrolls is filled with tension and drama. There were seven scrolls in Cave 1. In early May 1948, E. L. Sukenik, a leading scholar who was also the father of the great Israeli archaeologist Yigael Yadin, wanted to acquire these scrolls for Hebrew University. He raised some money, even mortgaging his own home. At that time his son was the head of the Haganah, the underground shadow army of the Israeli government that was being formed. Jerusalem itself was under Arab siege. Sukenik told his son, the head of the army, that he wanted to go to Bethlehem to acquire the scrolls. He now had the money and thought he could make a deal. His son, however, told him not to do it; it was too dangerous; Bethlehem was an Arab city. But Sukenik did not listen to his son's advice. He disobeyed his son. He got a pass to go through the line to the Arab side of divided Jerusalem and he got on a bus to Bethlehem – he was the only Jew on the bus – and then he returned to Jerusalem.

The day he did this was the day before the United Nations, by a two-thirds vote, passed the resolution creating the Jewish state. On the trip back to Jerusalem he carried with him, in a brown paper wrapper, three of the seven scrolls. The next day the United Nations passed this resolution. It is almost messianic. At the same time, literally within a 24-hour period, the state of Israel was created and Hebrew University acquired a scroll of the prophet Isaiah that was 1,000 years older than anything that had been known up to that time.

The four scrolls that Sukenik did not obtain ended up in the hands of an Assyrian cleric, the Metropolitan Samuel. There were all kinds of unsuccessful negotiations for the sale of these scrolls. Eventually the Metropolitan took them to New York, hoping to dispose of them in America at a better price. This turned out not to be so easy. It is a question as to why it was so difficult to sell these scrolls; the answer may have something to do with the fact that his title was unclear to

129

prospective American purchasers. So he ended up putting a classified ad in the *Wall Street Journal* for four old scrolls.

As luck – or as God – would have it, when the blind ad, hardly recognizable, appeared in the *Wall Street Journal*, years [it was in 1954] after the discovery of the scrolls and the creation of the state of Israel, Yigael Yadin was in New York, and someone pointed out the ad to him. Yadin knew that the Metropolitan would not sell the scrolls to an Israeli, so Yadin used some fronts through whom he negotiated. When the final deal was struck and delivery was to be made, Yadin could not show up to examine the authenticity of the scrolls himself because the Metropolitan, Yadin feared, would back out. So Yadin called Professor Harry Orlinsky, whom many of you here know of, who lives today in Columbia, Maryland. Orlinsky was just leaving to go on a vacation. He came back into his house because he heard the phone ring. Yadin told him to come to New York; he couldn't tell him why, but it was very important. So Orlinsky changed his vacation plans and went to New York. Yadin told him that he was to be Mr. Green. He was to examine the scrolls for authenticity. This is a cloak-and-dagger business and it is very easy to get fooled; someone with Orlinsky's expertise was needed. So Orlinsky went to a warehouse and identified himself as Mr. Green, looked at the scrolls and authenticated them."[11]

It would be difficult to imagine a set of circumstances more *providential* than those that surround the discovery and publication of the Dead Sea Scrolls. It seems that a number of things "happened" just at the right time and place when just the right individuals were available. It is difficult not to believe that God allowed these valuable manuscripts to become available and give their witness to a Hebrew text that is 1,000 years earlier than any available up until 1948 (the majority had been copied by A.D. 68)! The Lord chose to use providential circumstances rather than supernatural events to preserve His words.

The story of the final publication of most of the Dead Sea material (in 1991 by Robert Eisenman and James Robinson, published by the Biblical Archaeology Society) is a mystery story in itself, but when all is said and done there are about 900 (225 biblical documents) original documents fully or partially represented. In addition to this there are probably around 100,000 fragments on papyrus or leather.[12] Martin Abegg, Jr., writes:

At Qumran, nearly 900 manuscripts were found in some twenty-five thousand pieces, with many no bigger than a postage stamp. A few scrolls are well preserved, such as the *Great Isaiah Scroll* from Cave

1 (1QIsa[a]) and the *Great Psalms Scroll* from Cave 11 (11QPs[a]). Unfortunately, however, most of the scrolls are very fragmentary. The earliest manuscripts date from about 250BC, while the latest ones were copied shortly before the destruction of the Qumran site by the Romans in 68 CE. Approximately forty-five more manuscripts were discovered at the other sites: about fifteen at Wadi Murabb`ât, eighteen at Nahal Hever, and twelve at Masada.[13]

Abegg continues, "The Dead Sea Scrolls include more than 225 'biblical' manuscripts, about 215 of which were found at Qumran. . . . Parts of every book of the Jewish and Protestant Old Testament are included, with the exception of Esther and Nehemiah" (Vermes says just Esther).[14] One can read through the book by Abegg, Flint, and Ulrich, *The Dead Sea Scrolls Bible*, and actually see how the Bible reads based on the translation of the Scrolls! A large majority of the text is very similar to the Masoretic Text, especially the Great Isaiah Scroll and the Psalms Scroll.

> The most frequently represented Old Testament books among the Dead Sea Scrolls are Genesis, Exodus, Deuteronomy, Psalms, and Isaiah. The oldest text is a fragment of Exodus dating from about 250 B.C. The Isaiah scroll dates from about 100 B.C. These ancient witnesses only confirm the accuracy of the Masoretic Text and the care with which the Jewish scribes handled the Scriptures. Except for a few instances where spelling and grammar differ between the Dead Sea Scrolls and the Masoretic Text, the two are amazingly similar. The differences do not warrant any major changes in the substance of the Old Testament.[15]

Some recent authors would argue for more fluidity or variation in the text types at Qumran. Brotzman, for example, writes:

> While the Qumran documents have certified the overall faithfulness with which the text was copied, they also point out that the text in the last two centuries B.C., and up through at least a part of the first century A.D., existed in various text types rather than only one. . . . The finds at Qumran have provided actual manuscripts with which the text critic can work. The great majority support the Masoretic Text, but there are also manuscripts that support the readings of the Septuagint and Samaritan Pentateuch, as well as others that are not aligned with any previously known text type.[16]

In conclusion, many Hebrew copies of the OT text have been preserved for us today through the careful preservation of the Masoretes and through the several thousand existing manuscripts. God has used many unusual events and people to preserve His words for us.

NEW TESTAMENT COPIES

The preservation history of the Greek New Testament copies is quite a bit more detailed than the OT. There are over 5,000 partial or whole manuscripts of the New Testament books that are in existence today. Our choice of manuscripts in this chapter is based on the availability of the historical trails, not on the textual value of the manuscript. Perhaps a note is in order about the corruption of early texts. It is evident from the writings of the early Fathers that there were those who were intentionally changing texts to promote a particular view of some doctrine. John Burgon feels very strongly that corruption started at that time and exists in manuscripts today. But even Burgon, when writing about the chief Alexandrian manuscripts says, "Of fraud, strictly speaking, there may have been little or none. We should shrink from imputing an evil motive where any matter will bear an honorable interpretation."[17] Robinson and Pierpont agree: "Heretical corruption of texts is not here in view; indeed, the existing New Testament manuscripts show no consistent marks of such alteration as is reported in the early Fathers concerning manuscripts produced by the heretics Marcion or Tatian."[18] The New King James Version has done a great service for the Christian who has no knowledge of the Greek language. The textual notes record variations between text groups both in the Old and New Testaments. With a little bit of study of the NKJV introductory material, one can see for himself whether or not variants represent a form of corruption.

Copies of the New Testament fall into five main categories: papyri, uncials, minuscules (cursives), lectionaries, and early Church Fathers (technically not copies, but they do witness to the preserved words of the New Testament). We discussed *papyri* in some detail above. Nearly one hundred of these "ancient paper" New Testament manuscripts have been found so far, many dating between the second and fourth centuries. By the fourth century parchment began to replace papyrus as the primary writing material. The parchment manuscripts are called *uncials* and they use rather formal and square letters similar to our capital letters. The nearly 300 uncial manuscripts date from the fourth to the tenth century. By the tenth century a new style of writing, much more like cursive handwriting, began to be used for manuscripts. These manuscripts are called *cursives* or *minuscules*. Most Greek manuscripts are minuscules. *Lectionaries* are manuscripts of weekly or special Scripture reading lessons with selected portions of Scripture used in church services. Some scholars believe that churches started to use them as early as the first century, but most date the existing ones starting with the fourth century. The early *Church Fathers* have left many commentaries and other writings with thousands of Scripture quotations which, with proper care, can be used as legitimate sources of textual study.

The Alands list the following places where Greek manuscripts are today: Cambridge (66), Grottaferrata (69), Florence (79), Patmos (81), Moscow (96), Jerusalem (146), Oxford (158), Leningrad (233), London (271), Sinai (301), Rome (367), Paris (373), Athens (419), and Mt. Athos (900).[19] The whole collection of New Testament manuscripts can be divided into two major text groups, Alexandrian and Byzantine. I realize that some would add the Western and Caesarean text types, but more and more it seems scholars are questioning these as text families.[20] For this paper, we will limit the discussion to the Byzantine (sometimes called Majority, Syrian, Koine, or Traditional) and the Alexandrian (sometimes called the Ecclectic, Neutral, Critical, Westcott/Hort, Nestle, or United Bible Society). In addition, the manuscripts used to construct the Received Text (TR), a text based on a small group of Byzantine manuscripts, must be considered.[21] A form of the TR (although the name TR had not yet been used) was used as the primary basis of the KJV, and almost every English translation up until 1881 was based on the TR.[22] Except for a few like D. A. Waite,[23] all writers have recognized Desiderius Erasmus as the initial editor of what became the TR.

Our intention in the remainder of this paper is to trace the history and providential preservation of the manuscripts behind three text groups: Alexandrian, Byzantine, and Received Text (a subset of the Byzantine).

ALEXANDRIAN MANUSCRIPTS

The historical backgrounds of the primary Alexandrian manuscripts are by far the easiest to trace simply because there are very few of them (in comparison to the Byzantine) and most have been found fairly recently. Many of the Alexandrian manuscripts were relatively unknown until a number of European manuscript hunters began poking around in the deserts of Egypt where they had heard of ancient documents preserved in the dry climate. We will trace the history of a few of them, taken in the order in which they usually appear in a listing of New Testament manuscripts.

First in consideration, then, would be some of the papyri documents. David Allen Black lists the following papyri as demonstrating the Alexandrian text type:[24] p^{20}, p^{23}, p^{45}, p^{46}, p^{47}, p^{50}, p^{66}, p^{72}, p^{74}, p^{75}. The first two of these were found among the papyri at Oxyrhynchus, Egypt (about 100 miles south of Cairo on the Nile river). In 1897 Bernard Grenfell and Arthur Hunt went to Oxyrhynchus to search for Christian documents preserved in the dry

Egyptian climate. They were aware that Christians had settled and built churches in the area as early as the second century. They found a number of papyrus documents, including some twenty-eight containing portions of the New Testament, most of which dated between A.D. 200 and 400. The ancient practice was to put old worn out manuscripts in "rubbish heaps," and Grenfell and Hunt were able to locate such a place that yielded the largest find of papyri ever discovered.[25] According to Philip Comfort, p^{20} is dated in the third century and contains James 2:19-3:9. It does not offer any significant variations in its text. P^{23} is also dated in the third century and contains John 15:25-16:2, 21-32. It is similar to Codex Sinaiticus.[26]

P^{45}, p^{46}, and p^{47} come from the Chester Beatty collection. No one knows for sure exactly where these important documents were found, except that they came from along the Nile just south of Cairo. They probably belonged to a wealthy Christian family, a monastery, or Christian church. Some were purchased by Chester Beatty, and others by the University of Michigan from the same antiquities dealer, Phocion J. Tano.[27] They contain much of the Old Testament in Greek and in the New Testament the Gospels, Acts, Paul's Epistles, and the Book of Revelation. They reside in the Chester Beatty Library in Dublin, Ireland, and the University of Michigan library in Ann Arbor. Most scholars suggest that p^{45} and p^{47} have texts that are mixed (more than one text tradition), whereas p^{46} is similar to the Alexandrian text.

P^{66}, p^{72}, and p^{75} are part of the Bodmer collection. P^{66} and p^{75} date in the second century, and p^{72} to the third or fourth century. P^{66} contains the Gospel of John and has a mixed text. P^{72} contains 1-2 Peter and Jude and also has a mixed text. P^{75} contains most of Luke 3 through John 15 and is generally considered similar to Codex B (more about this one later). Philip Comfort tells the story (adapted from James Robinson) of their discovery:

> In broad daylight a Muslim peasant named Hasan (presumably from Abu Mana Bahari) went out near the cliffs beyond the limits of arable land (in an area a few miles south of Cairo) looking for *sabakh* (fertilizer), but this may have been an excuse for seeking treasure. While digging with a mattock, Hasan found some ancient books, but he was not particularly impressed with his find. He gave some of the books away to bystanders and took the rest home (presumably in a jar). The villagers knew of the discovery, which occurred around the time of the fall of King Farouk (July 23, 1952). Not knowing the value of these ancient Greek and Coptic manuscripts, Hasan burned some of the leaves – to light a water pipe or just to smell the fragrance of burning papyrus. Hasan attempted to barter the papyri codexes for

cigarettes or oranges, but the villagers were not interested – deeming the books worthless.

Word of the discovery soon reached communication and trade centers outside of the village. Middlemen emerged who wanted to sell the papyri to antiquity dealers in Alexandria or Cairo. The first purchaser of the Bodmer papyri was a goldsmith from Dishna. The goldsmith's son was a teacher at the same parochial school as the former owner of Codex III in the Nag Hammadi manuscripts, which had been sold to the Coptic Museum. When the goldsmith's son showed the papyrus to the Coptic Museum, it was nearly confiscated. From then on, the goldsmith was virtually under house arrest. But the papyri were safe from police search because they had been put in the house of a Coptic priest, who then became a coconspirator in the clandestine operation to traffic the manuscripts to Cairo. It took the goldsmith three years to sell off the papyri – at a very good price (due to the good market of the Nag Hammadi manuscripts). A Cairo dealer, Phocion Tano, bought and sold both Nag Hammadi manuscripts and Dishna manuscripts – many to Martin Bodmer of Geneva, Switzerland, some to Chester Beatty of Dublin, Ireland, and a few to other buyers.[28]

We will discuss more about the papyri when we get to the Byzantine manuscripts, but perhaps now would be a good time to say some things in general about the text witnessed by papyri documents. Matthew Black quotes Aland, "The simple fact that all these papyri, with their various distinctive characteristics, did exist side by side, in the same ecclesiastical province, that is, in Egypt, where they were found, is the best argument against the existence of any text-types, including the Alexandrian and the Antiochian."[29] Aland's position seems to be that at the time of the writing of the papyri documents there were no definite text types, but that witnesses to major text types were observable. Even the liberal *Interpreter's Dictionary of the Bible* agrees:

> Without exception, the papyrus NT MSS which are extant today were found in Egypt and undoubtedly were written there. Many of them are too small to be of much value textually. Their cumulative evidence, however, is of value. They prove conclusively that in Egypt, particularly in the second, third, and fourth centuries, no one type of NT text was dominant. In those early centuries many types of text flourished side by side.[30]

One final general point about the papyri manuscripts is mentioned by Comfort, "The early New Testament papyri contribute virtually no new substantial variants, suggesting that all of the New Testament variants are preserved somewhere in the extant manuscript tradition."[31]

ALEXANDRIAN UNCIAL MANUSCRIPTS

Next to consider are some of the uncial (capital letter) manuscripts that reflect the Alexandrian text type. Constantin von Tischendorf accomplished the most astounding of these finds in 1844. Tischendorf was an evangelical Christian trying to find evidence to fight against the rationalistic attacks on the Bible. Even the liberal Matthew Black called him a "defender of the faith"[32] for his book written in 1864 defending orthodoxy against the attacks of Strauss, Renan, and the Tubingen school on the historical foundations of the Christian faith. D. A. Waite libelously calls him an apostate.[33] "Only in this context can Tischendorf's life's work be fully appreciated," writes James Bentley. He continues:

> He was passionately determined to refute those who were destroying the faith of the Christian world. Many Christians desperately longed for such a refutation. In a pamphlet published in March 1864 Tischendorf wrote, 'May my writing serve this end: to make you mistrust those novel theories upon the Gospels – or rather, *against* them – which would persuade you that the wonderful details which the Gospels give of our gracious Saviour are founded upon ignorance or deceit.' Tischendorf's pamphlet sold out the entire edition of 2000 copies within three weeks. [34]

According to Tischendorf's son-in-law, "to prove the early existence and authenticity of the Gospels his main aim was to go in search of manuscripts that would afford this proof."[35] To this end Tischendorf scoured the libraries of Europe (Holland, London, Oxford, Cambridge, Basle, Naples, Florence, Venice, Modena, Milan, Turin, Rome), monasteries in Cairo, Libya, Mount Sinai, Jerusalem, Samaria, monastic communities by the Dead Sea, the library at Patmos, Constantinople, Vienna, and Munich, and other places, to collect hundreds of Greek manuscripts.[36]

Tischendorf's most famous manuscript find was the uncial Codex Sinaiticus or Codex 01 (uncials are numbered with a prefixed zero before the Arabic numerals). The Sinaiticus discovery is another exciting story that magnifies the preserving hand of God. He had heard that there were ancient manuscripts at the Greek Byzantine monastery of St. Catherine on Mount Sinai. Tischendorf describes what happened on May 24, 1844:

> In visiting the monastery in the month of May 1844, I perceived in the middle of the great hall a large and wide basket full of old parchments; and the librarian who was a man of information told me that two heaps of papers like these, mouldered by time, had been already committed to the flames. What was my surprise to find amid this heap of papers a considerable number of sheets of a copy of the Old

Testament in Greek which seemed to me to be one of the most ancient that I had ever seen. The authorities of the monastery allowed me to possess myself of a third of these parchments, or about forty three sheets, all the more readily as they were designated for the fire. But I could not get them to yield up possession of the remainder. The too lively satisfaction which I had displayed had aroused their suspicions as to the value of the manuscript. I transcribed a page of the text of Isaiah and Jeremiah, and enjoined on the monks to take religious care of all such remains which might fall their way.[37]

Believing that there were still more manuscripts like these at the monastery, Tischendorf returned in 1853 but was unsuccessful in finding them. He returned a third time in 1859:

By the end of January he was in the monastery. By his own account, he 'devoted a few days in turning over the manuscripts of the monastery, not without alighting here and there on some precious parchment or other.' But of his old discovery, he saw nothing.

On 4 February he told his Bedouin to prepare to leave for Cairo three days later. That evening he took a walk with the young Athenian steward of the monastery and then went for some refreshment in the steward's cell. Then the steward said that he too had read the Greek version of the Old Testament, and he took down from the corner of his cell a bulky parcel, wrapped up in a red cloth, and laid it before Tischendorf.

Tischendorf took it to his own rooms. It contained not simply the eighty or so leaves he had seen in 1844. Altogether he held in his hands 346 parchments, all in the same handwriting and from the same volume.[38]

Through rather clever diplomatic negotiations Tischendorf was able to eventually secure the codex, which is the only complete uncial copy of the New Testament, for Czar Alexander II of Russia, by whom he had been commissioned to seek the manuscript. The manuscript remained in Russia until 1933 when the Marxists who had little interest in Bible manuscripts, except for their cash value, sold it to the British. The story is intriguing:

In 1931 the British antiquarian bookseller Maurice L. Ettinghausen led a deputation of three to Moscow, to persuade the Russian authorities that it was folly to try to sell, say, three or four copies of a first edition of Homer all at once. Ettinghausen made friends with the head of the Russian department for the exchange of books, who happened at that time to be a Hungarian. He was introduced to the Vice-Commissar for Foreign Trade, who had been Quartermaster-General of the Red Army. And in the former Imperial Public Library, to one side, on a dusty lectern, he saw a square leather box, with a leather cover lettered 'Codex Sinaiticus Petropolitanus.'

As a joke, Ettinghausen told the Vice-Commissioner for Foreign Trade that if he ever needed money, he should tie Sinaiticus up in a brown-paper parcel and send it to Ettinghausen in London. The Vice-Commissar said he had never heard of the manuscript.

Two years later the Hungarian head of the department for the exchange of books was in London. In the autumn of 1933 he came to see Ettinghausen and asked him if Codex Sinaiticus was worth a million pounds. Maurice Ettinghausen replied that he did not know, but if ever the Russians wished to sell the codex, he would be prepared to find a buyer in the west. A few weeks later the Russian cultural attaché in Paris, Comrade Ilyin, informed Ettinghausen that the Soviet government was prepared to sell the codex for £200,000. Ettinghausen immediately informed Sir Frederic Kenyon of the British Museum.[39]

The document was eventually purchased for 100,000 pounds and arrived at the British Museum in December of 1933 where it remains to this today. The original 43 leaves of the Old Testament, which Tischendorf acquired in 1844, are now in the University Library in Leipzig. The manuscript is usually dated in the fourth century and classified as Alexandrian.

The origin of the manuscript has been of some question: Rome, Caesarea, or Alexandria have been suggested. *The Cambridge History of the Bible* gives arguments for Caesarea and Alexandria, but favors Alexandria.[40] Burgon and Bentley favor Caesarea.[41] Bentley is almost certain that it was one of the fifty codices that Eusebius of Caesarea produced for Constantine in approximately A.D. 332. He believes that it was taken to Sinai when the Arabs took Caesarea in 638. In a recent article Theodore Skeat argues strongly that Sinaiticus was written in Caesarea. He connects it with the letter of Constantine to Eusebius in 330 requesting 50 copies of the Holy Scriptures. He believes that, because of its size, it was left incomplete and unbound in the scriptorium at Caesarea for 200 years and later moved to the Sinai monastery.[42]

The second Alexandrian uncial manuscript to be discussed is the Alexandrinus, which is normally dated in the fifth century. It is, however, Byzantine in the Gospels. Writers who favor the Alexandrian text type usually show their bias when discussing this manuscript with such comments as, "The text is of uneven value (based on exemplars of different types in its different parts), inferior in the Gospels, good in the rest of the New Testament . . . ."[43] Most agree that it was given to the Patriarch of Alexandria in 1098, and was brought to Constantinople in 1621 by Cyril Lucar. Lucar, murdered for trying to guide his church toward Reformation doctrines, was Patriarch of Alexandria and later of Constantinople. Lucar sent Alexandrinus to England as a gift to James I (sponsor of the KJV), but it did not arrive until 1627 during the reign of Charles I. It became property of the British Museum in 1757 and remains there today. Hills points out that Alexandrinus in the Gospels is another witness to the early existence of the Byzantine text in Egypt.[44]

Another Alexandrian uncial, Codex B, or Vaticanus, is considered to be the oldest uncial (middle of 4th century) and therefore the best New Testament manuscript, in the opinion of those who favor the Alexandrian text. Metzger writes about it:

> The manuscript was written about the middle of the fourth century and contained both Testaments as well as the books of the Apocrypha, with the exception of the books of Maccabees. Today there are three lacunae [missing portions] in the codex: at the beginning almost forty-six chapters of Genesis are missing; a section of some thirty Psalms is lost; and the concluding pages (from Heb ix.14 onwards, including 1 and 2 Timothy, Titus, Philemon, and Revelation) are gone.

> The writing is in small and delicate uncials, perfectly simple and unadorned. Unfortunately, the beauty of the original writing has been spoiled by a later corrector, who traced over every letter afresh, omitting only those letters and words which he believed to be incorrect. The complete absence of ornamentation from Vaticanus has generally been taken as an indication that it is slightly older than codex Sinaiticus. On the other hand, some scholars believe that these two manuscripts were originally among the fifty copies of the Scriptures which the Emperor Constantine commissioned Eusebius to have written (see pp. 7-8 above). Indeed, T. C. Skeat of the British Museum has suggested to the present writer that codex Vaticanus was a 'reject' among the fifty copies, for it is deficient in the Eusebian canon tables, has many corrections by different scribes, and, as was mentioned above, lacks the books of Maccabees apparently through an oversight. Whether 'reject' or not, however, the text which it contains has been regarded by many scholars as an excellent representative of the Alexandrian text-type of the New Testament.[45]

Vaticanus has been in the Vatican since at least 1475 when it was noted in the earliest catalogue of the Vatican Library. The *Catholic Encyclopedia* says that it belonged to Pope Nicholas whose library in 1455 "contained 824 Latin and 352 Greek manuscripts."[46] There is no agreement among scholars as to how the manuscript made its way to Rome or from where it originated. Skeat argues for a Caesarea provenance. He believes that it was one of the fifty Bibles ordered by Constantine in 330 and was taken to Constantinople and later to Rome.[47]

Another important Alexandrian uncial is H^p. Metzger gives some of the background:

> Codex Coislinianus [codices often have several titles] is an important codex of the Pauline Epistles written in a very large hand with only a few words in each line. The text is Alexandrian. Dating from the sixth century, it came into the possession of the monastery of the Laura on Mount Athos, where, after it began to be dilapidated, its leaves were used to supply materials for the binding of several other volumes. Forty-one leaves are known to exist today, divided among libraries at Paris, Leningrad, Moscow, Kiev, Turin, and Mount Athos. A note appended to the Epistle to Titus states that it was corrected from the copy in the library of Caesarea, written by the hand of the holy Pamphilus [founder of the ancient library at Caesarea] himself.[48]

ALEXANDRIAN MINUSCULES

There are over 2800 minuscule (cursive) manuscripts of the New Testament. Minuscules are numbered with regular Arabic numerals without the prefixed zero. At least eighty percent of them follow the Byzantine text. Most of the remaining are independent ("Caesarean" or "Western"), but some are Alexandrian. Their historical background is hard to find. There are few exciting stories to tell. We will mention a couple of minuscules and conclude this section on the Alexandrian manuscripts. Metzger relates some of the background of the Alexandrian minuscule Codex 1739:

> Containing the Acts and the Epistles, this tenth-century manuscript was discovered at Mount Athos [see below in the discussion of Byzantine manuscripts] in 1879 by E. von der Goltz, and is usually known by his name. It is of extreme importance because it contains a number of marginal notes taken from the writings of Iranaeus, Clement, Origen, Eusebius, and Basil. Since nothing is more recent than Basil, who lived from A.D. 329 to 379, it appears that the ancestor of this manuscript was written by a scribe toward the close of the

fourth century. A colophon indicates that for the Pauline Epistles the scribe followed a manuscript which contained an Origenian text. It is, however, not of the Caesarean type but presents a relatively pure form of the Alexandrian type of text.[49]

Minuscule 69 is "Caesarean," but we will include it here because Metzger provides a little bit of its history. It contains the entire New Testament and dates from the fifteenth century.It was copied by a man named Emmanuel, a Greek from Constantinople who worked for Archbishop Neville of York. It is now in the Museum of Leicester, England. It is a member of what is called "Family 13," because manuscripts 13, 69, 124, and 346 are so closely related textually. Metzger mentions that "they were copied between the eleventh and fifteenth centuries, and are descendants of an archetype which came either from Calabria in southern Italy or from Sicily."[50]

This completes our short survey of historical backgrounds of the Alexandrian manuscripts. We are going to postpone the discussion of the Fathers and Lectionaries witness to the Alexandrian text until after the discussion of the Byzantine texts. It is evident from this survey that the Lord has used many means in preserving the Alexandrian witness: explorers, ancient ruins, peasants, middlemen, priests, antiquity dealers, theologians, monasteries, politicians, czars, communists, patriarchs, kings, the Vatican, and even waste baskets.

BYZANTINE COPIES

We must now turn our attention to the documents that hold the most interest for those who argue for the exclusivness of the King James Version, the Byzantine documents. Studying these manuscripts leads us to the knowledge of how most manuscripts were preserved. Greek manuscripts were virtually unknown in the West (Northern and Southern Europe) until shortly before the Reformation. If they had been known, only a handful of scholars could have read them, because the Greek language was all but extinct in the West. Spence-Jones writes, "Very different, indeed, was the condition of the entire West, including Italy, France, Spain, Germany and England. In all these countries, for more than seven hundred years, the knowledge of the Greek language and literature was lost. The historian of the Middle Ages does not hesitate positively to affirm 'that for all the purposes of taste and erudition there was no Greek in Western Europe during the Middle Ages.'"[51] Because of the sack (by the West in A.D.1204 during fourth Crusade) and fall (by the Muslims in A.D.1453) of Constantinople thousands of people fled Greek Constantinople for the West, bringing with them the Greek language and the Greek manuscripts, including the New Testament.[52] These manuscripts ended up in monasteries, universities, private collections, and libraries throughout Europe. This is how most manuscripts that we have today were preserved.

One of the most famous monastery areas is Mt. Athos, located on a peninsula jutting out into the Aegean Sea off the coast of northern Greece. We discuss it here a bit because many Byzantine manuscripts are traced back to Athos. The first monastic life appeared on Athos around the middle of the tenth century, and in days to follow many Byzantine (Greek) monasteries were built. Today only about twenty survive. Constantine (4th century) actually built three churches on the peninsula, buildings that are still in use by the monastic community today. The Athos community has always been under the influence of the Greek Orthodox Church except from A.D. 1204 to 1261 when the Latins (Roman Catholics) took over and in the process looted most of its valuable treasures including manuscripts. There were many such monasteries throughout the ancient world.

The Crusades were responsible for much of the destruction and scattering of Greek biblical manuscripts. *The Cambridge History of the Bible* describes some of this:

> After the fifth century books became rare: there were in fact many losses from the store of extant classical (and also Christian) literature in this period. Various factors contributed to this, one which affected both classical and Christian literature being the century-long Iconoclastic struggle, in which the emperors of the Iconoclastic persuasion, as is often the case with tyrants, showed themselves antagonistic to literature and literary activity in general. . . . The penultimate cataclysm affecting the transmission of Greek literature is the sack and fifty-year domination of Constantinople by the Latins in the thirteenth century, when many precious manuscripts were destroyed and the activity of *scriptoria* came to an end. The Empire was fatally weakened by this barbaric episode but managed to survive for another two hundred years. In this last period many manuscripts were produced, some with all the scholarly material which the scribe could muster, others for private reading or for school teaching rather than for scholarly or official use. The growth of enthusiasm for Greek learning in the West and the growing threat of the Turk drove manuscripts and scribes to Italy and beyond.[53]

Of course, large amounts of Christian literature had been destroyed earlier during the Roman persecutions up until about A.D. 311. Burgon makes reference to the destruction of the libraries at Caesarea and Alexandria in the seventh century by the Muslims.[54] Birdsall mentions the library at Caesarea as being the place where Armenian and Georgian scholars and translators came for guidance.[55]

But even with all of the destruction, many copies of the Greek New Testament survived and began showing up in the growing libraries of Renaissance Europe. It is apparent that most of these came from Constantinople and the Greek Orthodox Churches. Geanakoplos mentions Greeks moving to Venice from Constantinople, Crete, and Venetian-held Greek colonies:

> Most prominent of the Greeks who later returned to Venice was Bessarion, Archbishop of Nicaea and subsequently Cardinal of the Roman Church. . . . Of significance is the fact that, despite his many years of residence in Rome and the great reputation of Florence as the leading humanistic center, he chose Venice as the permanent reposi-tory for his collection of manuscripts, most important of which were some 500 written in Greek. As is well-known, the latter constituted the greatest single collection of Greek manuscripts in the period of the Renaissance. . . . It was these Greeks, those that is with an exten-sive knowledge of Greek literature, who helped to carry Greek letters from Venice to many of the principal areas of western Europe. To cite only two examples: that of the Cretan, Demetrius Ducas, who was summoned from Venice to Spain to teach Greek at the University of Alcala and there supervised the Greek New Testament version of Cardinal Ximenes' celebrated Complutensian Polyglot; and also the Cretan Calliergis, who after establishing a press in Venice moved to Rome, where he became the pioneer printer of Greek in the papal capital. . . . When in 1563 King Philip II of Spain began the construction of the great Escorial, he began to collect there a large library, which included one of the finest collections of Greek manu-scripts in the world. Some forty calligraphers, we are told, worked at the Escorial making copies of old manuscripts for the Spanish monarch.[56]

Geanakoplos mentions the Cretan library of Margounios, which because of the Turkish conquest after 1669, was spread to many places including the Vatican, Mt. Sinai, Mt. Athos, The Patriarchal Library of Jerusalem, Oxford, Russia, and Constantinople.[57] *The Cambridge Modern History* enlightens us about the Vatican library:

> Another great library which first took shape in the fifteenth century is that of the Vatican. A papal library of some sort had existed from very early times, and had received from Pope Zacharias (741-52) a large addition to its stock of Greek manuscripts. This old collection had

been deposited in the Lateran. When the papal Court was removed to Avignon in 1309, the books were taken thither. The Great Schism, which began in 1378, was closed by the election of Martin V in 1417. The books were subsequently brought back from Avignon to Rome, and placed in the Vatican. Eugenius IV (1431-47), who came next after Martin V, interested himself in this matter. But his successor, Nicholas V (1447-55), has the best claim to be called the founder of the Vatican Library. ... During the eight years of his pontificate, he enlarged that collection with energy and judgment, adding to it several thousands of manuscripts. The number of Latin manuscripts alone was, at his death, 824, as is shown by a catalogue dated April 16, 1455. ... His successor, Calixtue III (1455-8), added many volumes brought from Constantinople after its capture by the Turks.[58]

Before we leave this topic something needs to be said about the large number of Greek manuscripts in Russia. More than one hundred years before the official establishment of Christianity in Russia, two missionaries (Cyril and Methodius) translated the Bible from manuscripts from Constantinople into the yet unwritten language of the Slavonic tribes. The modern Russian alphabet still gives evidence of this with its many similarities to Greek. Under Vladimir, the Russian church was begun with a mass baptism at Kieff in 988. For the first five centuries of the church in Russia all the Metropolitans were Byzantine. Around 1650 Patriarch Nicon sent scholars to Grecian monasteries to collect manuscripts to be used for collations of the sacred books.[59] The Russian church's interest in the Greek church continues into modern times. During the last half of the nineteenth century the Russians gained (not always welcomed) a large presence on Mt. Athos (a source of many Greek manuscripts) in Greece and has been influential in the monasteries there to this day. It is easy to see, therefore, why Russia has been the source of many Greek manuscripts used by modern translators.

BYZANTINE PAPYRI

At this point we need to turn our attention to the preservation of some particular Byzantine text manuscripts. We have discussed above the discoveries of the papyri. Many writers give the impression that the papyri give witness to the Alexandrian text type only. We have mentioned, however, that Matthew Black and the Interpreter's Dictionary take the position that the papyri argue against any particular fixed text type at that time. Harry Sturz has made a rather thorough study of the papyri and lists "some 150 distinctively Byzantine readings now found to have early Egyptian papyri supporting them. Distinctively Byzantine readings are readings which at the same time are opposed (or not supported) by the principal manuscripts and witnesses to the

Alexandrian and Western texts."[60] This is another area of textual criticism that needs more work, but at the present it seems as if the papyri give witness to both major text traditions.

BYZANTINE UNCIALS

As mentioned earlier in our discussion of the Alexandrian manuscripts, uncial Codex A is normally dated in the fifth century. It is, however, Byzantine in the Gospels. As mentioned, most agree that it was given to the Patriarch of Alexandria in 1098, and was brought to Constantinople in 1621 by Cyril Lucar. Lucar sent it to England as a gift to James I (of KJV time), but it did not arrive until 1627 during the reign of Charles I. It became property of the British Museum in 1757 and remains there until today. Hills points out, as already mentioned, that Alexandrinus in the Gospels is another witness to the early existence of the Byzantine text in Egypt.

Codex C (04, or Ephraemi) is a palimpsest (the original document has been "erased" and another document written over the original). Tischendorf was able to decipher the original manuscript which contains part of the Old Testament and portions of every New Testament book except 2 Thessalonians and 2 John. Even though the manuscript is quite early (fifth century) Metzger shows his bias by writing, "It seems to be compounded from all the major text-types, agreeing frequently with the Koine or Byzantine type, which most scholars regard as the least valuable type of the New Testament text."[61] The Anchor Bible Dictionary says that it agrees with the Byzantine more than any other text in the Gospels and significant numbers of agreement in the Acts, Paul's Epistles, and the Catholic Epistles. The Dictionary adds:

> Tischendorf suggested that the manuscript was written in Egypt. This is confirmed by Cavallo, who argues for the Nitrian Desert, associating the script (he is thinking, it appears, of the NT particularly) with those of the Freer manuscript of Deuteronomy and Joshua, the NT uncials 016 (its closest associate) and 027, and two Homer codices . . . . The text has been reworked by 2 correctors who, it is suggested, are to be placed in 6th-century Caesarea and 9th-century Constantinople. In the early 16th century the codex was brought to Italy, and passed into the possession of Catherine de Medici, with whom it went to Paris, where it has remained ever since [in the National Library].[62]

Codex E (07) is an eighth century Byzantine uncial manuscript of the Gospels. Both Hatch and the Interpreter's Dictionary of the Bible trace it to John of Ragusa who brought it to Basel in 1431 and presented it to the

Dominican convent (see discussion of Erasmus' manuscripts later on in this paper). It was added to the University Library in Basel in 1559 where it resides today. Tarelli suggests that Erasmus may have used it.[63]

Codex E^a is a sixth or seventh century Byzantine manuscript of the Book of Acts. Hatch writes:

> The manuscript was in Sardinia at some time after the destruction of the Vandal kingdom in Africa by Belisarius in 534. Early in the eighth century it was at Jarrow in England, whither it was probably brought from Italy by Benedict Biscop or Ceolfrid not long after the middle of the seventh century. It was used by the Venerable Bede in his commentary on the Acts. Later the codex was taken to Germany, probably by one of the English missionaries; and it may have been in a monastery at Wurzburg for several centuries. Wurzburg was captured by the Swedes in 1631, and the manuscript may have been part of the victors' booty. At any rate it was soon afterward acquired by Laud by his agents in Germany. He presented it to the Bodleian Library in 1636.[64]

These Byzantine uncial manuscript stories give us an idea of how the manuscripts have been preserved through the centuries for the use of translators today. Most uncial manuscripts would have similar historical trails if we could trace them.

BYZANTINE MINUSCULES

The history of individual Byzantine minuscule manuscripts is hard to find as well. William Hatch's *Facsimiles and Descriptions of Minuscule Manuscripts of the New Testament* is one of the best sources for such information.[65] We will list a few entries to give us an idea of the background of some of the Byzantine minuscules. The following information is taken from Hatch. Other Byzantine manuscripts will be discussed below along with Erasmus.

Codex 1 (Acts, Catholic Epistles, Pauline Epistles [including Hebrews], and Four Gospels; tenth to twelfth century; not Byzantine, but included here because it was one that Erasmus had access to but apparently did not use) — The codex was presented to the Dominican convent in Basel by John of Ragusa, who was procurator-general of the Dominican order and who opened the Council of Basel in 1431. It was incorporated in the University Library in 1559.

Codex 34 (Four Gospels with marginal commentary; tenth or eleventh century; Byzantine) — It is in the national library of Paris, but once belonged to the Monastery of the Stauroniketes on Mount Athos.

Codex 49 (Four Gospels; eleventh or twelfth century; Byzantine) — It was presented to a certain church in the year 1413 by one Demetrius. Sir Thomas Roe, who was ambassador to the Sublime Porte in the reigns of James I and Charles I, brought it from Constantinople to England along with Codex Alexandrinus and gave it to the Bodleian Library in the year 1628. It remains at the Bodleian at Oxford.

Codex 218 (Old Testament, Four Gospels, Acts, Catholic Epistles, Pauline Epistles [including Hebrews], and Apocalypse; thirteenth century; only the Apocalypse is Byzantine). — The codex was brought from Constantinople to Vienna by Ogier [or Augier] Ghislain de Busbecq, a scholar and diplomat, who was sent as ambassador to Suleiman the Magnificent by the Emperor Ferdinand I. He died in the year 1592. It is in the national library in Vienna. Codex 421 (Acts, Catholic Epistles, and Pauline Epistles [including Hebrews]; twelfth to fourteenth century; Byzantine) was brought to Vienna on the same trip.

Codex 565 (Four Gospels; ninth or tenth century; Byzantine in Matthew and in most of Luke) – The codex once belonged to St. John's Convent at Gumush-Khaneh in north-eastern Asia Minor. In 1829 it was presented to Czar Nicholas I by the archimandrite of this monastery, whose name was Sylvester. It is in the Leningrad Public Library.

Scrivener gives some background on Codex 95 of the Apocalypse, dated in the twelfth or thirteenth century. He writes, "The late Lord de la Zouche, then Mr. Curzon, found it in 1837 on the library floor at the monastery of Caracalla, on Mount Athos, and begged it of the Abbot, who suggested that the vellum leaves would be of use to cover pickle-jars."[66] Scrivener collated it in 1855.

These statistics may be boring, but they are necessary to get a general idea of the history of most of the minuscules. The Alands[67] list pertinent information (except historical background) on about 175 minuscules (almost exclusively Non-Byzantine). They then list numbers only (no information) for a whole host of Byzantine minuscules, followed by these words:

> All of these minuscules exhibit a purely or predominantly Byzantine text. And this is not a peculiarity of the minuscules, but a characteristic they share with a considerable number of uncials. *They are all irrelevant for textual criticism, at least for establishing the original form of the text and its development in the early centuries* (emphasis

mine). Admittedly no adequate history has yet been written of the Byzantine text – a text which is in no sense a monolithic mass because its manuscripts share the same range of variation character- istic of all Greek New Testament manuscripts. But this is a task we may well leave to a future generation, or to specialists particularly interested in it today, and consider our own generation fortunate if we can succeed in tracing the history of manuscripts with non-Byzantine texts, and that in its general outlines. . . . *In fact, the "Majority text" . . . may yet prove to hold a multiple significance for the history of the text* (emphasis mine).[68]

The Alands demonstrate once again their bias against the Byzantine text, but it is somewhat muted by the context. The Alands were leaders in the field of textual criticism, and I believe their statement about the future of the Byzantine text witness is prophetic for future New Testament text work. There is much work to be done on the New Testament text, and the place of the Byzantine text will become much more prominent. "It was an error of ear- lier years to dismiss the readings of this [Byzantine] text as in all respects worthless. Many of them are not innovations. Zuntz is at pains to demon- strate that Byzantine may be ancient, and he declares with justice that Byzantine readings which recur in Western witnesses must be ancient, since the two streams of the tradition never met after the fall of the Western empire," writes the Cambridge History of the Bible.[69] "To think that we have solved our problems is naïve: to despair is ridiculous in the light of the wealth of material and of available methods of investigation."[70] Again, "Original readings may be discerned in the various witnesses to the so-called Western text, while the Byzantine text (brusquely dismissed by most exegetes since the days of Westcott and Hort) often reflects the putative original in both vocab- ulary and word-order. This indicates that all the major text-forms have their roots in the second century."[71]

Part of the future work that needs to be done will necessarily involve more work on the minuscules, lectionaries, and early Church Fathers. The great majority of the minuscules and lectionaries agree with the Byzantine text. Because of this they have been neglected by most of modern day scholarship. As indicated above, there will be more work done in the future on these two categories. All of the 2800 minuscules need to be collated because there are many variant readings, even though most of them are Byzantine. There is diversity in the Byzantine tradition. A thorough examination of all the varia- tions will be helpful.

LECTIONARIES

Lectionaries, as stated earlier, are portions of Scripture put together for church services. Many questions remain as to the date of their origin and the date of the origin of the text that they represent. Nearly 2000 are minuscules, and about 300 are uncials. One thing most agree on is that the lectionary manuscripts represent a Byzantine text with few exceptions, and that they preserve a long-standing tradition of the Byzantine Church. The Alands list several recently discovered lectionaries, many from the monasteries on Mt. Athos. The lectionaries have been preserved through their constant use in the tradition of the Greek Orthodox Church. Their importance as a source for New Testament textual study will increase in the future.

CHURCH FATHERS

The quotations of the early Church Fathers are the last general group of New Testament manuscripts that preserve the ancient text. They are important because they give witness to the state of the text very early on in the history of the text. They testify to the existence of a certain reading at a definite time and place. Their testimony is somewhat diminished because of the often "free" and inaccurate quotations of the words of the Scripture. John Burgon did a great deal of work on the Fathers and concluded that they identify with the Byzantine text 60% of the time. Many would disagree with this figure (Gordon Fee, for example[72]), but much more work needs to be done in order to arrive at a definitive answer. Most Greek copies of the Fathers have the same historical background as the other manuscripts: many came out of Constantinople before the occupation by the Turks in 1453, and others through monasteries, convents, and churches.

In conclusion, the Byzantine copies of the New Testament Scriptures have been preserved in papyri, uncials, minuscules, lectionaries, and the Church Fathers. God has used the crusades, monasteries, the Greek Orthodox Church, the Roman Catholic Church, persecution, libraries, wealthy citizens, ambassadors, and czars to be channels of preservation for the manuscripts that are available today. Two Greek New Testaments have been published on the basis of the majority readings of the Byzantine text, one by Robinson and Pierpont and the other by Hodges and Farstad. We have yet to see an English translation of the Majority Greek Byzantine text.[73]

RECEIVED TEXT COPIES

We have one text group that yet needs to be discussed, the manuscripts behind the Received Text. The information presented above pictures for us a situation where, by 1450-1500, Greek biblical manuscripts were spread all over the world. With the onset of the Renaissance, many scholars became interested in what the manuscripts had to say. Desiderius Erasmus was the most outstanding example of the enlightenment scholars who began to delve into the glory and wisdom of the classic Roman and Greek civilizations. (Almost every fact about Erasmus is debatable and controversial. It seems that whatever one writes, there are those that are glad to give a rebuttal. We will try to be as accurate as possible.) He, like many others, scoured Europe and many other places to find and edit copies of the ancient texts. His primary purpose, unlike most of his contemporaries, was to find the best manuscripts of the New Testament and make them available to be translated into all the languages throughout the world, so that every man and woman could read the Scriptures for themselves. The Cambridge Modern History records the following about Erasmus:

> But that purpose which gave unity to his life-work received its highest embodiment in his contributions to biblical criticism and exegesis. . . . He wished to see the Scriptures translated into every language, and given to all. 'I long,' he said, 'that the husbandman should sing them to himself as he follows the plough, that the weaver should hum them to the tune of his shuttle, that the traveler should beguile with them the weariness of his journey.'[74]

The Spanish Index and Roman Index of the Roman Church eventually censured some of the works of Erasmus. "This censure," writes Margolin in *The Bible in the Sixteenth Century,*

> and its underlying reasons may be easily surmised from a quantitative analysis of the passages that were suppressed. Their pin-point precision – a word, an adverb, an extenuation, an expression that was deemed too questioning (or, on the contrary, too affirmative) – will be found to coincide generally, though not always, with the crucial, burning points of the Epistle to the Romans. These are the points – such as justification by faith, original sin, man's freedom, and God's foreknowledge, inter alia – that were at the heart of the great theological controversies of the time (and of times to come).[75]

Erasmus never, however, became an unfaithful son of the Roman Church. He never sided openly with Luther, although he agreed with much that Luther was saying. He claimed that he never deviated from the Church's teachings.[76] To transform Erasmus into one who became "an Anabaptist in his theology" is to distort history.[77]

Our interest in this chapter, however, is in Erasmus' Greek New Testament and particularly the Greek manuscripts that he used. The modern printed texts of today are different from the texts of either Erasmus or Westcott and Hort. The text debate should be a text debate and not a personality bashing. Erasmus had worked on an edition of the New Testament while in England using manuscripts available there and those that he had picked up in his many travels. He was early influenced by Lorenzo Valla (an Italian biblical scholar in the middle of the 15th century), John Colet's lectures on Paul at Oxford, and Jacques Lefevre's studies on Paul's Epistles. Colet, Thomas More, and William Latimer were students of Grocyn who had come to Oxford from Italy to lecture in Greek.[78] There is evidence that Greek manuscripts had made their way to England from as early as 668 when Theodore of Canterbury, a competent Greek scholar, was sent by Pope Vitalian to organize the English church.[79] Erasmus' first published Greek text was rather hurried because his printer, the famous Froeben, wanted to publish before the Complutensian Polyglot came out (although it is known that there were Greek manuscripts in Spain, the manuscripts behind the Polyglot are still a mystery). The Greek part of this first edition of 1516 was based on probably seven (some say four, and some say as many as ten) Greek minuscule manuscripts that were found in Basel, and because of the rush, the edition had many errors. Erasmus' prime interest was to improve the Latin New Testament, but in order to do so he wanted to publish an accompanying Greek text for reference[80] and to justify his changes in the Vulgate. He had notes with him from his earlier studies but was not fully prepared for his first edition. Where did the Greek minuscules that Erasmus found in Basel come from? This question is not easy to answer, but it seems that most of the manuscripts for the first edition came from the Dominican monastery in Basel. They had been given to the Dominicans in Basel "by Cardinal John Stojkovic of Ragusa, when he attended the council of Basle in 1431."[81] It is possible that the Cardinal had obtained them in Constantinople on a recent trip. H. J. de Jonge writes, "These seven manuscripts, are, in the Gregory numbering usual for New Testament manuscripts: 1^{eap}, 2^e, 817 for the Gospels; 2^{ap}, 4^{ap}, and 7^p for the Acts and the Epistles; and 1^r for Revelation. Those sent to the press were 2^e, 2^{ap}, and a new transcript of 1^r, which together made up all the books of the New Testament."[82] P. S. Allen says that Erasmus also used the Leicester Codex written by Emmanuel of Constantinople which was with the Franciscans at Cambridge early in the sixteenth century.[83]

In his later editions he was able to make use of other notes and manuscripts which he had collected from his travels. There seems little point in attacking the man relentlessly for his first edition work. Remaining to this day, however, and due to his influence, are several words in the Received Text which are found in no Greek manuscript. Edward F. Hills lists Erasmus as the first editor of the TR (followed by Stephanus, Beza, and the Elzevirs).[84] Robinson and Pierpont, and a host of others agree. The TR is a text based on a very small percentage of the Byzantine manuscripts, and thus differs in numerous places from the majority of the Byzantine family.

Many say that the text/version debate is a scholar's issue. The New King James Version, however, puts much of this information at the fingertips of anyone who can read English and is willing to study a few pages of introductory material and to examine the textual references. Anyone can easily see the primary places where the three texts (Alexandrian, Byzantine, Received Text) disagree. The happy conclusion for the one who takes the time to examine them is that there is very little difference in these texts. World famous archaeologist Sir Frederic Kenyon wrote, "The number of manuscripts of the New Testament, of early translations from it, and of quotations from it in the oldest writers of the Church, is so large that it is practically certain that the true reading of every doubtful passage is preserved in some one or other of these ancient authorities. This can be said of no other ancient book in the world."[85] To say that God has preserved His words in a particular manuscript or collation of several manuscripts is to go beyond what God has revealed in His Word, and beyond the results of history and biblical study. To claim that one bases his decision on faith is to make his faith choice the standard for himself and those who follow him. Hills chooses the text behind the KJV published by Scrivener.[86] He explains that there are several forms of the TR, and that he is guided by the "common faith" in choosing the correct one.[87] Waite says that God has preserved His words "in the TR which underlies the KJV."[88] He does not specify (as Hills does) which TR. He leaves his readers with the false impression that there is but one fixed TR, that which underlies the KJV. It is better to conclude that God has not chosen to preserve His words in one particular place, text-type, or manuscript, but through the thousands of manuscripts that agree so closely. A comparison of all the manuscripts shows incredible agreement, and where differences do occur, we are usually left with two good choices and so must determine the best reading and maintain the other as a variant reading, knowing that God's words are preserved in them. This enforces the fact that God has truly preserved His words for us today.

CONCLUSION

It is evident that the Lord has used unique events to preserve for us both the Alexandrian and Byzantine witnesses to the New Testament text. His providential hand is seen in both of these great traditions. As a result we have over 5,000 partial or whole Greek manuscripts available to study today. Just as clearly we can see His hand in preserving the over 3,000 manuscript witnesses to the Hebrew Old Testament text. He has used wars, "accidental" finds, professional manuscript hunters, biblical scholars both liberal and conservative, Greek Orthodox and Roman Catholic institutions and people, museums, universities, politicians, and many other means in preserving these copies of the biblical texts. Praise God for the preservation of His words in these manuscripts.

---

[1]Harry Gamble, "Codex," in *The Anchor Bible Dictionary*, ed. David Noel Freedman et al. (Garden City, NY: Doubleday, 1992), 1:1068.

[2]Frederick Fyvie Bruce, *The Books and the Parchments* (London: Pickering & Inglis Ltd., 1963), p. 117.

[3]Brotzman (Grand Rapids: Baker Books, 1994), p. 56.

[4]A. A. MacRae, "Text and Manuscripts of the Old Testament," in *The Zondervan Pictorial Encyclopedia of the Bible*, ed. By Merrill C. Tenney (Grand Rapids: Zondervan Publishing House, 1975), 5:691.

[5]Ibid., pp. 694-95.

[6]Ibid.. pp. 690-91.

[7]David Noel Freedman (ed.), *The Leningrad Codex, Facsimile Edition* (Grand Rapids: William B. Eerdmans Publishing Company, 1998), pp. x-xi.

[8]Ibid., p. xiv.

[9]Brotzman, pp. 56-57.

[10]Freedman, *Leningrad*, p. xv.

[11]Hershel Shanks, *The Dead Sea Scrolls After Forty Years* (Washington, D.C.: Biblical Archaeology Society, 1991), pp. 4-7.

[12]Geza Vermes, *The Complete Dead Sea Scrolls in English* (New York: The Penguin Press, 1997), p. 10.

[13]Martin Abegg, Jr., Peter Flint, and Eugene Ulrich, *The Dead Sea Scrolls Bible* (San Francisco: Harper San Francisco, 1999), pp. xiv-xv.

[14]Ibid., 16. Vermes, p. 11.

[15]Mark R. Norton, "Texts and Manuscripts of the Old Testament," in *The Origin of the Bible*, ed. Philip Wesley Comfort (Wheaton: Tyndale House Publishers, Inc., 1992), p. 162.

[16]Brotzman, pp. 95-96.

[17]John William Burgon, *The Traditional Text of the Holy Gospels Vindicated and Established* (London: George Bell and Sons, 1896, reprint Collingswood, N.J.: Dean Burgon Society Press, 1998), p 33.

[18]Maurice A. Robinson and William G. Pierpont, *The New Testament in the Original Greek According to the Byzantine/Majority Textform* (Atlanta: The Original Word Publishers, 1991), p. 20, note 26.

[19]Kurt and Barbara Aland, *The Text of the New Testament*, 2d ed. (Grand Rapids: Eerdmans, 1989), p. 79.

[20]Matthew Black and Robert Davidson, *Constantin Von Tischendorf and the Greek New Testament* (Glasgow: University of Glasgow Press, 1981),p. 39. See also Aland, *Text, p* 55. Moisés Silva even uses the phrase "supposed 'Alexandrian' text type" in "The Text of Galatians: Evidence From the Earliest Greek Manuscripts," in *Scribes and Scripture*, ed. David Alan Black (Winona Lake, IN: Eisenbrauns, 1992), p. 25.

[21]Many overlook or refuse to accept the fact that the Majority Text and the Received Text are quite different.

[22]See F. H. A. Scrivener's *The New Testament in the Original Greek According to the Text Followed in the Authorized Version* for the choice of Greek words used by the King James translators. The text behind the King James is not identical to the Received Text.

[23]D. A. Waite, for example, writes, "It is gross mis-information to say that the Textus Receptus began with an edition of Erasmus." *Fundamentalist Mis-information on Bible Versions* (Collingswood, NJ: The Bible for Today Press, 2000), p. 68. Waite does not agree with Edward F. Hills, "Hence although the Textus Receptus was based mainly on the manuscripts which Erasmus found at Basel, it also included readings taken from others to which he had access," p. 198. Again, "God works providentially through sinful and fallible human beings and therefore His providential guidance has its human as well as its divine side. And these human elements were evident in the first edition (1516) of the Textus Receptus," p. 202 in *The King James Version Defended.* 4th ed. (Des Moines: The Christian Research Press, 1984). Again Waite writes, "The '*Textus Receptus*' is a Greek Text of the New Testament that has been handed down from generation to generation. It had its origination in the Apostolic era, when the New Testament was written. Erasmus merely put these Traditional Text manuscripts into print in A.D. 1516," (*Mis-information*, p. 42). This disagrees with John Burgon, "Since the sixteenth century – we owe this also to the good Providence of God – one and the same text of the New Testament Scriptures has been generally received. I am not defending the 'Textus Receptus'; I am simply stating the fact of its existence. That it is without authority to bind, nay, that it calls for skillful revision in every part, is freely admitted. I do

not believe it to be absolutely identical with the true Traditional Text," *Traditional Text*, p. 15.

[24]David Alan Black, *New Testament Textual Criticism* (Grand Rapids: Baker Books, 1994), p. 64.

[25]E. G. Turner, *Greek Papyri* (Princeton: Princeton University Press, 1968), p. 33. Turner writes about the value of "non-literary" papyri: "For example, C. H. Roberts has pointed out that the words 'within you' (ἐντὸς ὑμῶν) in the saying of Jesus 'The Kingdom of God is within you' is a common turn of phrase in Greek popular speech. It means not 'inside you' in a physical sense, not even 'inside your number' in the sense of belonging to a group: but 'available', 'within reach'. A doctor asks for his cloak to be sent from the country so that he may have it 'within him', i.e. within reach." p. 151.

[26]*Early Manuscripts & Modern Translations of the New Testament* (Grand Rapids: Baker Books, 1990), pp. 39-40. Codex Sinaiticus is discussed below.

[27]Alfons Wouters, ed., *The Chester Beatty Codex AC 1499. A Graeco-Latin Lexicon on the Pauline Epistles and a Greek Grammar* (Leuven: Peeters, 1988), p. xii.

[28]*The Quest for the Original Text of the New Testament* (Grand Rapids: Baker Books, 1992), pp. 86-7.

[29]Black, *Constantin*, p. 58.

[30]M. M. Parvis, "New Testament Text," in *The Interpreter's Dictionary of the Bible*, ed. George Arthur Buttrick (New York: Abingdon Press, 1962), 4:596.

[31]*Quest*, p. 56.

[32]M. Black, *Constantin*, p. 20.

[33]*Defending the King James Bible* (Collingswood, N.J.: The Bible for Today Press, 1992), p. 60. David Sorenson agrees, p. 100 in *Touch Not the Unclean Thing* (Duluth, Minnesota: Northstar Baptist Ministries, 2001).

[34]*Secrets*, p. 37.

[35]Ibid, p. 44.

[36]M. Black, pp. 8-9.

[37]Matthew Black, pp. 10-11, quoting from Tischendorf's *When Were our Gospels Written* (London 1866), pp. 23-24. Some writers who favor the Received Text never cease to ridicule the idea that God could preserve His words in a wastebasket! The librarian had no idea of the value of these manuscripts. Indeed the pages in the basket were of the Septuagint, a Greek version of the Old Testament, but were part of the uncial Codex Sinaiticus which also contained the entire Greek New Testament.

[38]Bentley, pp. 93-94.

[39]Ibid, pp. 110-11.

[40]J. N. Birdsall, "The New Testament Text," in *The Cambridge History of the Bible,* ed. P. R. Ackroyd (Cambridge: The University Press, 1970), 1:360.

[41]Burgon, *Traditional*, 165. Bently, *Secrets*, pp. 75-87.

[42]Theodore Skeat, "The Codex Sinaiticus, The Codex Vaticanus, and Constantine," *The Journal of Theological Studies* 50 (1999), pp. 583-625.

[43]Aland, p. 109.

[44]Edward F. Hills, *The King James Version Defended,* 4th ed. (Des Moines: The Christian Research Press, 1984), p. 171.

[45]*Text*, pp. 47-8.

[46]William Barry, "The Renaissance," in *The Catholic Encyclopedia*, ed. Charles G. Herbermann et al. (New York: Robert Appleton Company, 1911), xii: 766.

[47]Skeat, pp. 583-625.

[48]*Text*, p. 53.

[49]*Text*, p. 65.

[50]Ibid, p. 61.

[51]H. D. M. Spence-Jones, *The Golden Age of the Church* (London: Society for Promoting Christian Knowledge, 1906), p. 292.

[52]The Byzantine princess Theophano "scandalized the German inhabitants by taking baths (then considered unhealthy by the westerners) . . . . And only a few years later Theophano's cousin, Maria Argyra, shocked the good Peter Damiani, an ascetic Italian monk, by introducing the use of forks to the city of Venice." Deno. J. Geanakoplos, *Byzantine East and Latin West: Two Worlds of Christendom in Middle Ages and Renaissance* (New York: Barnes & Noble, 1966), p. 39.

[53]Birdsall, pp. 312-13.

[54]*Traditional*, p. 174.

[55]Birdsall, p. 315.

[56]Geanakoplos, *Byzantine East*, pp. 115, 116, 126, 150.

[57]Ibid, pp. 178-9.

[58]R. C. Jebb, "The Classical Renaissance," in *The Cambridge Modern History*, ed. A. W. Ward et al. (New York: The MacMillan Company, 1907), 1:552.

[59]Arthur Penrhyn Stanley, *Lectures on the History of the Eastern Church* (New York: Charles Scribner's Sons, 1884), p. 338.

[60]Harry Sturz, *The Byzantine Text-Type and New Testament Textual Criticism* (Nashville: Thomas Nelson Publishers, 1984), pp. 61-62. Gordon Fee ferociously disagrees. See his review of Sturz' book in *The Journal of the Evangelical Theological Society* 28 (1985): pp. 239-242.

[61]*Text*, 49.

[62]D. C. Parker, "Codex Ephraimi Rescriptus," in *The Anchor Bible Dictionary*, ed. David N. Freedman et al. (Garden City, NY: Doubleday, 1992), 1:1073.

[63]C. C. Tarelli, "Erasmus's Manuscripts of the Gospels," *The Journal of Theological Studies* XLIV (1943): p. 159.

[64]William H. P. Hatch, *The Principal Uncial Manuscripts of the New Testament* (Chicago: The University of Chicago Press, 1939), plate XXXIII.

[65]Hatch, *Facsimiles* (Cambridge, MA.: Harvard University Press, 1951).

[66]F. H. Scrivener, *Six Lectures on the Text of the New Testament* (Cambridge: Deighton, Bell, and Co., 1875), p. 83.

[67]Aland, pp. 129-38.

[68]Aland, p. 142.

[69]Birdsall, p. 321.

[70]Ibid, p. 318.

[71]Ibid, pp. 343-44.

[72]Jay E. Epp and Gordon D. Fee, *Studies in the Theory and Method of New Testament Textual Criticism* (Grand Rapids: William B. Eerdmans Publishing Company, 1993), pp. 344-59.

[73]There are nearly 2,000 differences between the Received Text and the Majority Text. Some continue to write as though they are almost synonymous. For detail differences see *The Interlinear Bible*, ed. Jay P. Green, Sr. (Lafayette, IN: Sovereign Grace Publishers, 1986), pp. 967-74.

[74]Jebb, p. 570.

[75]Jean-Claude Margolin, "The Epistle to the Romans (Chapter 11) According to the Versions and/or Commentaries of Valla, Colet, Lefèvre, and Erasmus," in *The Bible in the Sixteenth Century*, ed. David Steinmetz (Durham: Duke University Press, 1990), p. 141.

[76]J. A. Froude, *Life and Letters of Erasmus* (New York: Charles Scribner's Sons, 1912), p. 253.

[7]As does David H. Sorenson in *Touch Not the Unclean Thing* (Duluth, MN: Northstar Baptist Ministries, 2001), p. 193.

[78]Spence-Jones, pp. 302-3.

[79]B. Colgrave, "St. Theodore of Canterbury," in *The New Catholic Encyclopedia*, Editorial Staff at the Catholic University of America (New York: McGraw-Hill Book Company, 1967), 14:17.

[80]Hank de Jonge, "Novum Testamentum A Nobis Versum: The Essence of Erasmus' Edition of the New Testament," *The Journal of Theological Studies* 35 (1984): pp. 394-413.

[81]Preserved Smith, *Erasmus* (New York: Harper & Brothers, Publishers, 1923), 163. See also Metzger, p. 269, note 99.

[82]De Jonge, p. 404, footnote 40.

[83]*The Age of Erasmus* (New York: Russell & Russell, 1963), p. 144.

[84]*The King James Version Defended*, p. 193.

[85]Frederic Kenyon, *Our Bible and the Ancient Manuscripts* (London: Eyre & Spottiswoode, 1958), p. 55.

[86]See footnote 22.

[87]*King James*, p. 223.

[88]D. A. Waite, *Defending The King James Bible* (Collingswood, NJ: The Bible for Today Press, 1992), p. 48.

BIBLIOGRAPHY

Abegg, Martin, Jr., Peter Flint, and Eugene Ulrich. *The Dead Sea Scrolls Bible*. San Francisco: Harper San Francisco, 1999.

Aland, Kurt and Barbara. *The Text of the New Testament*. 2d ed. Trans. by Erroll F. Rhodes. Grand Rapids: Eerdmans, 1989.

Allen, P. S. *The Age of Erasmus*. New York: Russell & Russell, 1963.

Barry, William. "The Renaissance." Vol. XII/ pp. 765-69 in *The Catholic Encyclopedia*. Edited by Charles G. Herbermann et al. New York: Robert Appleton Company, 1911.

Bentley, James. *Secrets of Mount Sinai*. Garden City, NY: Doubleday & Company, Inc., 1986.

Birdsall, J. N. "The New Testament Text." Vol. 1/pp. 308-76 in *The Cambridge History of The Bible*. Edited by P. R. Ackroyd. Cambridge: The University Press, 1970.

Black, David Alan. *New Testament Textual Criticism*. Grand Rapids: Baker Books, 1994.

Black, Matthew and Robert Davidson. *Constantin Von Tischendorf and the Greek New Testament*. Glasgow: University of Glasgow Press, 1981.

Brotzman, Ellis R. *Old Testament Textual Criticism*. Grand Rapids: Baker Books, 1994.

Bruce, Frederick Fyvie. *The Books and the Parchments*. London: Pickering & Inglis Ltd., 1963.

Burgon, John William. *The Traditional Text of the Holy Gospels Vindicated and Established*. London: George Bell and Sons, 1896, reprint Collingswood, NJ: Dean Burgon Society Press, 1998.

Colgrave, B. "St. Theodore of Canterbury." Vol. 14/p. 17 in *The New Catholic Encyclopedia*. Editorial Staff at the Catholic University of America. New York: McGraw-Hill Book Company, 1967.

Comfort, Philip Wesley. *Early Manuscripts & Modern Translations of the New Testament*. Grand Rapids: Baker Books, 1990.

_____. *The Quest for the Original Text of the New Testament*. Grand Rapids: Baker Books, 1992.

De Jonge, Henk Jan. "Novum Testamentum A Nobis Versum: The Essence of Erasmus' Edition of the New Testament." *The Journal of Theological Studies* 35 (1984): 394-413.

Epp, Jay Eldon and Gordon D. Fee. *Studies in the Theory and Method of New Testament Textual Criticism*. Grand Rapids: William B. Eerdmans Publishing Company, 1993.

Freedman, David Noel, ed. *The Leningrad Codex, Facsimile Edition*. Grand Rapids: William B. Eerdmans Publishing Company, 1998.

Froude, J. A. *Life and Letters of Erasmus*. New York: Charles Scribner's Sons, 1912.

Gamble, Harry Y. "Codex." Vol. 1/pp. 1067-69 in *The Anchor Bible Dictionary*. Edited by David Noel Freedman et al. Garden City, NY: Doubleday, 1992.

Geanakoplos, Deno J. *Byzantine East and Latin West: Two Worlds of Christendom in Middle Ages and Renaissance*. New York: Barnes & Noble, 1966.

Green, Jay P., Sr. (ed.) *The Interlinear Bible*. Lafayette, IN: Sovereign Grace Publishers, 1986.

Greenlee, J. H. "Text and Manuscripts of the New Testament." Vol. 5/pp. 697-713 in *The Zondervan Pictorial Encyclopedia of the Bible*. ed. Merrill C. Tenney. Grand Rapids: Zondervan Publishing House, 1975.

Hatch, William Henry Paine. *Facsimiles and Descriptions of Minuscule Manuscripts of the New Testament*. Cambridge, MA: Harvard University Press, 1951.

_____. *The Principal Uncial Manuscripts of the New Testament*. Chicago: The University of Chicago Press, 1939.

Hills, Edward F. *The King James Version Defended*. 4th ed. Des Moines: The Christian Research Press, 1984.

Jebb, R. C. "The Classical Renaissance." Vol. 1/pp. 532-584 in *The Cambridge Modern History*. Edited by A. W. Ward et al. New York: The MacMillan Company, 1907.

Kenyon, Frederic. *Our Bible and the Ancient Manuscripts*. London: Eyre & Spottiswoode, 1958.

MacRae, A. A. "Text and Manuscripts of the Old Testament." Vol. 5/pp. 683-697 in *The Zondervan Pictorial Encyclopedia of the Bible*. ed. Merrill C. Tenney. Grand Rapids: Zondervan Publishing House, 1975.

Margolin, Jean-Claude. "The Epistle to the Romans (Chapter 11) According to the Versions and /or Commentaries of Valla, Colet, Lefèvre, and Erasmus." Pp. 136-66 in *The Bible in the Sixteenth Century*. Edited by David C. Steinmetz. Durham: Duke University Press, 1990.

Metzger, Bruce M. *The Text of the New Testament*. 2d ed. New York: Oxford University Press, 1968.

Norton, Mark R. "Texts and Manuscripts of the Old Testament." pp. 151-178 in *The Origin of the Bible*. Edited by Philip Wesley Comfort. Wheaton: Tyndale House Publishers, Inc., 1992.

Parker, D. C. "Codex Ephraimi Rescriptus." Vol. 1/pp. 1073-74 in *The Anchor Bible Dictionary*. Edited by David Noel Freedman et al. Garden City, N.Y.: Doubleday, 1992.

Parvis, M. M. "New Testament Text." Vol. 4/pp. 594-614 in *The Interpreter's Dictionary of the Bible*. Edited by George Arthur Buttrick. New York: Abingdon Press, 1962.

Robinson, Maurice A. and William G. Pierpont. *The New Testament in the Original Greek According to the Byzantine/Majority Textform*. Atlanta: The Original Word Publishers, 1991.

Scrivener, F. H. *Six Lectures on the Text of the New Testament*. Cambridge: Deighton, Bell, and Co., 1875.

Shanks, Hershel. *The Dead Sea Scrolls After Forty Years*. Washington, D.C.: Biblical Archaeology Society, 1991.

Silva, Moisés. "The Text of Galatians: Evidence From the Earliest Greek Manuscripts." pp. 17-25 in *Scribes and Scripture*. Edited by David Alan Black. Winona Lake, Indiana: Eisenbrauns, 1992.

Skeat, Theodore. "The Codex Sinaiticus, The Codex Vaticanus, and Constantine." *The Journal of Theological Studies* 50 (1999): 583-625.

Smith, Preserved. *Erasmus*. New York: Harper & Brothers, Publishers, 1923.

Sorenson, David H. *Touch Not the Unclean Thing*. Duluth, MN: Northstar Baptist Ministries, 2001.

Spence-Jones, H. D. M. *The Golden Age of the Church*. London: Society for Promoting Christian Knowledge, 1906.

Stanley, Arthur Penrhyn. *Lectures on the History of the Eastern Church*. New York: Charles Scribner's Sons, 1884.

Sturz, Harry A. *The Byzantine Text-Type and New Testament Textual Criticism*. Nashville: Thomas Nelson Publishers, 1984.

Tarelli, C. C. "Erasmus's Manuscripts of the Gospels." *The Journal of Theological Studies* XLIV (1943): 155-62.

Turner, E. G. *Greek Papyri*. Princeton: Princeton University Press, 1968.

Vermes, Geza. *The Complete Dead Sea Scrolls in English*. New York: The Penguin Press, 1997.

Waite, D. A. *Defending the King James Bible*. Collingswood, NJ: The Bible for Today Press, 1992.

_____. *Fundamentalist Mis-information on Bible Versions*. Collingswood, NJ: The Bible for Today Press, 2000.

Wouters, Alfons (ed.). *The Chester Beatty Codex AC 1499. A Graeco-Latin Lexicon on the Pauline Epistles and a Greek Grammar*. Leuven: Peeters, 1988.

ARE COPIES RELIABLE?

Keith E Gephart

INTRODUCTION

In 1677 the Baptist authors of *The London Confession of Faith* stated that "the Old Testament in *Hebrew* . . . and the New Testament in *Greek* . . . being immediately inspired by God, and by His singular care and Providence kept pure in all Ages, are therefore authentical."[1] In the nineteenth century, however, a well-known liberal scholar made this statement:

> We will never be able to attain the sacred writings as they gladdened the eyes of those who first saw them, and rejoiced the hearts of those who first heard them. If the external words of the original were inspired, it does not profit us. We are cut off from them forever. Interposed between us and them is the tradition of centuries and even millenniums.[2]

Both of these statements cannot be true. The contributors to this book argue forcefully that God has indeed preserved His Word. But a review of the materials published on the topic of preservation reveals that there is much disagreement about the method God used and which existing materials can be identified as those that God preserved.

Recently I received a manuscript by e-mail from a fundamentalist friend. He is a very good man who stands with me on most biblical positions. I find that his perspective on the textual-translation issue is typical of a multitude today. He claims that the "King James Only" controversy is really a battle over "two different Bibles." He assumes that the Textus Receptus is the faithfully preserved manuscript tradition and that anything else is a perverted tradition which ought to be anathema to all Bible believers. He then proceeds to vilify two men, Westcott and Hort, attempting to show that they were liberals, unsaved, worshippers of demons, and "gross modernistic heretics."[3] Then he concludes that the textual work which they have done is necessarily tainted and corrupted by their liberal bias.[4]

This is a common view, but we need to determine whether it reflects the facts. As we make a brief survey of the work of textual collators and critics through the centuries we hope to show that many have played an important role in this process. Some were Roman Catholic, some liberal, and some conservative. However, we must evaluate their work objectively on the basis of the finished product, not on the basis of our preconceived ideas. Some of those honored by proponents of the Textus Receptus or Byzantine Majority Text[5] were far worse theologically than commonly acknowledged, and some of those criticized by the same people were not nearly as bad as commonly understood. The bottom line is that God has remarkably preserved His word in whatever tradition one follows. It is a commonly recognized fact that 80-85 percent of all the manuscript evidence is in total agreement even on such matters as spelling and punctuation.[6] The majority of the variant readings are quite trivial and do not at all affect the meaning of the verses in question. It is true that there are numerous verses (but an extremely small percentage overall) whose meanings are affected by the variants; some of these variants do affect the theology of those particular verses. But even in these instances, our doctrine is not affected since there are so many other verses which teach the doctrine in question.

THE OLD TESTAMENT TEXT

We seldom hear much discussion on the text of the Old Testament; its accuracy is astounding. Robert Dick Wilson, a conservative scholar with remarkable academic credentials, noted that there are few variant readings in the Old Testament manuscripts supported by more than one out of the 200 to 400 manuscripts in which each book is found. This excludes the difference between the full or defective writing of the vowels, which generally does not affect the meaning of the text.[7] This may seem to be an overstatement. Ernst Wurthwein recognizes the existence of a large number of variants but states, "A relatively simple picture can be given on the whole for 𝕸 (Masoretic text) whose manuscript variants are found in Kennicott, de Rossi and Ginsburg, because real variants are rare."[8] William Henry Green, nineteenth century Princeton seminary professor of Old Testament, shows that we have no other ancient work which has been preserved as accurately as the Old Testament.[9]

THE NEW TESTAMENT TEXT

The accuracy of the New Testament text is also remarkable—especially when compared with other ancient documents. The number of extant manuscripts containing all or part of the Greek NT continues to grow with new discoveries. It is generally conceded that there are well over 5000 known manuscripts. It is the most remarkably preserved book in the ancient world. Many of these manuscripts are very close in time to their originals. Compare Caesar's *Gallic Wars* with 10 extant manuscripts, the oldest 900 years later than the original; Thucydides' *History of the Peloponnesian War* with 8 manuscripts about 1,300 years later; Herodotus' *History* with only 8 extant manuscripts again 1300 years later than the original; Tacitus' *Histories* and *Annals* have only two manuscripts, one from the ninth century and one from the eleventh.[10] The earliest manuscript of the New Testament is a portion of the eighteenth chapter of the Gospel of John from the early second century. F. F. Bruce notes that the ink on the original would hardly have been dry by that time![11] In 1994 a German scholar named Carsten Peter Thiede discovered that certain papyrus fragments of the Gospel of Matthew kept in the Magdalen College Library at Oxford, England may actually date to about 70 A.D. If his findings prove accurate, these would become the earliest surviving fragments yet discovered from the New Testament.[12] The student of New Testament textual criticism, in comparison with other textual critics, is almost embarrassed by the wealth and quality of material available for his work. In fact, John H. Skilton has remarked:

> Surely if scholars justly feel that they have essentially the original text of classical works, which have comparatively few manuscript witnesses, may we not feel certain that in the vast and varied company of extant witnesses to the New Testament text (among which different early textual traditions are represented), the original text in practically every detail has been transmitted to us?[13]

One of the greatest textual critics of the twentieth century noted:

> The Christian can take the whole Bible in his hand and say without fear or hesitation that he holds in it the true Word of God, handed down without essential loss from generation to generation throughout the centuries.[14]

THE NEED FOR TEXTUAL CRITICISM

Then why do we need textual criticism at all? Is it necessary? Maybe it is even corrupt and damaging to our cause. Many believers maintain an extremely negative attitude toward textual criticism. That negative attitude is prompted by the fact that the theological position of some modern textual critics has been liberal and antagonistic toward supernatural Christianity, including the inspiration and inerrancy of the Scriptures. However, in the very nature of the case, textual criticism is mandated. Not only do we have various manuscript traditions, no two manuscripts within any tradition agree on every reading. Our copies are not inspired in the same sense as the originals, and the Lord did not guarantee that copyists and translators would never make mistakes. They were human and have manifested human frailties. Anyone who compares various readings and makes decisions concerning the best readings is practicing textual criticism. In fact, the publication of *The Greek*

New Testament According to the Majority Text[15] is evidence that theological conservatives can approach textual criticism reverently. Criticism was practiced by Erasmus, by the translators of the King James Version, and by anyone who chooses one manuscript tradition over another.

Criticism does not mean sitting in judgment upon the Bible. *The American Heritage Collegiate Dictionary* defines criticism as "scientific investigation of literary documents (such as the Bible) in regard to such matters as origin, texts, composition and history."[16] As applied to the text, criticism refers to the consideration of all available evidence in an effort to determine, in so far as possible the reading of the original documents of Scripture. Of textual criticism Green writes:

> Its function is to determine by a careful examination of all the evidence bearing upon the case the condition of the sacred text, the measure of its correspondence with or divergence from the exact language of the inspired penmen, and by means of all available helps to remove the errors which may have gained admission to it from whatever cause, and to restore the text to its pristine purity as it came from the hands of the original writers.[17]

Reverent textual criticism is the friend of the believer. For as John R. Rice noted, the problem of copying, translating, preaching, and interpreting the Bible is left "to frail, fallible men, led and empowered by the Holy Spirit, but always, on the whole, preserving His word forever."[18] Did Rice then argue for the primacy of a particular translation of Scriptures? Indeed not. In fact, he said that "each translation is primarily the Word of God," and that "translations by reverent, responsible groups of scholars are more reliable than one-man translations." Rice went so far as to say that "all the translations together are the Word of God" and that the same is true of all the manuscript copies.[19] Skilton noted that the believer will engage in textual criticism not "in spite of his view of the Bible, but because of it. Believing that every word of the original manuscripts was breathed by the Holy Spirit, the consistent Christian scholar will be eager to recover every word of those originals."[20] Even though he knows that "no doctrine rises or falls with a disputed reading and that most variations are relatively unimportant, the conservative will nevertheless realize that not one jot or tittle of the law of God is actually unimportant (Matt. 5:18) and that our Lord held that even with regard to a brief statement in the Old Testament the Scripture cannot be broken (John 10:34, 35)."[21] Therefore, Christian scholars must strive to recover "the exact form of words and phrases used in the original."[22]

The believer cannot rest on the subjective inner witness of the Holy Spirit in order to determine the proper reading of Scripture. Rigorous study is required. Nor may he rest simply in the authoritative pronouncements of modern-day experts, whether real or supposed, as to the accuracy of a particular reading or manuscript tradition. There are numerous examples from the past of such authoritative pronouncements.[23]

SURVEY OF THE HISTORY OF TEXTUAL CRITICISM

The Early Period: up to A.D. 325

It is necessary to take a brief survey of the textual criticism of the New Testament.[24]   In the Early Period the making of books was a laborious process of hand-copying by scribes. These scribes either copied visually from an exemplar or wrote as they listened to readers dictate from a "master" copy. Either method was difficult and exhausting and was prone to manifold errors. Contrary to what we might have expected, much of the copying was done rather casually and unsystematically, and the result was the "largely unintentional creation of various readings."[25]   In this period there was some "conscious, though very elementary, selection and editorial revision."[26]   Most of the textual problems which require resolution arose in this period. Persecution complicated matters; many manuscripts were destroyed and the work of copyists was not encouraged by many rulers.

The Middle Period: 325-1516

Circumstances changed during the Middle Period (roughly 325-1516). The "conversion" of Constantine made Christianity the officially recognized religion of the Roman Empire. Copying centers arose in various parts of the empire in order to disseminate the sacred Scriptures. Generally, the work during this period was more careful and was much more extensive, but still extremely laborious. Two important circumstances had profound influence upon the developing form of the New Testament text after A.D. 400. The demise of the Alexandrian patriarchate and the rapid rise and spread of Islam throughout northern Africa greatly diminished the influence and spread of the kind of text used in that region. Second, Latin became the dominant language in the West; production of Greek texts practically ceased there. Because of these two circumstances, the transmission of the Greek New Testament occurred largely in the Eastern church.[27] The number of confused Old Latin readings had led to the adoption of another "authorized" translation for the West—the Latin Vulgate by Jerome beginning in 384.

Jerome's work was not well received initially. When he was asked by Damasus to work on the Latin Bible, he at first set about to make a simple revision of the Gospels in the Old Latin. When Jerome moved to the Psalms and other Old Testament books he discovered a large number of irreconcilable differences between the Hebrew and the Septuagint translation of the Hebrew. Therefore, he abandoned the revision and began a fresh translation. His work continued through twenty years.

Augustine strongly opposed Jerome's efforts. Although Augustine was a brilliant scholar and had memorized huge portions of Scripture in the Latin, he did not know Hebrew and had a limited knowledge of Greek. Because Augustine considered the Septuagint to be inspired, at times he went so far as to correct the Hebrew by the Greek! He used many of the same arguments which are so popular today for the exclusive use of the Textus Receptus or the King James Version: The Septuagint was without error; the Holy Spirit had given its authors unique understanding and ability in producing their translation. How could Jerome venture to correct these readings? Church tradition had supported the readings in the Septuagint for generations; how could Jerome change them? Moreover, the new version would create public unrest and would undermine confidence in the Word of God. Besides, the Septuagint readings were familiar to the ears and tongues of the people.[28]

It took about two centuries for Jerome's Vulgate to become the dominant Latin translation. Over the centuries of its dominance the Vulgate become thoroughly corrupted and confused. Several vain attempts were made to purify the text. Today there are more extant manuscripts of the Vulgate than of the Greek New Testament—over 8,000! Eventually, the Roman Catholic hierarchy under Pope Sixtus V, in 1590, and then under Pope Clement VIII in 1592 made officially sanctioned editions of the Vulgate which could not be altered nor spoken against under the threat of excommunication. Clement's "bull" hindered the serious advance of the textual criticism of the Vulgate for centuries.[29] In fact, translations into other languages were based upon the Vulgate readings and not upon the readings of the original languages.[30]

The Period of Printed Greek New Testaments: 1516-1633

The crucial turning point in the history of the text was the invention of the printing press by Johannes Guttenberg in 1450. Now the work could continue with less labor, more accuracy, and vastly increased speed. This invention introduced the third period of Printed Greek New Testaments that extended roughly from 1516-1633. However, a printed edition of the Greek New Testament was not the first major product of Guttenberg's printing press; Jerome's Vulgate has that distinction. In fact, over the next fifty years at least one hundred editions of the Vulgate were issued by various presses. The first edition of the complete Hebrew Old Testament was printed by the Soncino press in the Lombardy region of northern Italy in 1488. Bibles were printed in several vernacular languages of western Europe before 1500, but only a few short extracts of the New Testament in Greek appeared before the year 1514.

There are two primary reasons for this delay. The production of Greek fonts was extremely difficult and expensive. There were at least two hundred different characters for alternate forms of letters and many combinations of *two or more letters*. But, the principal cause for delay was the prestige of Jerome's Latin Vulgate. A publication of the Greek New Testament would provide scholars a tool with which to critique and evaluate the accuracy of the official Latin Bible of the church, a version considered by many to be inspired and inerrant.

Erasmus was not the first to print an edition of the Greek New Testament. In 1514 the first of six volumes of the Complutensian Polyglot[31] was the Greek New Testament with a Greek glossary. However, the last volume of the Old Testament did not appear until 1517, and the entire project did not attain the sanction of Pope Leo X until March 1520; even then distribution did not occur until about 1522. Meanwhile Froben, a printer at Basle, Switzerland, heard of the work of Francisco Ximenes de Cisneros (1437-1517), the cardinal primate of Spain, on the Complutensian Polyglot and determined to anticipate its publication by hiring Desiderius Erasmus of Rotterdam (1469-1536), the finest Greek scholar of the day. These men agreed on this project in March of 1515; Erasmus began his work in July of 1515, finishing by March of 1516! Such speed was detrimental to both thorough research and accuracy. Erasmus had only seven very late manuscripts (none earlier than the eleventh century) for his research and primarily relied upon two of them.[32] He simply entered corrections in these manuscripts where he believed necessary and sent them to the printer for typesetting. In fact, Erasmus himself admitted that his edition had been "thrown together rather than edited."[33] Erasmus' single copy of the book of Revelation was missing its last leaf containing the final six verses of the book; for these verses as well as for a few others throughout the book Erasmus translated from the Latin Vulgate into Greek! The result was the invention of some Greek readings found nowhere else in any Greek manuscripts.[34] The Baptist Greek scholar A. T. Robertson remarked, "If Erasmus had known that he was working for the ages, instead of getting ahead of Ximenes, he might have taken more pains to edit his Greek Testament."[35] Moreover, the printed edition contained hundreds of typographical errors; Scrivener declares that Erasmus' first edition was "in that respect the most faulty book I know."[36]

It is important to recognize these facts about the relatively poor quality of the initial work done by Erasmus, especially in light of the constant biting criticisms made against the quality of the so-called Alexandrian text. We must also recognize that Erasmus was until his death a Roman Catholic by conviction; he never renounced the foundational doctrines of his church. There is a remarkable inconsistency in those who criticize Westcott and Hort for having Roman Catholic sympathies (while not being Roman Catholic) and who remain silent concerning Erasmus' religious convictions. Erasmus did criticize the priestly establishment for some of their immoral lifestyle, but staunchly remained within the Catholic faith and refused to stand with Luther and others within the Reformation.

But even Erasmus was the brunt of suspicion and hostility from many—especially from those within the church. Erasmus had prepared a fresh Latin translation along with the Greek text. (In fact, his *Annotations on the New Testament*—philological[37] comments on the Vulgate—were his original primary objective.)[38] Many were incensed that his Latin translation differed from Jerome's *Vulgate in* numerous readings. A man name Sutor stated,

> If in one point the Vulgate were in error the entire authority of Holy Scripture would collapse, love and faith would be extinguished, heresies and schisms would abound, blasphemy would be committed against the Holy Spirit, the authority of theologians would be shaken, and indeed the Catholic Church would collapse from the foundation.[39]

Erasmus, in arguing with another incensed person, stated, "You must distinguish between Scripture, the translation of Scripture, and the transmission of both. What will you do with the errors of copyists?"[40] Erasmus was truly a textual critic; he corrected the text, introduced various readings, and retranslated passages from the Greek into a new Latin version. The Catholic Church had been using the Latin Vulgate for over 1,000 years. It was considered sacrilege to use a different translation or even to rely on a different Greek text! One priest wrote to Erasmus:

> Now I differ from you on this question of truth and integrity, and claim that these are qualities of the Vulgate edition that we have in common use. For it is not reasonable that the whole church, which has always used this edition and still both approves and uses it, should for all these centuries have been wrong.[41]

Somehow, these ancient arguments sound very modern. Priests were even more angry at his numerous caustic comments against them found in his philological notes.

Erasmus produced four more editions of his Greek New Testament in which he made corrections and improvements (1519, 1522, 1527, 1535). His fourth edition is considered to be his definitive one. It contains three parallel columns: the Greek, the Latin Vulgate, and his own Latin version. Erasmus wisely decided to make use of Ximenes' Polyglot Bible in making numerous revisions in his own text, including about ninety within the book of

Revelation. Because Erasmus' edition was less expensive and more convenient in its form, it attained wider circulation and exerted a much greater influence than did the Complutensian Polyglot.

Many editions followed those of Erasmus. I will list only some of the more significant. The Aldine press published the first edition of the entire Bible in Greek in 1518 at Venice; this edition slavishly followed Erasmus' first edition—even including many of the typographical errors![42] The first new edition was that of Colinaeus (Simon de Colines) in 1534; this edition utilized the Complutensian text and some additional Greek manuscripts and manifested numerous differences from Erasmus. Nicolinis de Sabio produced a beautiful pocket-sized edition in two volumes at Venice in 1538.

Robert Estienne (or Stephanus, Stephens), a well-known printer and publisher in Paris, exercised the greatest influence during the sixteenth century. He issued four significant editions of the Greek New Testament in 1546, 1549, 1550, and 1551 (the last edition at Geneva). The text was chiefly that of Erasmus' fifth edition of 1535 with some use of the Complutensian and of fifteen additional manuscripts. Stephanus' third edition in 1550 had a revised text and marginal variants from his additional sources. This was the first edition to utilize a critical apparatus. With only slight modifications, this is the edition which has become today's "received text." Stephanus' fourth edition was the first to utilize our modern verse divisions. It is significant to note that this work was done with only about 1/100 of the Greek manuscript evidence which we now have available to us; moreover, we have many thousands of additional readings of church fathers and of various versions.

Theodore de Beze (Beza, 1519-1605), who was John Calvin's successor in Geneva, published nine editions of the Greek New Testament between 1565 and 1604 (a tenth appeared posthumously in 1611). Five of these were reprints; the editions of 1565, 1582, 1588-89, and 1598 were independent. These editions contained his own Latin version, the Latin Vulgate, and some textual information taken from several Greek manuscripts collated by Beza and from some collated by Henry Stephanus, son of Robert Stephanus. His Greek text differs little from that of Stephanus' fourth edition of 1551. However, Beza's work greatly popularized and strengthened the Textus Receptus. The King James translators of 1611 made liberal use of his 1588-89 and 1598 editions.

The greatest influence during the seventeenth century was that of the publishing house of Elzevir in the Netherlands. Bonaventura Elzevir and his nephew Abraham published a small New Testament in 1624 which was based upon Beza's first edition (1565) and upon that of Stephanus. They issued a second edition in 1633 in which they put a publishing "blurb": "Therefore thou hast the text (*textum*) now received (*receptum*) by all, in which we give nothing altered or corrupt." From these words we derive *Textus Receptus* or the Received Text.[43] This Elzevir text of 1633 became the standard for the European continent, as did the 1550 text of Stephanus for Britain. The Elzevirs published seven editions altogether.

The Period of Collection and Collation: 1633-1831

The fourth period in the history of the transmission of the New Testament text extends from 1633 to 1831 and primarily concerns the collection and collation of materials—Greek manuscripts, readings of versions (translations), quotations of the church "Fathers," and readings in the ancient church lectionaries.[44] Just as it is impossible in the space of a brief chapter to list all of the editions of the Greek New Testament, so also it is impossible to mention all of those who made significant contributions in this area. It is important to note that in most cases the TR was still followed even though many began listing variant readings in their critical apparatuses. Many were afraid to insert actual changes into the text because of the revered status of the TR and the likely criticism and even ostracism they would receive.

In 1657 Brian Walton, the Bishop of Chester, in the fifth volume of his London Polyglot added the readings of Codex A (Alexandrinus); in his sixth volume he included various readings from fifteen other manuscripts (in addition to the sixteen already used by Stephanus). For this service to the body of Christ Walton was attacked by another good brother, Dr. John Owen, the Puritan Dean of Christ Church, Oxford. Moreover, in 1667 the London Polyglot was placed on the Index of the Librorum Prohibitorum.[45] The Dean of Christ's Church and later Bishop of Oxford, John Fell, published a Greek Testament in 1675 which was based on the 1633 Elzevir edition; Fell's edition included a critical apparatus which gave readings from over one-hundred Greek manuscripts and from the Coptic and Gothic versions. But, the edition which is the basis of today's TR is John Mill's edition of 1707. Although Mill merely reprinted Stephanus' third edition with only a few changes, he did make a significant new contribution in his critical apparatus by using seventy-eight new manuscripts, including some very old ones. He also utilized variant readings from several ancient versions including the Syriac Peshitta, the Old Latin, and the Vulgate. Mill was the first to collect a substantial amount of evidence from the writings of the Fathers. Mill's efforts were attacked by Dr. Daniel Whitby, Rector of St. Edmund's, Salisbury. Whitby contended that the large number of variant readings collected by Mill was the equivalent of tampering with the text.[46]

The first to actually depart from readings in the TR in the preparation of an edition of the Greek text (between 1709 and 1719) was Dr. Edward Wells.

His edition departed from the Elzevir text two hundred ten times. The example of Wells encouraged Richard Bentley to go even further in his critical apparatuses. Bentley, Master of Trinity College and one of the greatest scholars of that age,[47] had the ambitious goal[48] of publishing a Greek and Latin text restored to their conditions in the fourth century. Bentley was overcome by the prodigious amount of work and died before he could accomplish his goal. Bentley believed that Stephanus' edition had become to the Protestants what the Vulgate of Jerome had become to the Roman Catholics. Meanwhile a Greek-English diglot edition was edited by Daniel Mace, a Presbyterian minister at Newbury. Mace selected readings from Mill's apparatus which he believed to be superior to the TR. Although Mace seemed to suffer from both pride and excess, he did propose some interesting suggested readings. However, as usual, his efforts were "either vehemently attacked or quietly ignored" so that his work was soon practically forgotten.[49]

With the work of Johann Albrecht Bengel came a turning point in the history of the textual criticism of the New Testament. Bengel was a staunch conservative and a Pietist. He strongly held to the plenary inspiration of the Scriptures. However, his faith was disturbed by the more than 30,000 variants which Mill had published in his edition of the New Testament. Bengel determined to study this issue thoroughly in order to determine whether these variant readings undermined the convictions of himself and others concerning the inerrancy and authority of the Bible. Through his extensive study this brilliant and thorough scholar determined that the variants were fewer in number than could be expected and that they did not "shake any article of evangelic doctrine."[50] Bengel published an important edition of the Greek New Testament in 1734. Although using primarily the TR, he did make a few changes in the text. Moreover, Bengel developed five classes of marginal readings: genuine readings, those better than the text, those just as good, those not as good, and those which ought to be rejected. As the result of his massive labor, Bengel is often considered the father of modern textual criticism. He recognized the need to divide manuscripts into groups (sometimes called families) and also noted that manuscripts needed to be weighed and not merely counted. Bengel also favored the principle that usually the more difficult reading is to be preferred.[51]

It is extremely important to remember that Bengel was always a very strict conservative in his theology. Yet, it is he that developed many of the critical principles followed by the majority of textual critics today — principles often criticized as being "liberal" and "unbelieving." Even in his own day Bengel was treated by many as though he were an enemy of the Scriptures. One of his opponents was J. J. Wettstein of Basle, Switzerland. He held (as do many today) that all the most ancient manuscripts were contaminated and that the later ones used by Erasmus and his followers were more reliable. Wettstein collated as many as one-hundred manuscripts and eventually published (1751-52) a Greek New Testament in two volumes based on the Elzevir text and containing various readings and much illustrative material from classical and Jewish sources. He was the first to use the modern method of notation of manuscripts by using capital letters for uncials (manuscripts written in all capital Greek letters) and Arabic numerals for minuscules (manuscripts written in Greek "longhand" in smaller case letters). However, even Wettstein himself was regarded as having a liberal agenda and he was "deposed from his pastorate and driven into exile."[52]

Of course, not all early textual collators and critics were conservatives. J. S. Semler further developed Wettstein's methodology and classified Greek documents into a threefold classification of 1) Alexandrian, 2) Eastern, and 3) Western. Many regard Semler as "the father of German rationalism." It was shortly after the work of Semler that two English scholars took steps to abandon some of the readings of the TR in their critical editions of the New Testament: William Bowyer, Jr. in 1763 and Edward Harwood in 1776. Since Harwood abandoned the TR readings frequently, some might regard him as having little regard for the inspiration and authority of the Scriptures. Nothing could be further from the truth. In his preface he states that he adopted only those readings which "to my judgment appeared to be best authenticated: my meaning is, that I espoused only those which I verily believed to be the very words which the inspired authors originally wrote."[53] It is interesting to note that the first printed text in America[54] was the *Textus Receptus*. It was done by the Rev. Caleb Alexander under the auspices of the famous printer Isaiah Thomas, Jr.

One of the key figures in the transition to the methodology commonly used in the modern critical period is Johann Jakob Griesbach (1745-1812). He was a pupil of Semler who adopted and extended Semler's methodology. He greatly enlarged the assignment of manuscripts to the Eastern family of manuscripts,[55] but considered the readings of this group to be late and not as important. He published three editions of the Greek New Testament in 1774-77 with an excellent critical apparatus. He also elaborated a theory of textual criticism which challenged the TR. He is noted for developing the critical principle of the superiority of the shorter textual reading under usual circumstances. Griesbach was the first one in Germany to abandon the TR in many readings of the Greek text. Soon after his first edition was published several other scholars published collations of materials of Greek manuscripts, versions, and the Fathers which expanded the work of New Testament textual critics; these included C. F. Matthaei of Russia who favored the text of the TR,[56] F. K. Alter of Vienna, Austria, Andrew Birch of Denmark (who also favored the text of Stephanus), and J. M. A. Scholz who was a Roman Catholic dean of theology in Bonn, Germany. The latter added 616 manuscripts to those previously known. He regarded the more recent manuscripts as superior to those older ones of the Alexandrian family. He claimed that these older manuscripts had survived only because they were seldom used.[57]

The Period of Constructive Criticism: 1831-1881

The final transition from this fourth period of collection and collation of manuscripts to what is called by Miller and Fee the Period of Constructive Criticism[58] took place with the publication of a critical edition of the Greek text by the German Karl Lachmann in 1831. Lachmann was the first important scholar to make a clean break with the TR. His goal was not the restoration of the original text—a task which he regarded as impossible—but the restoration of the text to its condition at the end of the fourth century. Lachmann was extreme in his opposition to any use of the Eastern or Byzantine manuscripts, using no minuscule (ninth century and later) readings in his edition. His text was seldom based on more than four Greek codices, and often on only three, two, or even one!

But the man to whom we owe the most in the development of modern textual criticism is Lobegott Friedrich Constantin von Tischendorf. This man was prodigious in his labors, publishing at least twenty-two volumes of texts of Biblical manuscripts and eight critical editions of the New Testament between 1841-1872. His total of separate publications exceeds 150. Tischendorf's seventh edition leans more strongly toward the TR. However, his eighth edition reflects his discovery of Codex Sinaiticus and is largely based upon the readings of this manuscript. His eighth edition differs from his seventh in 3369 places![59] Lest we think that Tischendorf had little reverence for the text of the Scriptures, we need to hear him describing his efforts to his fiancee: "I am confronted with a sacred task, the struggle to regain the original form of the New Testament."[60]

Following the same principles in England as Tischendorf in Germany was S. P. Tregelles. His critical principles closely resemble those of Karl Lachmann even though he was totally unaware of Lachmann's work. Tregelles gave most recognition to the readings of the ancient manuscripts— not based merely on the age of the manuscript but on the age of the text which it contained. He published his edition of the Greek New Testament between 1857 and 1872; his edition is not as full as Tischendorf's, but the two are very similar. Tregelles accomplished his massive and tiresome textual labors despite ill health, poverty, and strong opposition. To him this textual work was an act of worship which he considered to be service to God and to His church. Yet, the attacks upon Tregelles were fierce. The following quote from

Tregelles not only evidences this but also makes extremely clear the similarities between Tregelles' adversaries and many contemporary proponents of the TR or KJV only viewpoints:

> These things are not very encouraging to those who, with solemn and heartfelt reverence for God's Holy Word, desire to serve Him, and to serve His people, by using intelligent criticism in connection with the text of the New Testament. . .But indeed the defenders of that traditional modern Greek text of the later copyists and of the early editors who followed them, often seem to think that no courtesy of any kind is due to those scholars who recur to ancient authority at all. . .[his critics] have shown with great skill what can be done by imputing evil motives, and misrepresenting principles, and that, too, in language most studiously offensive. . .Those who maintain the traditional text often invent or dream their facts, and then draw their inferences . . . .

> They do thus advance allegations as facts, which are not such; and by such invented premises, they draw conclusions of the most unfavorable kind against the ancient documents of every sort and region,— against the text which rests on such documents; and they speak against the critics who value them and bring them forward, as if they were both devoid of all acumen, and had no moral conscience with regard to Holy Scripture. This renders discussion almost impossible for it is not a question of principles, but often simply of facts.[61]

Another man who advanced the cause of textual criticism was Henry Alford. Alford was a poet, painter, musician, preacher, biblical commentator[62], scholar, critic, and philologist. At first Alford supported the TR, but in the sixth edition of his Greek New Testament with a commentary he utilized the principles of Tischendorf and Tregelles. He came to oppose the TR because he believed it to stand "in the way of all chance of discovering the genuine word of God."[63] F. H. A. Scrivener was another English scholar and textual critic who collated and examined Greek manuscripts, evaluated previously printed Greek New Testaments, participated in the English Revised Version (1870-81), published several editions of Stephanus' Greek text, and wrote a significant book on New Testament textual criticism. The Scrivener edition of the TR was published by Cambridge University Press in 1894 and 1902; his edition is followed by the present day Greek New Testament published by the Trinitarian Bible Society. However, his personal position was closer to that of the present day Byzantine Majority text view.

This Period of Constructive Criticism came to its climax with the work of two men who have had the most significant influence upon the recent history of textual criticism: Brooke Foss Westcott (1825-1901, Canon of

Peterborough and Professor of Divinity at Cambridge, later Bishop of Durham) and Fenton John Anthony Hort (1828-92, Professor of Divinity at Cambridge). For thirty years these two men devoted themselves to the study of the New Testament Text—first independently, then together. In 1881 they issued their edition of the Greek New Testament entitled, *The New Testament in the Original Greek*. Volume 1 contained a revised Greek text without a critical apparatus but with critical notes on special passages. Volume II (by Hort) contains the Introduction, an appendix, and Notes on Select Readings. The pre-published text was in the hands of the English revisers who were influenced by it. Almost all subsequent textual criticism is defined in relationship to the work of these two men. Even their adversaries recognize how much influence they have had. According to Fee, their forte was the "refinement and rigorous application of a scientific methodology to the New Testament text."[64] They utilized both internal evidence[65] and external evidence.[66] Many have disagreed with certain positions of Westcott and Hort while still following in the main their critical procedures; others have rejected their findings. One thing is certain, however. The ultimate goal of these men was not to destroy the text of the Bible, nor to undermine its authority. Their goal was to get at the readings of the autographs of Scripture!

This is one thing that all these persons have had in common—they all had a deep concern to find the most accurate readings of the Scriptures. Some of these persons were Roman Catholics; some were Anglicans, Presbyterians, Lutherans, and various sorts of Protestants. Some were clearly believers; others were skeptics and liberals; of some we are uncertain. But the sovereign Lord who gave us His Word has used these people to help preserve the text of the Scriptures. Erasmus may not have been a true believer, but does anyone doubt that God used him in this process? Cannot the same be said for the others? Skilton has suggested that since unsaved man has been made in the image of God he can recognize facts and principles which can be of help even to believers.[67] In contrast many have argued that Westcott and Hort (hereafter W & H) were unsaved. We certainly should not take the position as their judge in light of clear Scripture warnings to the contrary. How can some critics, more than one hundred years later, be so certain of their spiritual condition? Even if they were unsaved, should we necessarily reject their critical conclusions without serious evaluation? These men had their critics in their day; but, as far as can be ascertained, they were not criticized by their contemporaries as either unregenerate or as heretics. Dean Burgon strongly opposed the critical theory of W & H but never once attacked their character or their theological beliefs. Charles Haddon Spurgeon, a strong defender of the faith, even commended Westcott on various occasions. Samuel Tregelles did not take these men to task; but he did do so with some contemporary liberal scholars.

177

G. A. Riplinger in *New Age Bible Versions*[68] devotes an entire chapter to W & H, seeking to show their Satanic and unscriptural connections. Many others have followed her lead. Unfortunately, many of Riplinger's statements are either taken out of context or misquoted.[69] We have read many criticisms of W & H. Some are true; the vast majority are false. These men were not perfect in life or doctrine. Like the KJV translators, W&H were Anglicans and held to typical Anglican doctrines such as infant baptism and baptismal regeneration. However, they were not apostate deniers of the deity of Christ and of the authority of the Scriptures. Anyone who will read carefully Westcott's commentaries will be impressed with Westcott's reverent and careful treatment of the Word of God. One will disagree with some teachings in these commentaries, but unless he misunderstands the words or takes them out of context he will have difficulty finding anything which gives the impression that Westcott is a liberal or an apostate! Quite the opposite; he defends the deity of Jesus Christ.[70] If Westcott was a "closet liberal," he certainly never came out! His commentaries miserably fail to prove him a liberal scholar.

The Period of Dominance for the "Critical Text": 1881-the Present
The Final Period in the study of the transmission of the text is from 1881 to the present. W & H received some sharp criticism for their textual work and theories. One of the most outspoken was John William Burgon, Dean of Chichester. Dean Burgon was a learned textual critic and collator of manuscripts. He made this analysis of the work of W & H: "With regret we record our conviction, that these accomplished scholars have succeeded in producing a Text vastly more remote from the inspired autographs of the Evangelists than any which has appeared since the invention of printing."[71] Prebendary Edward Miller championed the Byzantine Majority text along with Dean Burgon. They argued largely upon the ground of the immense number of witnesses for the Byzantine Majority text from the fourth century on, and because of the remarkably uniform character of these witnesses. They could only account for such by the deliberate care given by the church for the preservation of these manuscripts. F. H. A. Scrivener and George Salmon were far more temperate in their criticisms of W&H than were Burgon and Miller. Scrivener objected to Hort's near total rejection of the Syrian (Byzantine, Eastern) text; Salmon thought that more consideration should have been given to the Western readings.

In the early years of the twentieth century, Bernhard Weiss of Berlin edited a three volume edition of the New Testament in Greek. Despite the fact that Weiss utilized internal evidence almost exclusively for the determination of his readings, his text had a remarkable resemblance to that of W&H.

Alexander Souter's edition of the New Testament was issued in 1910; his apparatus was his key contribution—especially the relatively full evidence which he includes from the Church Fathers, particularly the Latin Fathers. Souter used the Greek text produced by one of the British translators, Edwin Palmer, a text based on that of Stephanus and revised toward the text presumably underlying the English Revised Version of 1881. Souter produced a second edition in 1947. One of the most monumental editions of the Greek New Testament appearing in the twentieth century was that of Hermann Freiherr von Soden in two volumes, 1910 and 1913. Von Soden's prolegomena which sets forth his views of the history of the text is 2,203 pages in length! Though his system of classification of manuscripts was entirely too complicated, "his edition remains a monument of broad research and immense industry which, with the extensive prolegomena dealing with the history of the transmission of the text, must be taken into account by every serious textual critic."[72] His edition closely approaches the TR.[73]

It is evident that the TR has not lost all appeal, despite the near triumphal comments of many textual commentators such as Kurt and Barbara Aland. On page 19 of *The Text of the New Testament* the Alands state, "Despite their clamorous rhetoric, the champions of the Textus Receptus (led primarily by Dean John William Burgon) were defending deserted ramparts. But the battle was not conclusively lost until the *Novum Testamentum Graece* of Eberhard Nestle (1851-1913) was published in 1898 by the Wurttemberg Bible Society." It is true that the Nestle text has had an extremely significant and widespread impact since its publication. It is now in its twenty-seventh edition. Aland remarks again that 1904 marked the "final defeat" of the TR when the British and Foreign Bible Society adopted the Nestle text. "Voices have been raised recently in the United States claiming superiority for the Textus Receptus over modern editions of the text, but they are finding little favorable response outside some limited circles. The wheels of history will not be reversed."[74] It seems clear that Aland does not find himself within the "circle" of fundamentalists where many still adopt the TR, and that he does not consider the beliefs and practices of fundamentalism in general to be very significant. In order to produce his text, Nestle compared the texts of Tischendorf and W&H; when the two differed he consulted the second (1892) edition of Richard Francis Weymouth prior to 1901 and the edition of Bernard Weiss (1894-1900) after 1901. Nestle's text summarized the results of nineteenth century textual scholarship while eliminating the extremes of both Tischendorf (in his preference for Sinaiticus—or Aleph) and W&H (in their partiality for Vaticanus—B). Amazingly, the dominance of this text has endured over one hundred years.

After Eberhard Nestle's death, his work was continued by his son Erwin Nestle (1883-1972). Beginning with the thirteenth edition in 1927 a critical note apparatus was added which included significant variants supported by the Greek manuscripts, the versions, and the Fathers. The twenty-second edition included the name of Kurt Aland, who was given the job of verifying the correct readings by consulting the manuscripts and the patristic writings. Thus, all subsequent editions have relied on original sources only. As later editions of the Nestle-Aland testament were produced the editors moved away from identification with and dependence upon Westcott and Hort and Tischendorf. "This text (cf. App. II p.7l7ff.) differs from the text of Westcott-Hort in numerous and quite significant points. Besides, the whole manuscript scene has changed since their day.... Neither Codex Vaticanus nor Codex Sinaiticus ...can provide a guideline we can normally depend on for determining the text. The age of Westcott-Hort and of Tischendorf is definitely over!"[75]

There have been many other editions of the Greek New Testament, such as those of Augustin Merk (1933, 1984—10th ed.), Joseph Vogels (1922, 1955—4th ed.—closer to the TR), and Jose Maria Bover (1943, 1968—5th ed.) All three of these were Roman Catholics. Others were produced by Protestants: R. V. G. Tasker (1964—based on the English text of the New English Bible); George Dunbar Kilpatrick (a new edition of Nestle's text); and S. C. E. Legg (on Matthew and Mark, 1935, 1940). No one can be certain how many editions of the Greek New Testament have appeared since 1514; according to Edward Reuss in 1869, already there had been approximately 853 editions (mostly of the TR at that time!). Metzger estimates that by early in the twentieth century "it is altogether probable that the 1,000 mark was passed."[76]

In 1955 the translation secretary of the American Bible Society, Eugene A. Nida, established a committee to prepare an edition of the Greek New Testament in order to meet the needs of several hundred Bible translation committees. They wanted a reliable Greek text with variants noted only where important for translators and interpreters. They also wanted to know the degree of certainty which the variants have in comparison with the printed text. The scholars assigned to the editorial committee were Matthew Black (St. Andrews, Scotland), Bruce Metzger (Princeton), Allen Paul Wikgren (Chicago), and Kurt Aland (Munster in Westphalia). It is significant to note that Aland still worked with the new Nestle text. The first edition of the United Bible Societies' text (hereafter UBS) was published in 1966. At first there were numerous differences between Nestle and UBS, but many of these had been resolved by the second edition in 1968. Now the fourth edition of UBS and the twenty-seventh edition of Nestle are equivalent in text;

they differ in style, format, and in their textual apparatuses. This unification was made possible when the same editorial committee was chosen for both editions in UBS 3rd and Nestle 26th: Kurt Aland, Black, Martini, Metzger, and Wikgren; later the committee was expanded to seven with the inclusion of Eugene Nida and Barbara Aland. The third and fourth editions of the Nestle-Aland text have the most extensive range of materials in their critical apparatuses which has ever been assembled. But Von Soden still has the most detailed collection of variants, and Tischendorf still has the most accurate presentation of evidence for them.

However, not all agree with the textual theories of Nestle-Aland and UBS. In 1982 Zane C. Hodges and Arthur L. Farstad produced an edition of the Greek New Testament called *The Greek New Testament According to the Majority Text*. It is sad that Kurt Aland's only comments concerning this significant edition are: "One should beware of *The Greek New Testament According to the Majority Text* by Arthur L. Farstad and Zane Hodges (1982) as an anachronism in every respect."[77] Hodges and Farstad do not pretend "that the text of this edition represents in all particulars the exact form of the originals."[78] They consider their work to be both "preliminary and provisional."[79] Their premises include: 1) Any reading receiving overwhelming attestation by the manuscripts is likely the original; 2) final decisions about readings must be made on the basis of their history in the manuscript tradition.[80] The text contains two sets of apparatuses: the first shows where their text differs from the Oxford TR of 1825; the second indicates the other places where this text differs from Nestle-Aland and UBS. The text rests heavily upon von Soden.

Another edition based upon the majority text appeared in 1991 entitled *The New Testament in the Original Greek According to the Byzantine/Majority Textform*, by Maurice A. Robinson and William G. Pierpont.[81] Robinson-Pierpont[82] criticized Hodges-Farstad[83] as being neither a "majority" text nor "solely a Byzantine text."[84] Their position is that the "Byzantine textform more closely represents the original autographs than any other text type. . . This text, as currently printed, reflects the closest approximation yet produced to a true Byzantine Text edition of the Greek New Testament."[85] For their text they, like H-F, follow Von Soden (and Herman C. Hoskier on the book of Revelation). The differences between themselves and H-F are primarily due to 1) "their particular interpretation of identical data"; 2) "their use or rejection of additional data;" 3) some items in the Von Soden apparatus were "neglected or misinterpreted" by H-F.[86] Moreover, they reject outright any use of the history of the manuscript tradition—what they call the "stemmatic approach." favored by H-F. Instead they seek to follow carefully the seven-fold critical canons of John W. Burgon.[87] This edition includes no critical apparatuses, no capital letters, accents, breathing marks, punctuation, or paragraph divisions. Their overall view is not strictly a "majority text" approach, but a "Byzantine-priority" approach in those few cases wherein the majority reading is not strictly equivalent to the Byzantine reading. R-P show that there are about 1,500 differences between any TR edition and either their edition or that of H-F. R-P disclaim any "hidden agenda" for either the TR or the KJV. They say that they would welcome a good modern translation based upon the Byzantine Textform. They also stress that people using recent translations like the New American Standard Bible and the New International Version are not heretics, but are "only somewhat disadvantaged."[88]

CONCLUSION

What have we seen as the result of this historical survey of the work of textual collators, editors, and critics? Certainly we should be able to see the sovereign hand of God in His remarkable use of multiple persons over many years from variant backgrounds with diverse convictions and principles. The end result is a plethora of textual information to enable us to come to very intelligent and accurate decisions about the correct textual readings of the New Testament Scriptures. Rene Pache in *The Inspiration and Authority of Scripture* has put it this way: We need "to reconstruct from all the witnesses available to us the text essentially preserved in all, but perfectly preserved in none."[89]

It is obvious from history that the Lord has remarkably preserved His Word for us; however, it is also quite obvious that no one manuscript nor group of manuscripts has all the right readings. We could choose to bury our heads in the sand and argue for the infallibility of a particular Greek text type or of a particular revision of a translation, or we can take the best alternative left to us—study all of the manuscripts available to us rather than depend on one "authoritative" text.

Until recent years, fundamentalists have never argued that belief in an inspired and inerrant original text demands the preservation of an infallible present text in either the Greek or our vernacular. Listen to the words of Dr. James M. Gray, great early fundamentalist, former dean of Moody Bible Institute, and contributor to *The Fundamentals*:

> The record for whose inspiration we contend is the original record—the autographs. . .and not any particular translation or translations of them whatever. There is no translation absolutely without error, nor could there be, considering the infirmities of human copyists, unless God were pleased to perform a perpetual miracle to secure it.[90]

As Bengel demonstrated, the variants in the text do not affect any essentials of biblical teaching. The TR and the KJV are the Word of God; in them we meet and hear God and are brought into saving fellowship with Him. However, it is also true that the W-H text, N-A text, the UBS text, the H-F text,and the R-P text are the Word of God. Moreover, the NKJV and the NASB and the NIV are the Word of God. "'THE BIBLE AS WE NOW HAVE IT, IN ITS VARIOUS TRANSLATIONS AND REVISIONS, WHEN FREED FROM ALL ERRORS AND MISTAKES OF TRANSLATORS, COPYISTS AND PRINTERS, (IS) THE VERY WORD OF GOD, AND CONSEQUENTLY WHOLLY WITHOUT ERROR.'"[91]

Concerning the need to revise the KJV, even Charles Haddon Spurgeon, more than 150 years ago, stated:

> It was a holy thing to translate the Scriptures into the mother tongue; he that shall effect a thorough revision of the present translation will deserve as high need of honour as the first translators. Despite the outcry of reverend doctors against any attempt at revision, it ought to be done.[92]

In the search for a good text, our piety and love for God cannot replace sound knowledge and scholarly judgment. The resolution of questions raised by divergent textual readings is not solved by prayer or by some special illumination of the Holy Spirit. We can be thankful that through the centuries the Lord has equipped men with knowledge and textual skill and that He has blessed us with the fruit of their labors. How foolish to criticize and debunk the praiseworthy efforts of these remarkable servants who have exerted such labors over the text of our Scriptures. Even the great Baptist preacher and theologian of the eighteenth century, John Gill, clearly argues this point:

> Here I cannot but observe the amazing ignorance and stupidity of some persons, who take it into their heads to decry learning and learned men; for **what would they have done for a Bible, had it not been for them as instruments?** and if they had it, so as to have been capable of reading it, God must have wrought a miracle for them; and continued that miracle in every nation, in every age, and to every individual; I mean the gift of tongues, in a supernatural way, as He bestowed upon the apostles on the day of Pentecost; which there is no reason in the world ever to have expected. Bless God, therefore, and be thankful that God has, in His providence, raised up such men to translate the Bible into the mother-tongue of every nation, and particularly into ours; and that He still continues to raise up such who are able to defend the translation made against erroneous persons and enemies of the truth; **and to correct and amend it in lesser matters,**

in which it may have failed, and clear and illustrate it by their learned notes upon it.[93]

As the result, we can have the utmost confidence in the accuracy of the Bibles which we hold in our hands, read, preach, teach, and obey. Allow Gray to conclude the matter:

> Nor is that original parchment so remote a thing as some suppose. Do not the number and variety of manuscripts and versions extant render it comparatively easy to arrive at a knowledge of its text, and does not competent scholarship today affirm that as to the New Testament at least, we have in 999 cases out of every thousand the very word of that original text? Let candid consideration be given to these things and it will be seen that we are not pursuing a phantom in contending for an inspired autograph of the Bible. [94]

---

[1]As found in William L. Lumpkin, *Baptist Confessions of Faith* (Valley Forge: The Judson Press, 1969), p. 251. Note that the Baptists adopted their statement from the *Westminster Confession of Faith*; this was the mainstream view of conservatives in the seventeenth century.

[2]C. A. Briggs, "Critical Theories of the Sacred Scriptures in Relation to their Inspiration," *The Presbyterian Review*, II (1881), pp. 573 ff.

[3]Private e-mail received by author.

[4] Such attacks attempt to discredit their work and publications and the work and publications of others who labor to place into print reliable Biblical texts. Whether one accepts or rejects their views and work it must be remembered that the source documents that they used were Bibles or a portions of Bibles used and trusted by someone as the Word of God. [ed.]

[5]These two positions are not identical. A very small number of manuscripts lie behind the Textus Receptus which is the basis for the King James Translation; however, the readings of these manuscripts in most cases are very similar to those found within the Byzantine Majority Text manuscripts.

[6]Once minor differences in spelling and punctuation are eliminated, the percentage of agreement rises considerably.

[7]Robert Dick Wilson, *A Scientific Investigation of the Old Testament* (Chicago: Moody Press, 1959), pp 61-62. Wilson does admit on p. 61 that occasional emendation of the Hebrew is necessary.

[8]Ernst Wurthwein. *The Text of the Old Testament*. (Grand Rapids: William B. Erdmans Publishing Company, 1979) p. 112.

[9]William Henry Green, *General Introduction to the Old Testament—the Text* (New York, 1899), p. 181.

[10]See F. F. Bruce, *The Books and the Parchments* (Old Tappan, NJ: Fleming H. Revell Co., 1963), p. 180.

[11]Ibid., p. 181.

[12]Carsten Peter Thiede, *The Jesus Papyrus* (London: Weidenfeld & Nicolson, 1996).

[13]John H. Skilton "The Transmission of the Scriptures," in *The Infallible Word*, faculty members of the Westminster Theological Seminary (Philadelphia: Presbyterian & Reformed Publishing. Co., 1946), p. 161.

[14]F. G. Kenyon, *Our Bible and the Ancient Manuscripts* (London: Eyre & Spottiswoode, 1958), p. 23.

[15]Zane C. Hodges and Arthur L Farstad, *The Greek New Testament According to the Majority Text* (Nashville: Thomas Nelson Publishers, 1985).

[16]*The American Heritage Collegiate Dictionary*, Electronic Edition (Zane Publishing Company, 1996, 1997).

[17]Green, p. 162.

[18]John R. Rice, *Our God-Breathed Book* (Murfreesboro, TN: Sword of the Lord Publishers, 1969), p. 371.

[19]Ibid., pp. 375, 369.

[20] Green., p. 168

[21]Ibid.

[22]Ibid.

[23]See the discussion in Skilton (pp.171-73) concerning the 1590 decree of Pope Sixtus V on his published edition of the Latin Vulgate, and concerning the decree of Clement VIII of another edition.

[24]The outline followed here is basically that of H. S. Miller, *General Biblical Introduction* (Houghton, NY: The Word-Bearer Press, 1944), pp. 291 ff.

[25]Miller, p. 292.

[26]Ibid.

[27]See Gordon D. Fee, "The Textual Criticism of the New Testament," in *The Expositor's Bible Commentary* , Vol I, ed. Frank E. Gaebelein (Grand Rapids: The Zondervan Publishing House, 1979), pp. 425-76.

[28]See David Burggraff, "Paradigm Shift: Translations in Transition: We're Been Here Before," *Calvary Baptist Theological Journal*, 12 (Spring/Fall, 1996), pp. 105-115.

[29]See Skilton, pp. 171-173

[30]It is important to note that those who now translate into other languages from the KJV instead of from the original languages of Scripture are really following ancient Roman Catholic precedent.

[31]Named for the university town of Alcala, called Complutum in Latin.

[32]For a list of these manuscripts, see William W. Combs, "Erasmus and the Textus Receptus," *Detroit Baptist Seminary Journal*, I (Spring 1996), p. 45.

[33]See Kurt Aland and Barbara Aland, *The Text of the New Testament* (Grand Rapids: William B. Eerdmans Publishing Company, 1989), p. 4. I do not seek to minimize the significance of Erasmus' work, nor to imply that he did not put forth strenuous exertion in the completion of this project. But by scholarly standards, the work was extremely rushed!

[34]However, some of these non-Greek readings are still perpetuated in printings of the Textus Receptus and in the King James Translation. For non-Greek TR readings see Combs, op. cit., p. 47; for the KJV see e.g. Rev. 22:19 where the KJV reads "book" of life with the Latin mss. instead of "tree" of life found in all Greek mss.

[35]A. T. Robertson, *Studies in the Text of the New Testament* (Nashville: Sunday School Board of the Southern Baptist Convention, 1926), p. 36.

[36]F. H. A. Scrivener, *A Plain Introduction to the Criticism of the New Testament*, 2nd ed. (London, Deighton, Bell, and Co., 1874), p.383.

[37]Philology is the study of literature and the disciplines used in the study of language as used in literature.

[38]See Combs, pp. 40-44.

[39]See Doug Kutilek, *Erasmus: His Greek Text and His Theology* (Hatfield, PA: Interdisciplinary Biblical Research Institute), pp. 7-8.

[40]Ibid., p. 8.

[41]Combs, op. cit., p. 51.

[42] See Bruce M. Metzger, *The Text of the New Testament* (New York: Oxford University Press, 1968), p. 103.

[43]Hereafter abbreviated TR.

[44]Lectionaries were service manuals which contained extensive Scripture readings for various dates in the church calendar.

[45]"Prohibited Books"; see Metzger, op. cit., p. 107.

[46]Ibid., p. 108.

[47]Miller, op. cit., p. 295.

[48]Some might even consider it audacious!

[49]See Metzger, op. cit., pp. 111-112.

[50]Ibid., p. 112.

[51]See Ibid., pp. 112-113; Miller, op. cit., p. 295; Aland, op. cit., p. 9.

[52]Metzger, op. cit., p. 114.

[53]Quoted in Metzger, ibid., p. 117 fn.

[54]Worcester, Massachusetts in April, 1800.

[55]He called it Constantinopolitan.

[56]Unfortunately, Matthaei obtained a number of his manuscripts through "brazen thievery"; see Metzger, op. cit., pp. 121-122.

[57]See. Miller, op. cit., pp. 297-98.

[58]Or the Modern Critical Period by Metzger; op. cit., pp 119 ff.

[59]Miller, op. cit., 299.

[60]Metzger, p. 126.

[61]S. P. Tregelles, *An Account of the Printed Text of the Greek New Testament* (London: S. Bagster & Sons, 1854), pp. 262-64.

[62]His commentaries are still used with profit by many in the present day.

[63]Metzger, p. 128.

[64]Metzger, p. 427.

[65]Regarding both the human authors' usage and habits, and the habits of the copyists of the manuscripts.

[66]The quality of the documents, their family relationships, age of text, etc.

[67]See Skilton, op. cit., p. 179.

[68] (Ararat, VA: A.V. Publications Corporation, 1993), pp. 397-428.

[69]Much evidence could be produced; for example, see *The Lockman Foundation's Reply to New Age Bible Versions, by G. A. Riplinger* (May be obtained from The

Lockman Foundation, 900 South Euclid Street, La Habra, CA 90631.); James R. White, *The King James Only Controversy* (Minneapolis: Bethany House Publishers, 1995), pp. 95-108; John Ankerberg and John Weldon, *The Facts on the King James Only Debate* (Eugene, OR: Harvest House, 1996). pp. 25-26.

[70]Note his comments on John 1:1. In a section titled "The Word in His Absolute Being" he identifies the Word as being of the same essence as "God." *The Gospel According to St. John* (Grand Rapids: William B. Eerdmans Publishing Company, 1967 reprint), p. 2.

[71]See *The Revision Revised* (Paradise, PA: Conservative Classics, n.d.), pp. 25-26.

[72]Metzger, op. cit., p. 143.

[73]See an analysis of Von Soden in Aland, op. cit., pp. 22-23.

[74]Aland, p. 19.

[75]Eberhard Nestle, Erwin Nestle, Kurt Aland, et. al. *Novum Testamentum Graece*, 26th edition (Stuttgart: Deutsched Bibelstiftung, 1979), p. 43.

[76]Metzger, p. 146; he also has the information from Reuss. Note that we are now within the *twenty-first* century!

[77]Aland., p. 25.

[78]Nashville: Thomas Nelson, p. x.

[79]Ibid., p. x.

[80]However, the only two places where they have attempted to do this is in John 7:53-8:11 and for the book of Revelation.

[81]Atlanta: The Original Word Publishers, 1991.

[82] Hereafter known as R-P.

[83]Hereafter known as H-F.

[84]Ibid., "Preface," by Wm. David McBrayer, p. xi.

[85]Ibid., p. xiii.

[86]Ibid., p. xiv.

[87]Ibid.

[88]Ibid., p. xlii.

[89]Chicago: Moody Press, 1969, p. 197.

[90]Emphasis in the original; "The Inspiration of the Bible—Definition, Extent, and Proof," *The Fundamentals*, Vol. II (Grand Rapids: Baker Book House, 1980 reprint of the original 1917 ed.), pp. 12-13.

[91]Capitals in original; quoted by Gray from the 1893 General Assembly of the Presbyterian Church of America; ibid, p. 43. Few today recognize the fact that about half of the Scriptural quotations in *The Fundamentals* were from the American Standard Version.

[92]Spurgeon's "Preface" to *The English Bible*, Mrs. H. C. Conant (n.p. London: 1859), p. 7.

[93]John Gill, *A Body of Doctrinal Divinity* (Atlanta: Turner Lassitter, 1965, 3rd reprint), pp. 13-14; emphasis mine.

[94]Gray, p. 14.

BIBLIOGRAPHY

Aland, Kurt and Barbara Aland, *The Text of the New Testament*. Grand Rapids: William B. Eerdmans Publishing Company, 1989.

The American Heritage Collegiate Dictionary, Electronic Edition. Zane Publishing Company, 1996, 1997.

Ankerberg, John and John Weldon, *The Facts on the King James Only Debate*. Eugene, OR: Harvest House, 1996.

Bruce, F. F. *The Books and the Parchments*. Old Tappan, NJ: Fleming H. Revell Co., 1963.

Burgon, John William. *The Revision Revised*. Paradise, PA: Conservative Classics, n.d.

Burggraff, David "Paradigm Shift: Translations in Transition: We're Been Here Before," *Calvary Baptist Theological Journal*, 12. Spring/Fall, 1996.

Combs, William W. "Erasmus and the Textus Receptus," *Detroit Baptist Seminary Journal*, I. Spring 1996.

Fee, Gordon D. "The Textual Criticism of the New Testament," in *The Expositor's Bible Commentary*, Vol. I, ed. Frank E. Gaebelein. Grand Rapids: The Zondervan Publishing House, 1979.

John Gill, *A Body of Doctrinal Divinity*, 3rd rpt. Atlanta: Turner Lassitter, 1965.

Gray, James M. "The Inspiration of the Bible—Definition, Extent, and Proof," *The Fundamentals*, Vol. II. Grand Rapids: Baker Book House, 1980 reprint of the original 1917 ed.

Green, William Henry. *General Introduction to the Old Testament—the Text*. New York, 1899.

Hodges, Zane C. and Arthur L Farstad. *The Greek New Testament According to the Majority Text*. Nashville: Thomas Nelson Publishers, 1985.

Kenyon, F. G. *Our Bible and the Ancient Manuscripts*. London: Eyre and Spottiswoode, 1958.

Kutilek, Doug. *Erasmus: His Greek Text and His Theology*. Hatfield, PA: Interdisciplinary Biblical Research Institute, n.d.

The Lockman Foundation's Reply to New Age Bible Versions, by G. A. Riplinger. La Habra, CA: The Lockman Foundation, n.d.

Metzger, Bruce M. *The Text of the New Testament* New York: Oxford University Press, 1968.

Miller, H. S. *General Biblical Introduction.* Houghton, NY: The Word-Bearer Press, 1944.

Nestle, Eberhard, Erwin Nestle, Kurt Aland, et. Al. *Novum Testamentum Graece*, 26th edition Stuttgart: Deutsched Bibelstiftung, 1979.

Pache, Rene. *The Inspiration and Authority of Scripture.* Chicago: Moody Press, 1969.

Rice, John R. *Our God-Breathed Book.* Murfreesboro, TN: Sword of the Lord Publishers, 1969.

Robertson, A. T. *Studies in the Text of the New Testament.* Nashville: Sunday School Board of the Southern Baptist Convention, 1926.

Robinson, Maurice A. and William G. Pierpont. *The New Testament in the Original Greek According to the Byzantine/Majority Textform.* Atlanta: The Original Word Publishers, 1991.

Scrivener, F. H. A. *A Plain Introduction to the Criticism of the New Testament*, 2nd ed. London, Deighton, Bell, and Co., 1874.

Skilton, Robert H. "The Transmission of the Scriptures," in *The Infallible Word*, faculty of Westminster Theological Seminary. (Philadelphia: Presbyterian and Reformed Publishing. Co.), 1946.

Spurgeon, C. H. "Preface" to *The English Bible*, Mrs. H. C. Conant. London: 1859.

Thiede, Carsten Peter. *The Jesus Papyrus.* London: Weidenfeld and Nicolson, 1996.

Tregelles, S. P. *An Account of the Printed Text of the Greek New Testament.* London: S. Bagster & Sons, 1854.

Westcott, Bruce Foss. *The Gospel According to St. John*, Grand Rapids: William B. Eerdmans Publishing Company, 1967 reprint.

White, James R. *The King James Only Controversy.* Minneapolis: Bethany House Publishers, 1995.

Wilson, Robert Dick. *A Scientific Investigation of the Old Testament.* Chicago: Moody Press, 1959.

Wurthwein, Ernst. *The Text of the Old Testament.* Grand Rapids: William B. Erdmans Publishing Company, 1979.

THE VALUE OF THE COPIES OF SCRIPTURE

Daniel K. Davey

FUNDAMENTALISM AND THE PRESERVATION DEBATE

There are many voices in fundamentalism alleging with seeming authority and clamorous dogmatism that each has the correct view concerning the preservation of the text of Scripture. Clearly, all fundamentalists believe they have the *ipsissama verba* of the Holy Spirit in written form and most—if not all—are ready to defend their belief without compromise.[1] This is, in part, what defines us as fundamentalists.[2] We are absolutely and supernaturally convinced that the Bible we hold in our hands is the very Word of God. Contrarily, we do not believe the Bible merely contains the Word of God,[3] nor do we accept the premise that the Bible is truth—but in a restrictive sense,[4] and we flatly reject the view of those who accept the Bible as "inspired" but are inclined to see various levels of inspiration.[5]

All fundamentalists, then, view Holy Scripture through the following theological lens: (1) God has indeed spoken truth to man through the medium of human language (Hebrews 1:1-2); (2) What truth God wanted written down (*inscripturated*) He did so through human authors while protecting each human agent from recording error (2 Peter 1:19-21); (3) God's truth is understandable by man, and is written down for future generations to follow (Deuteronomy 31:9-13)—in other words, Christians today are able to identify what God proclaimed throughout the centuries (Romans 1:1-4; 1 Timothy 3:15; 2 Timothy 3:15); (4) This written truth from God is sufficient to prepare and equip each believer in Christ for every necessary good work (2 Timothy 3:17); and finally, (5) The truth of God in written form is complete (Revelation 22:18-19), and is the sole rule (authority) for the believer's faith and daily life (2 Timothy 3:16). If, therefore, fundamentalists agree to these specific tenets of truth, then why is there so much fury between fundamentalist brothers today over the Word of God? What could possibly divide and separate us who hold such a high view of the Bible? The answer is not to be found in a simple response because the issue is deeply rooted.

THE FRACTURING OF FUNDAMENTALISM OVER PRESERVATION

In the 1960s and 1970s, two very different but simultaneous biblical views of God's Word emerged and began to fractionalize fundamentalism into various groups. These so-called movements were actually pockets of men who were in basic agreement on the five tenets of Scripture as outlined previously, but found themselves in opposition to one another as to the method by which they believed God preserved His Word for today. In other words, while they held a high view of Scripture, agreeing on the Pauline truth of inspiration as delineated in 2 Timothy 3:16, they could not agree on its present-day application and implementation.

In the early days, as the various ideas were being formed into pamphlets, journal articles, and even books, there did not seem to be an overt intent by the defenders of these movements to segment fundamentalism. In fact, in most cases each believed their views needed to be heard to strengthen fundamentalism. Their goal was noble, but the end result is now realized as exactly opposite of their intended desire. Instead of cool heads, biblical exegesis, and theological discussion, the past few years are strewn with vitriolic language, damaged reputations, ungracious refusal to listen to the other's point of view, and even the relegating of solid, Bible-believing thinkers outside the domain of fundamentalism. These views have become entrenched within fundamentalism and the boundaries have become rigid. For this reason, the preservation issue has become a hostile theological battleground rather than a theme of unity.

The purpose, therefore, of these next pages is to seek to understand each of the contrary viewpoints on the preservation of Scripture. A few cautions will be offered for each view which need to be carefully measured by its advocates in light of the numerous copies of Scripture that are available to us. Finally, I will offer four reasoned principles of preservation which are an attempt to promote unity and offer healing within the fundamentalist community.

Preservation and the King James Version

The first movement is actually a reactionary development against what its advocates see as the depreciation (or downgrading) of the King James Version of the Bible. Indeed, no one familiar with the history of American fundamentalism would ever deny the fact that the KJV has been the translation of choice for the public proclamation of God's Word. For example, when I entered seminary in 1978, the president was Richard V. Clearwaters, a powerful figure in the fundamentalist movement. He was not only the president of the seminary I attended, but he was also my pastor. Pastor Clearwaters made it very clear that no English translation of the Bible could be used from his pulpit other than the King James Version. He was emphatic on this issue. However, from both his pulpit and writing ministries, he was equally as clear that the King James Version was not the best available English translation. In fact, he strongly asserted over forty years ago,

We know of no Fundamentalist . . . that claim the King James as the best English translation. Those in the main stream of Fundamentalism all claim the American Revised of 1901 as the best English translation.[6]

The reason R. V. Clearwaters held this view is best expressed in his own words, "Honesty compels us to cite the 1901 American Revised as the best English Version of the original languages. . . ."[7] Clearwaters, like most fundamentalists of his day, saw no conflict between preferring the public proclamation of the KJV in his ministry for its "clarity and style;"[8] and careful comparison of any English translation with the Hebrew and Greek texts of Holy Scripture to make sure he was accurately handling the truth.

Some today have misunderstood this time-honored practice of Clearwaters and his contemporaries. They have overlooked the supreme significance of the original languages and have staked their claim on the King James Version of the Bible as the God-inspired Bible for this present age. There seems to be little compromise on this matter for these supporters. Historically, the proponents of this view were somewhat obscure in American fundamentalism until the advent of a trilogy of books edited by David Otis Fuller, pastor of Wealthy Street Baptist Church in Grand Rapids, Michigan.[9] As Bauder accurately points out, Fuller's advocacy of the KJV only position in his work *Which Bible?* (1970) and his sequels *True or False?* (1973) and *Counterfeit or Genuine?* (1975) both popularized this view and brought considerable outrage among certain fundamentalists against the multiple translations of the English Bible.[10]

Though pastors, teachers, and historians are not in entire agreement over how this movement has risen to such national (even international) heights, one thing is clear, some today in fundamentalism make the use or non-use of the KJV a test of fellowship. A current vocal advocate shares his "concerns for fundamentalism" by asking, "Why would some want to move away from the tried and reliable 400 year heritage. . . ?"[11] This writer then quips, "Will fundamentalists who have accepted the *ASV*, and then the *NASV*, and now the *NIV*, some day end up promoting the *'Rap Bible Only'* movement?"[12]

While we applaud the desire of many of these fundamentalist brethren to stand against the spiritual compromise of this age and its deviation from God's Word, we question their unwarranted demand to adopt an English translation as the only preserved Word of God for this age. The ultimate textual issue never rests with translations—though all fundamentalists recognize the immediate issue of dealing with vague or inadequate translations of certain verses or passages; rather, the supreme issue relates to the acceptance or non-acceptance of the Word of God as given in its original form. In addition, we caution our brothers against making the KJV a key tenet for personal or ecclesiastical fellowship with one another. All fundamentalists recognize the beauty and grace of this translation, and we honor it as such. However, fundamentalists have historically allowed the exercise of individual soul-liberty in the matter of translations provided that that translation was nonsectarian and true to the original documents. This fact is part of the fabric of fundamentalism's elegant and beautiful tapestry.

Preservation and the Original Language-Text Manuscripts

The second movement supported by many fundamentalists is shaped by the conviction that all translations of Scripture are subject to, and must accurately manifest, the original language-text of the Scriptures. In other words, the supreme authority for any translation of any language is its conformity to the original Hebrew and Greek language-texts. Those who hold this view clearly distance themselves from the view that Scripture is preserved in a single translation.

This group, however, is far from monolithic because of the universal fact that none of the original language-texts of the Bible are extant today. So, the Word of God is available to us today through the multiple Hebrew and Greek copies of the original autographs. The number of existing copies is voluminous. The Hebrew copies of the Masoretic texts number more than 6,000,[13] and the Greek manuscripts number 5,487.[14]

On the positive side, students of Scripture have many witnesses to the authenticity of the Word of God. Yet, with all these witnesses available, one may seriously wonder if there is a single copy or grouping (family) of copies which best represents the original text as God gave it. The conclusions of such musings have divided fundamentalism into several distinct factions. These divisions may be identified as we separately consider the available copies of the original language-texts of the Old and New Testaments.

The Old Testament

The Old Testament Scriptures are viewed by some fundamentalists as preserved by God in the "Traditional (Masoretic) text which was printed at the end of the medieval period."[15] Hills seems to indicate that the King James Version of the Hebrew Scriptures was fully resting on the third edition (A.D. 1494) of the first printed Hebrew Bible (A.D. 1488).[16] Though his point is well intended, the facts of history do not fully support this conclusion. The translators of the 1611 King James Version included a four-page dedication to the King, followed by an eleven-page introduction entitled, "The Translators to the Reader." In their introduction they make the following statement,

196

Neither did we think much to consult the translators or commentators, *Chaldee, Hebrew, Syrian, Greek, or Latin;* no, nor the *Spanish, French, Italian,* or *Dutch* [German]; neither did we disdain to revise that which we had done, and to bring back to the anvil that which we had hammered: but having and using great helps as were needful, and fearing no reproach for slowness, nor coveting praise for expedition, we have at the length, through the good hand of the Lord upon us, brought the work to that pass that you see.[17]

In sum, the King James translators state that they were not translating their English text from any specific, single Hebrew textus receptus. In fact, they openly confess to their reliance upon several Hebrew texts, commentaries on the text, and various translations of the Old Testament. Rhodes and Lupas list over twenty texts that would have been available to the KJV translators from various language groups. At least seven of these texts were Hebrew including all three additions of *Biblia Rabbinica* (A.D. 1517, 1525, and 1548).[18]

Difficult Issues with the Hebrew Copies

When we concentrate on the copies of the Hebrew text, we must wrestle with two distinct but related issues: (1) The development of the Hebrew text from a consonantal, non-vocalized, non-paragraphed or versed text into a fully developed text with vowel points, accents, verse numberings and chapter divisions, and (2) The identity of the Masoretic text. While these issues deserve a lengthy study, time and space only permit a survey of their significance.

The Hebrew Scriptures existed for centuries as a consonantal text until "the golden age of the Masoretic tradition"[19] (A.D. 500 – 1000).[20] Since the Old Testament Scriptures were primarily a Jewish concern until after the time of Jesus Christ, the transmission of the Hebrew text was in a relatively few but reverent hands. Though there were linguistic developments (morphology, orthography, etc.) within the Hebrew language—as with any language of age—the consonantal text remained protected through several families or textual traditions.[21] Wurthwein writes, "Vowel signs were not added to the text until a later stage, when the consonantal text was already well established with a long history of transmission behind it."[22] When the golden age of the Masoretes arrived there arose a tradition of men who carefully developed vowel points, accents, marginal notes, and verse markings[23] (though chapter designations did not take place till later and were not of Jewish origin[24]) to preserve the readability of the consonantal text.

Contrary to myth, this group of Jewish scholars known as the Masoretes, was not a single grouping of men in a single geographical area. They worked in academies located in both Babylon and Palestine and produced multiple texts.[25] Before long the Masorete academy in Tiberias became the leading textual voice[26] (A.D. 780-930).[27] This probably was due to the lack of consistency in the others' vowel and accent markings while the Tiberian Masoretes maintained a "strict consistency in indicating pronunciation."[28] In any event, the work of Aaron ben Asher, one of the last of the Masorete scholars, is represented in the oldest full Hebrew text of the Old Testament that is extant (A.D. 1008).[29]

When history introduced the printing press about 450 years after the ben Asher text was completed, several Rabbinic Bibles were collated and edited by Jacob ben Chayyim,[30] and printed by Daniel Bomberg in Venice (1516/17 and 1524/25). The second Rabbinic Bible was an extensive work with both the marginal and end notes from the Masoretes, comments by several notable Rabbis of the day, and variant readings of other manuscripts ben Chayyim had collected.[31] For the next 400 years this Hebrew text was the textus receptus of the Hebrew Scriptures and was the basis for the first two modern Hebrew texts of (Rudolph Kittel's) *Biblia Hebraica* (1906 and 1912). Interestingly, the third edition of (Paul Kahle's) *Biblia Hebraica* (1937) returned to the ben Asher text and solely used this oldest of texts as its text of choice. Though textual variants exist between the ben Chayyim and the ben Asher texts, both are of the Masoretic tradition and they are in substantial agreement.

With the discovery of the Dead Sea Scrolls in 1947, the history of the Hebrew text takes a confident step forward underscoring the reliability of our modern versions. The impact of these discoveries are summarized by Brotzman into three propositional affirmations.[32] First and foremost, the Dead Sea Scrolls offer a look at the Hebrew text from a period that pre-dates the Leningrad Codex (A.D. 1008) by 1,000 years. Second, "[T]he Qumran scrolls, while being much earlier than the Masoretic text, generally support the fidelity with which the Masoretic text was copied."[33] Finally, while the Qumran documents certify the faithfulness of the Hebrew text, "they also point out that the text in the last two centuries B.C., and up through at least a part of the first century A.D., existed in various text types rather than only one."[34] Some of these alternative texts (though few in number) provide support for some Septuagint (Greek translation)[35] readings not supported by the Masoretic tradition.

Three Significant Conclusions

With this textual background appreciated, one may draw three essential conclusions concerning the copies of the Hebrew text. First, the Old Testament text has been painstakingly protected and carefully copied throughout the centuries of Jewish history so that through genuine comparison of the Masoretic texts, one can be assured that he possesses the Old Testament Scriptures in its original form. Second, while the ancient Scriptures were safeguarded as consonantal texts, they progressed into our modern versions with clear paragraph notations, vowel pointing, accent markings, verse numbers and chapter divisions. Therefore, what the Holy Spirit gave through the Old Testament authors, we understand today by means of human notations and vocalizations applied to the consonantal text. Third and importantly, there is no single standardized text passed down through the centuries by the various copyists. However, the thoroughness of our current texts in both Kittel's and Kahle's editions validate our confidence in the Hebrew copies so that we can safely say, "God has spoken, and we know what He has said" (Hebrews 1:1; 2 Timothy 3:15).

The New Testament

The most heated of textual controversies revolve around the surviving copies of the Greek New Testament. Though fundamentalist literature is scant on the Hebrew text of Scripture, it is abundant—overwhelmingly so—on the Greek New Testament. The voices that enter this debate are many, but there are basically three distinct groups which must be fairly understood if there is to be clear-headed dialogue within our ranks.

The first group holds to a *Textus Receptus* (TR) tradition, which is usually regarded as a single text tradition. For these supporters any accurate and viable translation of the New Testament (in any language) must come through this textual grid.[36] The second group broadens this single text tradition to include all Byzantine text-types of the New Testament which make up some 80% of all extant Greek texts of the New Testament.[37] Therefore, this group is identified as the *Majority Text* (MT) tradition. The final group holds to a more eclectic view than the MT tradition and gives greatest preference to the oldest existing copies of the Greek text which are sourced in manuscripts outside the Byzantine Empire. These supporters follow the *Critical Text* (CT) in their language studies.[38]

The Textus Receptus Position

Those who maintain a TR view benefit from a rich and varied history.[39] On March 1, 1516 the first edition of Erasmus' work rolled off the printing press. It was a massive 1,000-page volume that contained numerous typographical errors. Within three years Erasmus printed a second edition (1519)[40] and after this printing over 3,000 copies of his Greek New Testament were in circulation. By 1535 there were five editions of Erasmus' work and over thirty unauthorized reprints which were circulating in places like Venice, Basle, and Paris. Clearly, Erasmus' Greek New Testament had taken the world by a storm.[41] After the death of Erasmus, many men took up the mantle of copying, editing, and printing the Greek New Testament. Robert Stephanus printed four editions (A.D. 1546, 1549, 1550, and 1551) with his third edition being the first to include critical apparatus and his fourth edition the first to divide the text into numbered verses. Ultimately, 117 years after the first edition of Erasmus, Bonaventure Elzever (along with his brother, Matthew, and nephew, Abraham) printed his second edition of the Greek New Testament (1633) with the inscribed Latin words in the preface, *textum ergo habes, nunc ab omnibus receptum*, meaning, "You have therefore the text now received by all." The term *textus receptus* (from *textum . . . receptum*) was born and would dominate the textual landscape for the next two hundred years. Normally, this term is understood today as referring to all the editions from 1516 (Erasmus' 1st edition) to 1641 (Elzever's 3rd edition).[42]

TR advocates refer to a single text tradition that has providentially preserved the exact wording of the autographa (original autographs). Hills writes, ". . . the 3rd and 4th editions of Stephanus agreed closely with the 5th edition of Erasmus, which was gaining acceptance everywhere as the providentially appointed text."[43] However, textual evidence questions the *raison d'être* of such a statement.

Four historic challenges to the TR position

While the TR has been the dominant New Testament text for the past centuries, those who espouse this tradition today must squarely meet four challenges. First, there has not been a plain consensus as to which TR text is best. For example, while England followed Stephanus' 3rd edition (1550), and it eventually became the source for the Geneva Bible (1557), the European continent followed Elzever's 2nd edition (1633) which more closely aligned with Stephanus' 4th edition (1551). Therefore, however small the deviations, neither TR text is identical. Surely, both cannot be the pure representative of the autographa.

Second, when Theodore de Beza edited Stephanus' fourth edition in two separate editions (1588/89 and 1598), he did so making some changes to each text. It is very difficult to see how one writer could dogmatically conclude, "This author believes that Beza's 1598 Greek Edition of the New Testament is essentially equivalent to the very words of the NT *autographa*."[44] This is especially thorny when one considers that the 1611 KJV translators made extensive use of both the 1588/9 and 1598 editions of Beza.

Third, John Mills (1645-1707), a Greek scholar from Oxford, spent thirty years of his life studying thirty-two printed Greek New Testaments, nearly 100 manuscripts, and voluminous patristic citations of the New Testament.

His work was published two weeks before his death at age sixty-two (June 23, 1707). Using Stephanus' 3rd edition as his base he collected and calculated some 30,000 differences among the Greek texts and references.[45] His work is a critical blow to the entire TR tradition which seeks to find a consensus in some single text that fully and accurately reflects the autographa. Mills' research affirms that such a text did not exist in his day (almost 200 years after Erasmus' first edition).

Finally, with such observable data, TR supporters like Hills relegate the "changes" and "emendations" to Erasmus' 5th edition by Stephanus,[46] Calvin,[47] and Beza[48] as either "humanistic tendency"[49] or the overruling of the "common faith,"[50] which ultimately protected the TR text from their variant readings.[51] In their terminology, the TR has been supernaturally sheltered by God, and any textual changes (or protection from change) has been God-directed.

In addition, the problem of questionable texts with little or no credible manuscript support often surfaces. The TR supporters recognize that several readings in their text lack suitable manuscript confirmation (i.e. Ephesians 1:18, "understanding" and Ephesians 3:9, "fellowship" to use Hills' own examples).[52] In other words, the TR has some curious readings when compared to the other 5,487 copies. Since there is no consensus on this difficulty, the following statement is Hills' response to his own examples of unusual TR readings:

> Admittedly there are a few places in which the Textus Receptus is supported by only a small number of manuscripts. . . . We solve this problem, however, according to the logic of faith. Because the Textus Receptus was God-guided as a whole, it was probably God-guided in these few passages also.[53]

Hills' only support of these rare TR discrepancies is a blanket statement that these readings are "God-guided." What, then, is the difference between what the original writers experienced in 2 Peter 1:21 and the experience of the TR editors? Is this not a redefinition of θεόπνευστος" ("inspiration") as circumscribed by Paul in 2 Timothy 3:16? Hills' exuberance to defend his textual tradition has, in fact, led him away from a sound, Pauline understanding of this significant biblical term. Is there not a better line of attack?

The TR Contribution

Until the arrival of the TR tradition through Erasmus, the theological world was immersed in the Latin text—not considering the significance nor the authority of the Greek text. However, Erasmus, who is credited with stating, ". . . that he would the more readily spend money for Greek books than for clothes;"[54] indeed, spent tireless hours pouring over his Greek New Testament which became a key ingredient to the inauguration of the theological Reformation,[55] and eventually "would most profoundly shape the mind of the Western world."[56] Incredibly, the work of Erasmus would impact the English world for centuries to come, and yet, he could not speak a word of our language. One wonders where we would be today if the editorial labor of Erasmus had not initiated the fertile tradition of the TR. However, such is not the case, and we are forever grateful for the fruit of his work.

The Majority Text Position

The Majority Text advocates of the New Testament believe they have a broader and more appealing view of the New Testament text. They fully recognize the inconsistencies of the TR position and offer a stimulating alternative.

For background purposes, the terms "Majority Text" and "Byzantine Text" are used synonymously. Sturz writes, "'Byzantine' refers to that type of text which characterizes the majority of the later Greek uncial, semi-uncial and minuscule manuscripts of the New Testament."[57] The Byzantine texts—taking its name from the Byzantine Empire which is the origin of most of the manuscripts,[58] make up the vast majority of the 5,487 Greek manuscripts of the New Testament. Hence, the term most often applied to these texts is the Majority Text (MT).[59]

Two Important Textual Issues

Majority Text advocates are united on two major textual issues. First, though they have great appreciation for the traditional *Textus Receptus*, the preservation of God's Word must not be limited to this traditional text. Instead, the New Testament Scriptures are to be found within the entirety of the Byzantine tradition.

When Erasmus compiled his Greek text, the predecessor of the *Textus Receptus,* in Basel in A.D. 1516, he used "only four [Greek manuscripts] for his first edition and nothing earlier than the eleventh century."[60] These manuscripts were from the Byzantine tradition,[61] and in comparison with the rest of the manuscripts of the MT tradition, they were inferior texts.[62] Therefore, the MT "corrects those readings [of the TR] which have little or (occasionally) no support in the Greek manuscript tradition."[63] Wallace counts 1,838 times the MT differs from the TR.[64] This leads Pickering to call the TR "an excellent interim Greek text to use until the full and final story can be told;" meaning, the TR is acceptable, but only in the light of and with the support of the MT tradition.[65]

The second issue supporters of the MT affirm is that the textual approach of Brooke Foss Westcott and Fenton John Anthony Hort (W-H) is on tenuous ground.[66] Pickering says that the W-H theory of textual criticism is "erroneous at every point."[67] Though the MT position has historically maintained Pickering's view, some current MT scholars question the breadth of such a conclusion. It seems better to refurbish (or even discard) individual W-H principles which are in error than to throw out the entirety of their work. In any case, the MT position universally holds that there are several proposals and textual theories of W-H that have been too quickly embraced by modern textual scholars.[68]

Since this paper cannot deal with every W-H principle of textual criticism which the MT advocates question, I have chosen to briefly identify three of them. These will suffice to accentuate the great divide between the textual conclusions of the MT and those of W-H.

First, advocates of the Majority Text question the Westcott-Hort concept that equates the oldest manuscripts with the most reliable. They believe it is an *a priori* argument to equate the oldest manuscripts with the most reliable manuscripts. With such a textual bias, the Byzantine textual tradition will never be considered seriously since there are few Byzantine readings before the fourth century. In effect, W-H render 80% of all the available Greek texts inconsequential. Pickering counters that such a bias is a mistake, for it does not take into account that many early manuscripts are themselves unreliable. For example, he notes P66 (a papyrus codex containing portions of the Gospel of John written about A.D. 200) which has 216 careless errors,[69] many editorial insertions, and general sloppiness in fashion. "In short," writes Pickering, "P66 is a very poor copy—and yet it is one of the earliest!"[70] In addition, Pickering postulates that age is really not a factor at all, for any copy of a manuscript—by definition—must "contain a text older than it is."[71] So, the fact that there are Byzantine texts in the fourth century means that they were copied from some earlier text.

One word of caution needs to be considered. Though MT advocates may find fault with P66 (and other papyri as well) not all papyri can be looked upon with the same suspicion. In fact, the beauty of the 2nd and 3rd century papyri fragments is they are clear testimonials to the reality of the New Testament without unfolding the whole of the New Testament text. Many are credible witnesses to the historicity of the Greek autographa and must not be overlooked because of some textual agenda. If absolute commitment to a textual family is an "agenda," then does not this become the MT's own version of the W-H *a priori* argument?

A second charge against the W-H critical method battles the suggestion that since there is no extant Greek manuscript dated prior to the fourth century that can be clearly identified as belonging to the MT family, then a Byzantine text is always secondary to the earliest manuscripts. While the W-H tradition seeks to erode confidence in the MT by making it a late-date recension, Sturz (who does not embrace the MT position) has done an admirable job of laying this charge to rest.[72] He concludes there is no justification for not allowing the Byzantine text to speak as an independent and primary text on an equal basis with any other textual family (i.e. Alexandrian) because the MT does, in fact, have credible evidence in older readings.[73] His detailed work cannot be dismissed.

Finally, the advocates of the MT consider the W-H reliance upon two of the oldest uncials (about A.D. 325), Codex Sinaiticus (א) and Codex Vaticanus (B), to be unhealthy. Pickering argues "that these two MSS disagree over 3,000 times in the space of four Gospels."[74] Since these two codices disagree continually with each other this "seriously undermines their credibility."[75] Pickering also questions how these (and other) early manuscripts could survive if they had been in continual use. He writes, "Considering the relative difficulty of acquiring copies in those days . . . any worthy copy would have been used until it wore out."[76] The implication is clear—neither codex was of value in its day and should be considered as such today. "In short," Pickering concludes, "if the history of transmission presented herein is valid we should not necessarily expect to find any early 'Byzantine' MSS. They would have been used and worn out."[77] *It should be understood that though this contention has merit—maybe even be correct, at this point it is an argument from silence.* Such an argument should be held in reserve until time either verifies or alters it.

Two Contributions and One Concern of the MT Text

The MT position offers two significant considerations to the textual discussion. First, the sheer mass of Byzantine textual material must have some bearing on the identity of the New Testament text. Whether one agrees fully with Hodges' textual principles or not, one must honestly wrestle with his conclusion. He writes,

> The present writer would like to suggest that the impasse to which we are driven when the arguments of modern criticism are carefully weighed and sifted is due almost wholly to a refusal to acknowledge the obvious. The manuscript tradition of an ancient book will, under any but the most exceptional conditions, multiply in a reasonably regular fashion with the result that the copies nearest the autograph will normally have the largest number of descendants. The further

removed in the history of transmission a text becomes from its source the less time it has to leave behind a large family of offspring. Hence, in a large tradition where a pronounced unity is observed between, let us say, eighty per cent of the evidence, a very strong presumption is raised that this numerical preponderance is due to direct derivation from the very oldest sources.[78]

The second consideration is offered in the work of Sturz which argues that at the very least the MT should be granted independent status operating with basic equality with any other textual family. Clearly, the MT has proven accurate when other textual traditions have failed (e.g. Matthew 1:5,7,8,10),[79] so if it is accurate in the first chapter of the New Testament, why not allow it an equal "vote" throughout the rest of the chapters of the New Testament?

For those who champion this position, it is necessary to temper some MT arguments because of the comparative newness of its printed critical editions of the New Testament. The TR and the CT have had the benefit of time and multiple editions. To date there have only been two printings of the critical MT (1982 and 1985), and these have only been offered in the last twenty years.[80] Though the MT brings great benefit to textual issues it still is in need of maturity.

The Critical Text Position

This view states that God's Word is available to man through the multiple copies of the autographa. It treats both the Old Testament and the New Testament language-texts in much the same way. In effect, God gave His Word perfectly through human agents. These men were supernaturally protected as they wrote these words of God into human language. God expected His words to be copied (Deuteronomy 17:18) and even translated so that all nations might understand His commands and become disciples of His Son (Matthew 28:19-20).

An important and controversial ingredient to this view is that though God inspired and protected the inauguration of His written Word to man, He nowhere promises to preserve His Word through one specific text or family of texts. Sturz writes, "While God promised that His Word would be preserved, 'Heaven and earth shall pass away, but my words will not pass away' (Matthew 24:35), He did not stipulate in the Scriptures that He would keep Christian scribes from error or that the text-type with the most copies would be the best text."[81] He continues,

> Inspiration has to do with the very words which were originally God-breathed in the vocabulary and style of the original writers.

Providence has to do with all that God has allowed to come to pass in the preservation of that which was originally given by inspiration.[82]

Supporters of this view, however, differ on several significant issues. First, there is variation on which of the numerous manuscripts or manuscript families more closely preserves the original autographa, and second, there is some question as to whether one can emphatically say, as does Sturz, that Scripture speaks to its own preservation. As to the first, there is a remarkable difference of persuasion between the preservation of the Old Testament and the New Testament. The Old Testament often escapes scrutiny while battles continue to rage over the New Testament copies. The Alands[83] summarize the reason as follows:

> Until the beginning of the fourth century the text of the New Testament developed freely. It was a "living text" in the Greek literary tradition, unlike the text of the Hebrew Old Testament, which was subject to strict controls because (in the oriental tradition) the consonantal text was holy.[84]

Here is where the debate heightens, and it clearly focuses on the early copies of the New Testament autographa. For the Alands, the term "living text" means that the early copyists of the New Testament "felt themselves free to make corrections in the text, improving it by their own standard of correctness, whether grammatically, stylistically, or more substantively."[85] This stands opposite the history of the Hebrew consonantal text where careful and meticulous hands copied the writings of Moses and the Prophets. So, here lies the textual mountain which must be conquered.

Because the early New Testament manuscripts were not uniform—and many present a casual appearance—there was no standardized text until the third/fourth century.[86] The Alands' research determines that by the third/fourth centuries there developed two unmistakable textual families, and these are the Egyptian text family (Alexandrian), and the Byzantine text family.[87] The Alands see the vast majority of the earlier copies as forming the Alexandrian text. In their view the MT tradition was widely used because of the influence of the exegetical school at Antioch, and many church fathers like Eusebius, Athanasius, and Chrysostom—all using and promoting their text of choice; namely, the Byzantine text.[88]

To the Alands, the MT, which was the text of choice for centuries, became more readable than the Alexandrian because through time editors smoothed out difficult passages, conflated others, and polished those passages they deemed in need of clarification. Therefore, in the Alands' view, and many others who subscribe to the multiplicity of manuscripts ideal, the little used

Alexandrian textual family remained somewhat rough in its readings, and therefore, true to the original. In their view, then, the Alexandrian family of texts will always have precedence over the Byzantine family tradition—except in rare cases.[89] These so-called "rare cases" are due to the fact that the Alexandrian manuscripts do not agree with clarity on the original textual reading (e.g. Luke 11:14; Romans 5:1).

The million-dollar question then is this: Can one be emphatically certain that the original text is to be essentially sought in the Alexandrian textual family? This seems to be the unquestioned position of the majority of CT supporters. However, is this truly dealing with the multiplicity of manuscripts—weighing the value of each—or is it a mere rehearsal of the W-H *a priori* argument? For this reason, Sturz offers his research as a viable and significant option to balance the position of many CT advocates.[90] It seems somewhat duplicitous to espouse the multiple copy model and yet refuse to handle each text (or textual family) on equal footing. Therefore, Sturz's examination becomes a noteworthy caution that what one believes in theory he should practice in fact.

The second crucial issue of concern revolves around the statements of God (or lack of them) in His Word about the preservation matter itself. To put it another way, many hold that God has not promised in His Scriptures to preserve His Word. One author foregoes any Scriptural data and plainly writes,

> God has providentially preserved the text of Scripture in multiple manuscripts throughout history so that none of its doctrinal content is lost or affected adversely. However, one must remember that this conclusion is not based on an explicit verse of Scripture; it is based on the evidence of history. Therefore, we need to use all that historical evidence when we make decisions concerning the text of Scripture.[91]

In all due fairness, there are some within this movement who, though not as bold as Struz, disagree with the view of the above author, but do so tentatively. These do not courageously support their argument with unambiguous exegetical and theological data. They seem more apologetic than didactic. In effect, their timid voice is scarcely heard over the thunderous waves of those who emphatically declare there is no Scriptural support for the preservation of God's Word.

This, then, may be a second significant caution for those who maintain this view. Though all fundamentalists who embrace this view believe in an inspired autographa, they may not be arguing from an adequate platform. Authority rests in Scripture alone—its proclamation of exegetical truths and

207

patient explanation of theological precepts. Any view without such support finds itself at the mercy of historians and paleontologists. To put it more cogently, all arguments about Scripture and which concern Scripture must—in some respect—rest on exegetical and theological data. If we do not reason from Scripture, then we will reason around it, and this has inevitably led some fundamentalists to squabble more about historical information than discuss what the actual text and context of Scriptures declare. Though history is necessary, it is never the ultimate appeal—this alone belongs to the text of Scripture.[92]

A Call to Textual Realism and Biblical Preservation

The goal of this chapter, up to this point, has been to accurately digest the textual positions of fundamentalism relating to the preservation of Scripture, noting both strengths and weaknesses of each group. In review, there are two basic positions on the preservation issue with the second fragmenting into three varieties. The first position views the King James Version as the God-inspired text for this age. It typically has little regard for the original language-texts of the Testaments. However, the vast majority of fundamentalists hold to a variation of the second position which views the preservation of the Word of God as a language-text matter. The fragmentation which has occurred is the result of each group's ultimate conclusion as to which language-text copy, or family of copies, best preserve the original text.

Though there is little discussion concerning the preservation of the Old Testament text since most (properly or improperly) feel secure with the Masoretic text-type, there is a great deal of dialogue and printed material on the New Testament text. The TR, MT, and CT adherents have become entrenched and dialogue has seemingly come to a stalemate. Can there be a reasoned expression of compromise among fundamentalists who differ on this textual issue? I believe it can be done with two provisos: First, each view must be adequately heard and weighed for its strengths and weaknesses; and second, each group must view Holy Scripture in light of the nature of God, the purpose of written revelation, the multiple copies of each original language-text, and with the security that we possess the Word of God in written form. Since the first of the two conditions has made up the bulk of this chapter, the second will now be offered in the form of four reasoned principles. These principles are an attempt to encourage irenic discussion among fundamentalists within the boundaries of Scriptural logic. In clear terms, it is a call to textual realism offered in the spirit of Christian grace.

The starting place for discussion on preservation begins with the nature of God

Augustus Strong defined God as "the infinite and perfect Spirit in whom all things have their source, support, and end."[93] This definition mines several deep, but necessary facts about God. First, God is. He is the "first truth"[94] of all that exists, and Scripture introduces Him as the Creator of time, space, and matter (Genesis 1-2). Second, God is active in history. He is not an absentee God, as Deists would propose,[95] but as the Apostle Paul preached, "In Him we live and move and have our being" (Acts 17:28). Finally, God is active in history to bring about His desired ends. In other words, the God of the Bible "worketh all things after the counsel of His own will" (Ephesians 1:11) or as James said, "Known unto God are all his works from the beginning of the world" (Acts 15:18). He is not capricious or uncertain about anything in His created world. God is in complete and authoritative control. In truth, there is not a single atom in this universe or cell in one's physical body floating about without Divine knowledge or control. He is the Sovereign Creator and Sustainer of the created world, and His creation is following His plan—exactly.

Since the nature of God is both powerful and precise, it should be understood that His Word, whether spoken or written, manifests these same divine qualities. When God spoke in history, He did so fully expecting all that He said will accomplish all that He intended. Isaiah quotes the Lord saying, "My word. . .that goeth forth out of my mouth; it shall not return unto me void, but it shall accomplish that which I please, and it shall prosper in the thing whereto I sent it" (55:11). When God wanted His Word put in written form, He did so on His own initiative by transferring select eternal thoughts through the personalities of holy, human agents, causing each to record His words without distortion or error (2 Peter 1:20-21). For this reason the written words of God are affirmed by the biblical writers with such terms as, "the words of the Lord" (Exodus 24:4), "the Scripture of Truth" (Daniel 10:21), and "the Holy Scriptures" (Romans 1:2). Clearly, these men considered what they had recorded as directly and immediately from the mind of God.

God initiated and supernaturally guided the record of Truth into written form through human agents. He also took full responsibility in accurately sustaining His Word for future generations. The very nature of God demands His providential care for every matter in the created world so that His perfect and immutable ends are accomplished. Of course, this would also include His written Word.

Preservation rests upon the purpose of written revelation

Since God is perfect and infinite in His nature, He is far above the natural, finite limitations of man. "In this sense," writes Grudem, "God is said to be incomprehensible."[96] Therefore, of necessity, God must unveil Himself to man if man is to know anything about God. This unveiling is what is more plainly called revelation.

God's revelation of Himself to man takes two basic forms.[97] On the one hand, God uses general revelation (e.g. creation, Psalm 19; and moral consciousness, Romans 2:14-15) to manifest His glorious, supernatural nature to people of all nations and walks of life. However, on the other hand, God uses special revelation (e.g. Jesus Christ, John 1:1-18; and the written Word, Romans 1:1-4) to unfold His will and redemptive plan.

The widely-used term "Word of God" may refer to the Son of God (Revelation 19:13) because of His "role in communicating the character of God to us and of expressing the will of God for us"[98] (John 1:18). But, the definition most germane to this discussion relates to the literal speech of God or the specific statements of God given to man. This speech took four different forms in history: creative speech[99] (Genesis 1:3; Hebrews 1:3), direct speech[100] (Exodus 3:1-22), indirect speech[101] (Jeremiah 1:9 with 2:1-2f.; Luke 1:19), and written speech[102] (Exodus 24:4-7; 2 Peter 3:15-16).

For thinking people it should be apparent why God chose to preserve His speech in written form. First, truth inscripturated gives "a much *more accurate preservation* of God's word for subsequent generations."[103] Erickson concurs,

> It [revelation] could, of course, be preserved by oral retelling or by being fixed into a definite tradition, and this certainly was operative in the period which sometimes intervened between the occurrence of the initial revelation and its inscripturation. Certain problems attach to this, however, when long periods of time are involved, for oral tradition is subject to erosion and modification.[104]

The reliability of inscripturation is clearly seen by the way the New Testament authors quoted authoritatively the Old Testament text (Matthew alone does this sixty-two times),[105] and by the way they easily interchanged the terms "Scripture" and "God" (e.g. Galatians 3:8 and Romans 9:17).[106] In addition, Christ constantly maintained the reliability of the Old Testament text.[107] Several examples from the Book of Matthew are as follows: In 4:1-11, He authoritatively quoted Moses (e.g. Deuteronomy 8:3) and David (Psalm 91:11-12) to confront Satan. In 12:40, He gives unquestioned support to Jonah being swallowed by a large fish. He corrects a current, improper interpretation of the Law in 15:3-6. He affirms in 19:4-5 the historicity of Adam and Eve. He explains without contradiction the marriage covenant in 19:1-11 using both Genesis 2 and Deuteronomy 24. He confirms in 23:35 the fact of Abel's murder in Genesis 4; and in 24:37-38, He validates the universal flood in Noah's day. It should, then, be of no surprise that Christ calls God's Word "truth" (John 17:17) and calls His religious contemporaries to "search the Scriptures" (John 5:39), for He clearly considered the written text of His day verifiable and trustworthy.

Second, God's Word in written form allows "the *opportunity for repeated inspection* of words," writes Grudem, and "permits careful study and discussion, which leads to better understanding and more complete obedience."[108] Daniel is an excellent biblical example of this point. Chapter nine opens with the statement that Daniel was studying the word of God written by the prophet Jeremiah. Through his personal study Daniel writes, "I understood" the word which the Lord gave to Jeremiah that the captivity would be "seventy years" (9:2). This understanding led Daniel to fall on his knees and utter one of the most profound confessional prayers of the Bible. Jeremiah's preserved inscripturation of God's word accomplished in Daniel a significant purpose of the written Word of God; namely, through study of the text each child of God is drawn into a closer and more meaningful relationship with Himself. Apart from Scripture—preserved and available—there is no trustworthy divine-medium for personal growth in the lives of God's people (1 Peter 2:1-3).

Third, God's written words are "*accessible to many more people* than they are when preserved merely through [the] memory and oral repetition"[109] of a few. This can be clearly seen in the Apostle Paul's letter to the church at Colosse (Colossians 1:2). At the conclusion of this letter he writes (4:16), "And when this epistle is read among you, cause that it be read also in the church of the Laodiceans. . . ." In effect, the written Word of God is able to span both geographical boundaries as well as time without the aid of any person's memory or oral tradition. The written word, then, is God's indispensable method of transferring truth to large pockets of people without the need of the original human agent to whom God initially gave the message.

These three benefits of written revelation may seem obvious, but are mentioned here for their significant contribution. They are essential facts to assure man that God's written truth is of highest reliability, permanently established, and is widely available. For this reason, the Apostle Peter emphatically declares without embarrassment that God's word "liveth and abideth forever" (1 Peter 1:23).

Preservation depends upon the multiplicity of language-text copies

It is clear from both Scriptural and historical data that God does not designate any single manuscript or textual family as the "true text" by which all copies of the Holy Scriptures are to be measured. The plain fact is there is no single manuscript, in either Hebrew or Greek, that agrees completely with another. Is this a cause for concern? Should this fact bully us into an indefensible textual position that refuses to examine all textual data honestly? Is there not a reasonable answer that will promote unity within the ranks of God's people rather than divisive fragmentation? Here, then, is an important reasoned principle that if laid beside the other principles given above (and one yet to come), will allow us an adequate platform to deal objectively with the massive amount of textual material available today. For the sake of space, these next few paragraphs will focus on the hotly contested New Testament copies.

Of the 5,487 Greek manuscripts, Wallace calculates there "are approximately 300,000 textual variants among New Testament manuscripts."[110] This figure may seem overwhelming at first glance, but when the variants are analyzed by the CT editors of the UBS (4th revision) only 1,437[111] are deemed worthy of any consideration at all. Wallace compares the differences between the TR, MT, and CT texts and finds that these three texts are in agreement "almost 98 percent" of the time.[112] When these differences are weighed against one another "these differences are so minor that they neither show up in translation nor affect exegesis."[113] As Wallace compares the MT with the CT, he comes to the significant conclusion that "the majority text and the modern critical text are very much alike, in both quality [doctrinal purity] and quantity [textual agreement]."[114]

Wallace's conclusion can be illustrated by a careful study of the textual variants in the first chapter of the New Testament. Once these textual variants are identified, several observations become evident. Interestingly, when the variants of Matthew 1 are listed, the three Greek texts are not in harmony in their selection of textual differences. The TR, of course, lists no variants, the CT lists only seven, and the MT lists eighteen.

Here is a sampling of these variants to give an overview of the differences. In 1:5, the TR and the MT spell "Boaz," Βοόζ and the CT spells the same name, Βόες. In this case the TR and the MT agree with the LXX spelling (e.g. Ruth 4:21). In 1:6, the MT and the CT agree on the spelling of Solomon's name Σολομῶνα while the TR uniquely adds one letter Σολομώ ντα. Of great interest are the two names "Asa" and "Amon" (1:7-8, 10) in the kingly lineage of David. Again, the TR and the MT follow the LXX spelling (e.g. 1 Chronicles 3:10, 14) while the CT has two unique spellings that actually change the name-identity. Instead of "Asa"['Ασά] the CT reads "Asaph" ['Ασάφ], and in the place of "Amon" ['Αμών] the CT reads "Amos" ['Αμώς]. Finally, in verse 25, the CT does not include the words found in the TR and the MT, "her firstborn son" [τὸν υἱὸν αὐτῆς τὸν πρωτότοκον]

Before any conclusion is offered, five observations are in order. First, most of the text of Matthew 1 is in full agreement between the TR, MT, and CT. Second, the original text is identified only when the TR, MT, and the CT are viewed alongside each other and given equal merit. Third, the context of Matthew 1 (when cross-referenced with the chronologies of the Old Testament [LXX], i.e. 1 Chronicles 3) plays a role in setting aside variant readings when identifying the names of the kings in the lineage of David.[115] Fourth, if the CT reading is adopted in verse 25, verses 18-24 indisputably teach Mary's virginity; so obviously, Jesus would be "her firstborn." Consequently, the CT reading does not depreciate the biblical doctrine of the virgin birth, nor does the fuller reading of the TR and MT somehow heighten the doctrine in this specific passage. Therefore, the selection of either reading does not change the interpretation of this verse nor its contextual significance. Finally, through the full comparison of the multiple copies, the original text of Matthew 1 is identified and we can safely say we have the word of God in the first chapter of the New Testament.

We see that comparison of multiple texts of the New Testament is of great benefit in study of a passage. When the multiple copies are equally considered, one can gain confidence about the wording of the original language-text manuscript. In the small percentage of variants where the text does not seem clear (eg. Matthew 1:25), we can be assured that we know *exactly* where these difficult passages are, and we can also be assured that the general sense of that verse is not lost. In such rare cases, we must exercise patience with one another for not all the data is in—as of yet.

In light of this conclusion, it is imperative to understand that if some question persists about a certain textual variant, it is not the same thing as denying a biblical doctrine including the preservation of God's Word. We distinctly rest in the truth that God's providential care for His Word protects His purpose for His written revelation, so that it will not be altered. A thorough study of the available multiple manuscripts confirms this verity, and fully supports the statement of Christ when He says that His Word remains "unbroken" (John 10:34-35).[116]

The ultimate benefit of a proper understanding of preservation is the believer's security that he possesses the word of God

When the Scriptures are read, it is clear that the biblical authors fully accepted each other's writings as complete, true, and from the mouth of God. Though years and even centuries passed, time did not diminish the word nor cause the biblical authors to doubt that their copies of the Scripture were anything but pure and from God. The biblical writers unquestionably believed that they held the Word of God in their day.

The first writer of the Old Testament encouraged and even commanded copying of the documents of Scripture. Moses mandated copies of the law to be made for each future Israelite king so they might do "all" the Word of God (Deuteronomy 17:18-20). Joshua, having Moses' compositions (whether originals or not) was told by God to meditate on these writings "day and night" so that his way would be "prosperous" and "have good success" (Joshua 1:8). King David recognized the importance of the Word of God in his hands, and wrote that when God's Word is kept in his heart, "there is great reward." In the days of Ezra and Nehemiah (about 1,000 years after Moses), a great spiritual revival of God's people took place as they "were attentive unto the book of the law" (Nehemiah 8:3). Since the people could not understand the Hebrew, the Levites translated the Word of God into Aramaic "and gave the sense, and caused them to understand the reading" (8:8). Because of their translation of the Hebrew copy of the Word of God, all the people "understood the words that were declared unto them" (8:12), and they became obedient to the Word of God (8:17). The undeniable truth here is that the Old Testament writers believed they possessed God's Word, and whether through copies or translations of those copies, when the Word of God was read and proclaimed, the listener encountered God's truth, and spiritual revival was often the result.

Just as the Old Testament writers believed their copies of the Hebrew language-text were the very words of God, the New Testament writers follow suit. Over fifty times the writers of the New Testament used the term "Scriptures" [γραφή] to identify the Old Testament writings, and in each case the term refers to the *written revelation* of God.[117] The Apostle Paul calls these writings, "God-breathed" (2 Timothy 3:16). So, writes Grudem,

> Paul here affirms that all of the Old Testament writings are *theopneustos*, "breathed out by God" . . . breathing must be understood as a metaphor for speaking the words of Scripture. This verse thus states in brief form what was evident in many passages in the Old Testament: the Old Testament writings are regarded as God's Word in written form. For every word of the Old Testament, God is the one

who spoke (and still speaks) it, although God used human agents to write these words down.[118]

The New Testament writers and their writings were actually pre-authenticated by Christ when he said in John 14:26 and 16:13 that the Holy Spirit will "bring all things to your remembrance" and "guide you into all truth." When Luke set out to write his Gospel, he used "eyewitnesses" (1:2), but he clearly understood his work was of God when he wrote in 1:3 that his "perfect understanding" was "from above" ('ἄνωθεν). The Apostle Peter recognized the writing of Scripture to be the work of the Holy Spirit when he wrote that "no prophecy of Scripture is of any private [human] origin" (1:20). However, holy men were "moved by the Holy Spirit" (1:21) when they wrote down God's words. The Apostle Paul emphatically claimed, "If any man think himself to be a prophet, or spiritual, let him acknowledge that the things that I write unto you are the commandments of the Lord" (I Corinthians 14:37). The New Testament ends with the sobering words of the Apostle John, "For I testify unto every man that heareth the words of the prophecy of this book, if any man shall add unto these things, God shall add unto him the plagues that are written in this book" (22:18). There does not seem to be any doubt that the New Testament authors knew their words were from God and were on the same level as the Old Testament Scriptures (2 Peter 3:15-16).

It is clear that both the Old and New Testament authors believed they possessed the very words of God from previous biblical writers and were keenly aware that they themselves were instruments of God to record God's word in the same fashion as their counterparts. We may learn much today about biblical preservation by reviewing this fundamental conviction of the biblical authors. This calm and settled assurance of the biblical writers should also be our same guarantee. As the biblical writers believed they both wrote God's word and possessed His thoughts in written form from previous generations, so today, the believer's supreme joy is that he possesses God's very words in a written text and he, like the writer of Psalm 119:140, may confidently declare, "Thy word is very pure; therefore, thy servant loveth it."

CONCLUSION

The goal of this chapter has been to address the fundamentalist movement on the issue of biblical preservation. We who are fundamentalists by choice and conviction find ourselves fractured over the Word of God, and this is distressing given the high view of Scripture each one of us possesses. As initially stated, all of us agree to the fact that we possess God's Word in written form. We also strongly believe that the Word of God we hold in our hands is complete, without error, and sufficient to meet every spiritual need we have.

However, we find ourselves battling over our understanding of how God actually accomplishes the preservation of His word that enables us to boldly declare that we have His word in written form. Therefore, this chapter has been committed to carefully (and hopefully without bias) articulating the various views within our movement. It is important we understand each other's position on the text. In addition, there has been a desire to affirm openly both the contributions and the concerns the different preservation views present in light of the multiple copies of the Hebrew and Greek texts we possess today. Finally, four reasoned principles have been presented that seem (to this author) to be the most logical and sensible way of finding common ground based upon the facts that both history and Scripture afford us. The final outcome must wait, but in the middle of the debate on this issue it is hoped that we can address one another both factually and graciously. To this end this chapter is offered.

---

[1]The Latin phrase *ipsissima verba* means "the very words." It is used by C. H. Spurgeon, *Lectures to My Students*, 6th printing (Grand Rapids: Zondervan, 1976), p. 73: "Brethren, if you are in the habit of keeping to the precise sense of the Scripture before you, I will further recommend you to hold to the *ipsissima verba*, the very words of the Holy Ghost. . . ."

[2]A significant illustration of this high view of Scripture and its defense is found in the hundred-year-old published series called, *The Fundamentals.* James M. Gray wrote an article in this series entitled, "The Inspiration of the Bible—Definition, Extent and Proof," 1972 reprint (Grand Rapids: Baker), 2:2-60. Clearly, he considered the "authenticity and credibility" of the Bible an impregnable fact not to be undervalued. Fundamentalism today still maintains this high view of Scripture.

[3]Cornelius Van Til, *The New Modernism*, pp. 137-159 reveals the duplicitous and confusing language of Karl Barth who believed, "The text of the Bible, then, is a witness to revelation. It is an 'echo' of the voice of God." However, in the words of Carl Henry, "The Bible is no mere record of revelation, but is itself revelation." ("Divine Revelation and the Bible," p. 256, from Walvoord, *Inspiration and Interpretation* (Grand Rapids: Eerdmans, 1957). Also, see Ryrie's excellent small evaluation of Barthianism, *Neo-Orthodoxy* (Chicago: Moody Press, 1956).

[4]An example of this view, with lingering influence, is by Jack Rogers and Donald McKim, *The Authority and Interpretation of the Bible* (San Francisco: Harper & Row, 1979). Their "restrictive view" means that the function of inspired Scripture was to bring people to salvation not to educate its generation in matters of science and history. Since the Bible is not "a textbook of science or an academic tract" it may not be reliable in some of its nonsalvific statements (p. 26).

[5]D. A. Carson, "Recent Developments in the Doctrine of Scripture," in *Hermeneutics, Authority, and Canon*, eds. Carson and Woodbridge (Grand Rapids: Zondervan Publishing House, 1986), pp. 11-14, adequately disposes of Ian Rennie's argument which tries to separate "plenary inspiration" from "verbal inspiration" to support the thesis that the Bible contains various levels of inspiration.

[6]Richard Clearwaters, "Nothing to Explain—Nothing to Hide," *Central Bible Quarterly*, 3:1 (1960), p. 38. This article was reprinted in *The Great Conservative Baptist Compromise* (Minneapolis: Central Seminary Press, n.d.), pp. 186-200.

[7]Clearwaters, "Nothing to Explain—Nothing to Hide," p. 33.

[8]A statement I heard on several occasions from his pulpit ministry.

[9]In all three books Fuller acted more as an editor than an original writer. Of the 27 chapters that comprise his three books, only 5 are authored by Fuller (3, are the introductions to each book). The other 22 chapters are carefully selected and edited articles.

[10]Roy Beacham and Kevin Bauder, eds. *Only One Bible?* (Grand Rapids, Kregel, 2001), p. 14.

[11]Thomas Strouse, "Fundamentalism and the Authorized Version," an independent paper published in the mid 1990s by the author, p. 10.

[12]Strouse, p. 12.

[13]Emanuel Tov, *Textual Criticism of the Hebrew Text* (Minneapolis: Fortress Press, 1992), p. 23.

[14]Kurt and Barbara Aland, *The Text of the New Testament*, Erroll Rhodes translator (Grand Rapids: Eerdmans, 1987), p. 74. This number varies, according to the Alands, because uncial fragments which were once identified as a single manuscript are now properly identified and connected to its codex, some have been lost due to wars or natural disasters, and textual criticism continues to uncover new manuscripts though "it is unlikely that the future will bring any comparable increases" (p. 75).

[15]Edward F. Hills, *The King James Version Defended*, 4th ed. (Des Moines: Christian Research Press, 1984), p. 93. Of the 280 pages, Hills allots only nine pages (pp. 91-100) to the preservation of the Old Testament text. Regrettably, I found very little written material from this viewpoint on the preservation of the Old Testament text.

[16]Hills, p. 93.

[17]Erroll Rhodes and Liana Lupas, *The Translators to the Readers: The Original Preface of the King James Version of 1611 Revisited* (New York: American Bible Society, 1997), p. 57.

[18]Rhodes and Lupas, p. 57, footnote 172.

[19]Ernst Wurthwein, *The Text of the Old Testament*, trans. Erroll Rhodes (Grand Rapids: Eerdmans, 1979), p. 14.

[20]For a more detailed study, see Ellis Brotzman, *Old Testament Textual Criticism* (Grand Rapids: Baker, 1994), pp. 42-61. He divides the textual transmission of the Hebrew text into the following time periods: (1) Autographs – 300 B.C., (2) 300 B.C. – A.D. 135, (3) A.D. 135 – 500, (4) A.D. 500 – 1000, (5) A.D. 1000 – 1450, and (6) A.D. 1450 – present.

[21]Tov, pp. 106, 117, postulates the existence of five textual groups based upon his paleographical analysis of the Qumran documents dated from the middle of the second century B.C. to A.D. 68.

[22]Wurthwein, p. 14.

[23]Wurthwein, p. 14, "The *Sopherim* wrote out the consonantal text proper, the *Nakdanim* . . . added vowel points and accents to the manuscript, and the *Masoretes* added the marginal and final Masoretic notes."

[24]Brotzman, p. 47.

[25]Brotzman, p. 49.

[26]Brotzman, p. 50, "The Islamic conquest of Palestine in A.D. 638 made possible a revival of Jewish textual work in Tiberias, a city on the western shore of the Sea of Galilee."

[27]Wurthwein, pp. 23-24.

[28]Wurthwein, p. 24.

[29]The ben Asher codex is identified as the Leningrad manuscript B 19a.

[30]*Biblia Hebraica Leningradensia* (Boston: Brill, 2001), pp. vii-viii, furnishes the full name as Jacob ben Chayyim Ibn Adonijah, and provides additional information about his life and work. Also, Wurthwein, p. 37, footnote 65, observes that, "Jacob ben Chayyim was a Jewish refugee from Tunis who later became a Christian. He died before 1538."

[31]Wurthwein, p. 37.

[32]Brotzman, pp. 94-96.

[33]Brotzman, p. 95.

[34]Brotzman, p. 95.

[35]The Septuagint was initially translated several centuries before Christ. It is significant for several reasons (see Brotzman, p. 75), (1) It is the earliest translation of the Hebrew, (2) It contains the entire Old Testament, (3) It supports readings that

are not of the Masoretic tradition, and (4) It is quoted in the New Testament by the biblical writers.

[36]Edward F. Hills, *The King James Version Defended*, would be representative of this view.

[37]A representative of this view would be Wilbur N. Pickering, *The Identity of the New Testament Text,* revised ed. (Nashville: Thomas Nelson, 1980).

[38]The Critical Text is found in either the United Bible Societies, 4th revised edition of *The Greek New Testament* (1993), or Nestle-Aland's 27th edition of *Novum Testamentum Graece* (1994).

[39]I have consulted Edward F. Hills, pp. 95-106; Bruce Metzger, *The Text of the New Testament*, 2nd ed. (New York: Oxford University Press, 1968), pp. 95-106; and William Combs, "Erasmus and the Textus Receptus," *Detroit Baptist Seminary Journal*, 1:1 (Spring 1996), pp. 35-53.

[40]Metzger, p. 100, "The second edition became the basis of Luther's German translation." Additionally, Combs notes, p. 48, the title of the second edition was changed to *Novum Testamentum.*

[41]Ronald Bainton, *Here I Stand* (New York: Abingdon-Cokesbury Press, 1950), pp. 88, 125, reveals the impact of Erasmus' Greek New Testament upon Martin Luther. He writes, "The Latin for Matt. 4:17 read *penitentiam agite*, 'do penance,' but from the Greek New Testament of Erasmus, Luther had learned that the original meant simply 'be penitent.' The literal sense was 'change your mind'. . . . This was what Luther himself called a 'glowing' discovery. In this crucial instance a sacrament of the church did not rest on the institution of Scripture."

[42]This unity of tradition is portrayed in the "Preface" of Η ΚΑΙΝΗ ΔΙΑΘΗΚΗ by the Trinitarian Bible Society (which is the standard TR reproduction). It should be noted that the Elzevers produced seven editions of the Greek New Testament from 1624 to 1678. However, the Trinitarian Bible Society seems to consider only the first three editions of Elzever under this banner term of TR.

[43]Hills, p. 204.

[44]Strouse, p. 12.

[45]Metzger, pp. 107-108. Also, Alexander Souter, *The Text and Canon of the New Testament*, 2nd ed. (London: Gerald Duckworth & Co., 1954), pp. 89-90.

[46]Hills, p. 204.

[47]Hills, p. 204.

[48]Hills, p. 208.

[49]Hills, p. 204.

[50]Harry Sturz, *The Byzantine Text-Type and New Testament Textual Criticism*, (Nashville: Thomas Nelson, 1984), pp. 35, 37, sees Hills entire argument resting on one's faith in the providence of God. Sturz correctly replies, "With no intention of belittling faith or of treating Scriptural doctrines irreverently, there are elements in Hills' argument with which orthodox Christians may disagree." Faith in the providence of God is clearly taught in the Scriptures, but blind faith in someone's textual agenda cannot be equated with either biblical faith or providence.

[51]Hills, p. 204.

[52]In Ephesians 1:18 the TR reads, τοὺς ὀφθαλμοὺς τῆς διανοίας ὑμῶν, translated "the eyes of your understanding;" while both the CT (Critical Text) and the MT (Majority Text) read, τοὺς ὀφθαλμοὺς τῆς καρδίας ὑμῶν, translated, "the eyes of your heart." Also, the TR reads in 3:9, ἡ κοινωνία τοῦ μυστηρίου, translated, "the fellowship of the mystery;" while both the CT and the MT read, ἡ οἰκονομία τοῦ μυστηρίου, translated, "the dispensation of the mystery."

[53]Hills, p. 208.

[54]Ronald Bainton, *Erasmus of Christendom* (New York: Charles Scribner's Sons, 1969), p. 59.

[55]Bainton, *Here I Stand*, p. 125, "From the press of Forben in 1516 was issued a handsome volume, the Greek type reminiscent of manuscripts, the text accompanied by a literal translation and illumined by annotations. The volume reached Wittenberg as Luther was lecturing on the ninth chapter of Romans, and thereafter became his working tool."

[56]Bainton, *Erasmus of Christendom*, p. 97.

[57]Sturz, p. 13. In literary terminology, the uncial manuscripts are those printed in capital letters and are not connected to each other. These manuscripts are found between the 4th and 10th centuries. The minuscule manuscripts are those written in a running fashion, or in cursive, and are found from the 10th century onward. Harold Greenlee, *Introduction to New Testament Criticism* (Grand Rapids: Eerdmans, 1964), p. 29, says, "Approximately nine-tenths of the extant Greek N. T. mss. are from the minuscule period."

[58]Sturz, p. 13.

[59]Greenlee, p. 62, "Approximately 95 percent of the existing mss. of the N.T. are from the eighth and later centuries, and very few of these differ appreciably from the Byzantine text."

[60]Bainton, *Erasmus of Christendom*, p. 133. There is some controversy on the number of manuscripts used by Erasmus, and when he actually used them. Bainton maintains that Erasmus only had four for the 1516 edition, but made use of seven in later editions. Kurt and Barbara Aland, *The Text of the New Testament*, Erroll

Rhodes, trans. (Grand Rapids: Eerdmans, 1987), pp. 3-4, 72, agree with Bainton's conclusion. For another view see, Greenlee, p. 70, "Erasmus had been anxious to undertake such a task and set about it willingly, using no more than six mss. which happened to be available." In distinction to both Bainton and Greenlee, Combs, p. 45, pushes the number of manuscripts to seven. In any event, scholars are agreed that the manuscripts were of a late date and they came from the Byzantine textual tradition. Metzger, p. 99, adds that none of the manuscripts used by Erasmus contained the entire New Testament.

[61]Greenlee, p. 70, says that Erasmus may have had access to one manuscript outside the Byzantine tradition. He writes, "His only ms. which was non-Byzantine and of any antiquity was Cod. 1, and he does not seem to have leaned very heavily upon its text." The Alands, p. 4, disagree, "Erasmus relied on manuscripts of the twelfth/thriteenth century which represented the Byzantine Imperial text, the Koine text, or Majority Text—however it may be known. . . ."

[62]Metzger, pp. 99-103 examines the manuscripts available to Erasmus and shows the weaknesses of each.

[63]*The NKJV Greek-English Interlinear New Testament,* (Nashville: Thomas Nelson, 1994), p. x.

[64]Daniel Wallace, "Some Second Thoughts on the Majority Text," *Bibliotheca Sacra*, 146:3 (1989), p. 276.

[65]Pickering, p. 150.

[66]Pickering gives a lengthy chapter in his book (Chapter 4: "An Evaluation of the W-H Theory," 56 pages) trying to dismantle the entire W-H theory of textual criticism. This is central to his MT argument.

[67]Pickering, p. 96.

[68]Daniel Wallace is a current illustration of one who espouses the W-H tradition. Several articles that develop his views are: (1) "Some Second Thoughts on the Majority Text," (1989), op. cit.; (2) "Inspiration, Preservation, and New Testament Criticism," *GTJ*, 12:1 (1992), pp. 21-50; and (3) "The Majority-Text Theory: History, Methods and Critique," *JETS*, 37:2 (1994), pp. 185-215.

[69]Pickering, p. 123,. He quotes others to prove his point. For primary research on P66, see, Bruce Metzger, *Manuscripts of the Greek Bible* (New York: Oxford Press, 1981), p. 66. Also, note Metzger, *The Text of the New Testament*, p. 264.

[70]Pickering, p. 123.

[71]Pickering, p. 131.

[72]Sturz, pp. 55-131 supports the thesis that the Byzantine text type is as old as the Alexandrian text type. He lists Byzantine readings as early as the second century,

and concludes that the MT should be considered an independent voice in textual matters—not a secondary voice. In other words, "The Byzantine text should be given equal weight along with the Alexandrian and 'Western' texts, in evaluating external evidence for readings" (p. 130).

[73]Sturz, p. 130.

[74]Pickering, p. 126.

[75]Pickering, p. 126.

[76]Pickering, p. 129.

[77]Pickering, p. 133.

[78]Zane Hodges, "The Greek Text of the King James Version," *Bibliotheca Sacra*, 125:4, (1968), p. 344.

[79]These verses will be discussed in the next section.

[80]*The Greek New Testament According to the Majority Text*, 1985, inscribes these words on its jacket, "This publication of *The Greek New Testament According to the Majority Text*, marks the first time in the twentieth century that a critical edition of the Greek New Testament has used the vast bulk of extant manuscripts as a basis for its text."

[81]Sturz, p. 38.

[82]Sturz, pp. 39-40.

[83]Kurt and Barbara Aland are cited not just because of their scholarship, but as Holmes, "Reasoned Eclecticism in New Testament Textual Criticism," *The Text of the New Testament in Contemporary Research*, Holmes and Ehrman eds. (Grand Rapids: Eerdmans, 1995), p. 350, asks, "Why is almost no one (other than perhaps K. Aland) willing to claim, at least with any substantial degree of confidence, that with our current critical texts we have recovered the NT in the original Greek?" In addition to their appreciation of the autographa, they have also done an excellent job, in my view, in refining W-H proposals.

[84]Kurt and Barbara Aland, p. 69.

[85]Kurt and Barbara Aland, p. 69.

[86]Kurt and Barbara Aland, pp. 56, 64-67.

[87]The Alands see the Western text family as a "phantom" textual family (pp. 55, 68-69), and reject the existence of the Caesarean and Jerusalem textual families as well—"though the theoretical possibility of these must be conceded" (p. 66).

[88]Kurt and Barbara Aland, p. 65.

[89]Kurt and Barbara Aland, p. 4, view the Byzantine Imperial text as "the most recent and poorest" of the textual families.

[90]Sturz, pp. 9-10

[91]Glenny, *One Bible Only?* pp. 122-123.

[92]See chapter 3 of this book for evaluation of several texts that support the doctrine of preservation.

[93]Augustus Strong, *Systematic Theology*, 13th printing (Old Tappan, NJ: Revell, 1976), p. 52.

[94]Strong, pp. 52-62, traces this "first truth" idea through philosophy and theology.

[95]Strong, p. 414, "[Deism] represents the universe as a self-sustained mechanism, from which God withdrew as soon as he had created it, and which he left to the process of self-development." To put it another way, this view maintains "God is the maker, not the keeper of the watch."

[96]Wayne Grudem, *Systematic Theology* (Grand Rapids: Zondervan, 1994), p. 149.

[97] See, Millard Erickson, *Christian Theology* (Grand Rapids: Baker, 1986), pp. 153-198, for a helpful discussion on "revelation."

[98]Grudem, p. 47.

[99]This speech produces (creates) something that would not otherwise have been in existence.

[100]This relates to the statements of God given directly to man without the medium of another being.

[101]This is God's word given to prophets or angels or even a donkey for the benefit of others.

[102]This is God's word in written form, specifically referring to the Bible.

[103]Grudem, p. 50.

[104]Erickson, p. 200.

[105]I have used the count of UBS, 4th edition, *The Greek New Testament*, pp. 888-889.

[106]John Wenham, "Christ's View of Scripture," from *Inerrancy*, edited by Norman Geisler (Grand Rapids: Zondervan, 1980), pp. 21-22, makes this point.

[107]Gleason Archer, "The Witness of the Bible to Its Own Inerrancy", from *The Foundation of Biblical Authority*, edited by James M. Boice (Grand Rapids: Zondervan, 1978), p. 91-93 further develops this idea.

[108]Grudem, p. 50.

[109]Grudem, p. 50.

[110]Wallace, "The Majority Text and the Original Text: Are They Identical?" *Bibliotheca Sacra*, 148:2 (1991), p. 157.

[111]UBS has a variant itself on this issue. On page v the number 1,437 is used while on page 2 the number is increased by one (1,438).

[112]Wallace, p. 158.

[113]Wallace, p. 158.

[114]Wallace, p. 158.

[115]Wallace, "Errors in the Greek Text behind Modern Translations? The cases of Matthew 1:7, 10 and Luke 23:45," from his website, www.bible.org (1998), pp. 1-4, refuses to allow the full weight of all the manuscripts to help him decide the name readings. Therefore, he maintains the CT readings and explains that biblical writers "were more *creative* in their spelling than are we" since there was "no standard spelling guidelines in the ancient world" (p. 3). In distinction to Wallace, the translators of both the NASV and NIV, who normally favor the CT, forsake the CT readings in their main text for the obvious reading.

[116]See the satisfactory interpretation of this text by William Hendriksen, *The Gospel of John*, from the *New Testament Commentary Series*, 5th printing (Grand Rapids: Baker, 1972), p.128.

[117]Grudem, p. 74, writes that in each case γραφή is used it refers to God's word in written form. Most instances are references to the Old Testament while in at least two cases, 1 Timothy 5:18 and 2 Peter 3:16, some of the New Testament writings are included.

[118]Grudem, pp. 74-75.

BIBLIOGRAPHY

Aland, Kurt and Barbara. *The Text of the New Testament.* Translated by Erroll F. Rhodes. Grand Rapids: Eerdmans Publishing Company, 1987.

Bainton, Roland. *Erasmus of Christendom.* New York: Charles Scribner's Sons, 1969.

Barrick, William. "Ancient Manuscripts and Biblical Exposition." *The Masters' Theological Journal* 9:1 (1998): 25-38.

Beacham, Roy and Bauder, Kevin, eds. *Only One Bible?* Grand Rapids: Kregel Publishers, 2001

Boice, James Montgomery, editor. *The Foundation of Biblical Authority.* Grand Rapids: Zondervan Publishing House, 1978.

Borland, James. "The Preservation of the New Testament Text: A Common Sense Approach." *The Masters' Theological Journal* 10:1 (1999): 41-51.

Brotzman, Ellis. *Old Testament Textual Criticism.* Grand Rapids: Baker Book House, 1994.

Carson, D. A. "Recent Developments in the Doctrine of Scripture." *Hermeneutics, Authority, and Canon*, eds. D. A. Carson and John Woodbridge, 5-48. Grand Rapids: Zondervan Publishing House, 1986.

_____. *The King James Version Debate: A Plea for Realism.* Grand Rapids: Baker Book House. 1979.

Clearwaters, Richard. "Nothing to Explain—Nothing to Hide." *Central Bible Quarterly* 3:1 (1960): 186-200.

Combs, William. "Erasmus and the Textus Recptus." *Detroit Baptist Seminary Journal* 1:1 (1996): 35-53.

Comfort, Philip Wesley. *The Early Manuscripts and Modern Translations of the New Testament.* Grand Rapids: Baker Book House, 1990.

Fee, Gordon. "Modern Textual Criticism and the Revival of the *Textus Receptus*." *Journal of the Evangelical Theological Society* 21:1 (1978): 19-33.

Finegan, Jack. *Encountering New Testament Manuscripts: A Working Introduction to Textual Criticism.* Grand Rapids: Eerdmans Publishing Company, 1974.

Grudem, Wayne. "Part 1: The Doctrine of the Word of God." *Systematic Theology*, 47-138. Grand Rapids: Zondervan Publishing House, 1994.

Hodges, Zane. "The Greek Text of the King James Version." *Bibliotheca Sacra* 125:4 (1968): 335-345.

Holmes, Michael. "Reasoned Eclecticism in New Testament Textual Criticism." *The Text of the New Testament in Contemporary Research*, 336-360. Bart Ehrman and Michael Holmes eds. Grand Rapids: Eerdmans Publishing Company, 1995.

Greenlee, J. H. *Introduction to New Testament Textual Criticism*, seventh printing. Grand Rapids: Eerdmans Publishing Company, 1980.

Hills, E. F. *The King James Version Defended.* fourth edition. Des Moines: Christian Research Press, 1984.

Metzger, Bruce. *The Text of the New Testament.* second edition. New York: Oxford University Press, 1968.

_____. *Manuscripts of the Greek Bible: An Introduction to Palaeography.* New York: Oxford University Press, 1981.

Pickering, Wilbur. *The Identity of the New Testament Text.* revised edition. Nashville: Thomas Nelson Publishers, 1980.

Rhodes, Erroll and Lupas, Lina. *The Translators to the Readers: The Original Preface of the King James Version of 1611 Revisited.* New York: The American Bible Society, 1997.

Skilton, John. "The Transmission of the Scriptures." *The Infallible Word,* 141-195, By members of the faculty of Westminster Theological Seminary, third printing.Philadelphia: Presbyterian and Reformed Publishing Company, 1946.

Strouse, Thomas. "Fundamentalism and the Authorized Version." A paper presented at the National Leadership Conference, Landsdale, PA, February 1996.

Sturz, Harry. *The Byzantine Text-Type and New Testament Textual Criticism.* Nashville:Thomas Nelson Publishers, 1984.

Tov, Emmanuel. *Textual Criticism of the Hebrew Text.* Minneapolis: Fortress Press, 1992.

Wallace, Daniel. "Some Second Thoughts on the Majority Text." *Bibliotheca Sacra* 146:3 (1989): 270-290.

_____. "The Majority Text and the Original: Are They Identical?" *Bibliotheca Sacra* 148:2 (1991): 158-166.

_____. "Inspiration, Preservation, and New Testament Criticism." *Grace Theological Journal* 12:1 (1992): 21-50.

_____. "The Majority-Text Theory: History, Methods and Critique." *Journal of the Evangelical Theological Society* 37:2 (1994): 185-215.

_____. "Errors in the Greek Text behind Modern Translations? The cases of Matthew 1:7, 10 and Like 23:45." Taken from Wallace's website, www.bible.org. (1998): 1-4.

_____. "An Apologia for a Broad View of Ipsissima Vox." A paper presented at the 51st Annual Meeting of the Evangelical Theological Society, Danvers, MA., November 1999.

Wurthwein, Ernst. *The Text of the Old Testament: An Introduction to the Biblia Hebraica.* Translated by Erroll F. Rhodes. Grand Rapids: Eerdmans Publishing Company, 1979.

How Much Difference Do the Differences Make?

Mark Minnick

During the Fall of my freshman year of college I memorized the book of I John. It was an exhilarating, soul-satisfying experience finally to be able to quote its 105 verses straight through. But beyond that thrill I had another. I discovered that the effort to lock those verses into my memory had also unlocked much of their meaning to my spiritual understanding. Most of the book had come alive.

There were a few spots, however, that really left me puzzled. By one I was baffled. It was the second half of I John 2:23. The whole verse reads,

> **Whosoever denieth the Son, the same hath not the Father:** [*but*]
> *he that acknowledgeth the Son hath the Father also.*

It wasn't the meaning of those words that threw me; it was the fact that they were italicized. At that time I didn't know very much about Bible translations, but one thing I did know was that the italicized words in my King James Bible weren't that way for emphasis. They were that way because the translators had added them.

"Why did they add those words," I wondered, "and what gave them the right?"

Unwittingly, I had stumbled upon one of the most hotly contested issues in the modern text and translation debate. It concerns what are called *textual variants*. These are differences of wording between Hebrew or Greek manuscripts of the same biblical text.

Everyone engaged in the current text and translation debate agrees that these differences exist. But they disagree over just how important they are. One school of thought minimizes them. Another maximizes them. Some spokesmen for this latter position warn believers against any Greek text but the Textus Receptus and any English version but the King James. They allege that . . .

> *The old manuscripts behind the modern Greek text were influenced by heretics. The modern Greek text is a much different New Testament from the Textus Receptus. Every modern version based on the modern Greek text undermines major doctrines.*

If these charges are true then Bible believers are justifiably alarmed. But I want to resurrect Erasmus' question when he responded to similar criticisms by a professor named Martin Dorpius, *I beseech you to consider, most learned Dorpius, whether what you have written be **true***!

That's the question I want to address. Are these charges *true?* Do textual variants make that much difference? Do the older manuscripts betray the heretic's hand? Are modern Greek Testaments different Bibles than the Textus Receptus? Do modern versions erode major doctrines? Just how much difference do the differences make?

I'm going to attempt a factual but, in so far as possible, non-technical answer in nine points. For an indisputable first fact we're going to begin with the practice of the highly respected King James Version translators.

Fact #1: The KJV Translators Sometimes Employed Textual Variants.

(1) <u>Sometimes they employed variants from the Textus Receptus.</u>

Although it's conventional practice to identify the King James Version with the Greek text called the Textus Receptus (or TR), they are not technically one and the same. In fact, the King James translators couldn't use the TR. It wasn't published until 1633, twenty-two years after the first printing of the KJV.

The real Greek New Testament underlying the KJV appears to have been the one published in 1598 by the French reformer, Theodore Beza[1]. Not surprisingly, then, there are occasional variants between the King James Version, based on Beza 1598, and the TR, published twenty-two years later.

For instance, compare these examples.

(Mtt. 2:11)
And when they were come into the house they <u>found</u> the young child. (TR)
And when they were come into the house they <u>saw</u> the young child. (KJV)

(Rom. 12:11)
Not slothful in business; fervent in spirit; serving the <u>time.</u> (TR)
Not slothful in business; fervent in spirit; serving the <u>Lord</u>. (KJV)

(Heb. 9:1)
Then verily the first <u>tabernacle</u> had also ordinances. (TR)
Then verily the first *<u>covenant</u>* had also ordinances. (KJV)

Clearly, the KJV translators were not always translating the TR. In fact, sometimes they weren't translating Beza either.

(2) <u>Sometimes they employed variants from their own base text, Beza 1598.</u>

One example of this is the verse I stumbled across as a freshman (I John 2:23). Beza 1598 did not include the words, *but he that acknowledgeth the Son hath the Father also.* But the KJV translators discovered them in several previous texts. Hesitant to omit this clause entirely, but still uncertain of its authenticity, the translators deemed it wise to print it, albeit in italics.

I have lying here beside me even as I write a list of some 190 additional places where they opted for variants like this from texts or translations other than Beza 1598.[2] In all these cases they were obviously comparing manuscripts and then selecting from among the differing readings. And there's still another use which they made of variants.

(3) <u>Sometimes they included textual variants in their marginal notes.</u>

These were introduced by explanations such as the following:

"Many Greeke copies have. . ." (Mtt. 26:26)
"Many ancient copies adde these words. . ." (Lk. 10:22)
"This 36 verse is wanting in most of the Greek copies" (Lk. 17:36)
"Some copies reade. . ." (Jam. 2:18)

Other examples of such notes occur at Mtt. 1:11; Acts 25:6; Eph. 6:9; I Pet. 2:21; II Pet. 2:11 and II John 8. You can read these for yourself in the inexpensive "word-for-word reprint of the First Edition of the Authorized Version" published by Thomas Nelson Publishers, or in the marginal notes of a Cambridge Wide Margin King James Version, where they are faithfully reprinted to this day.

(4) <u>These variants recognized by the KJV translators have become significant.</u>

Most agree that the variants chosen by the KJV translators are textually and doctrinally insignificant. Not surprisingly, King James only proponents are the first to dismiss them. But it's for that very reason that they have *become* significant. Here's why.

Those who reject modern translations take exacting notice of their smallest deviations from the Textus Receptus.[3] Lists of such variants are published to convince readers that Greek texts differing from the Textus Receptus are fatally flawed, as are the translations from them. Verses in which modern translations don't include a name or title for deity are especially highlighted.

In such a climate, examples like Romans 12:11 (cited above), *where the TR itself omits the word "Lord,"* take on a heightened significance. So does the indisputable evidence that the KJV translators sometimes favored variants. Evidently, in the wise providence of God, believers have always been confronted with a small amount of textual uncertainty. But they didn't break fellowship over it nor charge one another with theological drift because of their translation preferences.[4]

This brings us to the question of today's Greek Testaments. How much difference exists between them? Let's fast forward the discussion up to modern times.

THE THREE DEBATED GREEK TEXTS (TESTAMENTS)
Much of the debate at this hour centers on differences between three Greek Testaments.

(1) the Textus Receptus (TR)

(2) the Majority Text (MT), sometimes called "Byzantine"[5]

(3) the 27th edition of *Novum Testamentum Graece* (NA27)[6]

NA27 is sometimes termed the "critical," the "eclectic," or the "Alexandrian" text.[7] It is also mistakenly called the "Westcott-Hort" text, a misstatement so common that I want to quote its emphatic denial by the editors of NA26.

> This text. . . differs from the text of Westcott-Hort in numerous and quite significant points. . . .The age of Westcott-Hort and of Tischendorf is definitely over (from the Introduction, p. 43*).

(1) The difference between the Testaments:

The foremost difference between these three Testaments is that NA27 generally favors the readings of the *oldest* Greek manuscripts. Though much fewer in number than those underlying the TR and the MT, they are nevertheless widely respected because of their nearness to the time of the autographs. Well over 50 of them are dated as early as the 2nd-4th centuries after Christ. This means that these Greek Bibles (that's what a manuscript was—someone's Bible) were being read by early Christians living, in some cases, less than a hundred years after the Apostles.

By contrast, the manuscripts whose readings the TR and the MT reflect seem to date back to no earlier than the beginning of the 5th century.[8] But the vast majority of them are even much later, dating from the 11th-14th centuries after Christ. So these are Greek Bibles separated, in most cases, from the autographs by well over a thousand years.[9]

(2) The difference between the TR and the MT:

The TR, as we have seen, was first published in 1633. It was a descendant of Erasmus' work over a century earlier, based on six or seven Greek manuscripts plus his own back-translating into Greek from the Latin Vulgate. The TR, then, is a Greek Testament combining the readings of just a few manuscripts, none of which contained the entire New Testament.[10] All were of relatively recent date. The two Erasmus relied upon most heavily were produced in the 12th century, a full eleven hundred years after Christ.

These manuscripts that Erasmus merged, whose readings appeared in the TR over a hundred years later, are a very small portion of a larger group. This larger group tends to agree together against the fewer oldest manuscripts when a reading is in dispute. As a result, this larger group is called the *majority*. The TR is a subset of it.

The TR and the MT are often hastily marshaled monolithically against NA27 as if their readings always side unanimously against it. But this is simply not the case, as a glance at the following table reveals.[11]

Words in the MT	Words in the TR
140,259	140,744

The TR numbers 485 words more than the MT. But what is not so easily seen is that the TR also differs from the MT in almost 1,400 additional places.[12]

Examination of these three New Testaments has led to two widely broadcast conclusions. One is that there *are* a great many words in question between them. The other is that there *are not* a great many words in question. I'd like to begin defending the latter view with a second factual statement.

Fact #2: The Greek Texts Contain Almost the Same Number of Words.

Here are the word totals for all three of these Greek texts.

WORDS IN NA27	WORDS IN THE MT	WORDS IN THE TR
138,019	140,259	140,744

The TR, as we have seen, has 485 more words than the MT. Now we also see that it has 2725 more than NA27. This appears to be a great many more, but calculate them in their entire New Testament context of some 140,000 words. From that perspective, it's apparent that no Greek text is alarmingly shorter than another. We have, for instance, no text in current usage which has 10% or even 5% fewer words than the others. If the TR is the point of reference, the percentages work out as follows.

TR	MT	NA27
100%	99.65%	98.06%

In other words, when it comes to the *total number of words*, the texts are better than 98% equivalent. And if the differences between the TR and NA27 were sprinkled evenly throughout an almost 700 page NA27 Testament they would occur at the rate of just 3-4 words per page.

We'll be identifying many of these words later. But I would argue thus far that considering the span of centuries over which the manuscripts were copied (16), the parts of the world in which they originated (scores), and the number being compared today (over 5,000), it's a truly remarkable act of God's providence that the *total number* of words in the New Testament is over 98% equivalent regardless of which text is being used. I would also anticipate, that given the very small percentage of total word difference between these testaments, it's more likely that they are going to be largely the same rather than much different from one another.

Now let's look more closely at these discrepancies between the word totals. What accounts for them?

Fact #3: There are a Few Verses Which NA27 or the MT Do Not Include in Their Texts.

Almost 10% of the 2725 TR words not included in NA27 are in just 17 passages. Three of these passages are not included in the MT either. Compare the three Testaments in these 17 passages.

INCLUSION OF THE QUESTIONABLE VERSES?			
Verses	**TR**	**MT**	**NA27**
Mtt. 17:21	Yes	Yes	No
Mtt. 18:11	Yes	Yes	No
Mtt. 23:14	Yes	Yes	No
Mk. 7:16	Yes	Yes	No
Mk. 9:44	Yes	Yes	No
Mk. 9:46	Yes	Yes	No
Mk. 11:26	Yes	Yes	No
Mk. 15:28	Yes	Yes	No
Lk. 17:36	Yes	No	No
Lk. 23:17	Yes	Yes	No
John 5:3b-4	Yes	Yes	No
Acts 8:37	Yes	No	No
Acts 15:34	Yes	Yes	No
Acts 24:6b-8a	Yes	Yes	No
Acts 28:29	Yes	Yes	No
Rom. 16:24	Yes	Yes	No
I John 5:7b-8a	Yes	No	No

These passages are highly publicized by Textus Receptus proponents as one of the most convincing pieces of evidence that the other Testaments are seriously flawed. This, however, does not necessarily follow. Here's why.

There are many very important manuscripts which do not include these verses. Some of the passages in question have almost *no* textual support. For instance, notice Acts 8:37, a verse that admittedly has become dear to Christians because of its usefulness to soulwinners.

And Philip said, If thou believest with all thine heart, thou mayest. And he answered and said, I believe that Jesus Christ is the Son of God. (KJV)

Despite its usefulness, this verse really has very little manuscript support. It doesn't appear even in the late medieval manuscript on which Erasmus depended most heavily. He later explained that he had made a personal decision to include it in his Testament because he found it in the *margin* of another manuscript.

In one sense, this is unwelcome news to all of us. We don't welcome the fact that a treasured passage, though completely orthodox, may in fact not actually be Scripture. I want to hasten to say that I'm not suggesting that Acts 8:37 isn't. All I'm pointing out is that most ancient Greek Bibles, used by believers for hundreds and hundreds of years, did not include this verse. Personal integrity demands, therefore, that we concede at least a measure of sympathetic understanding with those who question its authenticity.

For those who can decipher a textual apparatus,[13] the evidence, or lack thereof, for these seventeen questionable passages is available in precise detail in the Hodges/Farstad MT and NA27. There are also extended discussions in a volume entitled *A Textual Commentary On The Greek New Testament*, by Bruce Metzger.

Three of these passage are given no place in the MT because the vast *majority* of manuscripts do not have them. In the case of NA27, all 17 are omitted because they are not found in many of the *oldest* manuscripts.

To put it another way, the absence of these passages from NA27 is not due to a *contemporary conspiracy* but to the *ancient testimony* of Greek Bibles used by Christians living very close to the time of the Apostles. The editors of NA27 are merely providing us with a Greek New Testament whose books reproduce as closely as possible the ones those early believers read. In some cases their New Testament books simply did not have these seventeen passages. But having said that, let me proceed to a fourth point that should be very reassuring.

Fact #4: Every Questionable Verse Nevertheless Appears in the Footnotes of NA27 and the MT.

Though NA27 and the MT (in 3 cases) do not include these seventeen passages in their texts, they do print them in their footnotes. In addition, they also list the best manuscript evidence for each passage. In other words, there's no Greek New Testament being widely used today which *entirely* omits these passages. Today's New Testaments actually give *more* information about the age, source, and quality of the manuscripts in which these verses are found than has ever before been available to the Lord's people.

It is, therefore, unfactual to charge either of these Testaments with entirely omitting whole passages. In view of their stated purposes—providing New Testaments that reproduce either the oldest Greek Bibles (NA27) or the majority of Greek Bibles (the MT)—we couldn't rightly expect them to print these passages in their texts. Doing so would falsify the ancient evidence which it is their whole intent to display.

By including the disputed passages in their footnotes rather than their texts, NA27 and MT retain their own integrity but at the same time provide the reader with whatever evidence there may be for each verse.

Modern Translations

I want to transition now to the issue of how modern translations treat these same verses. Do they include them or omit them? Let's sample a few passages to find out.

For a start, we'll compare the wording of the KJV with that of the New American Standard Bible (NASB) for three of these passages.[14] The first passage in question is Matthew 17:21. Here it is in the KJV.

Howbeit this kind goeth not out but by prayer and fasting.

Now we turn to the NASB, and this is what we find.

["But this kind does not go out except by prayer and fasting."]

Even though Mtt. 17:21 is confined to the footnote of NA27, the NASB includes it in its text. But the translators do bracket it, thus indicating that in their judgment the words were *probably not in the original writings.*[15]

Note their use of *probably*. They're not dogmatic. They walk the cautious line between giving the reading the benefit of the doubt but also honestly alerting the reader to the fact that there is little, if any, older textual testimony for it. The alert comes in the form of the brackets plus an explanation in the footnote, *Early mss do not contain this v.* Judging by the similar approach of our highly respected KJV translators this seems fair enough.

Let's take another example, John 5:3b-4.

. . . waiting for the moving of the water. For an angel went down at a certain season into the pool, and troubled the water:

whosoever then first after the troubling of the water stepped in was made whole of whatsoever disease he had. (KJV)

And the NASB?

[. . . waiting for the moving of the waters; for an angel of the Lord went down at certain seasons into the pool and stirred up the water; whoever then first, after the stirring up of the water, stepped in was made well from whatever disease with which he was afflicted.]

Again the NASB has included the verse in its text, even though NA27 relegates it to a footnote. Again, however, the reading is in brackets and there is the explanatory footnote, *Early mss do not contain the remainder of v 3, nor v 4.*

One more example, Acts 8:37.

And Philip said, If thou believest with all thine heart, thou mayest. And he answered and said, I believe that Jesus Christ is the Son of God. (KJV)

[And Philip said, "If you believe with all your heart, you may." And he answered and said, "I believe that Jesus Christ is the Son of God."] (NASB)

This is one of the three verses that is not in the MT text either. Yet here again the NASB translators give it the benefit of the doubt.

How do other modern versions treat these passages? Here's a comparison of five modern translations: the New King James Version,[16] the New American Standard Bible, the Holman Christian Standard Bible,[17] the New International Version, and the English Standard Version.[18]

The versions are listed in the order of how *cautious* they are before bracketing a verse or relegating it to a margin. A [Yes] indicates that the verse is included in the text but bracketed. "Margin" indicates that although it is not in the text it is included in a marginal footnote.

How Modern Versions Treat the Questionable Verses				
	TR	**NA**		
Verses	**NKJV**	**NASB**	**HCSB**	**NIV**	**ESV**
Mtt. 17:21	Yes	[Yes]	[Yes]	Margin	Margin
Mtt. 18:11	Yes	[Yes]	[Yes]	Margin	Margin
Mtt. 23:14	Yes	[Yes]	[Yes]	Margin	Margin
Mk. 7:16	Yes	[Yes]	Yes	Margin	Margin
Mk. 9:44	Yes	[Yes]	[Yes]	Margin	Margin[19]
Mk. 9:46	Yes	[Yes]	[Yes]	Margin	Margin[20]
Mk. 11:26	Yes	[Yes]	[Yes]	Margin	Margin
Mk. 15:28	Yes	[Yes]	[Yes]	Margin	Margin
Lk. 17:36	Yes	[Yes]	[Yes]	Margin	Margin
Lk. 23:17	Yes	[Yes]	[Yes]	Margin	Margin
John 5:3b-4	Yes	[Yes]	[Yes]	Margin	Margin
Acts 8:37	Yes	[Yes]	[Yes]	Margin	Margin
Acts 15:34	Yes	[Yes]	Margin	Margin	Margin
Acts 24:6b-8a	Yes	[Yes]	[Yes]	Margin	Margin
Acts 28:29	Yes	[Yes]	[Yes]	Margin	Margin
Rom. 16:24	Yes	[Yes]	[Yes]	Margin	Margin
I John 5:7b-8a	Yes	Margin	Margin	Margin	No

The comparison reveals a fifth fact.

Fact #5: Modern Versions Include the Questionable Verses.

Only one translation, the ESV, entirely omits any of the questionable passages (I John 5:7b-8a). Otherwise, all five modern versions include, in some format, every one of the disputed verses.

I personally prefer putting these passages in brackets, as the NASB and the HCSB (in most cases) have done. This method candidly alerts the reader to their slim textual support. If anything, it errs on the side of giving the benefit of the doubt to them. Some would argue that this unnecessarily unsettles the reader. But this issue was addressed satisfactorily by the KJV translators centuries ago.

The translators faced this same criticism that they were unsettling people's confidence in the Word of God when they included marginal notes about textual or translational uncertainties. Their response was, . . . *doth not a margin do well to admonish the Reader to seek further, and not to conclude or dogmatize upon this or that peremptorily? For as it is a fault of incredulity, to doubt of those things that are evident; so to determine of such things as the Spirit of God hath left (even in the judgment of the judicious) questionable, can be no less than presumption.*[21] This response has stood the test of time and has always been the position of the vast majority of trusted Christian voices.

Fact #6: Modern Versions Give the Benefit of the Doubt to Other Disputable Passages as Well.

In addition to the 17 passages entirely absent from the text of NA27 there are 6 more encompassing at least one entire verse for which there is doubtful manuscript support. Some of these are single bracketed ([. . .]), to indicate *that textual critics today are not completely convinced of the authenticity of the enclosed words.* Others are double bracketed ([[. . .]]), to indicate *that the enclosed words. . . are known not to be a part of the original text.*[22]

These six passages include 31 verses. That's a substantial amount of material. But again, as in the cases of the absent passages, footnotes to the text and lengthy explanations in the supplementary *Textual Commentary* inform the reader of the textual evidence for omitting or including these passages. So there's no sleight of hand here.

But more importantly for our purposes, let's compare how some of the modern translations are dealing with these additional passages. They are again listed in the order of their caution about bracketing a passage or calling it into serious question (as the NIV does with two passages).

How modern versions deal with verses bracketed by NA27					
	TR	NA			
Verses	NKJV	NASB	HCSB	NIV	ESV
Mtt. 12:47	Yes	Yes	Yes	Yes	Margin
Mtt. 21:44	Yes	Yes	Yes	Yes	Yes
Mk. 16:9-20	Yes	[Yes]	[Yes]	Yes[23]	[[Yes]]
Lk. 22:43-44	Yes	Yes	[Yes]	Yes	Yes
John 7:53-8:11	Yes	[Yes]	[Yes]	Yes[24]	[[Yes]]
Rom. 16:25-27	Yes	Yes	Yes	Yes	Yes

Once more we see that none of the verses in question are actually omitted from these translations. In fact, no translation follows NA27 in even bracketing every one of them.

At this point, then, I'd like to offer a summary observation about the passages either absent from or bracketed in NA27. It becomes our seventh point.

Fact #7: Modern Versions Do Not Follow NA27 Slavishly.

Critics of NA27 commonly lump it and modern versions together as if they were identical. Our sampling of passages thus far demonstrates that they're not. It's therefore either ignorance or dishonesty that broadly brushes modern translations, especially the NASB, with the same criticisms one might have of NA27.

For instance, critics sometimes claim, "The modern versions are based on the critical text, and the critical text omits literally dozens of verses." The conclusion the hearer draws is that "the modern versions" *also* omit "literally dozens of verses." But this is not so in every case. In fact, it's not so of any version we've sampled if one is willing to look at the margins.

But this brings up an important question. Is a text or translation actually *more trustworthy* than another simply because it includes verses for which there is little manuscript support?

Fact #8: The Test of a Translation's Integrity Cannot be the Number of Questionable Verses It Prints.

Let me demonstrate this. As we have seen, the NASB displays commendable caution about omitting material, even when there is only doubtful manuscript evidence for it. It's evidently in keeping with this reserve that it also *includes* two additional verses to Mark 16 which are not found even in the KJV.

> [*And they promptly reported all these instructions to Peter and his companions. And after that, Jesus Himself sent out through them from east to west the sacred and imperishable proclamation of eternal salvation.*]

The NASB both brackets and italicizes these verses to indicate that they are almost certainly not original. Their inclusion at all is explained by the footnote, *A few late mss and versions contain this paragraph, usually after v 8; a few have it at the end of ch.*

Here's an instance of including material that almost no one would defend. We tend to agree, that even though there is *some* textual evidence for it, we would not be inclined to accept these verses as genuine. But why not? Their manuscript support is nearly as strong as that for a few of the disputed verses we've been examining. Yet all of us, no matter which postion we hold in the modern debate, tend to agree with omitting them. We all know that a text is not necessarily more accurate simply because it includes the greatest number of questionable verses.

To give another example, there are manuscripts of Acts, in fact an entire strain of them called the Western Family, which are nearly 10% longer than NA27. They include many readings which we've never seen in our versions. For instance:

> Simon the sorcerer **"did not stop weeping copiously"** (8:24)
> Peter and the angel **"descended seven steps"** (12:10)
> Paul argued daily in Tyrannus' hall **"from the fifth hour to the tenth."** (19:9)
> The seven sons of Sceva **"wished the same thing (they were**

accustomed to exorcise such persons). . . . They entered into the one who was demon possessed and began to invoke the Name, saying, 'We command you by Jesus. . . to come out.'" (19:14)

There's nothing heretical here. But few, if any of us would argue for retaining these readings.

I'm including these few examples in order to preclude our drawing a conclusion too hastily—that all questionable material should be given the benefit of the doubt. By that standard even the TR falls short.

The real issue should be the *quality* of the textual testimony to a verse. By that standard a few of the verses in our King James Version are almost as questionable as the two additional verses to Mark or some of the readings in the Western Family of Acts. We should not, therefore, automatically suspect a version because of its even-handed doubt about the one as well as the other.

ADDITIONAL VARIANTS

Thus far we've focused on word counts and the absence or presence of disputed passages that alter these. But even on pages where the word count of the three Greek texts might be precisely the same there are additional variants.

For instance, the MT differs from NA27 in about 6,500 places,[25] the vast majority of which we have not yet discussed. Many of these almost no one notices because of their very minor significance (as in the case of spelling errors). Others, however, warrant careful analysis. Accordingly, over 2,000 are discussed in the 2nd edition of Bruce Metzger's *A Textual Commentary on the Greek New Testament.*[26] Which of these actually affect what we read or preach?

I find myself confronted with this issue frequently during the course of systematic pulpit exposition. Let me explain.

My study every week begins with the Hebrew or Greek text. If it's the Greek text I hand copy it to a yellow note pad in a kind of diagram that displays the relationships between the various statements. When this display is completed I then begin the process of investigating the meanings of the words within their diagrammed context. Occasionally I may be investigating a word only to discover that there is some question about whether it was actually part of the original text as God inspired it. In other words, I've happened upon a textual variant.

Because of my expository approach to sermon preparation these variants become significant to me. I'm in lockstep with those who are insisting that every word of the Word of God is precious, and may, in addition, affect our exegesis.[27] That's my position precisely, and it brings us to a ninth fact.

Fact #9: Only a Small Percentage of Variants Affect Understanding Significantly.

Most KJV only or TR only proponents concede that some variants are more significant than others. For instance, I'm looking now at a pamphlet comparing the number of times certain English translations include/exclude names or titles for members of the Godhead. The author's intent is to demonstrate the inferiority of translations (and that of the Greek texts on which they're based) which have fewer references to diety than others.

Obviously, the pamphlet's author considered differences of this nature to be of greater significance to his case than those involving variations of spelling, conjunctions, or particles. He also assumed that this would be his readers' opinion. His pamphlet is therefore a concession that some differences are more important than others. I agree. But which ones?

I would contend that the significant issue here is whether a variant *affects what we read*. In other words, the most significant issue is not what Greek text underlies a translation, as some claim. Most people, many preachers included, will not and could not read a Greek text. What it says will always be "Greek to them." In addition, as we've seen (and widely disseminated misinformation compels me to emphasize this again), ***modern translations are not slaves to a particular Greek Testament***. Just as the King James Version occasionally varies from its base text, so do the modern translations.

The real issue, therefore, is *what a given translation is doing with its Greek text*. To display this, we're going to move now into an analysis of the variants in seven New Testament books by six different authors. Together, these seven books amount to over 25% of the entire New Testament. They give us, therefore, a sizable sample from which to draw our conclusions about the significance of variants.

A Sample Book: Jude

We'll note first the number of words in each text of Jude, a book in which NA27 actually has a *fuller* text than either the TR or the MT. This is the only New Testament book in which this is the case. It affords therefore a unique opportunity to illustrate certain facts.

NA27	TR	MT
461 words	454 words	450 words

Next, let's get the vital statistics on the variants among these words.

(1) There are 27 sets of variants in the Hodges/Farstad MT.[28]

(2) But only 12 sets seem to be affecting the NASB.

(3) There are just 26 Greek words involved in these 12 sets.

26 out of the roughly 450 words in Jude is about 6% of its text. But what percentage of these differences is even significant to an English reader?

To introduce us to a method of determining that, let's examine the first variant. It occurs in verse 1, where the MT has "sanctified" (ηγιασμενοις) but the NA27 has "beloved" (ηγαπημενοις). The KJV and the NASB differ accordingly.

Verse	King James Version	New American Standard Bible
1	. . . to them that are **sanctified** by God the Father, and preserved in Jesus Christ, *and* called:	To those who are the called, **beloved** in God the Father, and kept for Jesus Christ:

Comparing the two translations we notice the following differences.

(1) the first word, "**To**," is capitalized by the NASB to begin a new sentence
(2) "**them**" is "**those**" in the NASB
(3) "**that** are" is "**who** are" in the NASB
(4) "**called**," the last word in the KJV, is the sixth word in the NASB
(5) "called" is preceded by the article, "**the**," in the NASB
(6) "**sanctified**" in the KJV is replaced by "**beloved**" in the NASB
(7) "**by**" is "**in**" in the NASB
(8) "and **preserved**" is "and **kept**" in the NASB
(9) "**in** Jesus Christ" is "**for** Jesus Christ" in the NASB

At first glance the number of differences between the two translations is unsettling to anyone just counting and comparing English words. But only *one* of the differences is actually due to a textual variant. The others are entirely acceptable English translations of the exact same Greek text. The TR and NA27 are *identical* except for the one variant in question. The reader may therefore choose whichever he prefers, but he may not argue for his preference on any textual grounds.

The only exception is that created by the textual variant. How important is it? In other words, how much *difference* does this difference make?

Well, neither reading is unorthodox. Both are equally true. We know this because each truth is taught elsewhere in the New Testament. So omitting one or even both readings from this verse would not affect the Bible's doctrinal content.

The difference, therefore, between these two readings is entirely textual, not creedal. That is, the issue is solely a question of which of these equally true New Testament doctrines are being taught in this *particular* verse. That's a textual issue.

But nevertheless, since the difference would alter what I preached from this text, I would classify the variation as significant (S). What then does a conscientious expositor do with the variant when he preaches?

All I can do is relate my own approach. I truthfully acknowledge the variant. I point out that both readings teach truth that is found elsewhere in Scripture. And then I give my sermonic emphasis to either one or both of the truths.

Lest this last practice—choosing to give sermonic emphasis to either one or both truths—should sound too subjective or arbitrary, we must acknowledge that most preachers make this same kind of choice anyway when they restrict themselves and their people to one version over another. My point is that we make the choice one way or the other. Either we elevate one version over all others or we choose between variants individually. Either way, we're exercising an element of personal choice that determines what our people hear.

With that example of the method I'm using behind us, let's move on to looking through the list of all variants listed in the Hodges-Farstad apparatus for Jude which affect the NASB. Since two sets are complex I've divided them, giving us fourteen readings to examine.

1. vs. 1   **MT** substitutes "sanctified" (ηγιασμενοις) for "beloved" (ηγαπημενοις) (we looked at the wording of this in the example above)

2. vs. 3   **MT** omits "our" (της κοινης **ημων** σωτηριας)

   KJV   the common salvation

   NASB   **our** common salvation

3. vs. 4   **MT** adds "God" (τον μονον Δεσποτην **Θεον** και Κυριον ημων Ιησουν Χριστον αρνουμενοι)

KJV   denying the only Lord **God**, and our Lord Jesus Christ

NASB   deny our only Master and Lord, Jesus Christ

4. vs. 5   **MT**
(1) omits "all things" (ειδοτας υμας **παντα** οτι ο Κυριος απαξ)
(2) adds "this" (ειδοτας υμας απαξ **τουτο** οτι ο Κυριος)
(3) transposes "once" (απαξ)

KJV   ye **once** knew **this**, how that the Lord

NASB   you know **all things once for all**, that the Lord

5. vs. 12   **MT** omits "the men who" (Ουτοι εισιν **οι**)

KJV   these are

NASB   these are **the men who**

6. vs. 12   **TR** substitutes "carried about" (παριφερομεναι) for **MT** and **NA27** "carried along" (παραφερομεναι)

KJV   clouds *they are* without water, **carried about** of winds

NASB   clouds without water, **carried along** by winds

7. vs. 15   **MT** adds "among them" (παντας τους ασεβεις **αυτων**)

KJV   all that are ungodly **among them**

NASB   all the ungodly

8. vs. 22   **MT** substitutes "making a difference" (διακρινομενοι) for "who are doubting" (διακρινομενους)

KJV   And of some have compassion, **making a difference**

NASB   And have mercy on some, **who are doubting**

9. vs. 23   **MT** omits "on some have mercy" (ους δε ελεατε)

KJV   others save with fear, pulling them out of the fire. . .

NASB   save others, snatching them out of the fire; and **on some**

have mercy with fear. . .

10. vs. 23   **MT** places "with fear" with "save" (ους δε εν φοβω σωζετε, εκ πυρος αρπαζοντες)

           NA27 places "with fear" with "have mercy" (ους δε σωζετε εκ πυρος αρπαζοντες, ους δε ελεατε εν φοβω)

KJV   others **save with fear**, pulling them out of the fire

NASB   save others, snatching them out of the fire; and on some have mercy **with fear**

11. vs. 25   **MT** adds "wise" (Μονω σοφω θεω Σωτηρι ημων)

KJV   To the only **wise** God our Saviour

NASB   to the only God our Savior

12. vs. 25   **MT** adds "and" (Δοξα και μεγαλωσυνη)

KJV   glory **and** majesty

NASB   glory, majesty

13. vs. 25   **MT** omits "through Jesus Christ our Lord" (δια Ιησου Χριστου του Κυριου ημων)

KJV   To the only wise God our Saviour, be glory and majesty

NASB   to the only God our Savior, **through Jesus Christ our Lord**, be glory, majesty

14. vs. 25   **MT** omits "before all time" (προ παντος του αιωνας)

KJV   To the only wise God our Savior, be glory and majesty, dominion and power, both now and ever. Amen.

NASB   To the only God our Savior, through Jesus Christ our Lord, be glory, majesty, dominion, and authority, **before all time**, and now and forever. Amen.

As you can see, comparing variants is a tedious, painstaking undertaking. There's plenty of opportunity for error. I've worked through these as a "layman" to the science of textual criticism. A professional might discover an oversight somewhere. But in so far as I can see, as a preacher or reader of the KJV and the NASB, these are the only variations that make the slightest difference. Now just how significant are they?

The table below classifies the three kinds of variants which actually involve textual word changes affecting the NASB. Transpositions are omitted because in both cases where they occur (vv. 5, 23) their translation is similar or the same in both the KJV and the NASB. Whatever slight difference there may be results mainly from their connection with one of the variants below. Each variant is further classified as NS (not significant), SS (slightly significant), or S (significant). My classifications are based on the following considerations.

Reader's understanding unaffected	**NS** (not significant)
Reader's understanding influenced	**SS** (slightly significant)
Reader's understanding affected/altered	**S** (significant)

Here then are the classifications I would assign to the variants.

VS.	TR OR MT OMISSIONS/JUDE	TR OR MT ADDITIONS/JUDE	TR OR MT SUBSTITUTIONS/JUDE
1			"sanctified" for "beloved" (S)
3	"our" (SS)		
4		"God" (S)	
5	"all things" (S)	"this" (S)	
12	"the men who are" (NS)		"carried about" for "carried along" (NS)
15		"among them" (NS)	
22			"making a difference" for "who are doubting" (S)
23	"on some have mercy" (S)		
25		"wise" (S)	
25	"through Jesus Christ our Lord" (S)	"and" (NS)	
26	"before all time" (S)		

Analyzing these classifications results in the following summary.

Sets of variants	Sets affecting NASB	Variants in sets	S Variants	Greek words
27	12	16	9	20

To assess this, consider that out of the 27 sets of variants noted by Hodges/Farstad, only 9 variants in these sets really affect the reader's understanding. These 9, involving 20 Greek words, comprise only about 4½% of Jude's total text. Or, to say it the other way around, over 95% of Jude's text is the same for preaching and reading purposes, regardless of whether I'm using the KJV or the NASB.

A 4½% difference is initially a cause for concern. We're dealing here, however, with just one chapter of the Bible. In addition, and just the opposite of what we saw in the case of the questionable verses, it is *the TR's and the MT's omission* of three phrases which accounts for 14 out of the 20 significant word differences in Jude.

vs. 5	"all things"	(1 Greek word)
vs. 23	"on some have mercy"	(3 Greek words)
vs. 25	"through Jesus Christ our Lord"	(6 Greek words)
vs. 26	"before all time"	(4 Greek words)

Notice that these words include three names or titles for a member of the Godhead which the TR and the MT *omit*. Notice also that all of the questionable words are orthodox, appropriate to their contexts, and well supported by textual evidence. Therefore, exercising the same caution here that I did about the questionable verses earlier inclines me to retain them even though they are not found in my KJV. If I don't retain them my KJV is unaffected. If I do retain them they introduce nothing unorthodox. In fact, the truths of the passages are actually taught even more emphatically. But what I don't encounter, either way, is anything of the nature of false teaching or a misleading emphasis.

A SECOND SAMPLE BOOK: ROMANS

We're now going to look at a much longer book, considered by many to be Paul's greatest epistle. Here are the word totals for it.

NA27	TR	MT
7111 words	7208 words	7212 words

Here again, as in Jude, the total number of words in all three texts is very close. In this case, however, the MT, not NA27, has the longest text, though by just 4 words. NA27 is the shortest, numbering 97 words less than the TR. Using the TR as the point of reference the percentages work out as follows:

TR	MT	NA27
100%	100.05 %	98.65%

In Romans, then, there is less than a 2% variation in the total number of words between any of the three texts, with NA27 coming in just 1.35% shorter than the TR.

The variant totals for Romans are as follows.

(1) There are 246 sets of variants in the Hodges/Farstad textual apparatus.
(2) There are 86 sets which seem to be affecting the NASB.
(3) There are 139 Greek words in these 86 sets.

Out of space considerations we'll not list all of Romans' variants. Instead, I'll confine myself to only those I would classify as significant (S). Before doing so however, let me just give the first three that I would *not* classify as significant (S) so that you'll be able to judge for yourself whether the ones I'm ignoring would really affect your understanding as an English reader.

1:1   KJV (TR) **Paul, a servant of <u>Jesus Christ</u> . . .**

NASB (NA27) **Paul, a bondservant of <u>Christ Jesus</u> . . .**

Here is an example of what is called *inversion,* or "interchanging of position of words." As you can see, in this instance it makes absolutely no difference whatsoever to the meaning of the verse.

The second inconsequential variant in Romans occurs twenty-three verses later.

1:24   KJV (TR) **Wherefore God <u>also</u> gave them up. . .**

NASB (NA27) **Therefore God gave them over. . .**

This is an example of *addition*, in that the TR includes a word, "also," not found in the older manuscripts. Reading the statement in isolation from its context might give the impression that the "also" might be significant. But read from verse 23 right down through verse 24 and you'll see that the absence or presence of the word doesn't affect our understanding at all. I won't print the verses out here, but go ahead and pick up your New Testament and see for yourself.

The third inconsequential variant in Romans occurs in the same verse.

1:24   KJV (TR) . . . **to dishonour their own bodies between <u>themselves:</u>**

NASB (NA27) . . . **so that their bodies would be dishonored among <u>them.</u>**

This is an example of *substitution*, or "replacement of words with others." In some cases a substitution would be a significant variant. Here it makes no difference whatsoever.[29]

Let's now look at a table of the variants in Romans which have affected the NASB significantly.

REF.	TR OR MT OMISSIONS FROM ROMANS	TR OR MT ADDITIONS TO ROMANS	TR OR MT SUBSTITUTIONS IN ROMANS
1:16		"of Christ"	
1:29		"fornication"	
1:31		"implacable"	
3:22		"and upon all"	
4:19		"not"	
6:11		"indeed"	
6:11		"our Lord"	
7:14			"carnal" for "of flesh"
8:1		"who walk not after the flesh but after the Spirit"	
8:11	"Jesus"		
8:34	"Jesus"		

REF.	TR OR MT OMISSIONS FROM ROMANS (CONT.)	TR OR MT ADDITIONS TO ROMANS (CONT.)	TR OR MT SUBSTITUTIONS IN ROMANS (CONT.)
9:28		"For he will finish the work…in righteousness"	
9:31		"of righteousness"	
9:32		"of the law"	
10:15		"the gospel of peace"	
11:6		"But if *it be* of works, then is it no more grace: otherwise work is no more work"	
11:22	"God's"		
11:31	"now"		
13:9		TR addition here. MT divided. "thou shalt not bear false witness"	
14:6		"and he that regardeth not the day, to the Lord he doth not regard it"	
14:9		"and rose"	"revived" for "lived again"
14:21		"or is offended or is made weak"	
15:8		"Jesus"	
15:19		"of God"	
15:24		"I shall come to you"	
15:29		"of the gospel"	
16:5			"Achaia" for "Asia"
16:6			"us" for "you"
16:16	"all"		
16:18		"Jesus"	
16:20		"Christ"	

Totaling these classifications results in the following summary.

Sets of variants	Sets affecting NASB	S Variants	Greek words
246	86	32	77

Out of the 7208 words of the TR, then, only 77, or 1.07% would affect my preaching in any way. Or, to say it the other way around, almost 99% of the entire text of Romans will be the same for preaching and reading purposes, regardless of whether I'm using the King James Version or the New American Standard Bible.

A further matter worthy of notice involves those names or titles for members of the Godhead about which KJV and Textus Receptus advocates express concern.

The MT has a name or title where NA27 does not <u>8</u> times

But NA27 has a name or title where the MT does not <u>3</u> times (8:11, 34; 11:22)

The reason for calling attention to this is not to make the point that whichever text mentions a member of the Godhead by name or title the most times is most probably the original one. It is to demonstrate that NA27 is not a heretical text that purposely omits these names or titles in an effort to undermine the Trinity or the deity of Jesus Christ or some such thing. As we saw in the case of Jude, and again here in Romans, the older texts do, on occasion, actually include a reference to one or the other of the persons of the Trinity that the TR or the MT omits.

A THIRD EXAMPLE: HEBREWS

As in Romans and Jude, the total number of words per text is very close, with only a difference of 35 between NA27 and the MT, and 52 between NA27 and the TR.

NA27	MT	TR
4953 words	4988 words	5005 words

Using the TR as the point of reference the percentages are as follows.

TR	MT	NA27
100%	99.7%	98.96%

(1) There are 190 sets of variants in the Hodges/Farstad textual apparatus.
(2) There are 47 sets which seem to be affecting the NASB.
(3) There are 69 Greek words in these 47 sets.

Even though there are over 40 variants affecting the NASB, there are very few that do so significantly. In fact, Hebrews may have as few such cases per chapter as any New Testament book.

Ref.	TR or MT Omissions from Hebrews	TR or MT Additions to Hebrews	TR or MT Substitutions in Hebrews
1:3		"by himself"	
1:12	"like a garment"		
3:1		"Christ"	
7:21		"after the order of Melchisedec"	
8:12		"and their iniquities"	
10:9		"O God"	
10:30		"saith the Lord"	
10:34		"my"[30]	
10:34		"in heaven"	
10:38		"my"	
11:11		"was delivered"	
12:20		"or thrust through with a dart"	

Sets of variants	Sets affecting NASB	S Variants	Greek words
190	47	12	26

These S variants total out as follows. Of the 4988 words of the MT, only 26, or .5% would affect my preaching in any way. Or, to say it the other way around, better than 99% of the entire text of Hebrews will be the same for preaching and reading purposes, regardless of whether I'm using the KJV or the NASB.

A FOURTH EXAMPLE: MATTHEW

Our next example is Matthew. I count 918 variants in the Hodges/Farstad apparatus. Of these, 300 seem to be affecting the NASB. And of these 300, 105 might be classified as significant. I'm going to begin our analysis with a table including all 105.

REF.	TR OR MT OMISSIONS FROM MATTHEW	TR OR MT ADDITIONS TO MATTHEW	TR OR MT SUBSTITUTIONS IN MATTHEW
1:25		"her firstborn"	
5:27		"by them of old time"	
5:44		"bless them that curse you"	
5:44		"do good to them that hate you"	
5:44		"despitefully use you, and"	
5:47			"Gentiles" for "publicans"
6:1			"alms" for "righteousness"
6:4		"himself"	

Ref.	TR or MT Omissions from Matthew (cont.)	TR or MT Additions to Matthew (cont.)	TR or MT Substitutions in Matthew (cont.)
6:4		"openly"	
6:6		"openly"	
6:15		"their trespasses"	
6:18		"openly"	
6:33		"of God"	
6:34		"the things"	
8:15			"them" for "him"
8:18			"great multitudes" for "crowd"
8:29		"Jesus, thou"	
9:8			"marveled" for "afraid"
9:13		"to repentance"	
9:14		"oft"	
9:36			"fainted" for "were distressed"
10:3		"Lebbaeus, whose surname"	
11:2		"two"	
11:19			"children" for "deeds"
11:23	"not"		
12:4			"did eat" for "they ate"
12:15		"multitudes"	
12:35		"of the heart"	
13:36		"Jesus"	
13:40		"this"	
13:51		"Jesus saith unto them"	

257

REF.	TR OR MT OMISSIONS FROM MATTHEW (CONT.)	TR OR MT ADDITIONS TO MATTHEW (CONT.)	TR OR MT SUBSTITUTIONS IN MATTHEW (CONT.)
13:51		"Lord"	
14:14		"Jesus"	
14:22		"Jesus"	
14:24			"was not in the midst of the sea" for "was already a long distance from the land"
14:25		"Jesus"	
14:30		"boisterous"	
15:6			"and honour not" for "he is not to honour"
15:8			"draweth nigh" for "honors"
15:30		"Jesus"	
16:3		"hypocrites"	
16:20		"Jesus"	
17:4			"let us make" for "I will make"
17:11		"Jesus"	
17:11		"first"	
17:20		"Jesus"	
17:20			"unbelief" for "little-ness of faith"
17:22			"abode" for "were gathering together"
18:2		"Jesus"	
18:15		"against thee"	

Ref.	TR or MT Omissions from Matthew (cont.)	TR or MT Additions to Matthew (cont.)	TR or MT Substitutions in Matthew (cont.)
18:26		"Lord"	
18:29		"all"	
18:35		"their trespasses"	
19:9		"and whoso marrieth her which is put away doth commit adultery"	
19:16		"good"	
19:17			"why callest thou me good" for "why are you asking me about what is good"
19:17			"none" for "one"
19:17		"God"	
19:20		"from my youth up"	
19:29		"or wife"	
20:7		"and whatsoever is right that ye shall receive"	
20:16		"for many be called, but few chosen"	
20:22		"and to be baptized with the baptism that I am baptized with"	
20:23		"and be baptized with the baptism that I am baptized with"	

REF.	TR OR MT OMISSIONS FROM MATTHEW (CONT.)	TR OR MT ADDITIONS TO MATTHEW (CONT.)	TR OR MT SUBSTITUTIONS IN MATTHEW (CONT.)
20:26			"let him be" for "you shall be"
20:27			"let him be" for "you shall be"
21:12		"of God"	
22:7		"when heard"	
22:13		"and take him away"	
22:30		"of God"	
22:32		"God"	
22:37		"Jesus"	
23:4			"footstool" for "beneath"
23:4		"and grievous"	
23:7		"Rabbi"	
23:8		"Christ"	
23:8			"master" for "teacher"
23:19		"fools and"	
24:2		"Jesus"	
24:6		"all"	
24:7		"and pestilences"	
24:36	"nor the Son"		
24:36		"my"	
24:42			"hour" for "day"
25:6		"cometh"	
25:13		"wherein the Son of man cometh"	

Ref.	TR or MT Omissions from Matthew (cont.)	TR or MT Additions to Matthew (cont.)	TR or MT Substitutions in Matthew (cont.)
25:31		"holy"	
26:3		"and the scribes"	
26:28		"new"	
26:42		"cup"	
26:42		"from me"	
26:50			"wherefore art thou come" for "do what you have come for"
26:59		"and elders"	
26:60		"found they none"	
26:60		"false witnesses"	
27:2		"Pontius"	
27:24		"just person"	
27:35		"that it might be fulfilled which was spoken by the prophet, They parted my garments among them, and upon my vesture they did cast lots"	
27:41		"and Pharisees"	
27:42		"if"	
27:58		"the body"	
28:2		"from the door"	
28:6		"the Lord"	
28:9		"And as they went to tell his disciples"	
28:20		"Amen"	

At first glance this appears to be an alarmingly long list of significant variants. But let's put it into its context. Only Luke and Acts are longer than Matthew. Matthew's Gospel amounts to *a full 13%* of the entire New Testament! If you view the variants in that context the perspective changes.

WORDS IN TR OF MATTHEW	GREEK WORDS IN S VARIANTS OF MATTHEW	PERCENTAGE OF TEXT INCLUDED IN S VARIANTS
18,770	235	1.25%

This is actually a very small amount of significant variation in such a quantity of New Testament material. This is obvious when we compare Matthew with the other three books we've analyzed.

PERCENTAGE			
Jude	Matthew	Romans	Hebrews
4.4%	1.25%	1.07%	.52%

Again, as we've seen in the case of Romans and Hebrews, over 98% of the text is the same, regardless of which version we're using.

But this still leaves us with questions about that small percentage that is significantly different. To help answer our doubts, let's look more closely at some of the very significant variants in Matthew. For instance, one of the most disturbing might be the absence of the following words in both NA27 and every one of the four modern language versions we've used comparatively in this study (NASB, HCSB, NIV, ESV).

> **. . . that it might be fulfilled which was spoken by the prophet, They parted my garments among them, and upon my vesture they did cast lots** (27:35).

Admittedly, these are very significant words. But in order to understand why NA27 and modern language versions omit them, we need to note two facts. The first is that they are *not found in the MT either*—not even in brackets. The TR has them, but apart from it, almost the entire body of manuscript evidence testifies to their absence from this text.

I'm calling our attention to this one example in order to make the point that there are *facts* behind every significant variation. Those facts need to be given full consideration before we dismiss a Greek text or a translation simply because it involves a treasured truth, a great many words, or differs from what we have become accustomed to.

In this case, however, there is a second fact that is reassuring. That is that almost these same words are found in a passage about which there is no textual question at all, John 19:24.

It reads. . .

. . . that the scripture might be fulfilled, which saith, They parted my raiment among them, and for my vesture they did cast lots.

The question then, is not whether this statement is Scripture, but whether it is included in Matthew 27:35. The oldest manuscripts and the majority of all manuscripts say "no." It is for that reason alone that NA27, the MT, and modern versions do not include it.

Similar facts lie behind each of the other significant variants in Matthew. In each case there is manuscript evidence that justifies the readings of the MT or NA27 when they differ from those in the TR.

I want now to look more closely at the times a name or title for a member of the Godhead is found in the TR or MT but not included in NA27 and the NASB of Matthew. Here's the list according to the KJV.

Ref.	Name or Title in TR or MT only	Ref.	Name or Title in TR or MT only
6:33	God	18:2	Jesus
8:29	Jesus	18:26	Lord
13:36	Jesus	19:17	God
13:51	Jesus . . . Lord	21:12	God
14:14	Jesus	22:30	God
14:22	Jesus	22:32	God
14:25	Jesus	22:37	Jesus
15:30	Jesus	23:8	Christ
16:20	Jesus	24:2	Jesus
17:11	Jesus	25:13	Son
17:20	Jesus	28:6	Lord

Here are 23 instances in one book of the Bible where the King James includes names or titles for members of the Godhead which are omitted by NA27 (or modern versions).

NAME/TITLE OMITTED	NUMBER OF TIMES
Christ	1
God	5
Jesus	13
Lord	3
Son	1

Lists and statistics like this are sometimes publicized as proof that NA27 is defective or even unorthodox. Next to omissions of the word "God," for instance, the editors of such lists will sometimes write "denial of Diety." Next to omissions of "Christ," they assert, "denial of Messiahship."

But let's look at the list again. This time we'll include a portion of the KJV text and then parallel it with the NASB reading.

REF.	KING JAMES VERSION	NEW AMERICAN STANDARD BIBLE
6:33	seek ye first the kingdom of God	seek first His kingdom
8:29	What have we to do with thee, Jesus, thou Son of God	What business do we have with each other, Son of God
13:36	Jesus sent the multitude away	He left the crowds
13:51	Jesus saith unto them, have ye understood all these things? They said unto him, Yea, Lord	Have you understood all these things? They said to Him, "Yes"
14:14	Jesus went forth	He went ashore
14:22	Jesus constrained his disciples	He made the disciples
14:25	Jesus went unto them, walking on the sea	He came to them, walking on the sea

Ref.	King James Version (cont)	New American Standard Bible (cont)
15:30	cast them down at Jesus' feet	they laid them down at His feet
16:20	that he was Jesus the Christ	that He was the Christ
17:11	Jesus answered and said	He answered and said
17:20	Jesus said unto them	He said to them
18:2	Jesus called a little child unto him	He called a child to himself
18:26	Note: "Lord" here is not a reference to Jesus	
19:17	none good, but one, that is God	only One who is good
21:12	the temple of God	the temple
22:30	angels of God in heaven	angels in heaven
22:32	God is not the God of the dead	He is not the God of the dead
22:37	Jesus said unto him	He said to him
23:8	one is your Master, even Christ	One is your teacher
24:2	And Jesus said unto them	And He said to them
24:36	my Father only	nor the Son, but the Father alone
25:13	the hour wherein the Son of man cometh	nor the hour
28:6	Come, see the place where the Lord lay	Come, see the place where He was lying

Although the NASB, following its chosen Greek text, does admittedly omit these 23 names or titles, it is clearly not attempting to deny any member of the Godhead. In no case is there any question about who the particular verse is speaking of, whether it be Jesus Himself or the Father. If you have any lingering doubts about that fact, simply look up in an NASB the reference you're questioning and you'll see that within the context the referent is unmistakable. In fact, the NASB does what even the KJV does not—it capitalizes pronouns referring to deity (note, for instance, 15:30; 16:20; 18:2; 24:2; 28:6). The word "One" is also capitalized when it refers to deity (for instance, in 19:17). In one instance, 24:36, it includes the word "Son" when the KJV does not.

MORE SAMPLE BOOKS

I'm going to give now, almost without comment, the statistics for one more Pauline epistle and then the book of James and one epistle by John.

Ephesians

NA27	MT	TR
2422 words	2459 words	2469 words

Variants	Sets affecting NASB	Significant Variants
109	35	11

REF.	TR OR MT OMISSIONS FROM EPHESIANS	TR OR MT ADDITIONS TO EPHESIANS	TR OR MT SUBSTITUTIONS IN EPHESIANS
1:18			"understanding" for "heart"
3:6	"Jesus"		
3:9		"all"	
3:9			"fellowship" for "administration"
3:9		"by Jesus Christ"	
3:14		"of our Lord Jesus Christ"	
5:9			"Spirit" for "Light"
5:21			"God" for "Christ"
5:29			"Lord" for "Christ"
5:30		"of his flesh and of his bones"	
6:12		"this world"	

Significant variants	Words in S Variants	% of text	% of text unaffected
11	26	1.05%	98.95%

James

NA27	MT	TR
1742 words	1760 words	1765 words

Variants	Sets affecting NASB	Significant Variants
90	30	6

Ref.	TR or MT Omissions from James	TR or MT Additions to James	TR or MT Substitutions in James
1:19			"Wherefore" for "This"
2:19			"there is one God" for "God is one"
2:20			"dead" for "useless"
3:9			"God" for "Lord"
4:4		"adulterers and"	
4:12		"and Judge"	

Significant variants	Words in S Variants	% of text	% of text unaffected
6	11	0.62%	99.38%

I John

NA27	MT	TR
2141 words	2153 words	2187 words

Variants	Sets affecting NASB	Significant Variants
70	32	13

REF.	TR OR MT OMISSIONS FROM I JOHN	TR OR MT ADDITIONS TO I JOHN	TR OR MT SUBSTITUTIONS IN I JOHN
1:4			"your" for "our"
1:7		"Christ"	
2:7			"brethren" for "beloved"
2:20			"you know all things" for "you all know"
2:23	"the one who confesses the Son has the Father also"[31]		
2:27			"you shall abide" for "abide"
3:1	"and *such* we are"		
4:3		"Christ has come in the flesh"	
4:19		"him"	
4:20			"how can" for "cannot"

Ref.	TR or MT Omissions from I John (cont)	TR or MT Additions to I John (cont)	TR or MT Substitutions in I John (cont)
5:7b-8a		"in heaven, the Father, the Word, and the Holy Ghost: and these three are one. And there are three that bear witness in earth"	
5:13		"and that ye may believe on the name of the Son of God"	
5:18			"himself" for "him"

In evaluating I John it's important to remember that the words of I John 5:7b-8a are almost certainly not original.[32] They amount to 25 of the 57 words in significant variants in the book. Lets look at the statistics both with and without the words of this doubtful passage.

I John with 5:7b-8a

Significant variants	Words in S Variants	% of text	% of text unaffected
13	57	2.6%	97.4%

I John without 5:7b-8a

Significant variants	Words in S Variants	% of text	% of text unaffected
12	32	1.46%	98.54%

The words of this one reading, almost certainly not original, amount to a full 1.5% of the text of I John affected by variants. If we assume that it is spurious, we again have a New Testament book whose text is over 98% the same regardless of which text is being used.

CONCLUSION

This chapter has attempted to answer the question of how much difference the textual differences between Greek Testaments actually makes. Nine facts are now before us.

Fact #1: The KJV Translators Sometimes Employed Textual Variants.

Fact #2: The Greek Texts Contain Almost the Same Number of Words.

Fact #3: There are a Few Verses Which NA27 or the MT Do Not Include in Their Text.

Fact #4: Every Questionable Verse Nevertheless Appears in the Footnotes of NA27 and the MT.

Fact #5: Modern Versions Include the Questionable Verses.

Fact #6: Modern Versions Give the Benefit of the Doubt to Other Disputable Passages as Well.

Fact #7: Modern Versions Do Not Follow NA27 Slavishly.

Fact #8: The Test of a Translation's Integrity Cannot be the Number of Questionable Verses It Prints.

Fact #9: Only a Small Percentage of Variants Affect Understanding Significantly.

To demonstrate this last fact we have sampled 7 books, which combined, amount to over 25% of the New Testament. Compare the figures.

	New Testament	7 Sample Books	Percentage
Chapters	280	74	26.4%
TR Words	140,744	37,858	26.90%

Although I would like to have examined every New Testament book, it seems to me that what we have done provides a reasonably representative sample of what we could expect to find among the others as well. My analysis no doubt contains errors here and there. If I had caught them I would have corrected them. But nevertheless, even given the possibility of some small percentage of error, I'm confident that discovering it would not substantially alter the summary we'll view now.

Combining the statistics we've compiled for the seven sample books yields the following comparisons.

Book	TR Words	Variants	Significant Variants	Words in significant variants	Percentage of Significant Variation
Matthew	18,770	918	105	235	1.25%
Romans	7,208	246	32	77	1.07%
Ephesians	2,469	109	11	26	1.05%
Hebrews	5,005	190	12	26	.52%
James	1,765	90	6	11	.62%
I John	2,187	70	13	57	2.60%
Jude	454	14	9	20	4.40%
Totals	**37,858**	**1637**	**188**	**452**	**1.19%**

A total percentage of significant variation of only 1.19% for over 25% of the New Testament in two English translations made from two Greek texts is remarkably small. It's patently obvious that the two texts and the two translations are substantially the same.

This, of course, would not be the case if within that small amount of significant *textual* variation there were significant *doctrinal* differences. If one of these texts or translations, for instance, denied the deity of Christ, added works to faith for justification, denied the existence of Hell, called in question the resurrection, counseled unbelief, or promoted evil, then yes, we are looking at different Bibles. But *not a single variant in any way alters what Christians believe and practice.* Every variant could be included in our Bibles or every one could be omitted and it would not affect our faith or practice in the slightest way.

Yet still this very small percentage of significant variation may trouble someone who has followed this discussion right through to this point. Disappointed with the result, reassuring as it is, he may decide to reject every other Greek New Testament and cleave only to the TR. He has liberty before God to do so. *But he will still not escape the variants.*

No English translation, not even the King James, will reflect his preferred Greek text exactly. The King James translators themselves decided centuries ago that they were going to vary occasionally from every Greek New Testament in existence. The variants are woven seamlessly and invisibly right into the text of our King James Version.

"Oh," but you say, "there aren't many of them." How true. But by resorting to that argument you have yourself just conceded the whole point of this chapter—that there is *no such thing* as a perfect translation. At the end of the day, what really matters to every one of us is not the *existence*, but the *amount* and *kind* of variation in it.

Now it seems to me that for all practical purposes we've come to an agreement about that. We ought, therefore, to be able to discuss texts and translations without acrimony, without suspicion, and without accusation, but charitably. I'm not lobbying for any particular Greek text or English translation. What I am arguing is that in light of the facts no one in the debate should be allowed to level charges like the following without being vigorously challenged.

> *The old manuscripts behind the modern Greek text were influenced by heretics. The modern Greek text is a much different New Testament from the Textus Receptus. Every modern version based on the modern Greek text undermines major doctrines.*

I trust that by now it's apparent that whoever would make such allegations is either misinformed or dishonest. This chapter is being offered for the prayerful consideration of the former in the earnest hope that its findings will reasonably reassure and thus help ensure the "unity of the Spirit in the bond of peace."

---

[1]Beza published nine editions of the Greek New Testament between 1565 and 1604. Five of the nine, however, were reprints of earlier editions. His 1598 was the fourth *independent* edition. This was "more likely than any other to be in the hands of King James's revisers, and to be accepted by them as the best standard within their reach" (F. H. A. Scrivener, *The New Testament Greek and English.* Cambridge: The University Press, 1908, p. xxiv).

[2]See the appendix to F. H. A. Scrivener's *The New Testament Greek and English.*

[3]D. A. Waite, for instance, claims that he has counted "9,970 Greek words" where the Westcott-Hort text differs from the TR (*Fundamentalist Mis-information*, Collingswood, NJ: The Bible For Today Press, 2000, p. 11). Dr. Waite shows no awareness that thousands of these are so insignificant that they don't influence translation at all, nor awareness of the fact that the Westcott-Hort Testament is not the text of modern translators.

[4]The KJV translators wrote, *We do not deny, nay, we affirm and avow, that the very meanest translation of the Bible in English set forth by men of our profession. . . containeth the word of God, nay, is the word of God. . . No cause therefore why the word translated should be denied to be the word, or forbidden to be current, notwithstanding that some imperfections and blemishes may be noted in the setting forth of it* ("*The Translators to the Reader*," Holy Bible 1611 Edition. Nashville: Thomas Nelson Publishers, 1982, p. xix).

[5]In 1982, for the first time in history, an edition of the MT was made widely available to the public by two Dallas Seminary professors, Zane Hodges and Arthur Farstad.

[6]"NA" stands for its editors, Erwin Nestle and Kurt Aland. This text, with fewer footnotes, is identical to that also printed in the United Bible Societies 4th edition of the Greek New Testament (see the Introduction to NA27, p. 46*).

[7]As these labels are sometimes used disparagingly I'm going to confine myself to the designation "NA27."

[8]In *The Byzantine Text-Type and New Testament Textual Criticism*, Harry Sturz argues that some readings within this family date back as early as the second century (pp. 55-131). Most textual scholars, however, dispute this. D. A. Carson writes, *There is no unambiguous evidence that the Byzantine text-type was known before the middle of the fourth century. . . . I do not deny that readings found in the Byzantine text-type are found in the ante-Nicene period: but almost all of those readings are also found in other text-types* (*The King James Version Debate: A Plea for Realism*. Grand Rapids: Baker, 1979, p. 44).

[9]For an extended discussion of the evidence see Daniel B. Wallace, "The Majority Text and the Original Text: Are They Identical?" *Bibliotheca Sacra* 148, no. 590 (April-June 1991), pp. 158-166.

[10]As a result, even the TR is an "eclectic" text. Technically, there is no current Greek Testament which is not "eclectic."

[11]Word counts are generated from BibleWorks Version 4.0.

[12]Daniel Wallace reports 1838 differences between the two in "Some Second Thoughts on the Majority Text," *Bibliotheca Sacra* 146, no. 583 (July-September 1989), p. 276.

[13]This is the system of footnotes attached to the Greek Testaments. It displays the support for disputed readings in manuscripts, versions, and other ancient sources.

[14]The NASB generally reflects the NA27 text. As it is also one of the most literal modern translations it serves well for our comparative purpose.

[15]From the forward to the NASB Side-Column Reference Edition, p. vii.

[16]The New King James Version, in contrast to most modern translations, favors the TR.

[17]Copyright 2001 by Holman Bible Publishers. The Old Testament is still in progress. When completed the translation will be the work of 90 scholars representing 20 evangelical denominations. The publisher's goals for this translation include providing "English speaking Christians with an accurate, readable Bible in contemporary, idiomatic English," and affirming "the authority of the Scriptures as God's inerrant Word and its absolutes against the inevitable changes in culture" (from the Introduction).

[18]Copyright 2001 by Crossway Bibles, a division of Good News Publishers, a "not-for-profit organization that exists solely for the purpose of publishing the good news of the gospel and the truth of God's Word, the Bible." The ESV is "adapted from the Revised Standard Version of the Bible" (from the Copyright page).

[19]In this case the words of the verse are not printed. The note reads "Some manuscripts add verses 44 and 46 (which are identical with verse 48)."

[20]See note 19.

[21]"The Translators to the Reader." *Holy Bible 1611 Edition.* (Nashville: Thomas Nelson Publishers, 1982), p. xxiv.

[22]From the "Introduction," pp. 49, 50.

[23]These verses are separated away from vv. 1-8 by a horizontal line, several blank spaces, and the bracketed statement, "The two most reliable early manuscripts do not have Mark 16:9-20."

[24]These verses are separated from the verses preceding and following them by horizontal lines, several blank spaces, and the bracketed statement after 7:52, "The earliest and most reliable manuscripts do not have John 7:53-8:11."

[25]Wallace, "The Majority Text and the Original Text: Are They Identical?", p. 157.

[26]A hugely disproportionate number of these, nearly 550 of them, occur in just one book, Acts, due in large part to the Western Family additions I've just mentioned.

[27]Charles Surrett, for instance, a refreshingly irenic TR advocate, rightly observes, *For all those who desire to exegete God's Word in its original languages, the parsing of verbs, grammatical notations, kind and time of action, voice, mood, noun declensions, etc., will be affected by the texts from which such work is done.* (*Which Greek Text*. Kings Mountain, NC: Surrett Family Publications, 1999, p. 69).

[28]I chose the Hodges-Farstad apparatus for two reasons; one, because it is blessedly simple, and two, because the editors are especially interested in calling attention to the differences between their MT and what they call the "critical text" (essentially NA27). The number of their sets of variants is the number of their footnotes, but in some cases, as we shall see, there is more than one variant per footnote.

[29]The variant here is between εαυτοις, the third person reflexive pronoun, and αυτοις, the third person personal pronoun. Note the one letter of difference between them. It illustrates how easily variants crept into the handwritten copies, as well as the relatively insignificant nature of many of them.

[30]The inclusion or exclusion of the possessive pronoun here alters the testimony of the text. Its presence includes the author among those prisoners upon whom the readers had shown compassion. Its absence allows for the possibility that he was not among that number. I would therefore rate the variant S.

[31]This is the variant with which we began our study—the one that I stumbled across as a freshman in college.

[32]The words as they appear in our KJV are *in heaven, the Father, the Word, and the Holy Ghost: and these three are one. And there are three that bear witness in earth.* Though they contain no untruth, they are nevertheless unsupported by any credible texts. They seem first to appear in the work of a Spanish Latin writer, Priscillian, who died in 385. A few Old Latin manuscripts also contain them. But they were not even included in Jerome's Vulgate. Accordingly, Erasmus did not include them in his first two printed editions of the Greek NT (1516, 1519). The story of his being confronted by the Roman Catholic authorities with a sixteenth-century Greek manuscript which contained them has been told often (see F. F. Bruce, *The Books and the Parchments*, p. 210 for the account). To this day, these words are "absent from every known Greek manuscript except eight," and four of these carry it only as a variant written in their margins (Bruce Metzger, *A Textual Commentary on the Greek New Testament*, p. 647).

BIBLIOGRAPHY

Bruce, F. F. *The Books and the Parchments: Some Chapters on the Transmission of the Bible*. Westwood, NJ: Fleming H. Revell Company, 1963

Carson, D. A. *The King James Version Debate: A Plea for Realism*. Grand Rapids: Baker, 1979

Hodges, Zane C. and Arthur L. Farstad. *The Greek New Testament According to the Majority Text, Second Edition*. Nashville: Thomas Nelson Publishers, 1985.

The Holman Christian Standard Bible. Nashville: Broadman and Holman Publishers, 1999

Holy Bible, English Standard Version. Wheaton, Illinios: Crossway Bibles, Division of Good News Publishers, 2001.

Holy Bible, New King James Version. Nashville: Thomas Nelson Publishers, 1982.

Metzger, Bruce, *A Textual Commentary on the Greek New Testament*. Stuttgart: Deutsche Bibelgesellschaft, 1998, 2 nd edition, 2nd printing. United Bible Societies.

Nestle, Eberhard, Erwin Nestle, Kurt Aland, et.al. *Novum Testamentum Graece*, 27th edition. Stuttgart: Deutsche Bibelstiftung, 1994. American Bible Society, 2001.

Scrivener, F. H. A. *The New Testament Greek and English*. Cambridge: The University Press, 1908.

Struz, Harry A. *The Byzantine Text-Type and New Testament Textual Criticism*. Nashville, TN: Thomas Nelson, 1984.

Surrett, Charles L. *Which Greek Text? The Debate Among Fundamentalists*. Kings Mountain, NC: Surrett Family Publications, 1999.

"The Translators to the Reader," *Holy Bible, 1611 Edition*. Nashville: Thomas Nelson Publishers, 1982.

Waite, D. A. *Fundamentalist Mis-Information on Bible Versions*. Collingswood, NJ: The Bible for Today Press, 2000.

Wallace, Daniel B. "The Majority Test and the Original Text: Are They Identical?" *Bibilotheca Sacra* 148, no. 590 (April-June 1991), pp. 158-166.

_____. "Some Second Thoughts on the Majority Text," *Bibliotheca Sacra* 146, no. 583 (July-September 1989), p. 276.

THE AUTOGRAPH[1] THOUGH DEAD YET SPEAKETH
On the Translation of the Copies

Hantz Bernard

It happened in Haiti. After five years of working on the translation of the New Testament (NT) into Haitian Creole (hereafter only Creole), I was finally holding a trial edition of seven selected books.[2] I stood in the pulpit of my church on a Sunday night at the customary time when the Scriptures are read during the service, opened the booklet to a passage in the Gospel of John, and began reading. Halfway through the selected reading, my speech stumbled. A troublesome question surreptitiously entered my mind and brought a chill to my spine, "Whose words are these?" When I ventured to respond that they were mine, I felt guilty of sacrilege. When I attempted to say they were God's, I felt presumptuous.

Though my formal education was primarily in French, I grew up speaking both French and Creole. I learned English as a foreign language only in high school. At the age of fifteen, I was saved through the witness of a missionary and began reading the Scriptures faithfully. For lack of a good translation in Creole, I used only the French version universally adopted among French speaking believers called *Version Louis Segond*, and I used it unreservedly. I memorized verses and even long passages from it. I studied it and preached from it. I led souls to the Lord through it. My church grew from it. I marked it and taught from it at a theological seminary. Formally revised in 1910,[3] the origin of this version was distant enough in the past that I used it without ever questioning its validity as God's Word. Its longevity gave me confidence in it and reverence for it.

However, this Creole translation[4] that I was reading bore the imprint of my labor and that of people I knew. In order to translate accurately gospel accounts of fishing scenes, I had interviewed fishermen by the seashore to gather specific vocabularies. I had done the same for all passages related to a specific trade or field of knowledge. I had conversed with monolingual speakers of Creole to ascertain the nuances of words. I had searched books. I had consulted linguists. I had studied Greek grammars, dictionaries, and lexicons. I had written and rewritten sentences. I had compared the translated verses with various translations in three other languages. I had subjected the translation to several checklists. I had checked it for style, accuracy, clarity, and naturalness. Linguists who specialized in Creole had reviewed it. Native believers trained in theology, biblical languages, and translation methods had edited it. Experienced translation consultants had verified it. Common people had proofread it. Even the trial edition of the seven books from which I was reading was printed with the understanding that it would later be submitted to various, more stringent editorial examinations. Whose words, therefore, was I reading?[5]

The translation process we followed was neither unusual nor wrong. Serious translations of the Word of God are always the fruit of studious research, careful examination, and meticulous testing. Throughout Christian history, translating the Word of God into the native tongues of believers stands as a landmark of conservative faith. The Reformation grew from the compelling drive to make the Word of God available to the common people in their own languages. The Christian faith developed around the world from translations of the Scriptures. Today, among the nearly 6500 languages spoken in the world, about 383 have a complete Bible, an additional 987 have a complete NT, and 891 more have some portions of the Scriptures.[6] Whatever the layperson has learned about God and the Scriptures themselves, whether the mysterious truths of the trinity or the foundational tenet of inspiration, has been learned from translated Scriptures.

Still, in considering these facts about all these translations, we cannot evade these crucial but troublesome questions: Whose words are they? By what Biblical means can we claim a translation of the Scriptures is God's Word, when the process that produces it is so heavily controlled by man's skills? What are the criteria by which one can judge a translation to be or not to be God's Word?

AN ASSESSMENT OF THE SITUATION

These questions focus our attention upon one very important need: proven criteria by which to judge whether a translation is the Word of God or not. The autographs were definitely God's Word. Both the copies of the autographs and the translations of the copies are, by their very nature, distinct from the autographs. God must have intended acceptable standards to insure the preservation of the Word-of-God nature of the autographs when they are transferred to copies and from copies into translations. I will call this concept *scripturalness*. By *scripturalness* I mean the character of copies of the autographs and of translations of the copies as meeting God's intended standards so that they may be called the Word of God.[7] Though the discussion in this chapter will refer to the copies, they will primarily pertain to translations of the copies.

The issues that have dominated Bible translation in the past decades have raised a new awareness of the necessity of defining the scriptural nature of manuscript copies and Bible translations as distinct from the autographs. During the last forty years, new Bible agencies have proliferated, and old ones have grown. This has generated new methods of translation, new approaches to Bible production and sales, and numerous books on Bible translation theory. Most of these books address the subject almost entirely from a linguistic point of view. Others have reacted to this tendency by presenting only theological dimensions to Bible translation. Both approaches have shed some light on the issue. And both have, in some ways, complicated it.

In evaluating a piece of literature, one must judge it according to its subject matter or content and the quality of its language or form. God superintended the writing of the Bible so that both of these aspects might be respected. The Biblical writers were led by the Holy Spirit to write genuine, divine revelation in proper human language. Translations of their writings must, therefore, be evaluated for both theological soundness and linguistic appropriateness. A translation can be theologically sound yet linguistically unsound. Conversely, it may be linguistically correct while theologically incorrect.

Failing to recognize this simple fact, many linguists are proposing *linguistic* answers to translation problems that are *theological* in nature. Similarly, many theologians are presenting theological answers to questions that should be dealt with linguistically.

The Theological Dimension of the Situation

Scripturalness of translations has not been an issue throughout the history of doctrine. The Bible carries with it a rich theological heritage. Our forefathers in the faith defended it valiantly. They have left us a wealth of literature that presents both internal and external evidence that substantiates the divine inspiration of the Scriptures. To use our own terminology, we might say they defended the *scripturalness* of the Scriptures. However, their arguments relate mainly to the first documents penned by the Biblical writers: the autographs. The same arguments may be applied to the copies of those documents. But our forefathers did not systematically address the *scripturalness* of Bible translations because it was not a relevant problem at that time. For example, *The Fundamentals: A Testimony to the Truth* published in 1917 are considered to be "the famous sourcebook of Foundational Biblical Truths" (as the cover of the 1990 abridged edition by Kregel terms it.) However, not one of its twelve volumes addresses the subject of *scripturalness* of translations. Any reference in it to preservation relates the doctrine to the copies of the autographs but does not even allude to translations.[8]

The core doctrines that conservative believers now accept and revere were not developed by the stroke of one pen in the early church. Yes, these doctrines have always been in the Scriptures, but they are not developed systematically in the Scriptures. The first believers presumed them but they were not defined. The doctrines we hold so dear have been systematized gradually throughout history, often as a reaction to false teachings. The dates when particular doctrines were defined can be found in any simple book on the history of doctrine.

Today, the *scripturalness* of Bible translations has become a pertinent issue. As our forefathers responded to the theological challenges of their days, the present generation of believers bears the same responsibility. It is time for us to produce internal and external evidence to defend what we mean when we hold a translation of the Bible and declare, "This is the Word of God."

Our theology books do not provide a definite explanation either. Most books of systematic theology treat the doctrine of the Scriptures under headings of revelation, inspiration, and illumination. Those tenets are vital, but they do not directly address the issue of the *scripturalness* of Bible translations. These books define inspiration as it relates to the very first manuscripts, and only the very first manuscripts, that the Biblical writers produced.

For example, Millard J. Erickson in his book *Christian Theology* begins his chapter on inspiration with the right definition, declaring that it is "that supernatural influence of the Holy Spirit upon the Scripture writers which rendered their writings an accurate record of the revelation or which resulted in what they wrote to actually being the Word of God."[9] He titled the chapter this way: "The Preservation of Revelation: Inspiration." He went on to say that "inspiration relates more to the relaying of that [revealed] truth from the first recipient(s) of it to other people, whether then or later."[10] This is confusing. If inspiration is the way by which revelation is preserved, if it is limited only to the autographs, and if no autograph is in existence, how then is revelation truly relayed to people who live later than the time of inspiration? This is the type of confusion that exists in most books of theology in regard to the *scripturalness* of translations and the inspiration of the Scriptures.

Moreover, *scripturalness* of translations does not depend simply on textual issues. None of the inspired autographs is extant. As a result, we must rely on copies of the autographs, copies made by fallible people. Some copyists were better than others. Therefore, some copies are more accurate than others but we do not have the autographs with which to compare the copies.

Throughout history, believers have dealt with the problem by attempting to reconstruct the autographs from the copies that they possessed. Scholars have defined standards by which to decide, in view of the evidence, the most likely reading of the autographs. After centuries of such work, certain copies and particular renditions of certain passages have come to be identified with, and grouped in, specific collections or texts that bear specific names. Names such as Textus Receptus, Majority Text, and Aland-Nestle have become more familiar to lay people, though most users of these terms know little about the texts that bear those names. Nonetheless, many Christians identify themselves according to the text they prefer.

We cannot escape the fact that whatever text one prefers, that text was the result of a logical system of evaluating and selecting copies. Some texts were produced primarily on the basis of historical tradition; others involve more systematic examination. All copies were the products of human skills.

Textual issues are not the primary subject of this chapter. Nonetheless, copies are all we have available today. No autographs are known to exist. The copies are the source of any translation, whether old or new, conservative or free. The fact that the autographs are inspired does not make the copies inspired. Even if copies were inspired, that would not automatically make translations from those copies inspired.[11] Copies of the autographs, copies of copies, and translations of the copies are all products of human endeavor.

Like the history of doctrine and textual criticism, the doctrine of inspiration does not necessarily insure the *scripturalness* of translations. If inspiration were to include copies and translations it would still be necessary to define logical, Biblical, objective criteria that a translator should follow in order to guarantee that his translation would be inspired. In other words, if translations can be inspired, we must be certain that the translations we produce on the mission fields today are inspired. Once those criteria are determined we should be able to teach a course entitled "How to Produce Inspired Translations." That would allow a translator to declare without any fear of failure, "I am going to make an inspired translation. I have the formula." Of course, anyone who would make such a claim would be presumptuous and arrogant. Whether we are translators or readers of translations, we would like to have standards that can be applied to any translation in any language to determine whether or not it is the Word of God. The fact that systematic criteria have not been defined does not grant us the license to impose our own criteria and claim inspiration for a translation.

That lack of formal, definitive criteria makes this a sensitive issue in the practice of our faith. We recognize that Bible translations have influenced humanity in ways that are impossible for human literature to do. They have shaped the whole history of Christianity. They have fashioned our own spiritual experiences. In essence, man-produced-translations have accomplished wonders that only God-given revelation could perform. How is that possible?

Many solutions to this question have been proposed. In an effort to protect the foundation of our faith some have sought a method by which we may identify translations as the Word of God and not the word of man. They have applied the term inspiration to translations for fear that there is no other way for a translation to be the Word of God, that is, possess the quality of *scripturalness*.

It is impossible to defend Biblically the assumption that translations are inspired. The weight of theological literature on the subject during the past 200 years has convincingly confined inspiration to the autographs. Applying the term inspiration to translations in general creates a false comfort zone. That, in turn, complicates the problem. Applying the term to one translation per language would not advance the cause either. For then we would be astonished by the different semantic nuances among those translations. The same passages in different languages require different ways of expressing the same thing. That fact alone would disrupt our mistaken comfort.

Finally, translation sectarianism does not solve the problem of *scripturalness* of translations either. Some believers have refused to face the problem. They have withdrawn into a corner with one translation of their own choosing. They have built their comfort zone around it. Some among them may even go as far as reviling anyone who does not adopt their translation. They may defend it by establishing some equivalence between it and their preferred Biblical language copies. They may declare their chosen translation to be inspired because it speaks to them, and because it has been around too long to be considered any other way. If we deal with the subject this way, we are corrupting the very precious doctrine of inspiration. In my presentation, should I have stood in the middle of my church and declared to my people, "This is the inspired Creole translation I have produced?"

The history of doctrine, textual criticism, the doctrine of inspiration, and translation sectarianism do not provide adequate solutions to the problem of *scripturalness* of Bible translations. Today we face a crucial theological problem. Some Bible agencies have taken such latitude in translating the Scriptures that they offend the piety of conservative believers and undermine Biblical truth. In reaction, some believers have exalted translations to a level that has generated new theological problems. In either situation, we evade the truly appropriate issue: establishment of the criteria for ascertaining that whether any translation, in any language, is the Word of God or not.

The Linguistic Dimension of the Situation

The linguistic perspective of Bible translation is the other side of the same coin. Proponents of linguistics are often as unilateral in their perspective of Bible translation as those who consider only the theological dimension of it. Since the first official translation of the Old Testament (OT), the Septuagint (done in Greek, about the third century B.C.), until about forty years ago, no theory of, or methodology for, Bible translating had been systematically written. Throughout our history, a few languages have been graced with dozens of translations. French may number over 88 in its history. English may count up to 300. Thousands of languages today remain without the Scriptures. Two hundred years ago, at the dawn of the modern Bible society movement, the Bible had been translated into only 67 languages.[12] Translations were few and far between. But those that were produced depended mostly on the rare personal skills of born linguists rather than a pre-established theory.

Heidemarie Salevsky explains that in 1814 F.D.E. Schleiermacher was begging for "firm principles" of translation and that by 1960, no complete theory had been developed. She reported this statement from Schleiermacher:

> No consistent and coherent theory of translation resting on firm principles has made its appearance yet. What has been put forward is fragmentary. …The fact remains that as surely as there exists a science of the classical world, there must be a science of translation.[13]

The era of modern missions changed that perspective. As Christian communities sprouted among ethnic groups in Africa, Asia, and South America, the need for missionaries to learn new languages well and quickly, to reduce most of those languages to writing, and to translate the Word of God into them, produced many Bible agencies. In turn, the agencies developed methodologies for the multiple translations they were supervising. Nearly every missionary was a potential translator or medical doctor or both.

One famous example is William Cameron Townsend. In 1917, while selling Spanish Bibles in Guatemala, a Cakchiquel Indian challenged him, "If your God is so great, why doesn't He speak in my language?" Townsend took up the challenge. He moved to live among the tribe, learn their language, reduce it to writing, and translate the Bible into it. By 1931, the New Testament was available in Cakchiquel.

The experience established for Townsend the importance of linguistics in Bible translating. In 1934, he founded Wycliffe Camp to teach linguistics to students whom he would take with him to various fields with the goal of multiplying among many ethnic groups the successful experience he himself had had among the Cakchiquel tribe. Over the years, Wycliffe Camp grew to the three affiliates, Wycliffe Bible Translators, SIL International, and JAARS that greatly dominate the influence and nature of linguistics in Bible translating today.

This development within the Christian community coincided with the rise of linguistics as a science. During the 1950's, Noam Chomsky's theory of a universal grammar and a more scientific understanding of language structure among linguists stimulated the interest of Bible agencies. They began to mandate formal linguistic training for translators and translation consultants working under their auspices.

All this was good, but it came at the expense of theological training for those involved in Bible translation. Linguists developed a tendency of approaching the translation of the Scriptures as they would the translation of secular literature. They submitted it to the general principles of language analysis and translation, regardless of its uniqueness as divine revelation. The attitude intensified until even Eugene A. Nida, the father of the theory of Bible translation called *dynamic equivalence*, suggested that stylists should translate the Bible and Biblical scholars would only review the translation.[14]

Dynamic equivalence purported to solve, through linguistics, age-long theological and linguistic problems in translations. In time, the theory was expanded. Despite the warnings of the framers of that theory, many of the translators trained under those principles carried the theory much further than the framers intended.[15] Similar to the way computer software is modified to fit the specific tasks and purposes of the user, Bibles are being translated to appeal to particular social groups and different language levels. Thus, the focus has shifted from protecting the integrity of the Biblical text (as reflected in conservative translations) to satisfying the social inclinations of the reader.

Consequently, many conservative believers reacted by mistrusting Bible translators and rejecting altogether the modern translation movement. Some churches banned Bible translators from their mission programs. Other believers regarded linguistics with suspicion. And in striving to insure the perpetuity of the Scriptures, they clung to older translations or to a particular translation in a given language. Linguists, in turn, scoffed at them and accused them and their traditional translations of narrow-mindedness. Thus, passion has developed on both sides of the issue.

An Evaluation Of The Positions

The need for proven criteria of *scripturalness* still remains. In general, theologians have not adequately assessed the full value of linguistics in Bible translating. Neither have they determined from the Scriptures themselves the principles that might be foundational to a balanced, Biblical philosophy of Bible translation.

If a layperson were to ask a conservative theologian the criteria by which it was decided which book should be included in the Bible, the response would be Biblical, systematic, substantial, and conclusive. By contrast, if a prospective translator were to ask the same theologian specific criteria by which to assure that his translation will be the Word of God, the answer would be vague at best. Specific theological criteria by which we can ascertain the *scripturalness* of translations have yet to be developed from internal and external evidence.

Consequently, two problems arise: (1) The issue of the *scripturalness* of translations is often approached with strong passion rather than sound logic, with a partisan spirit rather than objective Biblicism. (2) Believers are unable to handle properly the theological "side effects" created by good linguistic principles in Bible translation. Just as good medicine has medical side effects, so linguistics has theological "side effects." No definitive theological prospectus has listed the warnings and proposed the appropriate use of this valuable tool. No satisfactory theological standards by which to curtail, prevent, or eliminate the side effects of linguistics as applied to Bible translation have been developed. The simple, yet troublesome, question of how to decide whether or not a translation is the Word of God remains unanswered.

Linguists, on the other hand, have not yet defined the distinctions between the translation of the Holy Writ and that of secular literature. That is, they have not yet clearly stated from the Scriptures the unique boundaries that must be placed upon linguistic modification in translating the Bible. In general, linguists would recoil from theological issues, adhere strictly to scientific analysis of languages, and remain oblivious to the theological side effects they generate. Some statements of the Scriptures may not appear to be linguistically correct but may be theologically sound. "I am that I am" transcends linguistics but is proper theology. In translating the Scriptures, it is necessary, but not sufficient, to understand the dictionary meaning of words and to be able to analyze languages. The Scriptures contain "things of the Spirit of God" that can only be "spiritually discerned" (1 Corinthians 2:14). Proper linguistics must take into account the unique character of Scripture and develop means by which to preserve it in translation.

Moreover, linguistics as a science is young. Many aspects of it are still highly hypothetical. Therefore, it should approach the work of the past with more respect and consider the future with more modesty.

In the first issue of *OPTAT: Occasional Papers in Translation and Textlinguistics*, Robert Longacre says in truth:

> The difficulty with translating the Bible—a difficulty especially felt by "people of the Book"—is that we are simply too close to the Bible and too emotionally involved with it to back off from it far enough to consider translation problems dispassionately.[16]

This evaluation may be applied to linguistic studies and to the unilateral linguistic approach to Bible translation as well. To be fair, both theologians and linguists must draw back a little for the sake of considering objectively the translation issues pertinent to both groups. Let us heed Longacre's admonition and try to consider some Biblical and linguistic answers to the problem of the *scripturalness* of Bible translation—dispassionately.

WHAT IS THE BIBLICAL BASIS FOR BIBLE TRANSLATION?

The translation of sacred literature has never been a small issue. Muslims, for example, believe that their sacred book, the Koran, loses its character when it is translated, and that it can be genuine only in Arabic. We Christians, by contrast, have tacitly accepted and promoted the translation of the Bible. We have assumed Bible translation to be theologically proper without really proving so from the Scriptures and without seriously developing the criteria that a translation must fulfill in order to be considered the genuine Word of God. Before ever arguing whether a translation is the Word of God, it would be helpful to look at the Scriptures themselves to determine whether they are translatable at all. Let us begin by establishing the Biblical perspective on languages themselves.

Biblical Perspective on Languages

Language is older than man. God, Himself, used language to create the universe. We read in Genesis that God spoke and this universe came into being from no previously existing material. Man, in turn, was created with language capacity both to receive and to convey information. He received vocal-audio instructions from God and used language to name the animals. At his first sight of a woman, he burst forth with eloquent poetic marriage vows. We may assume from limited Biblical data that the same language was used until the Tower of Babel. We can only speculate about the identity of this language.

At the Tower of Babel, God *confused or mixed* the languages. That mixture bore a few particularities: (1) Diversity in sounds and structure. Each language possesses its conventional sets of sounds and established structure to convey meaning. (2) Inherent similarity. Similar sounds, though in different associations or sets, occur in most languages. All languages display some arrangement of subject, verb, and object. They retain a natural possibility for equivalence among them. (3) Potentiality for change. The language spoken prior to Babel did not multiply. We have no way of knowing if it changed within itself. But after Babel, languages have continued to change throughout the ages. New languages are born. Old languages disappear. All languages are in constant mutation.[17]

Babel may not have introduced any essential change to languages apart from the characteristics just listed. The idea that imprecision entered languages at Babel is neither linguistically plausible nor theologically defendable. Imprecision (or ambiguity, as linguists term the concept) is not necessarily bad. It is meaning, albeit a controlled measure of meaning. Words like *several, little, few, immeasurable, eternal, indefinite,* and *infinite* are all imprecise in that they do not convey any delineated, definite, measurable entity. Yet, they do refer to verifiable concepts of reality. Thus, they communicate the *precise* meaning intended by their users. Anything that could have been said in the language before Babel can be said in the languages of today. Concepts relate to the mind and to experience. Languages are simply vehicles that move those concepts from one mind to the other, whether it be from God's mind to man's, or from man's to God's, or from one man's mind to another man's mind.

Throughout the Testaments, God has spoken in various languages. He spoke Hebrew to Moses and the prophets. He may have used a Canaanite dialect or Akkadian in speaking to Abimelech (Genesis 20:1-7), Chaldean to Nebucadnezzar (Daniel 4), Latin or Greek to Cornelius (Acts 10), and Greek or Aramaic to Paul. Nearly all of those languages exist today in some form. Therefore, there is no point in speculating that the language used by God in the Garden of Eden and by all humans until Babel was superior to those God, Himself, used later or those we humans are using today. Paul stated that even if we were to speak languages of angels, that would not make us superior in any way (1 Corinthians 13:1). God spoke the languages of man, respected their grammar, and used stylistic images. He wrote the Ten Commandments in a human language—Hebrew. He commanded the prophets to write His revelation, and later in history, He quoted some of those writings. It is therefore evident that God spoke various "common" languages. He read languages and wrote them as well.

From the beginning of creation, it has clearly been God's intention to perpetuate His thoughts through speech and writing. The fact that He used many languages indicates that all languages have the potential of receiving His

Word. He did not establish any qualitative value to any language or any form of any language. The beauty of a language pertains to style, not intrinsic quality.

God created man with an innate ability for language. Animals may communicate, but they cannot speak. Only man, created in the image of God, can speak languages. In fact individuals may learn dozens of languages at an early age, keeping separate the complexities of grammar in each one. Even today, we are uncertain how babies acquire languages.[18]

God has endowed His servants with linguistic abilities and has played upon the intricacies of language nuances to make specific theological points (cf. Galatians 3:16). Paul may have preached in at least four languages: Hebrew, Aramaic, Greek, and Latin. In his preaching, he may have quoted the OT by translating impromptu into the other three languages, even though his writings are all in Greek.

The primary medium for the propagation of the gospel is language. Preaching, evangelism, teaching, and witnessing all rely on the use of language. God's command for us to carry the great commission depends substantially upon our ability to use the different languages of "all nations" (Matthew 28:19).

Languages are God's handiwork. Man may "clone" languages, but he cannot create them. He may analyze them and systematize their grammar, but he cannot invent a new system. Attempts at inventing languages have been no more successful than attempts to produce life in test tubes. Scientists always begin with existing life. The result is of the same nature, the same "stuff," the same species as what God had made in the first place. Languages may undergo changes but they are always of the same nature as that which God originally created.

Languages and translations of the Scriptures are the means used by God to record and perpetuate His revelation. The linguistic and theological lesson to gain from Babel is not that languages are bad, but that they are so good, that God can use them (and has used them) as tools in compelling man to accomplish His purpose. God can use any language or any form of any particular language to receive and carry His revelation. And that language will have the potential to fulfill God's assignment adequately. God meant it that way.

Biblical Evidence for Translations of the Scriptures

The richness of languages, as God has purposed it, includes one fascinating phenomenon of activity among languages called translation. The Scriptures themselves contain numerous instances of Biblical texts in one Biblical language being translated into another Biblical language. But the fact that this interaction occurs between OT Hebrew (or Aramaic) and NT Greek does not make these languages superior to the others. Those languages (or their specific variations) were the ones God used because they were used by men in the social context in which He gave His revelation and inspiration. Had the social context been American, French, or Haitian, the same phenomenon would have occurred and the related languages would have been used adequately without attaching any special, spiritual value to them.

The events of the Day of Pentecost in Acts 2 readily catch our attention because they present effects that are the reverse from those of the Tower of Babel. They show that languages do not have an inherent moral or spiritual value. They simply accomplish the purposes of the users. In that passage, Galileans preached the Word in many languages, not to disperse people but to gather them, not to confuse them but to enlighten them. The format of preaching in the book of Acts seems to indicate that while the Galileans spoke the languages of the Parthians, the Medes, the Elamites, the Mesopotamians, the Judeans, the Cappadocians, etc., they must have quoted the Hebrew OT. Indeed, preachers in those days always quoted the OT to support their messianic view. Peter himself, seizing the opportunity, quoted from the Hebrew OT texts of Joel and the Psalms in his sermon. His quotations are recorded in Greek. And that day, he may have preached in Greek or Aramaic. That was translation![19]

In Nehemiah 8:8, the leaders read the book of the Law to the people in Hebrew and "gave the sense" (that is, they translated into Aramaic)[20] and then "caused them to understand the reading" (that is, they explained the sense).

The Biblical writers also translated as they wrote. They translated Hebrew and Aramaic names into their Greek equivalents (Mathew 1:23; John 1:38, 41, 42; 9:7; Acts 4:36; 9:36; 13:8). When Jesus spoke to the little girl in Aramaic ("Talitha Cumi"), Mark readily translated the sense in Greek for the readers (or listeners) to understand.[21]

Throughout the NT, the Biblical writers quoted the Hebrew OT, translating their quotations into Greek. Some of these quotations were formal. That is, they translated directly a Hebrew text nearly word-for-word. Others were allusions. That is, the writers used their own words to convey the meaning of an OT passage to substantiate the point of their writing.[22] Many translation principles may be deduced by evaluating objectively the translation practices of the NT writers. But the NT writers went further than translating their quotations from Hebrew into Greek. The majority of their quotations of the OT came from a translation, the Septuagint. A linguistic analysis of the quotations of the OT in the Epistle to the Hebrews and various other NT passages reveals a clear correlation between them and their equivalent passages in the Septuagint. The evidence is so overwhelming that Walter C. Kaiser, Jr., states,

> That the LXX [The Septuagint] was the principal Bible of the early church can hardly be refuted if one is to judge on the basis of the text from the OT most frequently used throughout the entire NT in quotations.[23]

This fact may provide the strongest evidence of the approval of translations of the Scriptures by the Scriptures themselves. Since the NT writers did not have to translate when they quoted the Septuagint, they remained closer in wording when they quoted it than when they quoted the Hebrew text. And not once did they declare that they considered their source to be inspired. Nor did they revile the Septuagint for its weaknesses—indeed, many parts of it were translated poorly.[24] If inspiration were the concern of the Biblical writers in regard to the Septuagint, they would have resorted to either one of the two reactions above, seeing that they passionately defended the purity of the Word of God wherever it was threatened and that they set forth the inspiration of the Scriptures in their writings of the NT. Instead, they simply quoted the Septuagint in the Inspired Records as the Word of God, with no comment about its character, whether positive or negative.

Thus, the Biblical writers wrote with the assumption that the Scriptures can be translated and still remain Scripture despite the presence of unintentional errors introduced by human fallibility in the process of transmission. How is it so? They did not explain systematically. Theological probing might enlighten us.

Theological Consideration of Bible Translations

We have established that God uses languages as a tool and that inspired Scripture has approved the translation of Scripture. Let us go one more step. How can we theologically appreciate translations of the Scriptures? In answering that question we will follow traditional tenets of the doctrine of the Scripture. We will do so by asking four questions to highlight the basic concerns anyone would have when faced with the issue of God revealing His mind to man.

Theological Necessity for Scripturalness

The first question one would ask is, "Can a man know the mind of God?" Yes, if God revealed His mind to him. And He did. The process by which God communicated His mind to man is called *revelation*.

This prompts us to ask a second question: Can a man be sure that God's revelation is accurately penned? Yes, if God controlled the recording of it. And He did. The process by which God insured that what He had in His mind was accurately recorded is called *inspiration*.

Third, can a man understand God's recorded revelation? The answer again is, "Yes." He can if God enables him. And He does. The process by which God enables the believer to comprehend His recorded revelation is called *illumination*.[25] Charles C. Ryrie explains the doctrine this way:

> Generally, the concept of illumination is related to the work of the Holy Spirit in making clear the truth of the written revelation. In reference to the Bible, revelation relates to the material, inspiration to the method of recording the revelation, and illumination to the meaning of the record. The unregenerate man cannot experience illumination in this sense for he is blinded to the truth of God (1 Cor. 2:14). The believer was promised this ministry of the Spirit by the Lord before his death (John 16:13-16), and can realize it to the extent dependent on the walk of the believer for full realization (1 Cor. 3:1-2).[26]

The writers who contributed to *From the Mind of God to the Mind of Man*, to which this book is the sequel, have adequately developed those traditional truths. For revelation, inspiration, and illumination to be relevant today two conditions must be fulfilled: (1) God's written revelation must have been kept secure throughout the centuries. (2) God must have provided a means by which His written revelation would retain its nature and character when it is transformed from the forms of the Biblical languages in which it was originally written, into the forms of the thousands of languages in existence throughout the centuries.

Therefore, between inspiration and illumination, another necessary process must be described. And this is exactly the concern we raise with this fourth question: Do we have today, and will the future generations have tomorrow, the same revelation that was recorded in the autographs? The answer is "Yes," if God *preserves* that recorded revelation for us. And I believe He does.

Man's Involvement in the Process

Generally, theologians have answered the last question above by defending the integrity of the Hebrew, Aramaic, and Greek copies. That is necessary and proper. But lay people do not read Greek, Hebrew, and Aramaic. These languages are "Greek" to them. They read translations of the copies. Their question is, "When I hold a translation of the Bible, do I really have God's Word in my hands?"

The doctrine of preservation provides the answer to that question. Through preservation, God insures the perpetuity of the Scriptures. Revelation and inspiration are completed actions of God. Their results continue today and will continue forever but, as a process, they are finished, fulfilled, accomplished. They were limited to the autographs. Illumination and preservation, however, are continuous processes that God applies to Scripture.

Through the Spirit's indwelling, today's believer can understand and properly apply the Scriptures. Though the Lord helps us by His Holy Spirit to understand His Word, He imposes upon us the responsibility of "rightly dividing the word of truth" (2 Timothy 2:25). Therefore, man is actively involved in the process.

The same happens with preservation. Yes, God watches over His Word so that it will always exist. But He has left the responsibility of perpetuating it to us. As a believer, I have to use my mind, my books, and all available resources in order to be certain what God means in the Scriptures. Likewise, I must apply all resources in partnership with God for the perpetuity of His Word both through reproducing the copies in the Biblical languages and through translating them.

The point is this: God has involved man in every step of the process of bringing His Word to man, from revelation to preservation. God precludes human error in inspiration, but He has not chosen to guarantee that level of perfection in preservation. He has operated in a way that, in spite of the imprint of human fallibility upon copies and translations, His Word would be His Word. But how has the process worked for preservation?

Preservation and Copies

We have previously stated the two conditions that must be fulfilled through preservation in order for revelation, inspiration, and illumination to be fully relevant today. They are (1) the preservation of God's Word through the copies and (2) the preservation of God's Word through translations of the copies.

Really, the first is less problematic. Examining manuscripts in the Biblical languages and ascertaining the authenticity of texts are difficult, scholarly processes. Still it is easier to prove the preservation of God's Word through the copies than through translations. Reproducing copies requires no changes in form. Because of that, the basic lines of arguments for the defense of God's preservation of the copies have generally been threefold: (1) Nothing of the autographs is lost: everything is preserved among the copies. (2) What differences there may be among the copies are minimal and solvable. (3) We have adequate methods for reconstructing the text satisfactorily where it does have divergences.

If photocopiers had existed when the autographs were produced, a copyist would only have needed to know how to operate one in order to reproduce the autographs. They would have sufficed as a tool for the preservation of the autographs in their original form. The copies would also have been perfect. But God did not purpose it to happen that way. He allowed human hands to copy the autographs knowing the potential for variation created by such a process. This objective aspect of the preservation of the Scriptures through the copies, we would call *duplicative preservation*.

Preservation and Translation

In contrast to the duplication of the copies, the translation of the copies requires a more involved process. My translation from Greek into Creole, like all translation, required great involvement of human skills and with that involvement an increased risk of human error. The first simple and obvious fact is that the forms, the characters used to record language, change. They change from those of one language into those of another. A second, more important, consideration is that, while the forms change when God's thoughts are transferred from the copies into the target language, they must remain God's thoughts as they were in the copies.

Translating the Scriptures may appear subjective, but in reality, it can be as much an objective process as the study of theology or hermeneutics. We define objectively what inspiration entails, which books are inspired, and which are not. We develop Biblical principles for the interpretation of Scriptures in order to discern what is true doctrine and what is heresy. We must seek to glean from the Scriptures definite principles by which to verify the preservation of God's Word through translations. Linguistics and theology are the tools we have in hand to objectively accomplish that task. I will call this aspect of the preservation of the Scriptures through translations *transformational preservation*.

Inspiration and transformational preservation bear striking similarities. By inspiration, the Holy Spirit enabled men to receive God's thoughts and write them down. He controlled their writing but only rarely dictated specific statements. The writers kept their personal writing styles and respected the linguistic parameters of the languages in which they wrote. They used logic. They often purposefully built their sentences in a particular structure or chose particular words to reflect specific nuances. Some even quoted from secular literature (Acts 17:28; Titus 1:12). Others even had to do research before writing (Luke 1:1-4).

Likewise, God according to His wise and holy counsel has allowed His Word to be perpetuated in a similar way (see table 1). God multiplied the languages. God allowed the NT writers to quote from a translation, the Septuagint. God has used translations throughout the centuries. The Holy Spirit's general ministry of illumination can aid the translators in their work. They make linguistic judgments. They analyze style. They choose words. They decide the length of sentences, etc. Can the similarity between inspiration and transformational preservation lead believers to recognize that a good translation carries the quality of inspiration leading to its popularity and longevity? [In the process of copying the words of the autographs can be preserved. In the process of transformation from one language to another it is impossible to preserve the words of the autographs, but the revelation recorded in those inerrant words can be preserved. Ed.]

TABLE 1: SIMILARITIES	
INSPIRATION OF THE AUTOGRAPHS	TRANSFORMATIONAL PRESERVATION
Divine guidance to writers by the Holy Spirit	Providential assistance by the Holy Spirit
Control by the Holy Spirit rather than dictation	Influence of the Holy Spirit rather than dictation
Utilization of human writing styles	Utilization of human writing styles
Respect of linguistic parameters	Respect of linguistic parameters
Logic in word choice, sentence structure, thought development, etc.	Logic in word choice, sentence structure, thought development, etc.

Inspiration and *transformational preservation* bear dissimilarities also (see table 2). The work of the Holy Spirit is different in each. Inspiration was a one-time operation, initiated by God, for a specific writing, so that God's thoughts would be written exactly as He intended. Preservation is a continuous, repetitive process under God's providential care. Inspiration functioned in a mysterious, subjective way; preservation uses objective, natural means to perpetuate Scripture. Inspiration is superintended directly by God; preservation is providentially accomplished by God. Inspiration precludes error; preservation does not nullify human fallibility. Using specific guidelines for evaluation, believers have recognized the books that are inspired. Adoption or rejection of translations is more subjective and believers have never reached consensus on guidelines for approval of translations.

TABLE 2: DISSIMILARITIES	
INSPIRATION OF THE AUTOGRAPH	*TRANSFORMATIONAL PRESERVATION*
One-time, historical action	Continuous, repetitive process
God actively triggers it.	God indirectly assists in it.
Style of the author	Effort not to impose translator's style but to preserve author's style
God personally selects the author.	God indirectly selects the translator(s).
Is activated according to God's direct purpose;	Is accomplished according to obvious need or God's indirect purpose;
Does not necessitate understanding of meaning;	*Heavily* relies on understanding of meaning: linguistically, through semantics; theologically, through illumination;
Precludes human error;	Does not nullify human fallibility;
Unique	Varied
Formal authentication by God's people	Informal approval or disapproval by God's people

Our conclusion from this comparison of inspiration and *transformational preservation* is threefold: (1) The rules that govern one cannot be imposed upon the other. They are different. (2) They have enough resemblance to suggest a similar, systematic approach of study. The characteristics listed in the two tables can serve as a starting point toward developing acceptable criteria by which to judge the *scripturalness* of Bible translations. (3) All things being normal, the involvement of human skills in translation will not corrupt the result or prevent it from being God's Word. God has always used man in every step in the communication of his word. We should try to develop guidelines by which we can differentiate true *transformational preservation* from corrupted *transformational preservation*.

Possibility of Objective Criteria

Many Biblical principles show that it is possible to define objective criteria by which to judge the *scripturalness* of translations. For one, God is able to guide us into understanding and defining what *transformational preservation* entails the same way that He helps us define sound doctrines. Like inspiration, preservation is a faith issue; but faith is not foolishness. We believe in inspiration because it is objectively revealed in the Scriptures. We need to establish that same basis of faith for preservation. At the same time, we should guard against imposing our own sectarian standard of preservation or basing our views upon feelings rather than objective research and study.

We also need to consider the nature of truth itself. Truth does not have to be inspired in order to be truth. Nor does it have to be inspired in order to be preserved as truth. One plus one equals two; that is truth. It is not inspired. It is simply truth. And it has been preserved as truth for ages. Human beings, even without the direct superintendence of God, possess the innate ability to preserve truths and hand them down from generation to generation, whether the truths relate to mathematics, agriculture, education, computers, or to the Scriptures. In *transformational preservation*, God prompts us to use that innate ability which He has given us.

In fact, God has used that innate ability of man even in relation to inspired Scripture. Many texts or allusions in the NT recorded by the inspired pen had been naturally handed down from generation to generation (i.e., Jude 9). Though we do not know how God superintended the oral transmission or how it occurred, we may confidently believe that God providentially protected or preserved those truths while they went from lips to ears for centuries. The same providential hand of God is evident throughout history in the wonderful ways the Scriptures have been translated, propagated, and used.

It is also comforting to know that God does not impose upon us standards that we cannot accomplish ourselves. For revelation and inspiration, He precluded error in the autographs in that He directly superintended the reception and the penning of His Word. In regard to *transformational preservation*, we see that the Septuagint, in spite of its obvious translation weaknesses, is quoted in the inspired autographs of the NT as God's Word. We may argue that those quotations did not have errors in them. I agree. But that does not negate the fact that the NT writers and speakers quoted from the Septuagint with the clear impression that they were quoting God's Word (i.e. Mark 4:12 // Isaiah 6: 9-10; Mark 15:34 // Psalms 21:2; 1 Corinthians 2:16 // Isaiah 40:13; Hebrews 3:15 // Psalms 95:7-8; 1 Peter 5:5 // Proverbs 3:34; etc.) And they did so even where the Septuagint differed with the Hebrew text (i.e. Matthew 19:19 // Leviticus 19:18; Matthew 23:39 // Psalms 118:26; Luke 8:10 // Isaiah 6:9; Acts 2:34-35 // Psalms 109:1; Galatians 3:6; Hebrews 4:3, 5; etc.). They did so even where the Septuagint differed from the Hebrew text (i.e. Matthew 19:19; 23:39; Luke 8:10; Acts 2:34-35; Galatians 3:6; Hebrews 4:3, 5).[27] Thus, in preservation God does not nullify human fallibility. He depends upon human ability. The problem is not so much the evidence of that reality, but the nature of it, the process of it, and the criteria that define its boundaries and character in translations.

Finally, God has declared that His Word will abide; it will be perpetuated; it will be preserved. God is of the same mind with us as we carry the responsibility of *transformational preservation* He has entrusted to us.

So what is the point? The first is that languages are tools that God Himself has instituted to carry the Scriptures. He has established their inherent character. And they do their job well. Second, the NT quotes from a translation, taking its *scripturalness* for granted. Therefore, God's Word can remain God's Word when translated. Third, preservation uses man's God-given skills. God used man to accomplish his purposes in revelation and inspiration. God also uses man to accomplish His purpose in preservation. Fourth, we need guidelines that will differentiate between good and poor transformational preservation. The comparison between inspiration and illumination provides basic elements that can lead to objective criteria of *scripturalness*.

Theological Perspective to the Translation Process

Let us seal the theological examination of Bible translating with one extended, true illustration. The Septuagint will serve again as the best example because, as best we can determine, it is the only *translation* that is quoted by the New Testament writers.

The historical records are inconsistent about the origin of the Septuagint. The account[28] generally considered the most reliable,[29] the *Aristeas Letter*, explains that King Ptolemy I Philadelphus (285-246 B.C.) summoned his librarian, Demetrius Phalereus, to collect for his library all the books of the world. Demetrius informed the King of a particular and valuable collection of Jewish books but argued that they would be of no benefit if not translated.

Ptolomey wrote to the Jewish High Priest requesting a selection of seventy-two translators. The King examined the translators that were provided and when satisfied assigned them a place to work. After some rituals of reverence to the Scriptures and requests for God's assistance, the translators gathered for consultation. According to Aristeas they completed the translation in seventy-two days.

Later, Philo, an Alexandrian Jew, narrated the story with the embellishment that the seventy-two translators were each assigned a separate cubicle and produced a separate translation that, when compared, were all identical. Philo assumed that the translations were also "identical" to the original Hebrew and that the Septuagint was produced by divine inspiration.

This view dominated the writings and the beliefs of many in the early church. It grew, not out of the Scriptures themselves, but out of an erroneous reconstruction of history, which in turn was generated by a passionate but improper devotion to a version. Then, in the third century, Origen produced his Hexapla containing the Hebrew text, the Hebrew transliterated into Greek letters, the Septuagint and three other Greek versions in parallel columns. The variations between the Hebrew and the Septuagint became obvious. If the Septuagint and the Hebrew text were both inspired and identical, why were there variations? Was God's revelation in conflict with itself?

By that time, Latin had become the lingua franca. A Latin version, the *Vetus Latina*, translated from the Septuagint, was commonly used by believers. The *Vetus Latina* became the basis of much of the scholarship of that era. Many peculiar beliefs developed from some of the unfortunate wordings in that translation.

When Jerome produced his own analysis of the Septuagint he rejected the view of Philo about its inspiration. He became convinced that the translation based on the Septuagint had to be replaced by a translation based directly on the Hebrew text. What Origen had tacitly presented in his Hexapla, Jerome exposed vividly. He concluded,

> I do not know who was the first who through his lies built seventy cells in Alexandria in which they [the translators] were separated and yet all wrote the same words; whereas Aristeas ... and long after him Josephus have said nothing of the sort, but write that they were assembled in a single hall and conferred together, not that they prophesied. For it is one thing to be a prophet and another to be a translator; in one case the Spirit foretells future events, in the other sentences are understood and translated by erudition and command of language.[30]

Jerome's views enraged many, including Augustine and other church fathers, who developed their beliefs and writings from particular wordings of the *Vetus Latina*. To defend the *Vetus Latina*, they resorted to ascribing inspiration to the Septuagint. They fought Jerome tirelessly but, in the end, vainly. Yet, their basic arguments are interesting because they resurfaced throughout history whenever a popular translation was passionately revered: (1) *Influence*. If it touches so many people, it must be divine. (2) *Longevity*. If it has withstood the test of time, it should never be changed or replaced. (3) *Tradition*. If you change it, you will destroy traditional beliefs and scholarship. Do you think you know more than all the fathers of old? (4) *Impressiveness*. It is so majestic that its wording cannot be matched.

Philo and Jerome exemplify the two basic views of the process of Bible translations. Philo believed Bible translation was accomplished through inspiration; Jerome insisted that Bible translation was accomplished using linguistics.

Jerome produced a new Latin translation from the copies of Biblical language manuscripts. It became known as the Vulgate and gradually gained the same revered position that had been held by the Septuagint and *Vetus Latina*. It was defended using the same arguments: influence, longevity, tradition, and impressiveness. When the Vulgate was examined the same way Jerome had examined the Septuagint, the Council of Trent, in 1546, felt threatened by the multiplicity of new translations and reacted by demanding that

> [T]he Vulgate approved through long usage during so many centuries be held authentic in public lectures, disputations, preaching and exposition, and that nobody dare or presume to reject it under any pretext.[31]

That did not deter the new surge of Bible translating born during the Reformation period. The reformers produced many Bibles with the intent that even a boy with limited education could understand them. The principles underlying them were those of Jerome, not those of Philo. Throughout the centuries, all Bibles have been translated with the same understanding. Some translations have been more thorough than others in their equivalence to the original copies.

What have we learned from this? Even the Septuagint, quoted in the NT, was produced according to analytical principles of linguistics, not by inspiration. Nevertheless, it was still the Word of God. Translations produced today, whether in English, French, Creole, Sara Kaba Naa, Dendi, Waali, Lamkaang, or any other language should be treated the way the writers of the NT treated the Septuagint. They understood that God preserved His Word both by *duplication* (copying the autographs) and though *transformation* (translating the copies). Yet, God's Word retained its *scripturalness* through both processes.

Does that mean linguistics is the master of all translation principles and the servant of none? We shall consider that next.

WHAT IS THE LINGUISTIC BASIS FOR BIBLE TRANSLATION?

The contest between Jerome and Philo shows that the *scripturalness* of Bible translations is not simply a theological issue. It is a linguistic issue as well. God instituted languages and established their special characteristics. He has used them as tools to accomplish His purpose. Therefore, study of the nature and structure of languages must play an important role in determining the criteria by which to judge the *scripturalness* of translations.

Linguistics helps us better understand what happened when God confused (mixed) the languages at the tower of Babel. We must learn to deal with the results of that phenomenon in order to accomplish God's purpose in the transmission of His Word. The study of linguistics reveals that when God *mixed* the language, He did so in a systematic fashion, adding new characteristics to those transferred from the language before Babel. Those changes include diversity in sounds and structure, and potentiality for change while retaining similarity. Linguistics is the study of the dynamics of those changes and all the other elements involved in the nature of language. An overview of some of the aspects of language will help us better understand the importance of linguistics in Bible translation and the role linguistics can play in preserving the *scripturalness* of translations.

General Characteristics of Languages

Linguistics as a science examines languages in general, not simply one language in particular. It presupposes that languages have many aspects in common and that many principles underlie them all.[32]

One of those common aspects is sound. Sounds in relationship to languages are like notes in music. The difference between one piece of music and another involves the selection and association of specific sounds. No piece of music has all the sounds that exist. Likewise, no language possesses all the possible language sounds. All languages exhibit some similarity in sounds; this similarity enables equivalence among languages. Thus, one may learn a new language and communicate in it properly. Since all the sounds are not the same in every language, the variation between the sounds to which one is accustomed and the sounds of the newly acquired language may produce a noticeable accent. Understanding sounds is important because languages are primarily "sounds." Written language is basically a conventional way of representing the spoken language on the page. If the sounds change, the language will eventually reflect those changes on the page as well.

Languages are also similar in their forms. All languages use units called words to convey meaning. Special terms are used to identify the functions of those words. In general, words are considered according to their function or position in a sentence. For example, some words may be termed subject (S), verb (V), or object (O), depending upon their role in helping their users convey meanings. Subject, verb, and object are essentially arranged in one of six ways: SVO, SOV, OSV, OVS, VSO, VOS. These patterns convey meaning. Some other words have the function of helping the basic SVO accomplish their linguistic tasks. In English, they are called adjectives, prepositions, pronouns, adverbs, etc. Their placement in a sentence is particular to each language.

French and English are SVO languages. Latin is an SOV language. Biblical Greek tends to be a VOS language. These patterns are extremely important in translating. For example, in transferring concepts from a VOS language to an SVO language, one must modify the word order. Below are a few sentences from John 3 translated word-for-word that illustrate this; I italicize the verbs and embolden the subjects.

Verse 1: "*Was* but a **man** out of the Pharisees ..."

Verse 2: "Rabbi, know-we that from God *have-come*-**you a teacher** ..."

Verse 3: "*Answered* **Jesus** and said to him, "Amen, amen, *say* **I** to you ..."

Verse 4: "*Says* to him **Nicodemus**, "*How able-is* a **man** to be born again ..."

Verse 5: "*Answered* **Jesus** ..."

Verse 9: "*Answered* **Nicodemus** and said to him, "How *able-are* **these things** to be?"

Obviously, those sentences do not reflect the natural word order of English. Greek and English both have subjects, verbs, and objects, but they do not necessarily use them in the same order. In translating from one language to the other, the word order of each language has to be respected if the meaning intended by the original language is to be preserved in the target language. Therefore, a word-for-word translation may be an inaccurate translation.

Another general aspect of languages is their mutation. All languages constantly form new words and discard old ones. The changes may even lead to the demise of a language or to a complete internal metamorphosis. There is no aspect of language that is sacred or unchangeable, whether grammar, structure, form, or meaning of words.[33] Not one language remains static. Each generation leaves its own imprint upon the language it has used.[34] One may see evidence of the shift in English by looking at the difference between the Elizabethan English of the 1611 King James Version (KJV), the 1769 revision commonly in use today, and the New King James Version (NKJV) recently published. Look at the passages in table three.

TABLE 3: SHIFT		
KJV 1611	**KJV 1769**	**NKJV 1982**
"My people are destroyed for lacke of knowledge: because thou hast reiected knowledge, I will also reiect thee, that thou shalt be no priest to me: seeing thou hast forgotten the lawe of thy God, I wil also forget thy children" (Hofea 4:6).	"My people are destroyed for lack of knowledge: because thou hast rejected knowledge, I will also reject thee, that thou shalt be no priest to me: seeing thou hast forgotten the law of thy God, I will also forget thy children" (Hosea 4:6).	"My people are destroyed for lack of knowledge. Because you have rejected knowledge, I also will reject you from being priest for Me; because you have forgotten the law of your God, I also will forget your children" (Hosea 4:6).
"The words of Agur sonne of Iakeh, euen the prophecy: The man spake vnto Ithiel, euen vnto Ithiel and Vcal, Surely I am more brutish then any man, and haue not the vnderstanding of a man" (Prouerbes 30:1-2).	"The words of Agur the son of Jakeh, even the prophecy: the man spake unto Ithiel, even unto Ithiel and Ucal, Surely I am more brutish than any man, and have not the understanding of a man" (Proverbs 30:1).	"The words of Agur the son of Jakeh, his utterance. This man declared to Ithiel – to Ithiel and Ucal: Surely I am more stupid than any man, and have not the understanding of a man" (Proverbs 30:1).

Whatever one's preference among the above versions may be, one fact is clear: they are from three different eras of English. The language has shifted. Because of that phenomenon, translations are generally brought up to date in accordance with the shifts, either by revision or by replacement.

A fourth general characteristic of language is the transfer of meaning. The forms within languages function as vehicles that transport packages of meaning from an original place (a source) to a destination (a receptor). The meanings are transported from one person's mind to the other's. In translation, one tries to carry the same package while switching from one vehicle (the forms of one language) to another vehicle (the forms of another language.) The part of linguistics that deals with meanings is called semantics. Expression of meaning is the reason that languages exist. The goal of any communication is to transfer concepts, meanings, from a source to a receptor. The source and the receptor may both be in the same language, but when they are in different languages translation is necessary.

Every part of the vehicle and every feature of the packages work together to give the packages a comfortable and safe ride from the source to the receptor. The features involved in the process may be styles, sentence structures, word order, or function words (conjunctions like *and* and *or*, prepositions like *in* and *of*, and pronouns like *you* and *I*). Other features may be tone and emphasis, metaphor, idiom, paraphrase, etc. All of these are phenomena that occur in all languages but no two languages handle them exactly the same way.[35] For example, a double negative signifies emphasis in Greek, but not in English. In Hebrew, one would say, "Dying, you shall die" (Genesis 2:17) to mean, in English, "You shall surely die."

God has made languages with innate similarities but with separate particularities. Similarities make translating possible; particularities make it difficult. At Babel, God mixed and multiplied those particularities enabling an increasing number of combinations. Each conventional set of mixtures produced a language of its own with the dynamics of mutation or shift. That complicates translation from one language to another, because the forms of those phenomena in the source language must be modified to fit their equivalent forms in the receptor language. Because of this constant shift in languages, translation becomes a never-ending process. Revisions have to be conducted periodically in order to bring translations into conformity with linguistic mutations. Linguistics enables us to sort out those intricacies and produce accurate translations of the Scriptures that convey the meaning of the original.

Some Linguistic Complexities Encountered in Translation

A few linguistic intricacies that one may encounter in translating will illustrate why a science is necessary in order to deal with them.

Complexities with Forms

One surprising discovery for a monolingual English speaker learning Creole, for example, is the absence of a passive voice in Creole. Similarly, most of the languages with which I have worked in Africa and a great percentage of languages in the world do not have a passive voice. Yet they do communicate "passive-voice" meanings in their own way. Look at these two simple sentences:

TABLE 4: ENGLISH/CREOLE EXAMPLES	
English	**Creole**
The mouse is eaten by the cat.	Chat la manje sourit la. *Cat the ate mouse the.*
What is written on the wall is accurate.	Sa k ekri sou mi an egzat. *That which writes on wall the exact.*

In the first sentence, the passive verb in English is rendered by an active transitive verb in Creole. The active verb of the second English sentence is translated by an active intransitive (or pseudo-passive) verb in Creole. If in translating those sentences one does not respect the grammar of Creole and tries to impose a passive voice upon it, the monolingual speaker of Creole will still naturally read the sentence as active. And instead of understanding, for example, that the cat ate the mouse, he will read that the mouse ate the cat.

With simple sentences like the two examples above, the modification from the form of English to the form of Creole is easy. But, when one is translating the long sentences of Ephesians, loaded with participles and passive voices (none of which occur in Creole,) the complexities are astounding.

Notice also in the translation of the second sentence another example of complexity: there is no verb "to be" as an equivalent to the "is" that appears in the English sentence. The verb "to be" is absent or has limited use in some languages. Generally, the languages deprived of a passive voice also have a limited use of the verb "to be." *You are beautiful* is rendered *Ou bèl* (You beautiful.) in Creole. Translating *I think, therefore I am* or *I am that I am* into Creole would involve great complexities. Some languages that use the verb "to be" as naturally as it is used in English may have ways to omit it and make perfect sense, whereas such an omission would confuse the sense of the same sentence in another language. Biblical Hebrew, especially in the Pentateuch and the poetic sections, uses many verbless clauses, sentences that require a verb (particularly the "to be" verb) in English but do not in Hebrew.

In one translation into Creole, the translator tried to challenge the non-existence of the passive voice in Creole and impose a passive voice upon the language.[36] Here are a few examples of the results:

		TABLE 5: FORCED PASSIVE VOICE	
Passage	English	Forced Creole Translation	Translation of Forced Creole Translation
Mark 14:27a	"And Jesus saith unto them, All ye shall be offended because of me this night:"	"E Jezu té di yo, Nou tou va ofansé nuit sa a pou tèt Mouin:"	"And Jesus had told them, You also will offend this night because of Me:"
Titus 3:3a	"For we ourselves also were some-times foolish, dis-obedient, deceived, …"	"Paské nou minm té foli kèk fwa, dezobeyisan, égaré, …"	"Because you were even foolishness a few times, disobedient, dumb…"
Ephesians 1:13b	" … in whom also, after that ye believed, ye were sealed with that holy Spirit of promise,"	" … nan Sila a nou té sélé avèk Sint Espri promès sa a apré nou té koué,"	" … in this One we put saddle with that Holy Spirit of promise after we had believed,"

A third interesting element in the examples is that in the word-for-word translation, the article is shown after the word it modifies. An article in Creole modifies the word that precedes it, not the one that follows it, as it is in English or French.

Here is a fourth interesting phenomenon: the use of pronouns in Creole. *Li* is the only personal pronoun for the third person singular. Consider the following sentences: "*He* reads" or "*She* reads" or "*He* reads *it*" or "*He* gives *it* to *him*" or "*She* received *it* from *her*" or "*His* book" or "*Her* book." Every one of the italicized pronouns in those sentences would be translated by the same word in Creole: *li*. Also, *we, us, our, ours, you, your, yours* are all expressed with the same Creole word: *nou*. You can imagine the difficulty in translating a sentence like this: "As also *ye* have acknowledged *us* in part, that *we* are *your* rejoicing, even as *ye* also are *ours* in the day of the Lord Jesus" (2 Corinthians 1:14 – italics mine). Every one of the italicized pronouns would be rendered by one word in Creole, *nou*.

In a few short, simple sentences, we see four grammatical aspects that are apparently insignificant phenomena in English yet that are completely different and even complex in Creole. John McWorther, a linguist who was a consultant for several major television networks at the rise of the *Ebonics* controversy, made a good point about the general nature of language when he said,

> [L]anguage is as sophisticated in all human cultures …. One might quite reasonably suppose that a First World culture … would have a grammatically 'richer' language, necessary to convey the particular complexities inherent to our treadmill to oblivion, whereas preliterate cultures such as, say, those in the Amazon rain forest would have 'simpler' languages for simpler lives. 'Bunga bunga bunga!!!!' as the 'natives' say in old cartoons.

> Ironically, however, if there is any difference along these lines, it is the opposite: the more remote and 'primitive' the culture, the more likely the language is to be bristling with constructions and declensions and exceptions and bizarre sounds that leave an English speaker wondering how anyone could actually speak the language without running the risk of a stroke.[37]

The list of complexities would be encyclopedic if we were to attempt to be exhaustive. The above examples adequately convey the difficulty involved in transferring meaning from the form of one language to that of another. Linguistics helps the translator sort out those complexities and assists him in finding the proper way the receptor language handles the concepts that he is translating. Thoughts that can be expressed in English can also be translated accurately into Creole or any of the most complex languages in existence, though not with the same structure of sentences as those in English. God has established in languages that innate faculty of equivalence among them alongside their separate particularities.

Thus, there cannot really be such thing as a word-for-word translation. It is linguistically impossible. Philo's idea that a translation can be "identical" to the original text or the present day calls of some Christians for word-for-word translations would require that the languages be *de-mixed*. If that could be done, there would then be only one language in existence and no need for, nor avenue for, translation.

Complexities with Meaning

Complexities in translation are not limited to the intricate forms and structure of languages. If they were the only linguistic difficulties encountered in translation, the task of translating would be an easy one. The forms are carriers of meanings. And decoding meaning from the forms of one language and encoding it into the forms of another is the most complex process of translation. In fact, that is what translation is all about. Even meaning itself is difficult to define. Linguists are still debating the meaning of "meaning." Most books on semantics devote an introductory chapter to defining *meaning*.[38]

Most people think of meaning as the way words are defined in a dictionary. But meaning involves more than the simple denotative definitions of a dictionary.[39] As one author argues, there are "other kinds of meaning (e.g., pragmatic, connotative, stylistic, affective, collocative, reflected, associative, thematic, relational, expressive, social, phatic, illocutionary, experiential, etc.)."[40] This abridged list may seem overwhelming and technical but it is not necessary to explain them here because any person uses these semantic features intuitively in communication.[41] However, it is important to realize the astounding challenge involved in insuring that translations are done accurately. Let me give another example:

A few years ago, I was conducting an Old Testament translation workshop on two Pentateuch books in Dendi, a language in Northern Benin. We arrived at Numbers 11:23a: "And the Lord said unto Moses, Is the Lord's hand waxed short?" The verse has an unusual idiom but, at first glance, it does not appear too difficult to translate. The translators rendered the verse, "And the Lord said to Moses, Did the hand of the Lord become short?" That sounded good. But there was one problem: their translation of the idiom "waxed short" corresponded to an idiom in their language with a different meaning. In essence, their translation was saying this: "And the Lord said to Moses: Is the Lord a crippled beggar?" Many "good" sermons could have sprung from that translation, but it was not an accurate translation.

We definitely had to find another translation. They came up with this: "And the Lord said to Moses: Isn't the hand of the Lord long enough?" It sounded like a good equivalence. Yet it corresponded again to an idiom in Dendi with a different sense. Upon further examination, we quickly changed it. Look at the story: God promised to feed the whole assembly of the Israelites. Moses asked Him where He was going to find enough food. God responded with the words of Numbers 11:23a. Now let me give you the meaning of the translation above and you will see why it had to be changed. For a speaker of Dendi "Isn't the hand of the Lord long enough?" meant "Am I not a big thief?" "Long hand" is idiomatic in Dendi for a thief so skillful that he could reach from afar, as it were, to steal and remain undetected.

The set of problems encountered in translating the verse into Dendi could be completely different from those one would face in translating the same verse into some other languages. In some languages, there might not occur any difficulty at all. In Dendi, we had six basic problems to solve in order to convey the meaning accurately and respect the conservative philosophy of translations set by our Bible society. Let us pinpoint them: (1) The Lord is speaking and addresses Himself in 3rd person instead of 1st; (2) the meaning of the metaphor in the word "hand;" (3) the meaning of the idiom "waxed short;" (4) the interrogative form that may be interpreted more as a request for information than a rhetorical question; (5) some complications with the passive voice, though not to the same extent as in Creole; (6) maintaining consistency with the whole Biblical record and the actual style of the author (or speaker).

This is how we managed it: We relied primarily on two linguistic principles. One is called "unpacking the metaphor." The other is called "crossing the bridge twice." The first insured that the metaphorical meaning was accurately translated. The second helped conserve the metaphor as part of the author's style. The final rendition was this: "And the Lord said to Moses: Is the hand of me, the Lord, not able to do it?" While the sentence may sound awkward in English, it sounded perfectly natural in Dendi. The metaphor of the "hand" is preserved, and its meaning of "accomplishment, action" is conveyed in "do." "Me" and "the Lord" are the same but without the weight of the sense borne by a third-person-meaning in "Lord." The interrogative form is kept but balanced by the negative "not." Using "not" kept the sentence from being perceived as a request for information and is also a reflection of the negative meaning in the word "short" in English. "Not able" stands for the presumed lack of ability expressed in "waxed short." So meaning and style are preserved.

This is linguistics in action. But it was not linguistics alone. There could have been other renderings that some might have judged linguistically appropriate but others might have regarded as theologically inappropriate. We will revisit the above illustration later and address that issue.

Dendi and Creole are not weird, isolated languages. In regard to semantics, all languages *behave* according to their *individual, particular temperament.* That creates complexities in translation. In oral communication, many factors help mitigate the complexities. We may rely on social context, facial expressions, gestures, and other factors in order to grasp the meaning intended by the speaker. But in translating a piece of literature more than two thousand years old, from a defunct culture and a dead language, especially in the case of sacred literature such as the Word of God, one's task becomes very complicated. Consequently, a clear understanding of how languages function and a reliable and balanced methodology proves valuable, even mandatory, in transferring God's Word into another language. Linguistics provides these tools—in our case, linguistics balanced with theology.

Examination of the Value of Linguistics in Bible Translation

In view of that conclusion, one might argue, "Bible translating preceded the Christian era, whereas systematic linguistic theories for Bible translations are children of the later part of the twentieth century. Numerous good translations were produced before the advent of linguistics as a science. If translations were done well without linguistics, why do we need it now?"

Linguistics and Translations in the Past

It is true that linguistics as a science is young and that good translations preceded the advent of linguistics. Nonetheless, Bible translating has always been done with an awareness of the nature and structure of languages. For example, in responding to Philo, Jerome declares strongly that in translation, in contrast to prophecy, "sentences are understood and translated by erudition and command of language."[42] This was stated at a time in history when the two best known translations were one in Greek and one in Latin. The linguistic theories recently developed shed light on the practices of the past two millennia of translation, showing their strength and revealing their weaknesses.

In order to manage the linguistic complexities in translation, one needs more than an intuitive knowledge of languages. A native speaker of a language has only a passive knowledge of that language until he or she studies it formally. That is why the American child who may express himself well in English must still study English throughout primary, elementary, and high schools. Enrolled in college, he or she still has to take English 101.

Likewise, the principles of linguistics have been in existence throughout history but never developed into a systematic science. Men gifted with unusual ability in languages have followed sound linguistic principles of translation even without ever writing down a formal theory. William Tyndale knew early in life that the Lord had blessed him with special gifts in languages. In nine months He produced a NT translation from which the 1611 King James NT has borrowed nearly ninety percent of its wording. Proponents of modern translation theories can see in Luther's writings evidence that he had followed the same principles in his translation as those they have recently developed and are presently advocating.[43] Yet he produced his German translation of the NT in three months without ever reading even a brochure on Bible translation principles or method.

We may add other names such as William Carey, generally acclaimed as the founder of the modern translation movement, and Adoniram Judson, who translated in Burma. We have rarely seen individuals with such ability in languages that they can produce a good translation quickly. Their translations, though good, did contain mistakes that might have been avoided had the principles we know today been available to them.

Thus, in their essence, most of the linguistic principles in Bible translation are not new but they have now been systematized into theories and developed into methodologies. The more we understand the nature and structure of languages, the more we will appreciate and comprehend the process of Bible translation; and in turn, the better equipped we will be as translators. As a result, we will also be closer to establishing objective criteria by which to verify the *scripturalness* of translations.

Linguistics is a good thing.

The principles of linguistics are deeply rooted in Bible translation history. As these principles were systematized their application to translating the Bible was initially good and well intentioned.

In 1961, James Barr spoke against the abuse of Biblical word studies.[44] His book did not propose any positive or systematic solution, either to word studies or to Bible translation. In 1964, Albert Eugene Nida published *Toward a Science of Translating*,[45] considered a classic and still a useful reference work. He presented the case for the theory of translation known first as *dynamic equivalence*, later as *functional equivalence*. In essence, he proposed a systematic way by which translating can be done with respect for the linguistic intricacies of the receptor languages. He developed principles to help translators handle them objectively and efficiently in Bible translation.

As such, dynamic equivalence was basically good. All the basic principles of dynamic equivalence are proper linguistic, grammatical principles. They can be adequately applied to translation. In fact, even the most conservative schools that offer some courses related to Bible translating use textbooks written by proponents of dynamic equivalence.

Nevertheless, as the theory gained advocates, it has deviated from its intended purpose. Different methodologies that emanated from it have corrupted the theory until the term came to be associated with the liberal aspects of translation (in many cases, rightly so). Consequently, the term is now being discarded by the very Bible societies that had promoted it in favor of the more candid qualifier, *meaning-based translation*.

Yet it remains the only theory of Bible translation to have been fully and scientifically developed. Some who adhere to a stricter approach of Bible translating have written in reaction to some of the liberal views that emanated from the corrupted version of the dynamic equivalence theory, but they have not developed a systematic theory of their own. If involved in the ministry of

Bible translation, they follow sound practices; they apply proper linguistic principles controlled by an awareness of the theological or Biblical implications of the linguistic modifications.

As an example, one may name the approach of James D. Price, a member of the translation team that worked on the NKJV. He proposes a framework that seeks to accommodate both Biblical accuracy and linguistic appropriateness and designates it *complete equivalence*.[46] The books on dynamic equivalence delineate methods of applying the theory, but Price does not provide a complete methodology by which to reach complete equivalence. In essence, his approach is the same as the one termed modified-literal translation in the *dynamic equivalence* system of categorization. For Arthur Farstad, "Complete equivalence is basically the literal method updated to include scientific insights from linguistic analysis."[47]

Another example is the approach of Leland Ryken, who served as literary stylist for the English Standard Version (ESV).[48] Though he claimed not to be an expert in Bible translation theories,[49] Ryken developed serious contentions against the dynamic equivalence theory with courage and scholarship and reached sound conclusions. His quest for literary qualities and theological soundness cannot be stressed enough. He presented numerous convincing examples of literary, modified-literal translations to support his arguments and defined valid qualities of a good translation.

All these are good. But Ryken did not delineate a scientific, predictable path by which to reach these results. His premise that "form is meaning" and that changing form is changing meaning[50] is not valid linguistically. One may argue rightly that form carries meaning or even that form has meaning (as in the structure of a book). But form in itself is not meaning. Otherwise, translation from any language into another would not be possible, for each language uses its own form to carry meaning. When one translates from an SVO language into an SOV language or renders with two words a meaning that is carried by one word in the Biblical language (or vise versa), one changes form. These phenomena occur in all translations. But is the meaning necessarily changed? Thus, the important ingredient neglected (but somewhat assumed) in Ryken's good recipe for Bible translation is sound linguistics. His proposals can serve more as ideals for Bible translation than a universally applicable theory.

From these examples, one may draw two points: (1) More literal translations are produced under the assumption that their *scripturalness* depends upon their affinity with the original text. But when is affinity achieved? Each theory of translation would define its own standards of evaluation based on literary, theological, or linguistic assumption or some combination of the three. Consistent standards of determining *scripturalness* will be established only when sound theological principles are gleaned from the Scriptures to delimit the application of linguistic methodologies. (2) While rejecting dynamic equivalence itself, the committees of both the NKJV and the ESV relied on the scientific, linguistic foundations that the dynamic equivalence theory had laid. The versions are both modified-literal translations, with one emphasizing literary beauty more than the other, thus showing that linguistics is inevitable.

That is why Bibles International, since its inception in 1981, has established careful principles that account both for the linguistic and Biblical dimensions of translations. It has developed wordcheck lists, consistency checks, back-translation methods, parallel-passage charts, model translations, electronic tools, and many other means by which to insure that the translations produced under its auspices around the world meet Biblical and linguistic standards. Linguistics is certainly a good thing. But are linguistics and dynamic equivalence interchangeable?

Linguistics is not Dynamic Equivalence.

The dominance of the dynamic equivalence theory underlies the third aspect of our examination of the value of linguistics in Bible translation. Many people, some of whom are well educated in Bible translation issues, confuse linguistics and dynamic equivalence.

Dynamic equivalence is a theory of Bible translating. Linguistics is the science of language. Since dynamic equivalence relies heavily on linguistics, the two are often subconsciously equated.

This confusion creates some serious problems. One of those is a tendency for many conservative believers who oppose dynamic equivalence to recoil from linguistics as it is applied in Bible translating. "Unclean! Unclean!" is the tacit cry in regard to linguistics. In reality, linguistics is a science that helps us discover the beauty, the splendor, the grandeur, the intricacies, and the usefulness of one of God's most magnificent creations: language.

Another problem is that proponents of dynamic equivalence often ridicule those who oppose their theory. They do so on the fallacious basis that those opponents are rejecting a well-proven science. One can uphold good principles of linguistics while rejecting the dynamic equivalence theory as a whole.

A third consequence is that those who are qualified to develop a more conservative theory of Bible translating often hesitate to do so, because many of the principles that they would include in their new theory would be the same as some of the principles of the dynamic equivalence theory.

Linguistics Alone Causes Theological "Side Effects."

Thus far we have said many good things about linguistics. It has permeated the practice of Bible translating from the outset of its use; its application as a science to translation was good and had good intent; and it is not to be equated with dynamic equivalence. All those are well deserved. Yet, applied alone to Bible translations, linguistics causes many "side effects." And that is the fourth element we must consider in examining its value in translation.

The best assessment of the side effects of linguistics is made by examining the results of translation practices that are based upon linguistics alone. The only theory that is based solely upon linguistics is *dynamic equivalence* (also known as *functional equivalence* and *meaning based translation*.)

The first side effect is that the classification of translations by a theory based solely on linguistics raises serious doubts. The widely accepted basic classification of translations is done by the proponents of dynamic equivalence and according to their views of Bible translating. It is based solely upon linguistic considerations. Some may distinguish translations according to their source-texts but the source of a translation does not predict the nature of the translation. Classifications of translations depend upon the existence of a theory and are developed within the framework of that theory. Classifications cannot stand unless there are well-developed theories to substantiate them.

When classified according to the dynamic equivalence theory, translations are generally labeled as formal, modified-literal, idiomatic or dynamic equivalent, and unduly free. Some books may add sub-categories to these main ones. According to these classifications, the KJV and NASB fall into the category of formal translations, those that seek painstakingly to preserve the form of the Biblical languages. The NIV, by contrast, is considered dynamic equivalent (though the most conservative of the dynamic equivalent translations in general.)

Proponents of the *dynamic* theory glean examples from the *formal* translations to show how obscure they are as a result of being too close to the wording of the original. In some instances, formal translations are indeed unclear. However, many factors, other than proximity of wording to the original, may account for certain apparently ambiguous wordings: the amount of information available to the scholarship at the time of the translation, the readers targeted, the nature of the original text itself, etc. Examples can be found in any translation, including the NIV and the KJV, that show that they are formal equivalent in some places, or modified literal, idiomatic, or unduly free in other places.[51]

In reality, even from a solely linguistic perspective, all *acceptable* or *non-overtly-bad translations* should be labeled "modified-literal" whether it be the KJV or NASB or even the NIV. In those translations, the forms and structure of the original language are *modified* to fit the forms and structure of the receptor language. These translations should not be categorized simply by the amount of structural modification introduced in transferring meaning. Some other qualifiers, including their theological assumptions, should be used to sub-categorize them.

In effecting modifications, the NASB places priority on the form of the source language as much as the receptor language permits. The NIV, in contrast, prioritizes the form of the receptor language as much as the source language allows. Handling the forms of the receptor language one way or another does not, in itself, predict the theological inclination of the translation. A so-called literal translation can be theologically liberal while an idiomatic translation can be theologically conservative.

Mentioning theological assumption as a factor in classifying translations may appear to be an aberration to a solely linguistic view of translation. Nonetheless, a translator's theological view will influence his work. Denial of the effect of theology in translation demonstrates a one-sided view of translation classification.

This leads us to *the second side effect of a theory solely based upon linguistics: undue emphasis upon the receptor language*. This can be a natural tendency for someone who is preoccupied solely by the intricacies of language. That is actually what happens to translations produced under the dynamic equivalence theory.

Translations are examined according to three common, basic standards: accuracy, clarity, and naturalness, all of which are linguistic elements. *Accuracy* pertains to this question: Has the translation preserved the intended meaning of the original text? *Clarity* implies that the readers of the translation understand it. *Naturalness* seeks to make the Biblical writers sound as they would have, if they had originally written in the language of the translation. According to dynamic equivalence, "a truly idiomatic translation does not sound like a translation. It sounds like it was written in the receptor language."[52]

The proponents of dynamic equivalence have established and defined those standards. They are good in proportion to the assumptions behind them. The problem of assumptions in translation parallels the approach of political campaigns today. Does a politician develop his or her agenda according to the poll (dynamic equivalence) or according to principle (stricter translations)?

Such assumption is most crucial in regard to accuracy. In determining the intended meaning of a Biblical passage, linguistics alone will not suffice. There must be theological considerations. Dynamic equivalence recoils from theological considerations and applies the three standards with the assumption that the response of the reader should be the final determining fact as to whether they have been achieved. But looking at Bible translation as a whole, response is not the only determining factor—not even the most important one. D. A. Carson declares in his article "The Limits of Dynamic Equivalence in Bible Translation" that

> [T]he hidden fallacy ... is the unwitting assumption that 'response' is the ultimate category in translation. Strictly speaking, that is not true; theologically speaking, it is unwise; evangelistically speaking, it is uncontrolled, not to say dangerous."[53]

What Carson is implying here is that theology or Biblicism is a valid and perhaps the most important assumption in Bible translating. All translations are based upon some sort of theological assumptions. In playing down doctrinal differences to produce an ecumenical Bible, one still translates according to a theological assumption. That theological assumption will influence every part of the translation, from the philosophy that energizes it, through the theory and methodology that govern it, to the structure of sentences and the choice of words (with their connotative nuances) that materialize it.

The history of a French translation provides an example. In 1874, Louis Segond produced the French translation that bears his name. It first appeared in portions but by 1880 Oxford published it in complete form. Dr. Segond was a liberal theologian. In spite of the opposition from conservative believers, he did not want to revise the translation to reflect conservative beliefs. Nevertheless, he gave permission that after his death, Bible agencies could do whatever they wanted with it. He died in 1909. One year later, a revision, which apparently had been in preparation even from before his death, appeared. It reflected conservative theological assumptions. Linguistically, the translation remained nearly the same. Theologically, it was different. That edition gained the acceptance of the French speaking world. Most conservative believers refer to the 1910 edition as the recognized date of origin for the *Louis Segond* they use. A formal revision in 1978 called *Segond à la Colombe* further enhanced the quality of the translation. Conservative believers accepted it gladly.

In parallel to the *Segond à la Colombe*, many leaders in the French religious world tried to promote the TOB translation, an ecumenical version produced in association between Roman Catholic and Protestant scholarship. Since the translation did not gain the popularity expected, they narrowed the ecumeni-

317

cal spectrum to Protestant denominations and gave particular attention to the charismatic groups. Again, the *Louis Segond* was revised in accord with the views of a target audience. In June 2002, the New Testament reached the market. This *Louis Segond* revision met opposition from conservative believers. Why was there frequent change of attitude toward the same version throughout its history? The theology reflected in it from revision to revision.

Conversely, uncontrolled theological assumptions may be as damaging as the imposition of solely linguistic reasoning. When I was conducting a workshop on the book of Genesis in an African language, a missionary wanted the translation of a particular passage in Genesis 2 to reflect his belief in dispensations. The matter was resolved by using this important principle: the goal of translating is that whatever one can reasonably and properly glean from studying the original text is to be accounted for in the translation, no more, no less, certainly not personal presuppositions.

Such personal presuppositions have lead to accusations that various good translations are weak on key doctrines of the conservative faith. If clear criteria existed by which to evaluate the *scripturalness* of translations, many of those claims could have been easily dismissed. The fact remains that theological assumptions always underlie translations. The character of those assumptions colors accuracy.

But accuracy is not the only quality of translation that undue emphasis upon the receptor language can influence. Clarity may also be influenced. The problem here is not that idiomatic translations are unclear but that, because of their emphasis on naturalness, more may be included in the translation than the Holy Spirit intended when He inspired the Scripture.

By reading the most conservative books on dynamic equivalence, one may think that the problem stated above is unfounded. They all issue warnings against adding meanings to a translation that cannot be substantiated in the source text. Eugene Nida and Charles Taber summarize it well:

> There should not be anything in the translation itself which is stylistically awkward, structurally burdensome, linguistically unnatural, and semantically misleading or incomprehensible, unless, of course, the message in the source language has these characteristics (the task of the translator is to produce the closest natural equivalent, not to edit or to rewrite).[54]

The problem is not the warnings; it is the imbalanced emphasis that, in turn, can lead beyond proper translation into *cultural equivalence*. In the quotation above as well as throughout the whole book, Nida and Taber emphasize the natural flow of the translation, not faithfulness to the source text. The objection to formal equivalence by advocates of dynamic equivalence is that "the literal approach to translation attempts to translate in such a form that the same number of possible interpretations [in the original] will be open to the reader" of the translation.[55] According to dynamic equivalence, such an attempt may create many problems. For one, the translation may be meaningless. Against that, Mildred Larson declares that the translator "certainly does not want to include information that carries no meaning at all."[56] Further, as Beekman and Callow argue, "it is relatively rare for the structure of the RL [Receptor Language] to be such that the ambiguity can be retained" and in trying to preserve the ambiguity of the original, "new ambiguities are inevitably introduced by the grammar or the vocabulary of the RL."[57]

All those concerns are real and valid. But the proposed solutions tend to go beyond the boundaries of the problem. Dynamic equivalence resolves to give a "clear meaning" to every part of a translation. No one can argue against eliminating ambiguities that are not genuine. But dynamic equivalence tends to go further than that. According to the theory, if a passage is ambiguous in the original, the translator should choose the meaning generally accepted by the greater constituency that will receive the translation or the meaning adopted by the consensus of scholars. Another solution would be to include one of the most recognized meanings in the text; the others would be included as marginal notes. (Of course, one's theological inclination influences which meanings are recognized and which one should be in the text rather than in the margins.) Many other similar options should be considered before a translator resolves to carry ambiguity that is present in the original into the translation.[58] The consequences of such a practice can be as vast as one's imagination.

Conversely, for a translation that balances linguistics with conservative theological concern, *proven ambiguity in the original should be treated as meaning in its own right*. If the original text is ambiguous, it is by the Holy Spirit's design, not by error. Therefore, the best translation would be the one that preserves the ambiguity in its original parameters, not the one that clarifies it for a better response from the readers. Any clarification introduced in the translation would reflect someone's view rather than the intended parameters set by the Holy Spirit.

This argument is obviously theological, not linguistic, in nature. It does show the necessity for theological considerations in Bible translating. To remove theological assumption in translation would be as unwise and dangerous as rearing a child apart from Christian influence and expecting him to grow up into a mature Christian.

The pivotal question is this: How far can naturalness go before it will undermine clarity and accuracy? When does a translation go beyond the boundary of proper *transformational preservation*? A strict translation could emphasize accuracy over naturalness to the extent that it loses clarity and, thus, accuracy itself. A free translation may emphasize naturalness to the extent that it corrupts accuracy or inflates clarity. What criteria could insure the proper balance?

To illustrate this whole issue, let me return, as promised, to the example of Numbers 11:23a in Dendi. As I stated earlier, in trying to translate this passage accurately, there could have been other renderings that some might have judged linguistically appropriate. Let me list a few here:

"And the Lord said to Moses: Do you think I am incapable?"

"And the Lord said to Moses: Am I not able to do it?"

"And the Lord said to Moses: I am able to do it, am I not?"

Some people could even accept the first rendition that we rejected ("And the Lord said to Moses: Is the Lord a crippled beggar?") An idiomatic translation might even use that rendering as long as it could be proven that the idiom in Dendi is communicating the *same intended meaning* of Numbers 11:23a.

The list of possibilities could be extended, but let us stop here to ask two questions. First, why did we go through all that painstaking analysis to insure accuracy of meaning? Linguistic concern! Metaphors and idioms function in certain ways. Linguistics helps determine the best way to handle them.

Second, why did we go to the extent of trying to preserve all the nuances as we did in the final choice of our translation? Theological concern! Because of theological concern, we sought to keep the consistency of God-intended images in the Bible. In Isaiah 50:2 and 59:1, God uses the same idiom (and God is always the user). Linguistics would focus only on the contextual meaning. Yet, in our judgment, we do not know all the aspects of intended meaning that God may have in mind beyond the contextual meaning. To a certain extent, just as the prophets of old may have written some things better than they knew, we must translate in a way that might be better than we understand. Therefore, we tried to keep the same range of options for the translation that the text would have in the original. We knew some of the associations in Numbers 11:23a with Isaiah but there are passages where we may not even recognize associations that might be hidden in them. Our Bible society has devised wordlists of various types so that words and expressions of the same meaning might be translated the same way in every occurrence.

Interestingly, many good translations that apply free variations for stylistic reasons would not pass our tests.

A final side effect that I may add is the choice of the target audience for a translation. Before writing any piece of literature, the writer must first determine its prospective, intended readers. Dynamic equivalence targets the common man in the street, not the common man in the church. In writing, targeting the average literacy level of an audience is a sound choice because it insures that the majority of people will understand the information conveyed. But should that literacy level pertain to people in the street or those in the church?

To answer that question, we should ask another one. Who are the primary readers to whom God addressed Scriptures? When we search the Scriptures we find statements that in time past, God spoke to our fathers in the faith by the prophets. In these days, called the last days, He speaks to us, His children, by One who is Son (i.e., Heb. 1:1-2). Moses wrote for God's people. The prophets wrote for God's people. The gospels were primarily intended for God's people. The epistles were addressed to saints and churches. This theological factor underlies stricter translations, because they target people in the church who are accustomed to vocabularies with which unsaved people in the street would be unfamiliar. One may end up with serious theological problems if the translator uses unsaved-man-in-the-street-vocabularies to express concepts intended for people with the Holy Spirit in their hearts.

The Bible provides a window through which those who are not saved may become God's people. Some people may have been saved by reading the Bible on their own. But it is rare for those who are unfamiliar with Biblical matters to be saved simply by picking up the Bible for the first time. Even when it occurs, it is an exception that magnifies God's grace, not a norm for Bible translation theories. The norm is what we see in everyday life and in the Scriptures. In every evangelistic situation in the Bible, the witnessing is done by someone "talking" the Word, not by someone handing a copy of the Scriptures to another. The Ethiopian Eunuch and Cornelius, who were acquainted with Scripture, needed someone to explain it to them. It was only after Theophilus had been saved that Luke wrote to him to establish his faith (Luke 1:4). The primary audience targeted in Scripture is God's people. God may use His written Word directly to bring one who is reading it to saving faith, but the primary use of the Bible is the establishing and maturing of believers. The audience to whom a translation is addressed will affect the work of translating.

The road throughout this section has been long and tedious but, I hope, profitable. Our discussion began with a question about the basis of linguistics in Bible translation. The answer is threefold: (1) Linguistics is absolutely necessary and inevitable for good Bible translating; (2) Linguistics alone is far from being an absolute standard for Bible translations. (3) Theology or Biblicism must balance linguistics in Bible translating, yet no such balanced theory has been developed to the point that it has gained wide acceptance among contemporary translators or that it has provided proven criteria by which to judge the *scripturalness* of translations.

FINAL PERSPECTIVE

When we consider the intricacies involved in translating the Scriptures, we can only marvel at what God has wrought. The Almighty, according to His wise and holy counsel, has instituted language and established its nature and character. He revealed His thoughts within the confines of human languages. He endorsed translating in the NT by allowing the writers of the Inspired Records to quote from a translation. In both inspiration and preservation, He has worked through men though in a different degree and a different way in each. Thus translations should be performed in a way that will reflect the way God Himself has used languages and the way He has revealed His thoughts: with respect to linguistic parameters and with respect to theological intent. Through what I have called *transformational preservation,* His Word remains His Word when it is translated, in spite of the imprint of human fallibility on it. He has devised this yet-to-be-fully-defined way so that every honest translation would retain the quality of *scripturalness* that is sufficient to be called the Word of God. Comparison between inspiration and *transformational preservation* provides objective guiding points in that quest.

Until definite criteria of evaluation are developed, it is wise to conduct Bible translating in a way that when the nature of preservation through translation is fully revealed, our translations will meet those criteria. May we translate as literally as the receptor language allows and as literarily (that is, with the literary qualities of clarity and naturalness of language) as the original language allows.

Let us add to that an attitude of humility like that of Luther who thanked God to have made him a translator, because otherwise he would have died with the false notion that he had been a wise man. God has chosen to perpetuate His Word in a way that defies human logic. That He should commit His precious Word to something as fragile as languages and to people as imperfect as we are may seem unthinkable. We should be cautious not to raise the standards higher than where God Himself has set them lest we be like Peter who tried to impose his own view of God's plans upon the Lord. He said defiantly to Him, "Be it far from thee, Lord: this shall not be unto thee." In that case we are aware of the Lord's immediate reproof and Peter's subsequent denial. Rather, let us be like Mary and say, "Behold the handmaid of the Lord; be it unto me according to thy word." God's way of working is to entrust heavenly treasures unto earthen vessels.

Yet, we must also approach Bible translating with care and respect. It is wise to refrain from statements or attitudes that may indicate that we are casual about the translation process. A statement commonly quoted from *The Translators to the Reader* (the preface of the 1611 edition of the KJV) says this:

> [W]e do not deny, nay, we affirm and avow, that the very meanest translation of the Bible set by men of our profession ... containeth the word of God, nay, is the word of God.[59]

The expression "the very meanest translation" raises linguistic and theological concerns, regardless of the meaning of "meanest." Taken in its social context of 1611, "the meanest translation" of that day may have been acceptable. In contrast, I doubt any conservative believer would apply the statement favorably to, let us say, the Cotton Patch translation where the names of the cities to which the epistles were sent are replaced by the names of modern-day cities. Is that the Word of God?

We face the responsibility of defining sound criteria by which we can verify the *scripturalness* of translations. Whatever the criteria, they should be potentially applicable to translations in any and all of the nearly 6500 languages God has allowed to exist. Just as there is not one revelation for English people and one for Japanese, and just as the plan of salvation is the same both for Europeans and for Africans, so must the criteria for Bible translating be applicable to every ethnic group of the world.

God has been providentially using men for millennia in order to transmit His Word in the form of translations. That is why today we can use many translations, whether those of the past or those of today, whether in English or in Creole, for personal devotions, teaching, or preaching. We can use even the translations that we produce ourselves, stand with them in the pulpits at our churches, read them, preach from them, and marvel, when we see the results, that the autograph though dead yet speaketh.

---

[1]The autographs are the first manuscripts that were written by the Biblical authors. The word is generally plural in number to indicate that there were originally sixty-six autographs. Here, it is purposefully singular to indicate the corpus of inspired revelation written by the collective group of Biblical authors.

[2]The selected New Testament books in this trial edition were Mark, John, Romans, James, 1 John, 2 John, and 3 John.

[3]The translation *Louis Segond* appeared for the first time in 1874 in portions. A conservative revision dated 1910 gained general acceptance of the French speaking world. Consequently, most conservative believers refer to the 1910 edition as the origin of the Louis Segond they use.

[4]The word "translation," unless otherwise qualified, refers throughout this chapter to translation of the Bible.

[5]W. Schwarz captures well the struggle of the translator of the Scriptures by bringing up the questions that haunt him as he consciously works on translating the Word of God into a vernacular language. *Principles and Problems of Biblical Translation* (London: Cambridge University Press, 1955), pp. 6-7.

[6]*United Bible Societies: World Annual Report 2000*, 190/191 (England: United Bible Societies, 2001), p. 338.

[7]Robert J. Dunzweiller addresses this issue in two papers ("The Inspiration and 'Inspiredness' of Scripture: A Proposal," 1977, and "Inspiration, 'Inspiredness' and the Proclamation of God's Word Today: A Modest Second Step," n.d.) He proposed "inspiredness" as a term for the same concept. However, he presents "inspiredness" as a quality of inspiration whereas in this chapter *scripturalness* is discussed as a quality of preservation. For us, even if a copy were to be identical to the autographs (that we do not have), the very fact that it was a copy would relay it to the category of preservation.

[8]Reuben A. Torrey and A.C. Dixon, eds. 1917 Reprint. (Grand Rapids: Baker Book House, 1998). Even Benjamin Breckinridge Warfield, at the height of his debate to defend the inspiration of the Scriptures against higher criticism, has not addressed the *scripturalness* of Bible translations. See, for example, his *The Inspiration and Authority of the Bible* (Phillipsburg: Presbyterian and Reformed Publishing Company, 1948).

[9]Grand Rapids: Baker Book House, 1985, p. 199.

[10]Ibid., p. 200.

[11]Dunzweiller made a valid point in his paper ("The Inspiration and 'Inspiredness' of Scripture: A Proposal") about inspiration of copies. He argues that when the NT referred to inspired Scripture in such passages as 2 Timothy 3:15; John 10:35; 1 Peter 2:19-21, all the writers (or speakers) knew and had ever seen were copies of the OT autographs, not the autographs themselves. They were not in existence then. Therefore, in their mind, those copies were inspired. Hence, he requested a redefinition of inspiration that would include, to some degree, copies and translations.

[12]Nida, Eugene A. "The Book of a Thousand Tongues," in *The New Testament Student and Bible Translation*, vol. 4, ed. John H. Skilton and Curtiss A. Ladley (Phillipsburg: Presbyterian and Reformed Publishing Co., 1978), p. 1.

[13]"Theory of Bible Translation and General Theory of Translation" (*The Bible Translator* (hereafter TBT), 42:1 [1991] pp. 101-102).

[14]Eugene A. Nida, "Bible Translation for the Eighties," *International Review of Mission* 70 (1981) pp. 136-37. Freddy Boswell presents a candid view of the need for Biblical training for Bible translators in "Do Bible Translators Need Formal Biblical Training?" *Notes on Translation* (hereafter NOT), 11:3 (1997), pp. 1-8.

[15]John Beekman and John Callow have repeated numerous warnings to translators that they should limit their translation only to genuine implicit information. See, for example, chapter 2, "Fidelity in Translation," in *Translating the Word of God* (Grand Rapids: Zondervan Publishing House, 1974). Eugene A. Nida and Charles R. Taber have similar warnings dispersed throughout their *Theory and Practice of Translation* (Leiden: E.J. Brill, 1969).

[16]Longacre, Robert. "OPTAT," *Occasional Papers in Translation and Text Linguistics*. 1 (1987), p.1.

[17]The English language, for example, has gone through progressive, yet drastic changes that can be marked in periods of about two hundred years. Consequently, old translations in English have been revised within each period to reflect the new grammatical and phonemic changes. If one goes far enough in the past, French would turn back into Latin. Cf. John McWhorter. *The Power of Babel* (New York: Henry Holt and Company, 2001) pp. 17-18. The French Bible *Louis Segond* that appeared in 1874 was revised in 1910, in 1954, and again in 1978 due mostly to the changes in the French language. Important changes continue to occur in French. In spite of the safeguards set upon the language by the French Academy, they have to regularly acknowledge new words that have entered French from other languages, especially English, and new grammatical rules. Likewise, any attempt at preserving old Bible translations in defiance to, or in denial of, the inevitable developement occurring within the languages in which they were produced would cause several problems and would eventually end up in a fiasco. At the Tower of Babel, God initiated in languages the potential to change. If not God, who else? When one resists the changes in languages, he or she not only challenges the potential God Himself has established but also falls prey to the hand of evolutionists who argue that mutation within languages proves the theory of evolution. See Robert T. Pennock, *Tower of Babel: The Evidence against the New Creationism* (Cambridge: A Bradford Book, 1999), pp. 117-46. See also McWhorter, pp. 1-15.

[18]See discussion by Donald N. Larson and William A. Smalley in *Becoming Bilingual* (Lanham: University Press of America, 1972), pp. 7-21.

[19]On a more technical approach, some linguists would call Peter's act an interpretation rather than a translation. They use "interpretation" for oral transfer of meaning from one language to another, and translation for written transfer from one language to another. Nancy Costello, "On Translation Theories" *NOT*, 6:2 (1992), p. 64.

[20]That the Hebrew word used here has been a technical term for interpretation (oral translation) from one language to the other is supported by a wealth of evidence. See the entry in Raymond Philippe, *Dictionnaire d'Hébreux et d'Araméen Bibliques* (Le Cerf: Société Biblique Française, 1991).

[21]William L. Gardner, "Toward a Theology of Translation" NOT, 5:3 (1991), p. 18. The title of the article announces much more than what is developed therein. Having given a few examples of translation in the Scriptures, Gardner went on to defend Dynamic Equivalence. The title could have been more accurately rendered, "Toward a Theory of Bible Translation."

[22]Walter C. Kaiser, Jr. *The Uses of the Old Testament in the New*. (Chicago: Moody Press, 1985), pp. 2-7.

[23]Ibid., pp. 4-5.

[24]The reader might appreciate the simple, succinct, but informative article about the limitations of the Septuagint as a translation tool by Gerhard Tauberschmidt, "Concerns about the Septuagint as a Basis for Old Testament Decisions" NOT, 11:4 (1997), pp. 52-56.

[25]Some conservative believers would rather define illumination as "the process by which God enables the believer to comprehend the *certainty* and the *spiritual significance* of the Scriptures." The nuances in this definition do not contradict the traditional, conservative expression of the doctrine as stated in the text. Millard Erickson says, "Revelation is God's making his truth known to man. Inspiration preserves it, making it widely accessible. Inspiration guarantees that what the Bible says is just what God would say if he were to speak directly. One other element is needed in this chain, however: For the Bible to function as if it is God speaking to us, the Bible reader needs to understand the meaning of the Scriptures, and to be convinced of their divine origin and authorship" (p. 246).

[26]Charles C. Ryrie. "Illumination," *Baker's Dictionary of Theology,* Everett F. Harrision, ed. (Grand Rapids: Baker Book House, 1973), p. 277.

[27]The OT references are according to the sequence of chapters and verses in the Septuagint not in the Masoretice Text. Gleason L. Archer and G.C. Chirichigno. *Old Testament Quotations in the New Testament: A Complete Survey*. (Chicago: Moody Press, 1983.)

[28]For the basic historical information in this section, I am indebted to W. Schwarz, pp. 17-44. His book is particularly helpful in that he has carefully analyzed the ancient texts themselves that are related to the subject instead of quoting the views of other writers about them.

[29]A colleague of mine has pointed out that the *Aristeas Letter* must have been considered as the first treatise on Bible translation since it is quoted very often throughout the centuries whenever questions arise about methodology of translating the Bible. Being so close in time to the Septuagint, it would deserve a special study that might prove very enlightening to the subject that we are considering.

[30]As quoted by Schwarz, p. 33.

[31]Ibid., p. 10.

[32]For a discussion of language universals presupposing an application to Bible translation, see Peter Cotterell and Max Turner, *Linguistics and Biblical Interpretation* (Downers Grove, IL: InterVarsity Press, 1989), pp. 19-24. Read also Bernard Comrie, *Language Universals and Linguistic Typology*, 2nd. ed. (Chicago: The University of Chicago Press, 1989), pp. 1-32.

[33]John McWorther, p. 12.

[34]Ralph Fasold. *The Sociolinguistics of Society* (England: Blackwell, 1984) pp. 213-217.

[35]Books that present the basic semantics of languages have proliferated during the later part of the twentieth century. I may recommend these two, the first for its down-to-earth approach, the second for its newness: Victoria Fromkin and Robert Rodman, *An Introduction to Language*, 4th ed. Fort Worth: Holt, Rinehart and Winston, Inc., 1988), pp. 122-241. And *Language Profiles: Materials for an Introduction to Language and Linguistics*, 8th ed. Thomas W. Stewart, Jr. and Nathan Vaillett, eds. (Columbus: The Ohio State University Press, 2001), pp. 111-240.

[36]*Nouvo Testaman Sin An*, 1985.

[37]John McWorther, p. 6.

[38]See Geoffrey Leech, *Semantics* (Great Britain: Hazell Watson & Viney Ltd., first print. 1974, reprint. 1975), pp. 1-7.

[39]Greg Thomson has produced various interesting articles on different essential aspects of meaning under the title "What Sort of Meaning is Preserved in Translation?" in four issues of *NOT* (2:1, 1988; 3:1 and 4, 1989; 4:1, 1990).

[40]H. Howard Hess. "Towards a Referential Base," *Journal of Translation and Textlinguistics*, 6:1 (1993), p. 5.

[41]Leech, pp. 10-27.

[42]W. Schwarz, p. 33.

[43]Ernst R. Wendland, a Lutheran professor and a translation consultant, wrote this: "In part 1[of two articles], five principles of functional equivalence that Martin Luther employed in translating the German Bible were presented: (1) the priority of meaning; (2) the need to change linguistic form; (3) expression of implicit information; (4) retention of the original unnatural form in places; (5) the importance of discourse analysis to exegetical study. In part 2 there are five more such principles: (6) the importance of context; (7) monitoring the reception of the message; (8) the value of readers' helps; (9) the team approach; and (10) need for revision." From "Martin Luther, the Father of Confessional, Functional-Equivalence Bible Translation," NOT, 9:2 (1995), p. 47. The first part of the article occurs in 9:1 (1995), pp. 16-36.

[44]*The Semantics of Biblical Languages* (London: Oxford University Press, 1961).

[45]Leiden: E. J. Brill.

[46]James D. Price, *Complete Equivalence in Bible Translation* (Nashville: Thomas Nelson Publishers, 1987), p. 5. [Recently, Price has preferred the designation *optimal equivalence* lest "complete" be understood as "perfect." Email from James D. Price ed.]

[47]Arthur L. Farstad, *The New King James Version in the Great Tradition* (Nashville: Thomas Nelson Publishers, 1989) p. 124.

[48]*The Word of God in English*: Criteria for Excellence in Bible Translation. (Wheaton, Illinois: Crossway Books, 2002.)

[49]Ibid, p. 9.

[50]Ibid, p. 31.

[51]Mildred L. Larson, though a proponent of dynamic equivalence, admits "translations are often a mixture of a **literal** transfer of the grammatical units with some **idiomatic translation** of the meaning of the text. It is not easy to consistently translate idiomatically. A translator may express some parts of his translation in very natural forms and then in other parts fall back into a literal form. Translations fall on a continuum from very literal, to literal, to modified, to near idiomatic, to idiomatic, and then may even move on to be **unduly free.**" *Meaning-Based Translation: A Guide to Cross-Language Equivalence.* (Lanham: University Press of America, 1984) pp. 16-17.

[52]Ibid., p. 16.

[53]*NOT*, 121:10 (1987) p. 7. The reader would benefit much from reading this article. D.A. Carson does not reject dynamic equivalence as a whole. But he pinpoints the weaknesses and expresses concern. He has come short of formulating a complete

theory of translation that would include the positive aspects of dynamic equivalence and regulates those that are lacking to dynamic equivalence.

[54]*The Theory and Practice of Translation.* (Leiden: E. J. Brill, 1982), p. 163.

[55]John Beekman and John Callow, p. 31.

[56]Larson, p. 437.

[57]pp. 55, 31.

[58]Ibid., p. 32.

[59]Erroll F. Rhodes and Liana Lupas, eds. (New York: American Bible Society, 1977), p. 47.

BIBLIOGRAPHY

Archer, L. Gleason, and G. C. Chirichigno. *Old Testament Quotations in the New Testament: A Complete Survey*. Chicago: Moody Press, 1983.

Barr, James. *The Semantics of Biblical Language*. Oxford: Oxford University Press, 1961.

Beekman, John, and John Callow. *Translating the Word of God*. Grand Rapids: Zondervan Publishing House, 1974.

Boswell, Freddy. "Do Bible Translators Need Formal Biblical Training?" *Notes on Translation*. 11:3 (1997):1-8.

Bradley, Virginia. "Assumption Involved in Interpretive Decisions." *Notes on Translation*. 5:3 (1991):23-33.

Buber, Martin, and Franz Rosenzweig. *Scripture and Translation*. First published in German, 1936. Translated by Lawrence Rosenwald and Everett Fox. Bloomington: Indiana University Press, 1994.

Carson. D. A. "The Limits of Dynamic Equivalence." *Notes on Translation*. 121 (1987):1-14.

Comrie, Bernard. *Language Universals and Linguistic Typology*. 2nd ed. Chicago: University of Chicago Press, 1989.

Costello, Nancy. "On Translation Theories." *Notes on Translation*. 6:2 (1992):15-20.

Cotterell, Peter, and Max Turner. *Linguistics & Biblical Interpretation*. Downers Grove: InterVarsity Press, 1989.

Devitt, Michael, and Kim Sterelny. *Language & Reality: An Introduction to the Philosophy of Language*. Cambridge: The MIT Press, 1987.

Dunzweiller, Robert J. *"The Inspiration and 'Inspiredness' of Scripture: A Proposal."* Philadelphia: Interdisciplinaey Biblical Reserch Institute, 1977.

_____."Inspiration, 'Inspiredness' and the Proclamation of God's Word Today: A Modest Second Step." n.d.

Erickson, Millard. *Christian Theology*. Grand Rapids: Baker Book House, 1985.

Farsol, Ralph. *The Sociolinguistics of Society*. London: Blackwell, 1984.

Farstad, Arthur L. *The New King James Version in the Great Tradition.* Nashville: Thomas Nelson, 1989.

Fromkin, Victoria, and Robert Rodman. *An Introduction to Language.* 4th ed. Fort Worth: Holt, Rinehart and Winston, Inc., 1988.

Gardner, William L. "Toward a Theology of Translation". *Notes on Translation.* 5:3 (1991):15-22.

Giglioli, Pier Paolo, et al. *Language and Social Context.* London: Penguin Books, 1972.

Hess, H. Howard. "Toward a Referential Base." *Journal of Translation and Textlinguistics.* 6:1(1993):1-55.

Kaiser, Walter C. *The Uses of the Old Testament in the New.* Chicago: Moody Press, 1985.

Larson, Donald N., and William A. Smalley. *Becoming Bilingual: A Guide to Language Learning.* Lanham: University Press of America, 1984.

Larson, Mildred L. Meaning-Based Translation: *A Guide to Cross-Language Equivalence.* Lanham: University Press of America, 1984.

Leech, Geoffrey. *Semantics.* First published in 1974. Reprint. England: Penguin Books, 1975.

Longacre, Robert. "OPTAT." *Occasional Papers in Translation and Textlinguistics.* 1(1987) 1-2.

McWorther, John. *The Power of Babel.* New York: Henry Holt and Company, LLC, 2001.

Nida, Eugene A. "The Book of a Thousand Tongues." *The New Testament Student and Bible Translation.* Vol. 4. ed. John H. Skilton and Curtiss A. Ladley. Phillipsburg: Presbyterian and Reformed Publishing Co., 1978.

_____. *Toward a Science of Translating.* Leiden: E. J. Brill, 1964.

_____. "Bible Translation for the Eighties." *International Review of Missions.* 70(1981):132-8.

_____ and Charles A Taber. *The Theory and Practice of Translation.* Leiden: E.J. Brill, 1982.

Nouvo Testaman Sin An. 1985.

Pennock, Robert T. Tower of Babel: *The Evidence against the New Creationism.* Cambridge: The MIT Press, 1999.

Philippe, Raymond. *Dictionnaire d'Hébreux et d'Araméen Bibliques*. Le Cerf: Société Biblique Française, 1991.

Price, James D. *Complete Equivalence in Bible Translation*. Nashville: Thomas Nelson Publishers, 1987.

Rhodes, Erroll F., and Liana Lupas, ed. T*he Translators to the Reader –The Original Preface of the King James Version of 1611 Revisited*. New York: American Bible Society, 1997.

Ryken, Leland. *The Word of God in English: Criteria for Excellance in Bible Translation*. Wheaton, Illinois: Crossway Books, 2002.

Ryrie, Charles C. "Illumination," in *Baker's Dictionary of Theology*. Everett F. Harrision, ed. Grand Rapids: Baker Book House, 1973.

Salevsky, Heidemarie. "Bible and General Theory of Bible Translation." *The Bible Translator.* 42:1(1991):101-113.

Schwarz, W. *Principles and Problems of Biblical Translation*. London: Cambridge University Press, 1955.

Skilton, John H., and Curtiss A. Ladley, ed. *The New Testament Student and Bible Translation*. Vol. 4. Phillipsburg: Presbyterian and Reformed Publishing Co., 1978.

Stewart, Thomas W., Jr., and Nathan Vaillette, ed. *Language Files: Materials for an Introduction to Language and Linguistics*. 8th ed. Columbus: The Ohio State University Press, 2001.

Tauberschmidt, Gerhart. "Concerns about the Septuagint as a Basis for Old Testament Textual Decisions." *Notes on Translation*. 11:4(1997):52-6.

Thomson, Greg. "What Sort of Meaning is Preserved in Translation?" *Notes on Translation*. 2:1(1988):1-24; 3:1(1989):26-48; 3:4 (1989):30-54; 4:1(1990):21-31.

Torrey, Reuben A., and A. C. Dixon, ed. T*he Fundamentals: A Testimony to the Truth*. 4 vol. 1917. Reprint. Grand Rapids: Baker Book House, 1998.

United Bible Societies: *World Annual Report 2000*. London: United Bible Societies, 2001.

Warfield, Benjamin Breckinridge. *The Inspiration and Authority of the Bible*. Phillipsburg: Presbyterian and Reformed Publishing Company, 1948.

Wendland, Ernst R. "Martin Luther, the Father of Confessional, Functional-Equivalence Bible Translation." Notes on Translation. 9:1(1995):16-36; 9:2(1995):47-60.

Williams, James B., ed. *From the Mind of God to the Mind of Man:* A Layman's Guide to How we Got Our Bible. Greenville, SC.: Ambassador-Emerald International, 1999.

Preserved for Our Proclamation and Transformation

Michael Harding

Introduction

The great translator of the English Bible, William Tyndale, was burned at the stake on October 6, 1536, because he dared to translate the Bible into English so that the common person could read it. Tyndale understood that no doctrine connected with the Christian faith is more important than the one that has to do with the basis of true religious knowledge. When all is said and done, the only true and dependable source for Christianity lies in the book Christians call the Bible.

Biblical Christianity consists of both belief and behavior. God preserves His Word in order that His people might glorify Him in their doctrine and practice. Serious departures from the preserved *message* in Scripture are occurring in some Evangelical and Fundamental circles today, including churches which espouse a King James Only position. These departures include a subjective non-theological approach to preaching; a man-centered understanding of the Gospel; an over-simplification of saving faith; an outright denial of biblical repentance; a hedonistic[1] tendency in worship; serious confusion regarding bibliology (doctrine of Scripture); increasing worldliness in the personal lives of professing believers; and a weakening of ecclesiastical separation by local New Testament (NT) churches.

Adherence to a particular English translation does not insulate a pastor, church, or school from these deviations. Some have erroneously assumed that if they use the King James Version of the Bible (KJV) their ministry is protected from theological error or aberrant Christian practice. A number of these believe that if a pastor or church uses a conservative English translation other than the KJV, they have departed from the Faith and are headed toward ecclesiastical, theological, or personal compromise. However, a proper understanding of the certainty of Scripture and the doctrine of inspiration along with its corollary of preservation is foundational for living a life characterized by doctrinal integrity and moral purity. This chapter maintains that a clear understanding and application of orthodox bibliology corrects the defects of Fundamentalism and the serious compromises of Evangelicalism more effectively than exclusive loyalty to one biblical text, one textual family, or one English translation.

THE BELIEVER'S CERTAINTY OF SCRIPTURE

The believer's certainty regarding the truthfulness and authority of the Bible can only come by appealing to the self-authenticating nature of Scripture in conjunction with the internal witness of the Spirit. The Scriptures are *self-authenticating* in that they claim divine authority for themselves. Paul, for example, claimed that his words were taught by the Spirit (1 Cor. 2:13). Scripture cannot appeal to some higher authority outside itself for authentication. God is the author of Scripture; there is no greater authority to which one may appeal. The Holy Spirit is not *revealing* anything to believers in this regard, only *illuminating* their minds to see the truth which has already been revealed as to its certainty and significance. A systematic study of all sixty-six books of the Bible will lead genuine Christian believers to the conclusion that those books form an organic whole—the canon of Scripture.

The basic Christian presupposition is that the one living and true God has revealed Himself in the sixty-six books of the Bible. Why is it necessary for a true Christian to hold this presupposition? Because all discussion and argumentation by necessity come down to a primitive starting point, a truth that is accepted as self-evident, an authority for which no greater evidence can be given. Consequently, all facts must be tested and interpreted in light of that authority the Bible. Only then can men understand that truth is whatever God has said, would say, or could say about any fact in the universe. Every affirmation of truth must be evaluated by the standard of God's truth recorded in Scripture.

Unregenerate man, on the other hand, assumes that he has the right to direct his life according to his own will and that his intellect is the final authority for truth. An unregenerate mind, however, cannot approach any subject neutrally. The Scriptures affirm that the "carnal mind is enmity (hostile) against God" (Rom. 8:7). Man in his fallen condition does not *welcome* the truth of God for the simple reason that the natural man does not possess the Spirit of God (1 Cor. 2:14). Consequently, the unbeliever suppresses the certainty, importance, and personal implications of God's truth upon his life by his unrighteousness in thought and deed (Rom. 1:18). In light of man's intellectual depravity which theologians call "noetic sin" (sin of the mind), any experiential attempt to *verify* the Scriptures to the unregenerate mind is doomed to failure. Unless the Holy Spirit illumines the mind of the individual he will never understand [or grasp] the true nature of the Word of God which is self-evidencing, self-attesting, and self-authenticating. The true believer's faith rests in the Spirit's power to open his eyes, enlighten his mind, and convince him of the Scriptures' truthfulness and significance to his life (1 Cor. 2:4–5; Eph 1:18; 1 John 2:20).

G. Campbell Morgan, a man who became a well-known expositor of God's Word, spoke of the supernatural power of God's Spirit upon his own mind. He confessed that he had experienced a time in his life where he was confused and perplexed about the accuracy and authority of the Word of God. At the height of this personal crisis, he left his house and went to a bookstore down the street, purchased a new Bible, and began to study it with a submissive heart. Years later, Morgan commented about that day:

> The Bible found me . . . I began to read and study it then in 1883. I have been a student ever since, and I still am [1938].[2]

Morgan emerged from that test convinced by the Holy Spirit that the Bible is none other than the Word of the living God. Like Morgan, every believer knows the certainty, truthfulness, and significance of God's written Word because of the miraculous work of illumination.

THE BELIEVER'S CERTAINTY OF THE DOCTRINE OF INSPIRATION

Since the apprehension of both the certainty and significance of Scripture is based on the illuminating work of the Holy Spirit, it is necessary to understand what the Scriptures teach concerning their own origin, inspiration, preservation, and relevance. Without an exegetical[3] and systematic understanding of bibliology, any discussion as to the relevance of Scripture is fruitless. Therefore, a careful examination of 2 Timothy 3:16 along with its necessary implications will set the framework for applying the practical benefits of the Word of God in the life of every true believer.

The Content Of 2 Timothy 3:16

All historic, orthodox Fundamentalists believe that the Bible is plenarily and verbally inspired. Plenary-verbal inspiration defines both the extent and nature of biblical inspiration. "Plenary" speaks of the divine authorship of *all* Scripture by the Holy Spirit. "Verbal" applies the concept of inspiration to the "very words of Scripture."[4] Warfield gives the classic definition:

> Inspiration is, therefore, usually defined as a supernatural influence exerted on the sacred writers by the Spirit of God, by virtue of which *their writings* are given Divine trustworthiness [emphasis added].[5]

In 2 Timothy 3:16 Paul establishes *the Scriptures' own claim to divine authority and relevance to sound belief and behavior.* Paul warns Timothy not to be deceived by false teachers and impostors, but instead to continue in what he has learned, having been fully "convinced" of Scripture's truthfulness and authority (2 Tim 3:15).[6] Both his grandmother, Lois, and his mother, Eunice, taught Timothy the "Holy Scriptures" (lit. "the sacred writings") from his early childhood. The Scriptures made Timothy "wise unto salvation" (2 Tim. 3:15). Paul argues that the oracles of God are the divinely ordained means to both regenerate and sanctify a man's soul through the work of the Holy Spirit. The Old Testament (OT) Scriptures referred to by Paul set the foundation for the NT Scriptures which will accomplish God's redemptive purpose in the life of Timothy and other believers:

> All scripture is given by inspiration of God, and is profitable for doctrine, for reproof, for correction, for instruction in righteousness: That the man of God may be perfect, [throughly] furnished unto all good works (2 Tim. 3:16–17).

The Meaning of "All Scripture"

"All Scripture" (πᾶσα γραφή) refers to the whole of Scripture. The discussion of this phrase centers on whether one should adhere to the collective interpretation of *pasa* as "all" or to the distributive interpretation of *pasa* as "every." Whereas the rendering "every Scripture" encompasses the entire Bible in its component parts, the collective translation "all Scripture" best describes the Bible as a whole.[7] The context and language both indicate that the Scriptures *in their entirety* are profitable for doctrine, reproof, correction, and instruction, thereby equipping the man of God for every good work.

"Scripture" (γραφή) has several important connotations in the interpretation of 2 Timothy 3:16. Most importantly, *graphe* refers to "the sacred writings" of the Old Testament *and all future New Testament writings*. The New Testament writers use this term over fifty times "exclusively with a sacred meaning of Holy Scripture."[8] For instance, when Paul writes, "the Scripture says" (Rom. 4:3; 9:17; 10:11; 11:2), he regards this expression as God speaking, and the present tense of the verb indicates the continual relevance of Scripture's authority.[9] Paul and the other biblical authors regarded their own inspired writings as divinely given and authoritative (1 Cor. 2:13; 14:37–39; 1 Thess. 2:13; Luke 1:1–4; John 20:31). Furthermore, the apostle Peter corroborates the inspiration of the NT when he mentions that false teachers purposely distorted Paul's letters as they did "the rest of the Scriptures" (2 Pet. 3:15–16).[10] Hiebert explains Peter's comments:

> Clearly, Peter accepted the Pauline epistles as having the same authoritative character as the rest of the sacred Scriptures. From the first, the churches read the Pauline Epistles as an authoritative message for the Christian faith and practice, and this attitude was obtained even in those churches which were not their direct recipients (Col. 4:16; 1 Thess. 5:27). Like the books of the Old Testament, *his*

> *epistles were accepted as revealing the mind of God*
> [emphasis added].[11]

Equally important, the term "Scripture" indicates that the *"writing,"* not the *"writer,"* was the object of inspiration. True, the sacred writers were the "organs of God for the infallible communication of His mind and will."[12] They spoke as they were "borne along" by the Holy Spirit (2 Pet. 1:20–21). The unity (confluence) of the Divine/human authorship is expressed in verse 20 which teaches that no prophecy of Scripture originates from one's own private interpretation.[13] Literally, "no prophecy of Scripture *'becomes'* (γίνεται)," referring to the origin of Scripture. Scripture does not originate from human initiative. On the contrary, the authors of Scripture were "moved" (φερόμενοι—"being borne or carried along") by the Holy Spirit (v. 21 cf. Acts 27:15, 17). *Pheromenoi* ("being borne along") is a present passive participle indicating that the *original authors* of Scripture were miraculously and continuously acted upon by God as they wrote. The apostle Peter does not imply that the human authors were passive in regard to their personalities while writing the autographs. Instead, he explains that in the relationship between God and the human authors, the human writers were not independent, much less, dominant. Scripture originated with God.

The Meaning of "Theopneustos"

The English word "inspiration" comes from the Latin *inspiro* which means to breathe *in*. Paul, however, asserts that all Scripture is "breathed *out*" by God (θεόπνευστος). This unusual word occurs only once in the NT. It is a compound of "God" (θεος) and "breathe" (πνεω). The lexical definition of *pneo* means to "breathe out."[14] Various Bible dictionaries and encyclopedias describe *theopnuestos* as "spiration," "spiring," or "breath," indicating a divine product of the creative-breath of God.[15] On this foundation of divine origin all the noble attributes of Scripture are built. Warfield has done the most exhaustive research on *theopneustos* and remains unmatched by past or contemporary scholarship. He explains the significance of *theopneustos* as follows:

> Everywhere the word ["God-breathed"] appears as purely passive and expresses production by God. . . . Let anyone run his eye down the list of compounds of "θεος" with the verbals "τος" as they occur in any Greek *Lexicon*, and he will be quickly convinced that the notion normally expressed is that of a result produced by God.[16]

Warfield's meticulous research on *theopneustos* concludes that Scripture is the immediate result of the creative breath of God.[17] God "spirated" the Scriptures. He did not "*in*-spire" an *existing* text but rather "*ex*-spired" or

339

"breathed-out" the text. Scripture is a direct production of God's immediate power, not something previously existing and then infused with the divine influence. Scripture is called *theopneustos* because it is the product of divine "spiration"—the creation of the Holy Spirit. The Scriptures, therefore, owe their origin to the activity of God, the Holy Spirit, and are in the highest and truest sense His direct revelation.

The Relationship of the Term "Scripture" to "God-breathed"

The question here relates to whether "God-breathed" ($\theta\epsilon\acute{o}\pi\nu\epsilon\upsilon\sigma\tau o\varsigma$) should stand in the predicate of the sentence as translated in most conservative translations, "All Scripture *is* inspired of God" or whether it should stand attributively, "Every Scripture inspired of God *is* profitable . . . ." The *Revised Version* of 1881 reverts to Tyndale's attributive interpretation of the construction: "Every Scripture inspired of God is profitable." Vine also interprets the phrase attributively along with the Wycliffe Bible, Coverdale, and the Great Bible.[18] It should be recognized that often translation work requires some amount of interpretation. Newport White in *The Expositor's Greek New Testament* states the case for an attributive translation.[19]

On the other hand, a comparison of this phrase in 2 Timothy 3:16a with the parallel construction in 1 Timothy 4:4 indicates that the proper translation should read "All Scripture *is* inspired of God" rather than "All Scripture inspired of God *is*." 1 Timothy 4:4 reads, "every creature of God [is] good and nothing to be refused" ($\pi\hat{\alpha}\nu\ \kappa\tau\acute{\iota}\sigma\mu\alpha\ \theta\epsilon o\hat{\upsilon}\ \kappa\alpha\lambda\grave{o}\nu\ \kappa\alpha\grave{\iota}\ o\grave{\upsilon}\delta\grave{\epsilon}\nu\ \dot{\alpha}\pi\acute{o}\beta\lambda\eta\tau o\nu$). This corresponds to the Greek syntax in 2 Timothy 3:16, "All [every] Scripture [is] God-breathed and profitable for teaching" ($\pi\hat{\alpha}\sigma\alpha\ \gamma\rho\alpha\phi\grave{\eta}\ \theta\epsilon\acute{o}\pi\nu\epsilon\upsilon\sigma\tau o\varsigma\ \kappa\alpha\grave{\iota}\ \dot{\omega}\phi\acute{\epsilon}\lambda\iota\mu o\varsigma\ \pi\rho\grave{o}\varsigma\ \delta\iota\delta\alpha\sigma\kappa\alpha\lambda\acute{\iota}\alpha\nu$). In light of this comparison, Warfield concludes that "on the whole, the preferable construction would seem to be, 'Every Scripture, *seeing that it is God-breathed*, is as well profitable.'"[20] In addition, if "God-breathed" carried an attributive use, then one would expect it to appear immediately before "Scripture" in the passage. However, "God-breathed" appears after "Scripture" and fits well as a predicate. Furthermore, words which are linked by the conjunction "and" should normally be understood together: "All Scripture [is] God-breathed *and* profitable." An attributive translation, on the other hand, sounds very awkward and leaves open a possible misinterpretation that some Scripture could be uninspired.

In summary, inspiration is the activity by which that portion intended by God of His special revelation[21] was put into written form by the supernatural agency of the Holy Spirit. Using the thought processes, literary styles, and personalities of certain divinely chosen men, the Holy Spirit moved in such a way that the product of their special labors in its entirety is the very Word of

God, including both the ideas and the specific vocabulary—complete, infallible, and inerrant in the original manuscripts.

The Necessary Implications of 2 Timothy 3:16

The Scriptures Are Free From All Error in the Autographs

E. J. Young defines "inerrancy" as "free from all error."[22] Inspiration and inerrancy were considered synonymous terms until recent times. Some, however, hold to a plenary view of inspiration, yet question the legitimacy of verbal inspiration. When Augustus Strong, for instance, asserts that "thought is possible without words," he opens the door to human error in the recording of the autographs.[23]

Whatever God *immediately creates*, however, must of necessity be without error factually, theologically, morally, historically, and scientifically. The source of God's Word is found in the Godhead, not human origin or instrumentality. The infinite perfections of God's very being demand inerrancy. When God speaks, He is veritable and veracious, credible and truthful. God will not lie (1 Sam. 15:20), cannot lie (Titus 1:2; Heb 6:18), and did not lie when He "breathed out" or "ex-spired" the sixty-six books of the Bible. The Spirit of truth (1 John 5:6) authored the Scriptures through human instrumentality, protecting the writings of the original authors from all error. Christ said, "I have given unto *them* the words which thou gavest to me" (John 17:8). The perfect God by the necessary demands of His own being communicates without error. The miracle of inspiration *via* the Holy Spirit guarantees an inerrant recording of that revelation.

The Scriptures Are Providentially Preserved

When Paul writes, "All Scripture is God-breathed," he refers *directly* to what the biblical authors themselves wrote, not to what someone copied or translated. The Scriptures recognize the vital distinction between what the original writer wrote and subsequent copies or translations made by others (Deut. 17:18; Neh. 8:8). Several Old Testament passages indicate that the human authors of the autographs were conscious that they were writing God's words: David said, "The Spirit of Jehovah [Yahweh] spake by *me*" (2 Sam. 23:2); Isaiah said, "Seek ye out . . . *this* book of Jehovah [Yahweh], and read" (Isa. 34:16); Jeremiah said, "[God's] words . . . even all that is written in *this* book" (Jer. 25:13). In similar fashion, Paul knew that the directly inspired text consisted of "The things *which I write* unto you . . . [they] are the commandments of the Lord" (1 Cor. 14:37 cf. 2:13; Acts 4:25).

The autographs have *primal* authority; copies and translations *derive* their authority from the original text rather than from an additional miraculous act of inspiration. The New Testament testifies to the necessary distinction between the autographs and copies. Jesus preached from accepted copies and translations of the original text such as the Septuagint, and He accepted them as authoritative Scripture (Luke 4:16–21). He regarded the extant copies of His day as so approximate to the original manuscripts (which no one possessed) that He appealed to those copies as authoritative (Matt. 19:4–7 cf. Gen. 2:24).

The criteria for all textual reproduction and examination is exemplified in Exodus 32:15–16. God wrote the first tablets of the Law, which later were destroyed. The second copy of the Law was written *according to the first writing* (Deut. 10:2, 4). In Jeremiah 36:28–32 the prophet explains that the only recording of the Jeremiah scroll had been destroyed; therefore, God miraculously gave all the words again to Jeremiah and enabled him through inspiration to record them. However, there is no promise in God's Word for a miraculous, immediate, divine working in the copyists or translators. Such a promise would necessitate continuous miracles each time the Bible was copied or translated. Claiming such a promise would be *adding a new doctrine* to God's Word. A biblically defined miracle is the *direct* application of God's power into the universe.[24] A work of providence, however, is indirect, as opposed to miraculous intervention. God has promised to preserve His Word through secondary causation (Ps. 119:152), but not through a *miraculous transmission* of the text.

Why is it necessary to make a distinction between the copies and originals in this regard? An error in a copy or translation reflects on a scribe, copyist, translator, or printer. An error in the original text, however, reflects on the *author*. Therefore, God commands His people to *carefully preserve* His inscripturated words, and He reserves divine judgment for those who intentionally corrupt the text either through addition, subtraction, or misrepresentation (Deut. 4:2; 12:32; Prov. 30:5–6; Dan. 12:4; Rev. 22:18–19). The safeguarding, preserving, and transmission of God's Word is one of the most serious and demanding responsibilities that God has given to His people, and it requires our utmost effort.

Equally contemptible in God's eyes as adding or subtracting from the original words of Scripture are attempts to corrupt the *message* of the Scriptures. The religious leaders of Christ's day set aside the commandments of God in order to keep their traditions (Mark 7:9). In so doing, they invalidated the Word of God (Mark 7:12). The rabbis had a superstitious attitude toward the text of the OT; however, when they intentionally *circumvented the message* of the text, they effectively corrupted the text itself. Disobeying the message or refusing to accept its truth as part of one's belief system equals "adulterating" the Word of God (2 Cor. 4:2; 2 Thess. 2:2; 3:14). Many who have held a Bible in hand have hated God in their hearts. Jesus said, "You search the Scriptures because you think that in them you have eternal life; it is these that testify about Me and you are *unwilling to come to Me* so that you may have life" (John 5:39–40, NASB).[25]

The teaching of preservation logically flows from the doctrine of inspiration; that is, it is a necessary corollary of inspiration. The corollary says that there is no real purpose or value in inspiring a document that is not preserved. Translations of the Scriptures derive their authority from the inspiration of the autographs necessitating the preservation of the text. **The original *text*, including its message, has been preserved in the totality of the Hebrew, Aramaic, and Greek manuscripts.[26] No particular translation, manuscript, codex, text type, or family of manuscripts can *scripturally* claim exclusive rights to the teaching of providential preservation *via* secondary causation**. For this reason the original translators of the KJV recognized in their preface that all translations, since they are done by *fallible* men, are not perfect and thus can be improved upon.[27] They also respected other translations as the Word of God. In actuality, only 31% of the KJV is new translation *per se*; the KJV translators borrowed heavily from previous translations such as Wycliffe, Tyndale, Coverdale, the Geneva Bible, the Bishop's Bible and even the Latin Vulgate.[28] Numerous NT quotations of the OT, including those of the Lord Jesus Christ, are from the Greek translation of the OT (Septuagint) rather than the Hebrew Masoretic Text. Following the example of the KJV translators, NT authors, and the Lord Jesus Christ, it is not wrong for a Christian to use translations of the Bible other than the KJV, provided of course that the translation is based on fidelity to the original text, orthodoxy in interpretation, relevance to the language of the time, and suitability for reading. The bottom line is this: God wrote the Bible in Hebrew, Aramaic, and Greek; every reproduction of God's Word in any other language is a translation, including the beloved and respected King James Version of the Bible.

THE BELIEVER'S CERTAINTY THAT THE SCRIPTURES ARE THE FINAL AUTHORITY FOR BELIEF AND BEHAVIOR

Paul declares that all Scripture is "profitable" or "useful" ($\dot{\omega}\phi\dot{\epsilon}\lambda\iota\mu o\varsigma$; 2 Tim 3:16) in the sense of yielding a practical benefit (1 Tim. 4:8; Titus 3:8). This benefit is delineated in four phrases.[29] These phrases are arranged in two pairs, each with a negative and positive aspect. The first pair of words deals with belief (creed) and the second pair with behavior (conduct). The Scriptures are for teaching the truth and refuting error—our belief. The Scriptures are also profitable for reforming one's actions and discipline in right living—our behavior. The Bible is fully sufficient for the salvation of man and the development of the believer into full maturity (2 Tim. 3:17).

The Scriptures construct our faith by establishing correct belief ("doctrine"), convict by exposing incorrect belief ("reproof"), correct by exposing incorrect behavior ("correction"), and counsel in order to establish right behavior ("instruction in righteousness"). The practical benefits that Scripture bestows indicate its inherent divine authority for belief and behavior, for doctrine and practice (cf. 2 Pet. 1:3–4).

The Scriptures Construct Our Faith by Establishing Correct Belief

The Word of God benefits believers by supplying the absolute truth-deposit from which Christians are taught the propositional truth-claims of God ($\pi\rho\grave{o}\varsigma$ $\delta\iota\delta\alpha\sigma\kappa\alpha\lambda\grave{\iota}\alpha\nu$, "for doctrine"; 2 Tim. 3:16). The Scriptures indoctrinate by means of setting forth the whole counsel of God, which is the systematic, unified, non-contradictory body of truth inscripturated in the Bible. Sound doctrine also includes the moral implications which necessarily result from genuine faith in the truth: "For whoremongers, for them that defile themselves with mankind, for menstealers, for liars, for perjured persons, *and if there be any other thing that is contrary to sound doctrine*" (1 Tim. 1:10*)*.

Doctrinal preaching has fallen on hard times in some sectors of Evangelicalism and Fundamentalism. The declining doctrinal emphasis in preaching, ministerial training, and ecclesiastical associations is hard to miss, but difficult to prove. Much too often God's objective, inscripturated truth is invalidated by a subjective, non-theological approach to preaching. Fundamentalism historically has used doctrine to define its beliefs and its relationship to a hostile world. The Fundamentalists' understanding of biblical truth has always led the movement to display a militant spirit against the naturalistic age. Christians who fail to recognize the gradual shift from an objective apprehension of truth to a subjective embracing of error are naive to the destructive power such a shift has over the historic Faith. The failure of the experiential to be anchored to biblical truth surrenders the historic Faith to the whims of human autonomy. Truth, for some comes by intuition and feeling, rather than by ascertaining God's viewpoint on a particular subject. "I feel" rather than "God says" is the current mantra to theological questions. The result is a loss of authority, accountability, and duty, all replaced by human autonomy, utility, and the false idea that "being good" essentially means "feeling good"— a counterfeit of Christian joy and contentment.

To make matters worse, ministers are now regarded as corporate managers and psychotherapists who no longer need precise and thorough theological training. As "professionals" who cater to the world's mind-set of what ministry should be, pastors have unwittingly produced a practical atheism in their congregations based on the erroneous assumption that truth for its own sake is neither relevant nor practical. Rather than theology coming from

God's Word, a democratized faith has developed in which each man's intuitions are granted equal value, extending a presumption of common wisdom to all. Like modern politicians, the best pollster today makes the best pastor, one who trims his preaching to fit the popularly held ideas of his audience rather than truth expressed in the text.[30] It is time for both pulpit and pew to have an understanding of the Faith rooted in an historical, contextual, grammatical, theologically accurate understanding of the specific biblical text and to correlate that truth with every other truth God has revealed in His Word. A strong revival of doctrinal instruction and preaching is necessary to cure the cancer that is eating away the paper-thin piety that passes for godliness today. In the absence of such a revival, our churches will continue to move toward an entertainment format which will result in losing the "reached" rather than reaching the lost.

The Scriptures Convict by Exposing Incorrect Belief

Paul's unique choice of words ($\dot{\varepsilon}\lambda\varepsilon\gamma\mu\grave{o}\nu$) which occurs only here in the NT has the sense of "reproof" or "rebuke" (2 Tim. 3:16b). In other words, a correct apprehension of Scripture refutes error. Paul expresses the identical concept in 2 Timothy 4:2, "Preach the word; be instant in season, out of season; reprove, rebuke, exhort with all longsuffering and doctrine."

Erroneous views of doctrine have developed into sharp, sometimes divisive controversies which in turn have led to emotional, acrimonious exchanges and unnecessary polarization. In bibliology, for example, there exists a wide spectrum of views regarding the King James Version. Some believe the heresy that the *King James translation itself* is *directly* inspired by God, and that it can be used to correct the Greek text when necessary. Others erroneously claim superiority for the *Textus Receptus* as a doctrine which must be believed by faith. And some cling by faith, not to an inspired translation as such, but to a *God-protected* text type such as the Byzantine or Majority text. Fundamentally, the solution reverts back to a correct apprehension of the doctrine of bibliology in order to understand precisely *what* was "God-breathed" when the Holy Spirit gave the Scriptures.

Another prevalent error regarding bibliology is the tendency to replace objective biblical truth with an unbiblical reliance upon personal experience as our spiritual authority. According to George Gallup, the current generation of Christians, instead of looking to the Bible, is seeking for direct communication by the Holy Spirit.[31] This accounts for an increase in "revelations" rather than genuine interest in God's recorded special revelation. Certainly this phenomenon occurs in charismatic circles. It also occurs in non-charismatic circles by use of careless cliches such as "God spoke to me," "The Lord told me," and so on. In fairness, many who utilize this terminology are speaking innocently concerning what the Lord is accomplishing in their lives. Nevertheless, the implications of this homespun theology diminish faith in the literal truth of the Bible. If God literally did "speak" to an individual Christian, then what He said would logically carry equal authority with the Bible as new revelation. Some even claim to receive a "special word" from the Holy Spirit in the interpretation of biblical passages. The effect of these "illuminations" essentially displaces the authority of the objective meaning of Scripture as determined by sound methods of exegesis and replaces it with a subjective inner experience.

Perhaps this yearning for the experiential in contrast to understanding His revealed truth sheds some light on the general decline in Bible reading in recent decades. The declining interest in the Bible as a *written document* is a popular trend. The 1991 Barna report compared the responses of 18–25 year olds with those 65 years old and above to several questions. First, both groups agreed in similar numbers with the statement, "The Bible is the written Word of God and is totally accurate in all it teaches."[32] When one examines actual practice with respect to the Bible, however, significant differences begin to appear. For example, when asked whether they had read the Bible one time within the preceding seven days, 61% of the senior citizens said yes. The percentage, however, declined with each succeeding age group: 52% of those age 55–64 to 32% of those 18–25. When asked whether they read the Bible on a daily basis, 31% of the senior citizens said yes; only 4% of the younger generation (18–25) responded affirmatively.[33] Barna conducted the same survey one year later, and the results indicated an even greater decline in Bible reading.

If Bible reading further declines in the years ahead, what authority will people rely upon for matters of faith and practice? More than likely they will rely on personal experience, secular ideology, pop psychology, or at best, church services. In light of the increasing biblical illiteracy in our culture and churches, the responsibility to include sound biblical content, interpretation, and application in preaching is greater now than it was in a more biblically literate culture. Yet the trend is toward skits and rock music in lieu of preaching and teaching. To the extent that people rely upon the presentation, whatever form it may take, it will be the functional authority. Eventually, dilution of belief in the authority of the Bible is inevitable.

It is one thing to read the Bible; it is quite another matter to interpret it correctly. One cannot "reprove" without proper interpretation and application. In 1937 Henry Cadbury wrote a book entitled *The Peril of Modernizing Jesus*. Twelve years later he produced a sequel in the form of a journal article entitled "The Peril of Archaizing Ourselves."[34] These titles taken together illustrate the twin-dangers of modernism and isolationism. A *true* biblicist avoids both dangers by retaining the distinctive message of the Bible according to the intent of its author (authorial intent) while relating that message to the present world. The Bible can never mean today what it never meant yesterday. What Paul wrote in Romans, God wrote. What God meant in Romans, Paul meant. Otherwise, every passage could possibly mean two different things at the same time, essentially destroying the authority of Scripture. If a passage can literally have two *different* meanings simultaneously, then why not three or four meanings? Believers can legitimately disagree as to what a passage means, but none can logically disagree with the truth that the Scriptures should mean today what they meant when they were written. If not, then the interpreter has essentially banished the author from his own thoughts and words.

Furthermore, careful attention must be given to discern between descriptive truth and prescriptive truth when interpreting Scripture. Not everything God's Word describes is intended as a prescription for life. Numerous examples could be given. Methods of childbirth (midwives), betrothal in marriage, the acquiring of concubines, and other such matters simply provide the setting of the message in the Bible. Context, the overall message of Scripture, the analogy of Faith, plus specific commands and principles help distinguish the descriptive elements from the prescriptive ones. God has progressively revealed His truth through successive stages which provide a staircase effect of one truth building upon another. These truths, principles, and commands carry forward the progressive unfolding of God's dispensational program with regard to both Israel and the Church. Truths and commands that are rooted in the unchanging character of God and the created order are not confined to one stage of God's program, particularly when they are repeated or adjusted for the Church in the New Testament age. Application, on the other hand, compares the unchanging truth with the ever-changing world. The universality of Scripture must be maintained unless the Bible itself treats it as limited. The greater the parallel that exists between the current situation and the biblical text, the greater the authority there is in the application.

Pragmatism in the ministry also tends to redefine the message of Scripture by virtue of the results produced. "What works," the most vital concern to modern pragmatists, becomes the ultimate guide in ministry. Pragmatists, consequently, nullify the authority of Scripture through "Jesuit casuistry"—the end justifies the means. Usually, the alteration of the message occurs subtly by emphasizing obscure elements in Scripture and minimizing obvious truths such as the holiness of God. While the Bible lays out a basic methodology in ministry of assembly, prayer, worship, preaching, teaching, witnessing, and serving, it also specifies significant principles governing how these activities are to be done. In the current church growth movement and mission techniques, scriptural methods and principles are being displaced by pragmatic considerations. Rather than going to the Bible, many "ministries" draw primarily on the behavioral sciences instead of biblical truth.[35]

This increasing pragmatism in both Evangelical and Fundamental churches can be seen in the current hymnody emerging out of the cacophony of Contemporary Christian Music (CCM), resulting in the diminishment of biblical truth. The New Testament local church must teach and admonish with psalms, hymns, and spiritual songs as a result of being richly indwelt with the Word of God (Eph. 5:18–20; Col. 3:16). After all, when people leave the church service, they are humming the songs not the sermon. Believers are indoctrinated through the hymnal as well as the pulpit. Unfortunately, many Christian songs are chosen on the basis of how they make one feel as opposed to what they teach. Pay careful attention to the doctrinal affirmations and omissions of what Christians sing today, and one will ascertain not only what people currently believe, but more importantly what they *will* believe.

The direction of today's theology can be seen in some popular chorus books. Overall there is a narrowing conception of God as revealed in the Scriptures. In the popular songs of today's church one finds a diminishment of God's holiness, righteousness, and His demands upon His people. Virtually nothing about the idea of divine judgment, repentance, confession of sin, and the need for cleansing is mentioned, much less emphasized. The sense of sinfulness, unworthiness, and guilt is seemingly absent from today's positive worship. Instead, there is a considerable emphasis on intimacy between the believer and God, suggesting moral continuity rather than discontinuity between God and His creatures.

The modern pop music of the CCM movement, with its trickle down effect into the Fundamentalist environment, often preaches a *moral immanence*[36] between the creature and the Creator. The signs are obvious: celebration replaces meditation; praise choruses supplant doctrinal hymns; sloppy attire is purposely worn instead of respectful clothing. Ultimately, one sees a "detheologized" view of the Lord Jesus Christ, an overemphasis on His humanity, and a de-emphasis of His deity and authority.[37] As long as He is the friend and helper who fills human needs, Christians will worship the Son of God with a "Jesus is my boyfriend" demeanor and lyric. A generation from now when large portions of "believers" begin to question either in belief or practice the Lordship, deity, and atoning death of Christ, the "theological mush" of the CCM movement will carry some of the responsibility. One can only hope that this continuous detheologizing of the Christian salvation experience will soon reveal its shallowness for what it is. Only then will a renewed emphasis upon doctrinal preaching and biblical evangelism which calls sinners to a true conversion motivate believers to reverentially express their faith with songs delineating the full spectrum of biblical truth.

If the Gospel *message* (truth) is to be preserved along with the *text* (words), pastors must continually clarify both in song and sermon exactly what the essence of saving faith is. The heart of the matter is a true understanding of saving faith whereby the convicted sinner receives the Lord Jesus Christ with repentant faith *via* a complete reliance upon His finished cross work that precludes all vestiges of self-help. Emphasizing the preservation of the text to the exclusion of the message misses the entire point. If doctrinal truths remain only on the written page and are not thundered from Christian pulpits, the text will be preserved, but the truth will be lost.

The Scriptures Correct by Exposing Aberrant Behavior

"Correction" (ἐπανὸρθωσιν, 2 Tim. 3:16c) is used in the sense of "setting something right," most likely with reference to conduct as it was sometimes used in extra biblical literature.[38] God's Word has the authority to regulate personal and public conduct.

Attitudes and behavior among "Christian" young people toward things once considered wrong and sinful are gradually changing. There has been a noticeable shift in attitudes toward smoking, drinking alcoholic beverages, objectionable Hollywood movies, questionable entertainment, rock-music, modern dancing, gambling, romantic physical involvement outside of marriage, androgyny,[39] and public immodesty. James Hunter in *Evangelicalism: The Coming Generation* considers certain aspects of this shift as "moral reposturing."[40] Generally speaking, there has been a decline in personal separation from the world in Evangelical colleges and universities, among Evangelical preachers and leaders, and even among everyday Christians. Richard Quebedeaux, a self-professed new-evangelical, admits in *The Worldly Evangelicals* that "Evangelicals are making more and more compromises with the larger culture." He adds that "Evangelicals have become harder and harder to distinguish from other people" pointing out that Christian "business people, professionals, and celebrities have found it necessary (and pleasant) to travel the cocktail-party circuit in Beverly Hills." Finally, he mentions with approval that "Evangelicals have often discovered the pleasure of alcohol and tobacco while studying and traveling in Europe."[41] The status of these traditional taboos has undergone alteration in Christian circles. They are regarded less as sins that displease God and are described only in terms related to their dysfunctional or unwise character. In some respects Fundamentalism lags about ten to fifteen years behind such Evangelical trends.

What has contributed to this decline? I suggest that a lack of commitment to the doctrinal and ethical message in the Scriptures carries much of the responsibility. Christian pulpits and educational institutions have retreated from the position where God *judges* the unrepentant sinner and the sin, to loving the sinner and hating the sin, to loving the sinner and condoning the sin.[42] The absence of doctrinal, authoritative preaching on sin and the complete depravity of fallen humanity has hastened the moral decline in both Western culture and individual Christians. In 1991 a survey of non-Christians and professing born-again Christians revealed a striking ignorance regarding the biblical understanding of sin. The respondents were asked whether or not they agreed with the following affirmation, "People are basically good." As one would expect, 83% of the non-believers agreed with that statement. Shockingly, 77% of the "believers" agreed with it[43]—people may sin, but perhaps they are not sinners after all!

A "dysfunctional" view of sin has also revamped preaching and evangelistic strategy. Words like "sin," "guilt," and "wickedness" are being replaced with euphemisms such as "mistake," "estrangement," "maladjustment," "indiscretion," or "imprudence." "Sin," in today's religious world, is no longer against God, but against oneself. Selfishness, rather than being the essence of all sin, has become the goal of redemption. Ministers appeal to self-interest in their preaching because they know that self is what really motivates people. Human-need now beckons the unfulfilled to receive "wholeness" at the foot of the cross. How, one may ask, can anyone actually repent in such an environment? The regression is from the biblical position which says, "I'm *not* O.K., you're *not* O.K.," to the popular notion of the seventies, "I'm O.K., you're O.K.," culminating in the current self-esteem craze, "I'm O.K., I'm O.K."—a kind of schizophrenic Pelagianism.[44] Consequently, sin has not been a popular subject for Christian authors or pastors. A virtual paucity on the subject exists today.[45]

The Scriptures correct these popular misconceptions regarding sin by exposing the extent that human nature has been spoiled and impeded by the effects of sin. Sin is any lack of conformity to the moral law and character of God, either in act, disposition or state (Rom. 5:12–14; 7:22–23; James 4:11–12). Sin is called an act (Rom 7:19), a disposition (Jer. 17:9; Ps. 51:5; Rom. 7:8–10, 17), a conscious or subconscious thought (Matt. 5:27–28; 15:19), an affection (Exod. 20:17; 1 John 2:15–17), an omission (James 4:17), an involuntary act (Luke 12:48; 2 Pet 3:5) or any combination of these. Personal, individual sin originates from the human heart (Mark 7:21–23; James 1:14) and is rooted in selfishness and autonomy (Isa. 14:12–14; 2 Thess. 2:3–4; Deut. 6:4–5). Adam's first sin, the one sin of the one man, comprehended the whole human race. Depravity, condemnation, and death resulted. Depravity is total in that it has penetrated and affected the entire race of human beings (Gal. 3:22; Rom. 3:10; Ps. 4:1–3; 1 Kings 8:46) and the whole of man's being (Isa 1:6; Eph 4:17–19). Depravity has affected (1) man's body, resulting in entropy[46] and death (Rom. 8:10; Eph. 4:19); (2) man's mind in that he refuses to think God's thoughts after Him (Titus 1:15; Rom. 8:5–7; 1 Cor. 2:14); (3) and man's will as revealed by his rebellion and stubbornness in disobeying the Word of God•(John 8:34; Jer. 13:23). All of these result in a depraved and wicked heart (Jer. 17:9). Human beings, therefore, have the native capability of committing the most vile sins (Rom. 1:18ff; 3:10–18). When an unregenerate man does a "good deed" *via* common grace (Gen. 6:3; Rom. 2:14–15; Matt. 7:11), it is for selfish purposes and not for God's glory (Isa. 64:6; Matt. 6:5; Prov. 21:4). Thus, man has no possible means of salvation or recovery within himself and is utterly incapable of meriting God's favor or contributing to his salvation (Matt. 19:25–26; Rom. 1:18; 7:18; Eph. 2:1, 8; Titus 3:5; Heb. 12:2).

The necessary doctrinal implications emanating from a biblical view of sin are often muzzled by an erroneous theology that is quite prevalent in some circles. The grace of God and the Gospel message are misrepresented in regard to repentance and the volitional aspect in saving faith. Leading advocates contend that repentance of sin is not needed for one to be saved. Such an understanding of saving faith is void of a change in the human will in regard to one's sin and following the Savior.

Fidelity to a particular text type or translation does not erase infidelity regarding the Gospel message. The doctrine of salvation by grace does not negate the fallen human condition. A message that man's will is universally "free" from the effects of sin and that he is searching for God misrepresents the Gospel and ignores the biblical demand for genuine repentance and a transformed life through the miracle of the new birth. It is hard to imagine a greater distortion of the preserved message of Scripture. Man will never bow his knee to Jesus Christ apart from a work of saving grace that transforms the human heart (Matt. 13:8, 23; John 3:1–16; 1 John 5:1). If people are invited to accept Jesus Christ just to have their needs met, it will be difficult, if not impossible, to expect something more of them later.

Preaching that ignores repentance of sin in the Gospel or "dumbs down" the volitional aspect of saving faith will supplant the Gospel of supernatural transformation. As a result, the basic constituency of the church will be compromised, culminating in a deterioration of the quality of church life and Christian service to mere externalism (eccentric emphasis on rules) or libertinism (e.g., "Christian" rock concerts, night clubs, sensual dancing, abandonment of dress and music standards, etc.). The Evangelical and Fundamental landscapes are strewn with the wreckage of churches and church members who have succumbed to a diluted and inevitably, a deleted message. At some point faithful ministers of the Gospel must recognize the need for speaking out against sin and proclaiming the absolute necessity for the miraculous work of *regenerating grace* in every believer. It is the worst kind of hypocrisy to insist on the exclusive usage of a particular translation of the Bible such as the King James Version or another conservative translation while simultaneously ignoring or adulterating its theological message.

The Scriptures Counsel by Establishing Correct Behavior

Finally, God's Word "trains" or "disciplines in righteousness" (πρός παιδεὶαν τὴν ἐν δικαιοσὺνῃ, 2 Tim. 3:16d). The training is designed to produce conduct whereby "righteousness" (δικαιοσὺνῃ) becomes a reality in the life of the believer. Holiness literally means "to cut," "to separate," or to be "set apart" as sacred by God's presence.[47] Holiness refers to the majestic transcendence of God by emphasizing the distinction between the Creator and the creature. Second, it means that God is separate in His being from all that is evil, impure, and defiled.

Righteousness relates to God's holiness in that it corresponds to God's purity. Righteousness entails moral integrity of action and disposition according to God's perfect standard of holiness. The term is used here in the simple sense of "right conduct" (1 Tim. 6:11; 2 Tim. 2:22; Rom. 6:13; 9:20a). Such training or discipline is designed to bring one's behavior into conformity to God's holiness.

Generally, God's love is emphasized today in Evangelical circles much more than His holiness and righteousness. God is love (1 John 4:7–16). Nevertheless, God's love is governed by His holiness; otherwise, His love would be reduced to capricious sentimentality. God's holiness necessitates His judicial wrath against that which is opposed to His character and commands. Psalm 97:10 says, "Ye that love the Lord, hate evil . . . ." God hates "every false way" (Ps. 119:104), "vain thoughts" contrary to His Law (Ps. 119:113), "lying" (Ps. 119:163), "a proud look," "wicked imaginations," and factious men who are heretical schismatics (Prov. 6:17–19; 1 Cor. 3:17). God "hates all workers of iniquity" (Ps. 5:5). The Psalmist, himself, says that he "hated the congregation of evildoers" (Ps. 26:5). The dictates of biblical separation and conformity to Christ can be summarized in Romans 12:9, "Abhor that which is evil; cleave to that which is good;" "Hate the evil, and love the good" (Amos 5:15); "And let none of you imagine evil in your hearts . . . for all these are things that I hate, saith the LORD" (Zech. 8:17).

Scripture has much counsel regarding the righteousness so desperately lacking in His Church today. There seems to be a significant ignorance as to the theological and practical aspects of worldliness among professing Christians. This is true in some churches no matter what translation they use. Churches and schools will herald their favorite translation of the Bible all the while they are departing from a faithful practice of righteous living in personal or ecclesiastical separation. The apostle John addresses this issue in his first epistle. In the context of 1 John, the beloved disciple distinguishes between those who know God and those who do not. Those who love God keep His Word (1 John 2:5), love other true believers in Christ, manifest the fruit of regeneration (1 John 2:10), and subsequently do not love the world (1 John 2:15). False teachers, who erroneously claim to be true disciples of the Lord Jesus Christ, cannot pass the objective standards evidencing true belief and repentance. They do not genuinely confess their sins, receive Christ as Lord and Savior, love the brethren, or evidence an increasing pattern of righteousness and a decreasing pattern of sin (1 John 2:1–4). Instead, Christian charlatans and false teachers love the world's system. Scriptural warnings not to love the world serve a twofold purpose for NT churches: (1) They eventually expose those who only profess to know Christ, but actually have *never known* Him. (2) They are the God-ordained means by which true believers continue in belief and behavior, evidencing that they are the true children of God who could never be plucked from the Father's hand.

What in the world is the world? "World" (κὸσμος) is mentioned six times in 1 John 2:15–17. The "world" in this context refers to a system or network of ideas, activities, and purposes. In this sense the world is an organized system of evil ordered against God at every point. Paul says, "the world by wisdom knew not God" (1 Cor. 1:21). He speaks of the "princes of this world" who crucified the Lord of Glory (1 Cor. 2:8). James declares that "friendship" with the world is the height of infidelity with God (James 4:4). God tells His people plainly, "Love not the world" (1 John 2:15), "have no fellowship with the unfruitful works of darkness" (Eph. 5:11), and "be not conformed to this world" (Rom. 12:2). The world is at total cross-purposes with God, because it is "not of the Father."

The term *kosmos* (world) emphasizes the *present*, meaning the present arrangement of things. The world is the current, secular mind-set with its ever-changing values, symbols, goals, and priorities. It always emphasizes the "now." Thus, the world is transient, always on the move, and "passing away." It believes in "change" for its own sake and the "becomingness" of all things. As such, the world is humanistic, being structured by autonomous man and his "I'm worth it" philosophy. It consists of the desires of modern man's sinful, fleshly, and prideful nature, his self-esteem and self-fulfillment

353

syndrome. Worldliness includes both those outward activities and inward affections for and attachment to some aspect of the present arrangement of things. This includes the world's thought patterns, amusements, fads, habits, philosophies, goals, friendships, practices, and lifestyles.

1 John 2:15–17 enumerates three aspects of the world that is conditioned by fallen humanity. First, John characterizes the world and its current age as the "lust of the flesh." Grammarians describe this expression as a subjective genitive. "Flesh" operates as the subject and the term "lust" acts as the verb. John is speaking of the flesh's passionate desires. The "flesh" is a complex of sinful attributes that comprises the sinful nature.

How does the believer combat worldliness in regard to the intellectual, volitional, and emotional aspects of this complex of sinful attributes called the flesh? First, Paul says, "make no provision for the flesh to fulfill the lusts thereof" (Rom. 13:14). The word "provision" ($\pi\rho\grave{o}voi\alpha v$) carries the idea of "forethought" which literally means "to have a mind before." The apostle commands believers not to use their intellect sinfully in order to discover various ways to fulfill the desires of the flesh. A man must yield to the Spirit of God and refuse to exercise a fleshly intellect by making forethought to sin.

In addition, believers are admonished to "cleanse ourselves from all filthiness of the flesh and spirit, perfecting holiness in the fear of God" (2 Cor. 7:1). Contextually, Paul is concerned with the influence of other people who are succumbing to fleshly activity (2 Cor. 6:14–7:2). In this case, believers are not to enter into a spiritual yoke or union with those whose lives are characterized by the fleshly nature. This principle carries over even into non-religious relationships to a lesser degree. One is in the world, but not of it. Believers are not to disassociate themselves altogether from sinners in this world. The goal of relationships with the unregenerate is the salvation of the lost, "plucking" them as branches from the fire, "hating even the garment spotted by the flesh" (Jude 1:23). Yet one must not enter into a yoke where it would be impossible to avoid being negatively influenced and having one's "temple" defiled.

Finally, the people of God are not to abuse or misuse their liberty in Christ as an occasion to fulfill the works of the flesh (Gal. 5:13). In this present age believers are not under the Mosaic Law as a governing constitution for the New Testament local church. However, every command and principle rooted in the unchanging character of God, the created order, and repeated or adjusted in the NT carries over into each new, succeeding dispensation. In this sense, the Law of Moses remains a corroborative witness to the will of God for believers in the NT church age. Paul's concern here is that believers not abuse their new standing in Christ by using the grace of God as a cloak for sinful, fleshly behavior. Paul revolted against such perverted thinking. Freedom from the Mosaic Law does not imply freedom from laws, commands, principles, precepts, directives, prohibitions, or standards.

Second, John mentions "the lust of the eyes" as an integral part of "all that is in the world." This entails the sinful cravings and desires stimulated by what is seen. The grammatical construction could be considered a genitive of means, namely that the eyes are the means by which sinful desires are stimulated. Fleshly lusts are aroused by that which enters the mind by means of the senses. In a day of billboard advertising, movie and television screens, and eye-catching magazine spreads, this aspect of the world is predominant. The world is filled with men who are exercising their fallen nature willfully, mentally, and emotionally. Others are looking upon the experiences, accomplishments, and creations of men exercising their fallen nature, and through their senses they are being enticed (James 1:14–15).

Third, and perhaps the most insidious of all, John describes the world as characterized by the "pride of life." There is a devilish progression from what one wants to what one has and boastfully displays. "Pride" parades the spirit of the "braggart" who extols his own virtues and possessions. The genitive "of life" ($\tau o\tilde{u}$ $\beta\acute{\iota}ou$) portrays an attitude of boastfulness and hollow self-exaltation. The goal of these fleshly desires is the celebration of earthly life in its possessions, achievements, indulgences, and self-promotion. Ultimately, John refers to men whose lives are filled with the self-congratulation of an independent life resting in self-sufficiency. Most of the bragging does not occur in an outward and obvious manner. Rather, it is the making and maintaining of an image that the world approves. Wherever there is this arrogance of lifestyle, this image that "all is well and prosperous with my life without God," there is "the pride of life."

The world will hear any minister who *speaks of the world*: "They are of the world: therefore speak they of the world, and the world heareth them" (1 John 4:5). This occurs in compromising pulpits, Christian rock concerts, and nearly everywhere that professing believers endeavor to blend with the world, rather than confront the world with God's truth and a biblical lifestyle. If a church, for instance, appeals to men's baser motives and creates a congregation made up of people dominated by self-interest, then that is a worldly church.

How does one recognize a church that is not speaking in such a way that the world approves of them? Is the atmosphere of that church conditioned by truth and obedience? Are the people serious about their Christian lives? Are they willing to set aside their selfish interests? Are their appeals designed to appease fallen human nature? This is how we are to evaluate a Christian ministry, not primarily by their exclusive allegiance to one text type or translation. Such a criterion is an insult to the Word of God itself.

How does one obey God's command not to love the world? By the "renewing of the mind" in the Word of God. This renewing of the mind is evidenced by the choices that "people of the Faith" make every day. By faith believers seek God's will through the Word of God in every decision (James 4:15). By faith believers reject worldly wisdom (1 Cor. 3:18).

Specific directives for personal separation from worldly attitudes and actions include the moral commands, precepts, and directives of God's Word (Exod. 20:1–17; 1 Cor. 5:9–13; 6:9–10; Gal. 5:16–21; Eph. 5:1–7; 2 Tim. 3:1–5). In addition, God lays down numerous principles by which believers are to make wise decisions regarding their behavior in the world:

1. The principle of enslavement (self-control)

   (1 Cor. 6:12) **"All things are lawful unto me** (Corinthian slogan of antinomianism[48]), but all things are not expedient: all things are lawful for me, **but I will not be brought under the power of any**."

   (1 Cor. 9:27) **"But I keep under my body, and bring it into subjection . . . ."**

2. The principle of offense

   (Rom. 14:13–16) "Let us not therefore judge one another any more: but judge this rather, that **no man put a stumbling block or an occasion to fall in his brother's way** . . . . {16} **Let not then your good be evil spoken of:"**

   (1 Cor. 10:32) **"Give none offence, neither to the Jews, nor to the Gentiles, nor to the church of God . . . ."**

3. The principle of God's glory

   (1 Cor. 6:20) "For ye are bought with a price: therefore **glorify God in your body, and in your spirit, which are God's.**"

4. The principle of a biblically educated conscience

   (Rom. 14:23) "And he that doubteth is damned if he eat, because he eateth not of faith: **for whatsoever is not of faith is sin.**"

5. The principle of Christ's name (authority)

(Col 3:17) "And whatsoever ye do in word or deed, **do all in the name of the Lord Jesus**, giving thanks to God and the Father by him."

6. The principle of corruption by association

(1 Cor. 15:33) "Be not deceived: **evil communications corrupt good manners**."

7. The principle of peace in the Body of Christ

(Col. 3:15) "**And let the peace of God rule in your hearts**, to the which also ye are called in one body; and be ye thankful."

8. The principle of edification

(Rom. 15:1–2) "We then that are strong ought to bear the infirmities of the weak, and not to please ourselves. {2} **Let every one of us please his neighbour for his good to edification**."

In summary, separation from the world grows out of the very character of God and His exclusive right to first place in all things; it is an expression of God's eternal holiness (Isa. 6:1–3). God could demand no other behavior in this regard and be consistent with Himself. God's holiness is His "apartness" or separation from all that is sinful, unclean, or profane, and His holiness regulates or qualifies all of His other moral attributes (Exod. 5:11; Isa. 6:1–11). Therefore, He demands that all people who name the name of Christ be like Him in character and conduct (Matt. 5:48; 1 John 2:1–4). It remains the responsibility of every believer and Christian organization not to compromise His character by any association or endeavor, attitude or attempt, that breaks down the absolute distinction between righteousness and sin, God's people and Satan's people, "day people" and "night people" (1 Thess. 5:1–11), obedient Christians and disobedient Christians, light and darkness, truth and error, right and wrong, or good and evil.

CONCLUSION

The Bible is fully sufficient for the salvation of man and the development of the believer into full maturity (2 Tim. 3:16–17). God's purpose is that the "man of God" be complete and sufficiently capable to meet all the demands placed upon him by his heavenly Father. The phrase "man of God" applies to Christians in general and to church leaders in particular. Scripture is given for the purpose of enabling all believers through the Spirit to meet the demands that God places on them. Through the assimilated Word of God, each believer in Christ is "fully equipped" by the Holy Spirit to do every kind of good work. God has ordained believers unto good works and calls on them to do good works (Eph. 2:10; Titus 3:1). God has given the Scriptures to instruct believers so that they may know either in precept or in principle what God expects them to believe and how God expects them to behave.

For those in vocational ministry, the magnificent truths in the Bible ought to motivate each "man of God" to preach the Word of God expositionally according to the original intention of the biblical writers and honestly apply the Word to the world believers live in today. Many churches are in poor health because they feed on junk food, artificial preservatives, and unnatural substitutes, instead of the milk and meat of the Word. Consequently, a worldwide spiritual famine has resulted from the absence of any genuine proclamation of the Word of God (Amos 8:11)—an absence which continues to run wild and almost unabated in most quarters of the Church. Unless there is a serious correction in the understanding of bibliology, hermeneutics, and homiletics, the NT Church of the Lord Jesus Christ will suffer increasingly from hazy preaching, muddled heads, fretful hearts, and paralyzing uncertainty. As my systematic theology professor often said, "A mist in the pulpit usually results with a fog in the pew."[49]

On the other hand, *the minister of the Gospel who possesses the true conviction of Scripture's origin, inspiration, inerrancy, certainty, significance, and preservation will submissively place himself under the Word of God, not over it, and deliver its message rather than his own in order to produce mature, fully equipped, Christ-like disciples for the honor and glory of God.* **Only then is the true purpose of the preservation of God's inspired revelation accomplished.**

---

[1] Hedonism is the philosophical view that pleasure or personal satisfaction is the chief good in life. It is manifested in the contemporary attitude prevalent in society, "If it feels good do it. Self-satisfaction is the goal in life." It is displayed in some so-called worship services by unrestrained emotional and physical release.

[2] Jill Morgan, *A Man of the Word: Life of G. Campbell Morgan* (Grand Rapids: Baker Book House, 1978), p. 10.

[3] "Exegetical" refers to the contextual, grammatical, historical, and theological interpretation of a particular passage of Scripture. "Systematic" refers to the harmonizing of exegetical conclusions with the totality of Scriptural truth—sometimes called the "analogy of Faith."

[4]Stewart Custer, *Does Inspiration Demand Inerrancy*? (Nutley, NJ: Craig Press, 1981), p. 10.

[5]Benjamin Breckinridge Warfield, *The Inspiration and Authority of the Bible*, ed. Samuel G. Craig (Phillipsburg, NJ: Presbyterian and Reformed Pub. Co., 1948), p. 131.

[6]Ralph Earle, "2 Timothy," *The Expositor's Bible Commentary*, 12 vols., ed. Frank E. Gaebelein (Grand Rapids: Zondervan, 1978), 11:409.

[7]A. T. Robertson, *A Grammar of the Greek New Testament in the Light of Historical Research*, 3rd ed. (Nashville: Broadman, 1931), p. 772.

[8]Walter Bauer, William F. Arndt, and F. Wilbur Gingrich, *A Greek-English Lexicon of the New Testament and Other Early Christian Literature*, 2nd ed. revised and augmented by F. Wilbur Gingrich and Frederick W. Danker (Chicago: University of Chicago Press, 1979), p. 165 (hereafter cited as BAGD).

[9]Warfield, *Inspiration and Authority of the Bible*, p. 348. Also, see pp. 299–318 for additional evidence of the interchange between "God" and "Scripture."

[10]The apostles considered the other NT authors of Scripture as equally authoritative as the words of Christ and the OT. For example, in 1 Timothy 5:18 Paul initially quotes Deuteronomy 25:4, "Thou shalt not muzzle the ox when he treadeth out the corn." Paul continues by quoting the Lord's words as recorded by Luke, "for the labourer is worthy of his hire" (1 Tim. 5:18 cf. Luke 10:7). Both "Scriptures" are joined together with a simple conjunction in 1 Timothy 5:18 and are placed together with *equal authority*. This example indicates that Luke's Gospel was already available to Paul in written form, and that it was regarded by the apostle as sacred Scripture.

[11]D. Edmund Hiebert, *Second Peter and Jude: An Expositional Commentary* (Greenville, SC: 1989), p. 175.

[12]Charles Hodge, *Systematic Theology*, 3 vols. (Grand Rapids: Eerdmans, 1977), 1:154.

[13]*Confluence* refers to the dual nature of the written Word of God. The Scriptures were penned by human authors in normal human language, demonstrating all the necessary aspects of human personality. Yet, at the very same time, those thoughts and words were breathed out by God the Holy Spirit Who miraculously superintended the writers of Scripture so that what they wrote was the God-breathed, inerrant, infallible, inscripturated sixty-six canonical books of the Bible. Confluence ultimately affirms one author with two aspects involving the human vehicle and the divine message.

[14]BAGD, pp. 685–86; Warfield, *"Inspiration and Authority of the Bible,"* p. 284.

[15]*Evangelical Dictionary of Theology*, s.v. "Inspiration," by C. F. Henry, ed. Walter A. Elwell, p. 145; *Theological Dictionary of the New Testament*, 1 vol. edition, s.v. "θεόπνευστος," by E. Schweizer, pp. 894–95; *International Standard Bible Encyclopedia*, s.v. "Inspiration," by B. B. Warfield, 3:1474.

[16]Warfield lists eighty-six compounds of this type and concludes that "at least seventy-five reflect quite simply the sense of a result produced by God" (Warfield, *Inspiration and Authority of the Bible*, pp. 272, 281–82).

[17]Ibid.

[18]*Vine's Expository Dictionary of Old and New Testament Words*, s.v. "Inspiration," by W. E. Vine, ed. F. F. Bruce (Old Tappan, NJ: Fleming H. Revell Co., n.d.), p. 262.

[19] Newport White, "2 Timothy" in *The Expositor's Greek New Testament*, 5 vols., ed. W. Robertson Nicoll (Grand Rapids: Eerdmans, 1967), 4:175.

[20] Warfield, *Inspiration and Authority of the Bible*, p. 134.

[21] All Scripture is special revelation. All special revelation, however, has not been inscripturated (Deut. 29:29; John 21:25 cf. Exod. 5:2 and 6:1; Rev. 10:1–4; Dan. 12:4, 9).

[22] Edward J. Young, *Thy Word is Truth* (Grand Rapids: Eerdmans, 1957), p. 113.

[23] Augustus H. Strong, *Systematic Theology*, 3 vols. (Valley Forge, PA: Judson Press, 1907), 1:217.

[24] The "universe" is defined as *all that is not God,* including everything involved in this time-space-mass continuum.

[25]The verb "search" can be translated either in the imperative or the indicative (The KJV translates this as imperative). The indicative makes better sense in the context. Here Christ is condemning the Pharisees for their supposed allegiance to the Scriptures while simultaneously rejecting the Lordship and deity of Christ.

[26] On rare occasions, ancient translations such as the Septuagint et. al. have contributed to our knowledge of the autographic text when resolving an apparent *copyist's* error. For example, in 1 Samuel 13:1 the Masoretic Text states that Saul was one year of age, בֶּן־שָׁנָה — lit. "son of a year" (a Hebrew idiom meaning one year of age), when he began to reign over Israel. Some ancient *Greek* manuscripts which pre-date the Masoretic Text read "thirty years" instead of "one year," thus harmonizing 1 Samuel 13:1–2 with 1 Samuel 13:3ff; 9:2; 10:1–6 and Acts 13. The Scriptures make it clear that Saul was a full-grown adult when he was anointed King of Israel. In looking at the apparatus in our Hebrew Bible (*BHS*) as well as some additional sources, it reveals that a few manuscripts from the Lucianic Greek recension translate 1 Samuel 13:1 by stating that Saul was "thirty" when he began

to reign. The *internal evidence* for supplying "thirty" originates from Scripture passages such as 1Samuel 13:3ff; 9:2; 10:1–6 and Acts 13. On account of my theological conviction regarding the inerrancy of the autographa, I believe the original Hebrew text also reads "thirty," even though we do not currently possess a Hebrew manuscript with that reading.

[27]William W. Combs, "The Translators to the Reader: Preface to the King James Version," *Detroit Baptist Theological Seminary Journal* 2 (Fall 1996): 269–290. Often in the current translation debate, *ad hominem* arguments against one who compiles and correlates the ancient manuscripts are dishonestly used to cast unnecessary dispersions upon a Greek text, manuscript family, or translation. If such arguments were legitimate (and they are not), the textual base of the KJV itself would have to be discounted. For instance, Erasmus, the Roman Catholic editor and initial compiler of the textual base underlying the KJV, was sharply attacked for some of his comments in the *Annotationes*. Erasmus was *justly criticized* because of his heretical view of inspiration. During the time he assembled his Greek text to parallel his Latin translation, he believed that inspiration protected the biblical writers in matters of *faith only,* and not in matters of history, science, or factual accuracy. In Acts 10, for example, Erasmus states in his notes that the *original words of the apostle were in error*, reasoning that divine inspiration extended only to their thoughts, and not to their words: "It was not necessary to ascribe everything in the apostles to a miracle. They were men, they were ignorant of some things, *and they erred in a few places*" (Erika Rummel, "An Open Letter to Boorish Critics: Erasmus' *Capita argumentorum contra morosos quosdam ac indoctos,"* *Journal of Theological Studies* 39 [October 1988]: 454).

[28]A. C. Partridge, *English Biblical Translation* (London: Andre Deutch Limited, 1973), p. 111.

[29]George W. Knight III, *Commentary on the Pastoral Epistles*, New International Greek Testament Commentary (Grand Rapids: Eerdmans, 1992), p. 449.

[30]Wells, David F. No Place for Truth : Or Whatever Happened to Evangelical Theology? (Grand Rapids: Eerdmans, 1993), p. 214

[31]Walter A. Elwell, "Belief and the Bible: A Crisis of Authority?" *Christianity Today* 24/6 (March 21, 1980), pp. 91–100.

[32]Approximately 51% of the senior citizens and 46% of the 18–25 year olds affirmed the proposition.

[33]George Barna, *The Barna Report: What Americans Believe* (Ventura, CA: Regal, 1991), pp. 292–94.

[34]Erickson, Millard J. *Where is Theology Going?* (Grand Rapids: Baker Book House, 1994), p.107.

[35]David J. Hesselgrave, *Today's Choices for Tomorrow's Mission: An Evangelical Perspective on Trends and Issues in Missions* (Grand Rapids: Zondervan, 1988), pp. 138–43.

[36] "Moral immanence" is a view that places man and God in an immediate relationship, ignoring the infinite gap between God and man and the separation created by sin.

[37]Erickson, *Where Is Theology Going?*, p. 41.

[38]"Επανὸρθωσιν" is only used once in the NT (BAGD, p. 282).

[39] "Androgyny" means the removal of male and female characteristics, roles, or dress.

[40]James Davison Hunter, *Evangelicalism: The Coming Generation* (Chicago: University of Chicago Press, 1987), pp. 59–62.

[41]Richard Quebedeaux, *The Worldly Evangelicals* (San Francisco: Harper and Row, 1978), pp. 12, 14, 118.

[42]God's judicial wrath is similar to the "wrath" of the court when it pronounces sentence on a condemned criminal. Out of the infinite perfections of God's being, He is able to both love and exercise judicial wrath on the condemned sinner at the same time (John 3:16–17).

[43]Barna, *What Americans Believe*, pp. 89–91.

[44]Pelagianism, a heresy that began early in Church history, denies the depravity and *moral* inability of the human will.

[45]Erickson, *Where Is Theology Going?*, pp.150–151.

[46] "Entropy" is the physical law that recognizes the disorder, gradual degrading, decline, wearing out, and eventual death of all physical systems.

[47]Francis Brown, S. R. Driver, and Charles A. Briggs, *A Hebrew and English Lexicon of the Old Testament,* reprint ed. (Oxford: Clarendon Press, 1972), p. 871.

[48] Antinomianism (literally: against law) it the title given to the view which espouses that because believers are under grace they are not bound by the moral principles and commands of God's Word, therefore they may sin with impunity because God's grace abounds. This view is refuted in Romans 6:1–2.

[49]Class notes from Dr. Roland McCune and Dr. William Combs have been utilized in the preparation of this chapter.

BIBLIOGRAPHY

Barna, George. *The Barna Report: What Americans Believe*. Ventura, CA: Regal, 1991.

Brown, Francis, S. R. Driver, and Charles A. Briggs. *A Hebrew and English Lexicon of the Old Testament*. Reprint ed. Oxford: Clarendon Press, 1972.

Bauer, Walter, William F. Arndt, and F. Wilbur Gingrich, *A Greek-English Lexicon of the New Testament and Other Early Christian Literature*. 2nd ed. revised and augmented by F. Wilbur Gingrich and Frederick W. Danker. Chicago: University of Chicago Press, 1979.

Combs, William W. "The Translators to the Reader: Preface to the King James Version." *Detroit Baptist Theological Seminary Journal* 2 (Fall 1996): 269–90.

Custer, Stewart. *Does Inspiration Demand Inerrancy?* Nutley, NJ: Craig Press, 1981.

Earle, Ralph. "2 Timothy." In *The Expositor's Bible Commentary*. 12 vols. Edited by Frank E. Gaebelein. Grand Rapids: Zondervan, 1978.

Elwell, Walter A. "Belief and the Bible: A Crisis of Authority?" *Christianity Today*, 21 March 1980, pp. 91–100.

Henry, C. F. "Inspiration." In *Evangelical Dictionary of Theology,*. Edited by Walter A. Elwell. Grand Rapids: Baker, 1984.

Hesselgrave, David J. *Today's Choices for Tomorrow's Mission: An Evangelical Perspective on Trends and Issues in Missions*. Grand Rapids: Zondervan, 1988.

Hiebert, D. Edmund. *Second Peter and Jude: An Expositional Commentary*. Greenville, SC: Bob Jones University Press, 1989.

Hodge, Charles. *Systematic Theology*, 3 vols. Grand Rapids: Eerdmans, 1977.

Hunter, James Davison. *Evangelicalism: The Coming Generation*. Chicago: University of Chicago Press, 1987.

Knight III, George W. *Commentary on the Pastoral Epistles*. New International Greek Testament Commentary. Grand Rapids: Eerdmans, 1992.

Morgan, Jill. *A Man of the Word: Life of G. Campbell Morgan.* Grand Rapids: Baker Book House, 1978.

Partridge, A. C. *English Biblical Translation.* London: Andre Deutch Limited, 1973.

Quebedeaux, Richard. *The Worldly Evangelicals.* San Francisco: Harper and Row, 1978.

Rummel, Erika. "An Open Letter to Boorish Critics: Erasmus' *Capita argumentorum contra morosos quosdam ac indoctos," Journal of Theological Studies* 39 (October 1988): 431–456.

Robertson, A. T. *A Grammar of the Greek New Testament in the Light of Historical Research.* 3rd ed. Nashville: Broadman, 1931.

Schweizer, E. "θεόπνευστος," In *Theological Dictionary of the NewTestament*, one volume edition, Gerhard Kittel, editor. Grand Rapids: Eerdmans, 1976.

Strong, Augustus H. *Systematic Theology*, 3 vols. Valley Forge, PA: Judson Press, 1907.

Vine, W.E. *Vine's Expository Dictionary of Old and New Testament Words.* Edited by F. F. Bruce. Old Tappan, New Jersey: Fleming H. Revell Co., n.d.

Warfield, B.B, "Inspiration." In *International Standard Bible Encyclopedia,* Edited by James Orr. Grand Rapids: Eerdmans, 1939

_____. *The Inspiration and Authority of the Bible*, Samuel Craig, ed. Phillipsburg, NJ: Presbyterian and reformed Publishing Company, 1948.

White, Newport. "2 Timothy" in *The Expositor's Greek New Testament.* 5 vols. edited by W. Robertson Nicoll. Grand Rapids: Eerdmans, 1967.

Young, Edward J. *Thy Word is Truth.* Grand Rapids: Eerdmans, 1957.

WHAT THE PRESERVATION ISSUE HAS TAUGHT US

Dr. Paul W. Downey

What has the preservation issue taught us about ourselves? If nothing else, we have discovered that we don't know as much as we assumed we knew about what the Bible says and does not say about the subject. Because there seems to be some legitimate room for disagreement, we ought to permit a measure of latitude among brethren on this issue. Rather than lining up with one well-known fundamentalist or another, or even with one school of higher learning or another, it behooves Christians to make sure we line up with the Word of God.

I am deeply concerned about the strife and division that is being caused by ignorance, intemperance, pride, or fear. The dispute over Bible versions has revealed three primary problems in fundamentalism that need to be addressed. First, we need to be more careful in adopting and articulating our doctrinal positions. Second, we need to be less conceited about our place in history and in the contemporary world. Third, we need to denounce the carnality that has often been displayed in the manner in which brethren have expressed their disagreement with one another.

WE NEED TO BE MORE CAREFUL

Develop Doctrine Properly

When Moses died, Joshua was appointed by God to lead Israel in the conquest of Canaan. Joshua was following all of God's instructions. He had brought the people across the Jordan, established the memorial heap in Gilgal, and circumcised the men (himself and Caleb being the only surviving men who had been circumcised in Egypt.) While the army was recovering from their surgery, Joshua was examining the situation at Jericho, the first city they were to conquer. While he was on a hill overlooking the city, "there stood a man over against him with his sword drawn in his hand: and Joshua went unto him, and said unto him, *Art* thou for us, or for our adversaries?" (Joshua 5:13). The man, whom we discover to be the Lord, gives a classic answer. When asked if he was for Israel or for her enemies, the Lord said, "Nay." He went on to explain that He came "as captain of the host of the LORD" (5:14). The issue is never whether the Lord is on your side or your adversary's, but whether you are on the Lord's side or His adversary's.

Our doctrinal positions must not be adopted or developed to agree with or oppose a particular preacher, teacher, or school. Our doctrine must agree with Scripture. It must be based upon careful study of what the Bible says. We must not be guilty of searching through the Bible in hopes of finding a text that will *support* our positions. Rather, we must use the Bible to *inform* our positions.

Influence of Emotion

A few years ago, I attended the funeral of a young man whose sister attended our church school. The pastor conducting the service encouraged people who knew the deceased to come down to the open casket and talk to him. He said he believed that the spirit of the deceased was present in the room and would be encouraged and blessed by the kind words people would say to him, so he wanted each one to give something of his own private eulogy addressed to the deceased. He said he believed that God would want the man to hear those things. Of course, he had no biblical basis for this; he believed it simply because it made him feel good. His theology regarding the disposition of the soul following death was developed emotionally, not biblically. Most fundamentalists would be quick to recognize the dangerous error of this emotion-based doctrinal position.

But we are not always so alert. The doctrine of the preservation of the Word of God has become an emotionally charged subject, with much being written and said about it that has been more inflammatory than illuminating. A position that elevates to the level of perfection a single English version, or even a single Greek text, has its emotional appeal. It feels like a stable alternative to the measure of uncertainty involved in making textual and translation choices based on evidence, and it sounds like a defense of the Bible we have been reading, memorizing, and preaching for years. But it is neither.

Interpretation of "Proof Texts"

We have all heard messages taken from a text that did not teach what the preacher preached. Some of those may have even been eloquent and doctrinally sound, but were just taken from the wrong text. Others have drawn wrong conclusions by misinterpretation of the texts. We would call either *eisegesis*—reading into the text what isn't there—as opposed to *exegesis*—drawing out from the text what is there.

Examples abound. Consider one that bears indirectly on the versions issue. When God gave instructions through Moses concerning the future monarchy, one of the commands issued was that the king must not "multiply horses to himself" (Deut. 17:16). God wanted the king to trust God, not the military, for the nation's defense. But the kings of Israel disobeyed this command. We are told specifically that Solomon "had forty thousand stalls of horses for his *chariots* and twelve thousand horsemen" (1 Kings 4:26), representing a significant shift in national defense policy. Years ago a man who is now quite a well-known preacher delivered a message on that theme. Unfortunately, he blamed the shift on David rather than Solomon because he used 2 Samuel 8:4 as his text: "And David took from him a thousand *chariots*: and seven hundred horsemen, and twenty thousand footmen: and David houghed all the chariot *horses*, but reserved of them *for* a hundred chariots." Now this preacher may have had a point had he blamed David for keeping a hundred of the horses for his chariots, but that is not how he applied the text. He did not know that the word "houghed" meant "hamstrung" (to make the horses useless by cutting their hamstrings). He pronounced it "hogged" and interpreted it colloquially, as if David had kept all the horses—"hogged" them—for himself.

Such a careless, and sometimes cavalier, approach to handling Scripture has characterized many who now espouse the King James Bible as the only preserved Word of God. The fact that so many of our fundamentalist brethren have been caught up in this rhetoric indicates the extent of our willingness to force the Scriptures to say what we want them to mean. Granted, many passages of Scripture touch on the subject of preservation, some more directly than others. But it is impossible to find a proof text that says exactly what some want it to say concerning the Biblical text as it exists today, transmitted over the centuries and translated into many languages. If we would be faithful in our handling of the Word of God, we must let it mean exactly what it says. We must not be guilty of trying to make it mean what we think it should say.

One of the errors of those who argue for a biblical doctrine of perfect preservation in a single manuscript tradition or a single English Bible is that they often assume that "God's Word" and "Scripture" are always synonymous. William W. Combs has observed:

> A glance at a concordance or lexicon will easily demonstrate that in the Old Testament the expression "the Word of God" (or Lord) is used almost universally of oral communication.... The phrases "the word of God" or "the word of the Lord" are used twenty-one times in Acts and in every case the referent is to the apostolic message of Christ, which was delivered orally. This is the normal usage in Paul's epistles as well. For instance, when Paul describes his enemies as those who "corrupt the Word of God" (2 Cor. 2:17, KJV), he is not making reference to the Scriptures, but the gospel message.[1]

Surely, "Scripture" is always God's Word, but "the word of God" does not always refer to documents. For instance, Hebrews 11:3 says, "By faith we know that the worlds were framed by the word of God." Clearly, that is not a reference to a manuscript. Thus, many references to the durability of God's Word may well have only an indirect relationship to manuscripts.

Consider Matthew 24:35—"Heaven and earth shall pass away, but my words shall not pass away." This is a verse cited by many as a promise that not one word of the King James Bible will differ from the autographic texts of the Greek New Testament and the Hebrew Old Testament. But that is not what Jesus said. He said that His words will outlast the physical universe. Actually, the implication of this verse is that even when every copy of the Scriptures will be destroyed when heaven and earth pass away, the truth and promises contained in His words will still exist. It is unlikely that Jesus was speaking of a written document, since it would be twenty to thirty years before the earliest of the Gospels would record His words. Furthermore, to argue that all of Jesus' words were recorded conflicts with the clear testimony of the Gospels. Passages like Luke 5:3-4, 9:11, and 13:22, tell us of times that Jesus "taught the people" without recording what He said. Did those words "pass away"? Did Jesus' promise apply only to the words that were eventually recorded in the Gospels, or did it apply to all of His words? It seems that a literal understanding of Matthew 24:35 requires the conclusion that nothing Jesus ever said could pass away—all will stand forever. Even those words not written down. Making this statement refer to a document would be too limiting. Jesus actually promised that everything He said will be fulfilled, even to the destruction of heaven and earth, and nothing can prevent the fulfillment of His words.

It would go beyond the scope of this chapter to enter into detailed examinations of all of the texts used in the versions debate. The passages used to develop a doctrine of the preservation of the Bible do constitute God's guarantee of both the eternal duration and the ultimate fulfillment of His every Word. But they do not say what some want them to say. They do not promise that *all* copyists and/or translators, or any *particular* ones, will be divinely guided to reproduce the originals flawlessly. Neither is there any promise of a perfect translation of the Bible in any particular language or in any particular generation. Combs correctly asserts,

> It was sufficient for God's purpose to preserve His Word in copies of the autographs whose exact wording contains some variation....It is proper, and not any sort of deception, to speak of different printed Greek and Hebrew texts, and different translations, as the Word of God even though they have differences among them. God has preserved the Scriptures in a state of what might be called "essential purity."[2]

Inconsistent Theology

Suspending Proper Hermeneutics in Resolving Difficulties in the Text

Unfortunately, in their efforts to defend their view of perfect preservation, some who claim to be in the mainstream of historic fundamentalism have gone to great lengths trying to explain discrepancies in the Old Testament. For instance, 2 Kings 8:26 says that Ahaziah was twenty-two years old when he ascended to the throne, but 2 Chronicles 22:2 says he was forty-two. It seems obvious that they cannot both be correct. Additional information in 2 Kings 8:17 tells us that Ahaziah's father, whom he succeeded to the throne, died at age forty. Since it would be impossible for Ahaziah to be forty-two when his father was forty, we can be confident that 2 Kings 8:26 gives his correct age as twenty-two. Apparently, the age of forty-two given in 2 Chronicles 22:2 represents a transcription error.

At least one advocate of the perfect transmission of the text disagrees. Admitting that his interpretation is based on his presupposition of perfect preservation, he says, "If one comes to the Bible believing that God has kept His promise to preserve His Word, he will find wonderful lessons that are hidden from the scoffers. Ahaziah was both twenty-two and forty-two."[3]   He argues that God was so angry with Ahaziah's wicked rule, which perpetuated the sins of his father, that God began counting his age with his father's birth (in 2 Chronicles, but not 2 Kings), holding him responsible for not just twenty-two years of evil, but for the years of his father's sin before him.

Unfortunately, the math doesn't work. For Ahaziah to be considered forty-two when he was only twenty-two, God would have had to start counting two years *before* his father's birth. Further, this argument fails to notice that God expressly says He does not calculate sin that way: "The soul that sinneth, it shall die. The son shall not bear the iniquity of the father" (Ezekiel 18:20). It is dangerous to be so committed to an erroneous view of preservation that one is willing to draw conclusions that conflict with the clear teaching of Scripture to support it. Even if claiming to "start from faith," any contention that concludes that *God meant something He did not say* and that *God said something He did not mean* amounts to the very method of interpretation used by the allegorists of medieval Catholicism, which the Reformers were attempting to correct.

Those who would call discrepancies like this one "scribal errors" are not casting doubt on the Word of God. Rather, they are so committed to the inspiration and infallibility of God that such a discrepancy must be attributed to the fallibility of the copyist. But those who take the position described above are so committed to the infallibility of the scribes who copied the text and to their own infallibility to interpret the text, that they must insist the discrepancy is accurate. In defending their position on the text, they have created far more serious conflicts than the one they were attempting to resolve. They have violated the Biblical doctrine of personal responsibility for sin and have adopted a dangerous hermeneutic.

Diminishing Human Responsibility for Handling the Text

The arguments for perfect preservation in a single text also seem to come into conflict with passages such as Deuteronomy 4:2, 12:32, Proverbs 30:6, Jeremiah 26:2, and Revelation 22:18-19 that issue warnings of judgment upon those who would tamper with the Word of God by adding to it or taking from it. These warnings present us with enormous implications to the concept of preservation: 1) man is capable of adulterating the Word of God, and 2) it is man's responsibility to guard the Word of God to maintain its purity.

Deuteronomy 29:29 says, "The secret things belong unto the LORD our God: but those things which are revealed belong unto us and to our children forever, that we may do all the words of this law." Jude 3 says, "Beloved, when I gave all diligence to write unto you of the common salvation, it was needful for me to write unto you, and exhort you that ye should earnestly contend for the faith which was once delivered unto the saints." Other passages, like 1 Corinthians 11:2, Philippians 2:16, 1 Timothy 3:9 and 15, 4:16, 5:17, 6:14 and 20, 2 Timothy 1:13 and 14, 3:14, and Titus 1:9, also challenge believers to carefully remember, guard, obey, and proclaim the doctrines of the Word of God. God has revealed His Word to us. He expects us to handle it with reverence and care forever, so we can obey all of His Word. This is true whether one is copying a manuscript in the original language, translating from the original language into another, or preaching, teaching, or writing about the Word of God.

Some have charged that those who would say such a thing have denied faith in God's control in favor of a naturalistic science with man in control. But there are problems with this charge. First, this "faith vs. science" proposition adopts the false dichotomy of Kierkegaard's "I believe it because it is absurd." But faith and science are not mutually exclusive. God provided evidence for everything He challenges us to believe. An obvious example is in the account of Jesus' resurrection.

> And the angel answered and said unto the women, Fear not ye: for I know that ye seek Jesus, which was crucified. He is not here: for he is risen, as he said. **Come, see the place where the Lord lay**. And go quickly, and tell his disciples that he is risen from the dead; and,

behold, he goeth before you into Galilee; **there shall ye see him**: lo,
I have told you. (Matthew 28:5-7)

The women and the disciples believed in the resurrection because they were
shown the empty tomb and they saw the risen Christ. Actually, Peter and John
did not take the women's word for it; they went to see for themselves (Luke
24:11-12; John 20:3-8). We criticize Thomas for insisting on evidence before
he would believe, but *none* of the disciples believed until Jesus "showed them
his hands and his feet" (Luke 24:36-41). Without such eyewitness accounts
the resurrection testimony loses credibility. Paul knew this, which is why he
listed eyewitnesses to validate the message in 1 Corinthians 15:5-8.

Second, acknowledging human responsibility for handling the text is *not*
the same as denying God's sovereignty and insisting that man is in control.
The whole concept of "providence" is based on the assumption that *God* is
always in control. But the fact that God is always in control does not mean
that every outcome is always perfect. Sin still has its effects. God's sovereignty permits Satan's devices and man's willfulness to cause a measure of
disruption, without ever threatening God's eternal purposes.[4] Further, it is
patently inconsistent to claim that Erasmus' redactions of the manuscripts
found in the library at Basle, Switzerland, illustrates God's providential care
in preserving His Word, but Tischendorf's discovery of a codex at a
monastery at Sinai[5] does not.

A third fallacy is the assumption that one man's belief that he can identify
the preserved Word of God by *counting* manuscripts is somehow less scientific than another's belief that he can identify the preserved Word of God by
dating manuscripts. Ultimately, this "faith vs. science" view is reminiscent of
the Roman Catholic charges against the Reformers in regard to the Mass.
When disavowing transubstantiation, the Reformers insisted that the bread
and wine were just bread and wine. The Catholic Church accused them of
replacing faith ("this is my body...and my blood") with science (only bread
and wine). But the Catholic Church was wrong. Idolatry is idolatry, whether
directed toward the elements of the Lord's Supper, or directed toward a particular copy of the Bible.

Ignoring God's Method of Transmitting the Text

Many want a doctrine that guarantees a line of transmission that permits no
influence of human fallibility, but we find that at some stage in the line of
transmission from the mouth of God to the heart of man, human fallibility
must become evident. We differ among ourselves not so much on that fact,
but on the stage in the line of transmission at which we accept the influence
of human weakness. We know that people accept Christ today in spite of an

imperfect understanding of Scripture given by an imperfect witness. We know that believers grow under the influence of imperfect teachers and their own imperfect understanding. So at what stage do we accept the introduction of human fallibility in the process of preservation and communication?

Theological liberals claim that human fallibility is evident in the originals. Even Erasmus, who produced the new Greek text that evolved into the *Textus Receptus*, expressed doubt that the *autographa* of the Gospels were inerrant. In his notes (Matt. 2, note 7 and Mark 1, note 2) Erasmus pointed out discrepancies in quotations from the Old Testament and suggested the possibility that "the evangelists themselves did not take testimonies of this kind from books but trusted to memory and consequently made mistakes." When Johann Eck accused him of undermining the authority of Scripture, Erasmus defended his notes, saying, "I deny that the presence of some mistakes must needs shake the credibility of the whole of Scripture."[6] This position denies the clear Biblical teaching on inspiration and inerrancy. This is a heretical view that we must not countenance.

Conservative theologians have historically insisted on the infallibility and inerrancy of the originals, but have recognized signs of human fallibility in copies and translations. This is based on the obvious fact of differences between copies. There are over 5600 Greek manuscripts or fragments of the New Testament, and they are substantially alike, but no two are identical in every respect. In fact, "there are between six and ten variations per chapter for the closest two manuscripts."[7] The vast majority of those differences involve variations in spelling or word order, so they have little or no material influence on the message of the text. But their existence argues against the notion of perfect preservation in a single manuscript. The agreement between those manuscripts is overwhelming, but not perfect.

Lately, some have begun to insist that God has guaranteed that a perfect copy of the original will be available forever. If so, only one of the many Greek manuscripts could be the perfectly preserved copy. But "it is easily demonstrable that every manuscript has scribal errors in it."[8] Not one manuscript has been found completely free of spelling errors, words dropped or added, or corrections made within the text. Besides that, we cannot compare any existing manuscripts with the originals, since they no longer exist. Some have concluded that we must accept by faith the latest edition of the Greek New Testament produced by Erasmus of Rotterdam in 1516, which came to be known as the *Textus Receptus* when so called by the Dutch printers named Elzivir in their 1633 edition. This is the position taken by Edward F. Hills in *The King James Version Defended* (1956) and those who accept what he has called "the logic of faith." This position actually amounts to *belief* that the

King James Bible is the perfectly preserved Word of God, despite the *evidence* to the contrary. This is not *biblical* faith, but fideism[9].

Still others are now insisting that a perfect copy in Greek is not enough. These are unwilling to admit the possibility of human weakness being introduced at the stage of translation. Since it is obvious that translations differ, even translations using the same Greek manuscripts, those who hold this position find it necessary to decide which translation is the exclusive edition produced by God's guidance. Some of the ancient church fathers believed this. They claimed that the Septuagint was the exclusive repository of God's preserved Old Testament in Greek, and that study of the Hebrew was unnecessary, even inappropriate. Augustine, speaking of "The Authority of the Septuagint Translation," said,

> For the same Spirit who was in the prophets when they spoke these things was also in the seventy men when they translated them, so that they could also say something else, just as if the prophet himself had said both, because it would be...divine power which filled and ruled the mind of the translator. [10]

For centuries the Catholic Church argued that the Latin Vulgate was God's preserved Word. [11] More recently, some have come to believe that the men who made the King James Version were the only translators so guided by God that their product was perfect. Generally, there are two reasons given for settling on the KJV: 1) It was translated from the *TR*, which they hold to be the perfectly preserved Greek edition[12], and 2) it was the most widely used English Bible for over three hundred years. Some who hold this position, most notably Peter Ruckman, recognize differences between the King James and the *TR*, but are so committed to belief in a flawless English translation that they teach that God supernaturally guided the translators of the KJV to "correct the Greek." Teaching what amounts to a doctrine of double inspiration, similar to the error of Augustine in regard to the Septuagint, Ruckman calls this "advanced revelation."[13] He has yet to produce an explanation consistent with his view as to why the King James has had to go through several revisions to date. Similarly, Arlin Horton, president and founder of Pensacola Christian College, recently denounced the position taken by the Fundamental Baptist Fellowship, saying, "[T]hey **do not believe** that **any Bible translation** or version **is infallible** (wholly trustworthy), **inspired, or inerrant**" (emphasis in original.)[14] While trying to deny that he has adopted Ruckman's heretical view of inspiration, Horton is contending for the same conclusion—an inspired *translation*. Horton apparently deals with the differences between the King James and the TR simply by denying that they exist.

Others are unwilling to stop at this step. They argue that if God has perfectly preserved his Word for us in copies and translations handed down through the centuries, surely He would not risk the possibility of *misunderstanding and misinterpretation* of the Word. It is precisely this rationale that led the Catholic Church to the theological position that the Pope and the Church Councils were infallible when speaking *ex cathedra*. They reasoned that if human fallibility were introduced at the point of interpretation and teaching, the Word is not fully preserved.

Even Catholicism goes no further. For centuries they tried to keep the Bible out of the hands of the laymen, in part because they believed that the common man would infect the Scriptures with his human fallibility. To protect the Word of God from such corruption by the mishandling of sinful men, the Roman Church kept the Bible securely in the hands of the clergy. They even forbade its translation into any language other than Latin, at least ostensibly because they feared that putting the Bible in the language of laymen would corrupt it with human frailty.[15] Catholic doctrine still insists that conversion of one's soul cannot be accomplished apart from the Church, even separate from human understanding.[16] Thus, the Roman Catholic position is the only one that holds to a theology of preservation that guarantees no possibility of human fallibility at any point in the chain of communication of the Word of God from the time it was breathed out by God to the original writers to the time that it accomplishes the work it was sent to do in conversion. We find ourselves to have come full-circle. We started with the Reformation principles of the priesthood of the believer and the perspicuity (clarity) of Scripture, and have found our rationale for the defense of the "preservation of God's Word in the infallible King James Bible" leading inexorably back to Roman Catholicism.

Denying God's Prerogative in Disseminating the Text

On the basis of Matthew 4:4—"man shall not live by bread alone but by every word that proceedeth out of the mouth of God" (and the parallel in Luke 4:4)—some are now insisting that God's justice demands complete availability of every word for which mankind is accountable. The assumption is that the Lord Jesus has said that a man cannot live without access to every word of the Bible. If that is true, then it is reasoned that God's people must have in their possession a Bible that is 100% pure. There must be "zero tolerance" for variations or omissions.

A couple of especially significant problems for this theory arise when one takes a look at the verse Jesus was quoting—Deuteronomy 8:3.

And he humbled thee, and suffered thee to hunger, and fed thee with manna, which thou knewest not, neither did thy fathers know; that he might make thee know that man doth not live by bread only, but by every *word* that proceedeth out of the mouth of the LORD doth man live.

First, notice that *"word"* is italicized in the King James Bible as an indication that *it is not found in the Masoretic text* of the Hebrew Bible. What the King James footnotes do not tell you is that the word "word" is supplied from the Septuagint. The fact that the word "word" has been lost from the Hebrew in this verse and recovered by the Greek translation argues eloquently against the very proposition mentioned above.

Second, note the context of Deuteronomy 8:3—the issue was not spiritual nourishment but physical provision. The people were hungry and God sustained them. Given the similarity of the context of Matthew 4:4, it seems unlikely that the Lord Jesus was withstanding the temptation to turn stones into bread near the end of a 40-day fast by claiming that He was being sustained by reading the Bible. That would have been foreign to the context He quoted and absurd in the setting in which He spoke. It is much more likely that the Lord was insisting that food was not necessary for His survival, since God had decreed it. That is, man does not live by bread alone, but by the word of God. It is consistent with what Paul says when he describes God as the One in whom "we live, and move, and have our being" (Acts 17:28) and Christ as the One by whom "all things consist" (Col. 1:17). The Lord Jesus is affirming the Sovereignty of God. He is not promising the perpetuity of a manuscript.[17]

But even if we were to spiritualize this verse and assume it means that our spiritual sustenance depends upon access to the Scriptures (which is the way most of us have taught this passage), we must remember that the Bible has only been complete for the last third of human history, and for about the first 2500 years of mankind's existence, not one verse of Scripture was available to *anyone*. Furthermore, access to complete copies or translations has been relatively rare throughout history. Even today many people have not a single word from God available in their languages, and no opportunity to learn the original (or any other) languages. We must not make the error of ascribing injustice to God simply because His dissemination of His Word does not conform to our view of fairness. It is only the grace and mercy of God that gives us access to *any* of God's Word.[18]

Aside from the obvious historical evidence to the contrary, there are additional problems with insisting that Matthew 4:4 (or Luke 4:4) promises the complete availability of every word of the Bible. First, the Lord referred to *"every word that proceedeth out of the mouth of God,"* which is not necessarily synonymous with "every word of the Bible." As already mentioned, not every word that Christ spoke was recorded. Also, Revelation 10:3-4 tells us that John was specifically forbidden to write the words uttered by the "seven thunders." It is also worth noting that the Lord Jesus referred to Abel as a prophet (Luke 11:50-51), but the Scriptures nowhere record a single word that Abel prophesied from God. It seems clear that even the complete and perfect Bible has never contained "every word of God."[19]

Confusing the Perpetuity of God's Word with the Durability of the Text

Consider Jeremiah 36:21-28. It recounts a time when Jehoiakim, King of Judah, was listening to the recitation of judgment pronounced upon Israel and Judah for sins against God. They were reading the prophecy of Jeremiah. Because Jehoiakim did not like the message, he cut it up and burned it a few pages at a time until the entire scroll was consumed. There were no copies. This was the one and only, original, inspired *autograph* communicated by God to Jeremiah. Did its destruction constitute the passing of a multitude of "jots and tittles"? Did its destruction mean it would "return void"? Was the "incorruptible Word of God" proven to be "corruptible" when the scroll turned to smoke and ash? Of course not. The written, inspired, inerrant, infallible *autograph* was physically destroyed. But the Word of God endured. The scroll was not protected by heaven, but God's Word was settled in heaven. God's Word transcends written documents, even the physical universe, and will be completely and ultimately fulfilled if not one copy remains. The power and effectiveness and duration of the Word of God, and man's responsibility to obey it, do not demand the presence or even the existence of any physical copy.

Missing the Parallel of Creation/Inspiration as Applied to the Text

There are significant parallels between God's creation and maintenance of the universe and His inspiration and preservation of His Word. The fact of creation does not necessitate its continuance in perfection. One of the challenges to the defense of creationism by using the argument from design is that the designs of various structures and processes in nature show evidence of decay. If a perfect and all-powerful God created perfectly, how do we account for such things as disease, deformity, and death? The answer, of course, is that sin and the subsequent curse predict the introduction of such flaws. We can even see biblical evidence for a gradual increase in these "errors" as we trace the decline in life spans. Once sin was introduced, the universe began to decay. We can easily identify many of these flaws as "errors" even though we do not have the original, pristine creation to compare with the world in which we now live.

How does this relate to inspiration/preservation? If a perfect and all-powerful God inscripturated His Word perfectly (inspiration), how do we account for such things as spelling errors, words dropped or added, and other discrepancies in later copies? The obvious answer is that sin and the confounding of languages at Babel predict the introduction of such variations. No man is capable of doing anything perfectly without the intervention of God, even copying manuscripts. Therefore, *textual* transmission of the *Word* of God is just as likely to introduce variation as is *genetic* transmission of the *image* of God. Further, it seems obvious that God's intentional act of confusing man's languages at Babel was so effective that God made it impossible to move from one language to another with absolute precision, making *perfect* translation impossible.

While the blemishes on creation are apparent, they do not materially affect the obvious truth that the universe was designed by an intelligent Creator, nor do they change the fact that man is still created in the image of God (Gen. 9:6). The variations are superficial, and do not represent real *change*. Just so, while the textual blemishes are evident, none of them materially affects the obvious truth that the text we have is the Word of God that is able to "make thee wise unto salvation" (2 Tim. 3:15). Virtually all of the textual discrepancies can be set right by carefully comparing the manuscripts—what is altered in one is intact in another. It is perfectly appropriate for Combs to assert:

> The essential message of Scripture has been preserved not only in the Byzantine text-type, but in the Alexandrian text-type as well; the KJV is the Word of God as well as the NASB. When we refer to either or both of these versions as the Word of God, we do so because we rightly assume they are tethered to the autographs and are thus sufficient representatives of them.[20]

It is tragic that so many who claim to defend the "preserved Word of God" have grossly and blithely misinterpreted, misconstrued, and misapplied the very Word of God they set out to defend. They boldly accuse textual transmitters and translators of tampering with the Word of God because of textual choices made in comparing manuscripts or translation choices made in communicating the Word in a new language, yet are often guilty of doing more violence to the text in their teaching, preaching, writing, and making of videos than any textual critic ever dreamed of doing.

Define Doctrine Precisely

No matter what doctrinal position we are talking about, precise definitions are important. By and large, fundamentalism has been rather careless about definitions—maybe not officially, but in our pulpits and our pews.

Refuse to Present Simplistic Solutions to Complex Issues

Consider, for instance, the question of "Calvinism." Whether you and I would consider one another a "Calvinist" depends almost entirely upon two factors: definitions and emphases. The theological implications of and the tension between the clear Scriptural teaching on God's sovereign will in election and man's responsibility to come to God in faith cannot be explained and resolved in a forty-minute sermon, let alone by a couple of half-baked clichés. What we owe one another is to explain the theological complexities the best we can without belaboring them, and admit the limits of our understanding. By so doing we may not resolve all of the doctrinal questions, but we will communicate proper Scripture study methods and demonstrate theological honesty.

Similarly, textual questions are not always easily explained. The average Christian seems to be under the impression that the King James Bible was translated exclusively from a single original-language Bible which was an exact replica of every Bible that came before it in its line of transmission. They have no idea that there are variations among the modern King James Bibles in use, that the King James translators used several resources in the process of translating, that translation decisions were sometimes based on political expediency rather than accuracy, and that the *Textus Receptus* (TR) itself is an oft-revised eclectic text in its own right.

After Erasmus finished his multiple revisions of the Greek New Testament that would later be called the TR, Estienne/Stephanus produced several of his own revisions. Then Beza published several more editions before the King James translators began their work. To have a perfect finished product at the end of this process, God must have supernaturally guided the editors to insure that over the course of at least eighty-two years the text was *corrected and restored* to autographic purity. That would also mean there was a period of about two generations during which the perfectly preserved text was unavailable. Even after all that, there are many places in the KJV where Beza's text is not followed. It seems obvious that the theory of perfect transmission in the TR/KJV is fatally flawed. To end up with a perfect finished product would require the miraculous intervention of God—God would have had to miraculously *restore* the text. Since there are no biblical promises of such direct divine involvement in the process of copying or translating the text of God's Word, and since the physical evidence demonstrates that translating is an imprecise science incapable of producing perfection *via* human agency, we must agree with the King James translators themselves:

[W]ee doe not deny, nay wee affirme and auow, that the very meanest [worst] translation of the Bible in English...containeth the word of God, nay, is the word of God....No cause therefore, why the word translated should bee denied to be the word, or forbidden to be currant [brought up to date in modern English], notwithstanding that some imperfections and blemishes may be noted in the setting foorth of it. For what euer was perfect vnder the Sunne, where Apostles or Apostolike men, that is, men indued with an extraordinary measure of God's spirit, and priuileged with the priuilege of infallibilitie, had not their hand?[21]

Refuse to Preach Specious Sermons for our Congregations

Much of the current controversy may well have been caused by the fact that many of today's preachers grew up never hearing their pastors *teach doctrine*. Many fundamentalist pastors emphasized a sort of high-pressure evangelism and church growth gimmickry to the exclusion of almost everything else. They may have occasionally taken the time to tell their congregations *what* they should believe, but they rarely bothered to make a careful, biblical case for *why* they should believe it. Whether or not it is intentional, that kind of specious preaching amounts to demagoguery. It is an affront to God, an assault on believers, and an abuse of the pastoral office.

Since God has seen fit to communicate with mankind by breathing out His Word for our admonition, we ought to treat His Word with profound respect and reverence. When studying, interpreting, or preaching the Bible we must never forget that we stand before the people as spokesmen for God. We are obligated to preach with integrity. How dare we take an oath in a court of law to speak "the truth, the whole truth, and nothing but the truth," but not consider ourselves so bound in our pulpits!

Our congregations are not really "ours." They are God's people, "the sheep of His pasture." We must not twist or distort the message of Scripture by feeding God's flock spiritual junk food, preaching sermons that are poorly researched, badly organized, barely prepared, and/or carelessly delivered. Not only do God's people need quality spiritual food; they also need a well-balanced diet. We must preach "all the counsel of God" (Acts 20:27), "teaching them to observe all things whatsoever I have commanded you" (Matt. 28:20). We need to emulate Ezra, who "had prepared his heart to seek the law of the LORD, and to do *it*, and to teach in Israel statutes and judgments" (Ezra 7:10). Only then could it be said that Ezra "read in the book in the law of God distinctly, and gave the sense, and caused them to understand the reading" (Nehemiah 8:8). That is the task of the shepherd who would give the flock what they need.

Most fundamentalist pastors spend hours each week on correspondence (e-mail and "snail mail"), phone calls, church and staff administration, counseling, and visitation (sick, shut-in, soul-winning). Much of that is part of our pastoral calling to care for God's flock. But none of those activities prepare us for our pulpit ministry. That requires many hours of Bible study and prayer. If we fail to block out adequate time for sermon preparation, we have neglected the most important aspect of our office. The pastor must give attention to being thorough in his preparation and accurate in his presentation of the Word of God. The "elders that rule well" and are considered "worthy of double honor" are "especially they who labor in the word and in doctrine" (1 Tim. 5:17). Perhaps one reason our theology is out of balance is that our ministries are out of balance. Or perhaps the reverse is true—unbalanced theology produced unbalanced ministry. I shudder to think how it must grieve the Lord to hear what comes out of our mouths on those occasions in which the pastor selected a text just hours, or even minutes, before he stepped into the pulpit.

The doctrine of the preservation of Scripture, and its implications for the versions issue, is complex. When dealing with inspiration and inerrancy, too many preachers have simply held up a King James Bible and proclaimed, "We believe that every word came from God" and "there are no mistakes or contradictions in it." They have underscored this when asking the congregation to turn to a particular passage of Scripture and quipping, "If you have the *right Bible*, you can turn to page...", and by making a point of insisting that "*my* Bible says..." After hearing such comments long enough, people began to assume that only the King James English was inspired. Any variation in the *English* from one translation to another was deemed to represent evidence that evil people are changing the Word of God.

So we find that to advocates of perfect preservation, admission of *any* variation causes problems. Wilber Pickering propounds a devastating *non sequitur* when he insists, "If we do not have the inspired Words or do not know precisely which they be, then the doctrine of Inspiration is inapplicable."[22] However, Pickering failed to mention that his own hero, John Burgon, writing in *The Traditional Text of the Holy Gospels* (1896), indicated the need for 150 corrections in the Gospel of Matthew alone. Zane Hodges, another TR/KJV advocate, has produced a *Revised Textus Receptus* which gives readings different from those found in the KJV "in about 1000 places."[23]

Those who hold to perfect preservation in the TR find it difficult to explain the following comments from Erasmus, who's Greek New Testament formed the basis for what became the TR:

I frankly admit that there are many things [in my New Testament] that could have been dealt with in a more learned fashion, and it is undeniable that my attention flagged and I was nodding in some places.[24]

Granted that the Greek books are just as corrupt as the Latin ones, yet by collating manuscripts that are equally corrupt one can often discover the true reading, for it frequently happens that what has been corrupted by chance in one is found intact in another.[25]

Now granted that the Greek and Hebrew manuscripts are as corrupt as ours [the Latin Vulgate], does it follow that we are deprived of any hope of ever emending what is found to be corrupted in our manuscripts? Does it not happen frequently that from several faulty manuscripts—though not faulty in the same way—the true and genuine reading is found?[26]

Advocates of a perfect TR must conclude that the editors must have been just as inspired as the original writers. Each one made textual choices. Erasmus selected what readings would appear in his first published edition, and even created some of the readings. If Erasmus, or any other editor or translator, received *one word* by divine direction, you have *new inspiration,* regardless of what you call it.

WE NEED TO BE LESS CONCEITED

An Appreciation for History

Knowledge of How the Bible Came to Us
No one would dispute the fact that God did not present Adam with a King James Bible in a black leather binding. But we need to face the implications of that fact. God communicated His Word to the original writers *via* inspiration, and 2 Peter 1:20-21 specifically *limits* this moving of the Holy Ghost to those "holy men of God," and He did so over time.

The first of the inspired writings came through Moses (unless Job were written by someone earlier than Moses), some 2500 years after creation. So, for at least the first third of human history, mankind had no written Word of God. It took another 1000 years for God to finish speaking to His people through the Old Testament prophets. Following was a period of about 400 years of silence before God revealed Himself in the Person of His Son, the Living Word. After the earthly ministry, crucifixion, resurrection, and ascension of the Lord Jesus, God directed the writing of the New Testament, which spanned another thirty to fifty years. And it was many years after that before *any* churches or individuals had entire collections of the New Testament writings.[27]

It is significant that God did not see fit to miraculously preserve the original manuscripts of the Bible texts as exemplars for all future copies and translations. No scroll written by the hand of a prophet or apostle remains. The *autographa* were subject to decay and destruction. But God's people made copies of the originals.[28] At least by the time of Daniel, Ezra, and Nehemiah, we know that the Jews commonly taught from the scrolls in synagogues scattered all over the Persian Empire, which would make authoritative copies necessary.[29] From the very start of the inscripturation of God's Word, Moses commanded all Israel to make copies when he said "thou shalt **write them** [the words of the Law] upon the posts of thy house and on thy gates" (Deut. 6:9). The copying of God's Word is a part of the process of preservation but is clearly distinguished from inspiration, because God never even implied that the copyist would be guided by the Holy Spirit to produce an error-free product.[30]

The time came when even faithful copies of the originals were useless to a reader who did not know Hebrew. It became necessary to translate those copies to other languages. The Old Testament was translated from Hebrew to Greek (the Septuagint, or LXX) nearly two hundred years before the birth of Christ. This was the version of the Old Testament most commonly used and quoted by Jesus and the disciples.[31] "This Greek version of the Old Testament…became the Christian Bible in the first century. About 80% of the quotations from the Old Testament found in the New Testament follow the readings of the Greek rather than the Hebrew text."[32] The earliest known translations of the entire Bible were from Greek to Coptic (Egyptian) and Aramaic (Syriac). Shortly after those translations came the early Latin versions.

Every translation ever made varies somewhat from all others. The primary reason for differences is that no target language ever captures every nuance of the original, so some variation is inevitable. Because translation work is inexact, and due to differences in the texts from which they worked, the 1611 edition of the King James Bible also had over 8400 marginal notations providing explanations and variant readings. There were at least 6637 such notes for the Old Testament, 767 for the New Testament, and 1018 for the Apocrypha.[33] Knowing they were going to be criticized for casting doubt on the text, the translators defended their inclusion by saying:

> Some peraduenture would haue no varietie of sences to be set in the margine, lest the authoritie of the Scriptures for deciding of the controuersies by that shew of vncertaintie should somewhat be shaken.

But we hold their iudgmet not to be so sound in this point....[I]t is better to make doubt of those things which are secret, then to striue about those things that are vncertaine....[D]oth not a margine do well to admonish the Reader to seeke further, and not to conclude or dogmatize vpon this or that peremptorily? For as it is a fault of incredulitie, to doubt of those things that are euident: so to determine of such things as the Spirit of God hath left (euen in the iudgment of the iudicious) questionable, can be no lesse then presumption. Therefore as S. *Augustine* saith, that varietie of Translations is profitable for the finding out of the sense of the Scriptures: so diuersitie of signification and sense in the margine, where the text is not so cleare, must needes doe good, yea, is necessary, as we are perswaded....They that are wise had rather haue their judgements at libertie in differences of readings then to be captiuated to one, when it may be the other.[34]

Admitting that there are "such things as the Spirit of God hath left...questionable" and that "some imperfections and blemishes may be noted in the setting forth of it," they recommend the "reader to seek further" profiting from "the variety of translations." Obviously, the translators of the KJV saw themselves as men responsible for the careful handling of the text of the Bible, not as men divinely guided to produce a flawless work by the miraculous leading of the Holy Spirit.

Knowledge of What Others Believed Before Us

Even if one could establish an unbroken line of perfect transmission from the autographs to the Hebrew Masoretic text and the Greek *Textus Receptus*, those manuscripts must still be translated into modern languages to be able to communicate God's Word to the average person. Are those translations perfect? John R. Rice did not think so.

A perfect translation of the Bible is humanly impossible. The words in one language do not have exactly the same color and meaning as opposite words in another language, and human frailty and imperfection enter in. So, let us say, there are no perfect translations.[35]

Translation is distinct from inspiration because "human frailty and imperfection enter in." Larry Pettegrew explains:

Translations do partake of derivative inspiration as long as they reflect accurately the original documents (2 Tim 3:15), but no translations are perfect and in themselves they are not God-breathed. Therefore, no translation of the Bible should be set up as a standard by which all other translations and manuscripts are judged.[36]

383

Fundamentalism has never identified the King James Bible as the standard by which all manuscripts and translations are to be judged. The traditional position of historic fundamentalism can be summed up in the words of R. A. Torrey, general editor of *The Fundamentals*:

> I have said that the Scriptures of the Old and New Testaments *as originally given* were absolutely inerrant, and the question of course arises to what extent is the Authorized Version, or the Revised Version, the inerrant Word of God. The answer is simple; they are the inerrant Word of God just to the extent that they are an accurate rendering of the Scriptures of the Old and New Testaments as originally given, and to all practical intents and purposes they are a thoroughly accurate rendering of the Scriptures of the Old and New Testaments as originally given. (emphasis in original)[37]

As far back as we look in our Bible-believing heritage, we find the same sentiments expressed repeatedly. In his *Baptist Catechism*, 17th century theologian Benjamin Keach says:

> The Word of God...is contained exactly and most purely in the Originals, and in all translations, so far as they agree therewith. Now though some translations may exceed others in Propriety, and significant rendering of the Originals: yet they generally, (even in the most imperfect that we know of) express and hold forth so much of the Mind, Will, and Counsel of God, as is sufficient, by the Blessings of God upon a conscientious Reading thereof, to acquaint a man with the mysteries of salvation, to work in him true faith, and bring him to live godly, righteously, and soberly in this world, and to salvation in the next.[38]

John Gill, premier Baptist theologian of the 18th century, says:

> Inspiration...is to be understood of the Scriptures, as in the original languages in which they are written, and not of translations: unless it could be thought, that the translators of the Bible into the several languages of the nations into which it has been translated, were under the divine inspiration also in translating, and were directed of God to the use of words they have rendered the original by; but this is not reasonable to suppose.[39]

> Whatever mistakes may be made, through the carelessness of transcribers of copies, they are to be corrected by other copies, which God in His providence, has preserved.[40]

Charles H. Spurgeon concurs:

I do not hesitate to say that I believe that there is no mistake whatever in the original Holy Scriptures from beginning to end. There may be, and there are mistakes of translation for translators are not inspired.[41]

John Dagg, 19th century Baptist theologian, adds his testimony:

Although the Scriptures were originally penned under the unerring guidance of the Holy Spirit, it does not follow, that a continued miracle has been wrought to preserve them from all error in transcribing. On the contrary, we know that the manuscripts differ from each other; and where readings are various, but one of them can be correct. A miracle was needed in the original production of the Scriptures; and accordingly, a miracle was wrought; but the preservation of the inspired word, in as much perfection as was necessary to answer the purpose for which it was given, did not require a miracle, and accordingly it was committed to the providence of God.[42]

James M. Gray, in one of the essays he contributed to *The Fundamentals*, says:

The record for whose inspiration we contend is the original record— the autographs or parchments of Moses, David, Matthew, Paul, or Peter as the case may be, and not any particular translation or translations of them whatever. There is no translation absolutely without error, nor could there be, considering the infirmities of human copyists.[43]

Another contributor to *The Fundamentals* was L. W. Munhall. In his essay, "Inspiration," he quotes passage after passage in support of the doctrine of plenary-verbal inspiration. He cites several scholars as men who defended the doctrine of inspiration, significantly juxtaposing quotes from Canon Westcott and Dean Burgon, not as adversaries, but as fellow defenders of the faith. Carefully checking Munhall's Bible citations will reveal that he quoted from several different translations, most frequently the American Standard Version (1901). In defense of inerrancy of the originals, he says,

[T]he critics are only throwing dust into the air when they rail against verbal inspiration and attempt to disprove it by pointing out the apparent errors and discrepancies of the authorized and revised texts....[T]hey know that no one believes that the translations and revisions are inspired.[44]

Still, there are those among us who persist in teaching a doctrine of divine supervision of copyists and translators. They quote Dean John Burgon for support, because his scathing yet scholarly critique of the work of the revisers is well known. They erroneously assume that Burgon believed that the *Textus Receptus* was a perfect replica of the divinely inspired originals. But that was not his position. He clearly repudiated such a view by saying:

> That a perpetual miracle was wrought for their [the Scriptures'] preservation—that copyists were protected against all risk of error, or evil men prevented from adulterating shamefully copies of the Deposit—no one, it is presumed, is so weak as to suppose.[45]

> Once for all, we request it may be clearly understood that we do not, by any means, claim perfection for the Received Text. We entertain no extravagant notions on this subject. Again and again we shall have occasion to point out that the Textus Receptus needs correction.[46]

The conclusion is inescapable. Those among us who make adherence to the *Textus Receptus* and the King James English a test of orthodoxy would do well to temper their rhetoric until they have read the views of their fundamentalist forebears. It may be that some will still believe that their understanding of Scripture demands that they renounce those views in favor of a perfect preservation in a single text position. If so, I will commend them for their integrity, but will insist that they admit they have adopted a novel position. They are redefining the doctrine of inspiration and are building a cult following. They are withdrawing from our ranks to establish a new and spurious adaptation of fundamentalism.

An Attitude of Humility

Recognize the Arrogance of Assuming English is God's Favored Language

It is unlikely that the *lingua franca* of heaven will be English. Why, then, do we act as if we believe that God's eternal purpose in communicating His Word reached its apex in an English translation made 400 years ago? Granted, English-speaking people have been richly blessed of God. His Word is more readily available in our language than in any other. But there are other large language groups to whom God would have His Word communicated clearly. The arguments of exclusivity for the King James Version do not hold up when applied to other languages. It is remarkably arrogant of English-speaking believers to assume that God intends to speak to the world today in King James English.

People who speak the living languages of earth need to hear the Word of God in their own tongues. This is, in fact, one of the not-so-obvious lessons we should learn from the way God has communicated His Word. God's original communication of His Word was in Hebrew when Israel spoke Hebrew, in Aramaic when that became the dominant language, and then in Greek when that language dominated. Jesus and the Apostles validated the work of translation by repeatedly citing the Greek version of the Old Testament. The Holy Spirit illustrated the work we are to do in proclaiming God's Word to the world by doing His own translating at Pentecost. But that phenomenon was temporary. Since then, it has been the responsibility of God's people to study other languages in order to be able to communicate God's Word coherently and universally. That task has not yet been fulfilled. There are many languages yet to be mastered, and many people to whom not one of God's words is yet accessible. And to the English-speaking masses, Elizabethan English is becoming increasingly unintelligible. To quote John Gill once again,

> To the Bible in its original languages is every translation to be brought, and by it to be examined, tried, and judged, and to be corrected and amended: and if this was not the case, we should have no certain and infallible rule to go by; for it must be either all the translations together, or some one of them; not all of them, because they agree not in all things: not one, for then the contest would be between one nation and another which it should be, whether English, Dutch, French, etc., and could one be agreed upon, it could not be read and understood by all....They [godly translators] have never failed of producing a translation worthy of acceptance; and in which, though they have mistook some words and phrases, and erred in some lesser and lighter matters; yet not so as to affect any momentous article of faith or practice; and therefore such translations as ours may be regarded as the rule of faith.[47]

There are some who claim that God promised perpetual availability of His Word to *every generation*. Citing verses like Psalms 33:11, and 100:5, they conclude that God would be showing favoritism if He made his Word available to some generations and not others. The fact that God is not a "respecter of persons" (Acts 10:34) relates to His authority to save whom He will, without regard for personal merit. If this impartiality argues for every *generation* availability of God's Word, it would also seem to require that it would be unfair if God's Word were not available to every *individual*. Again, we end up ascribing injustice to God on the basis of a fallacious human standard of fairness.

I would never dispute the general premise of the *durability* of God's Word, or the necessity of its *availability*. The Bible teaches both. But those who accept the notion that God must make His every word available to every generation have committed at least four errors. First, they have ignored the fact that some of God's words are available to no one. We've already noted that not all of Jesus' words were inscripturated; everything else He said is unavailable anywhere.

We've also noted that the Apostle John was allowed to hear the words uttered by the "seven thunders" and "was about to write: and I heard a voice from heaven saying unto me, Seal up those things which the seven thunders uttered, and write them not" (Rev. 10:4). We have no idea what those thunders said, because God has never made those words available. Further, we know that there are "secret things" (Deut. 29:29) that have never been revealed.

Second, they have forgotten that God sometimes limits the availability of His Word for judicial purposes. God announced through His prophet Amos,

> Behold, the days come, saith the Lord God, that I will send a famine in the land, not a famine of bread, nor a thirst for water, but of hearing the words of the LORD: and they shall wander from sea to sea, and from the north even to the east, they shall run to and fro to seek the word of the LORD, and shall not find it. (Amos 8:11-12).

Third, their conclusion that this "availability promise" supports the TR/KJV *exclusively* begs the question. Samuel Schnaiter makes the following observation:

> This would have to mean that God's Word was preserved for the Jews first in Hebrew and then in the Greek Old Testaments (after the Jews forgot their Hebrew.) It would have to mean that God's Word was preserved for the Latin speaking world in the Old Latin and Vulgate versions, for the Egyptian people in Coptic, for the Syrians in Syriac, and so on....If we start scrutinizing and comparing versions from different ages one to another, we are bound to find certain minor differences. But we will also find that God has been true to His promises...in spite of these minor differences.[48]

Finally, only a maximum of about 7% of the text produced by Westcott and Hort was different from the *Textus Receptus*, so 93% was still present in their Greek and Latin texts. The "every generation availability" argument assumes that even if the remaining 7% were available in other Greek texts, or in Syriac or Coptic versions, God's Word was "hidden from the public." Besides, nearly all of the differences in the text produced by Westcott and Hort represented abbreviated, not expanded, readings. Fears that they believed some of God's Word was hidden are groundless. If "hidden" to anyone, it was hidden to the Egyptians and Syrians. It has been aptly observed that

> many pro-KJV advocates have used only the KJV all of their lives and are resistant to any changes. While they can easily believe that God would allow others to have access only to a 'corrupt' text, they absolutely refuse to believe that God might also allow them to have an imperfect text.[49]

We must insist, however, that despite the presence of minor variations among the texts and translations of Scripture, we are absolutely certain that God's Word has been kept for us by God's providential care and is available to us today. Actually, God's Word is more readily and completely available to more people in our generation than ever before in history.

Recognize the Error of Elevating Tradition over Truth

If we were certain that the Lord would return for His people in the next few months, there may be some justification in saying that new translation work is unnecessary. But what if He surprises us by waiting longer than we expected? Are we prepared to insist that the world will be speaking English a century or two from now, and if so that Elizabethan English will still be intelligible? There are some who disparage supporters of Modern English versions of Scripture, accusing them of wanting to make the majestic and time-honored King James Bible a museum piece. But they have forgotten that Wycliffe's, Tyndale's, and other English Bibles that preceded the KJV, and upon which it was based, are already museum pieces (not to mention the Greek texts themselves.) There is nothing wrong with preserving important historical artifacts in museums. There is a great deal wrong with insisting that God's people be restricted to using those artifacts to do His work. It is no more spiritual to insist on using a Bible in Elizabethan English today than it was for Rome to insist on the use of the Latin.

We need to admit that we may never come to perfect agreement on this issue of English Bible versions. But we must also admit that perfect agreement is not necessary. The major difficulty today seems to be the multiplicity of choices in English translations. I am traditional enough to like the idea of a more or less universally recognized standard English version for ease and consistency of communication. But God certainly does not require such a thing.

Those who have exalted the King James Bible to the status of an icon will sometimes ask, "If you don't think the KJV is the Word of God for today, then which Bible is?" Our reply ought to be that we are troubled by attempts to bind the fundamentalist conscience to a single translation. That has never been the practice of the true church. That was certainly not the view of the King James translators. That was not the view of the theologians of fundamentalist heritage, whether they were Presbyterian, Methodist, Congregational, Anglican, Episcopal, or Baptist. It seems that we have at least three choices:

1. We can throw up our hands in despair over the many different English Bibles available, concluding that we are so confused that we cannot know for sure what God has said.

2. We can choose our favorite English version and denounce all others as "tools of Satan to cast doubt on" the version we've chosen.

3. Or we can rejoice that God's Word is so abundantly available to us that we are not restricted to a single edition. Just as the King James Translators recommended—"variety of translations is profitable for the finding out the sense of the Scripture"—we can compare among them to gain an ever more complete understanding of what God has said.

Jesus Christ, in whom resides all authority in heaven and in earth, has charged us with the responsibility to make disciples of every *ethnos*, teaching all of His Word in all the world (Matt. 28:18-20). The work of translating the Scriptures will not be completed until the Church's evangelical commission is ended by the return of the Lord. Our goal ought to be obvious: to communicate the Word of God clearly, accurately, and powerfully. That requires study of languages, including our own. By insisting that all God's people, or even the English speaking world, use the King James Bible exclusively we are in danger of making God's Word unintelligible to the 21st century "plowboy." We become the new elitists if we demand that the Scriptures can be read and studied only by those who understand the increasingly arcane grammar and syntax of 17th century English.

In the abundance of manuscripts (handwritten Greek or Hebrew Bibles), early versions (translations into Greek, Coptic, Syriac, and Latin), and the quotations in the writings of the early church leaders, we find a unanimity that leaves no room for doubt. While the Bible's preservation is not perfect in any one copy or translation, it is *complete in the entire body* of documents, and it is *sufficient in each* to be accurately called "the Word of God." God has kept His Word for us.

WE MUST DENOUNCE CARNALITY

Love the Brethren
Since the Bible says nothing that implies miraculous intervention in copying and translating the text of Scripture, and since good and faithful men have taken varied positions, we ought to allow for a little variety among ourselves without resorting to name-calling. Some among us believe the Bible makes no direct promise of its own preservation, that it only implies it by inference. Others believe it is promised. Some believe that God's Word is preserved in the multitude of manuscripts, and that each ancient Bible is a sufficiently accurate representation of the original to be confidently called "God's Word." Others believe that the *autographa* have been maintained in

a single manuscript tradition. We all believe we have the trustworthy, reliable, authoritative Word of God. We all ought to be about the business of proclaiming the truth of God's Word, rather than dividing over differences of opinion about the text of God's Word.

A word of caution is in order. While we must strive to be charitable in our tone, *we must not capitulate to those who would impose a new and erroneous theology of Scripture.* The versions issue is creating a line of separation between truth and error. We should not separate from one another because of preferences for different English translations, if those choices are made on the basis of sound doctrine. There are many English translations, but only a few that would commend themselves to men of orthodox faith. While they are all God's Word insofar as they are accurate renderings from the original languages, some are more accurate than others. It is not impossible, nor even that difficult, to narrow the range of choices to a handful of superior versions. Our own Baptist distinctives of soul liberty and individual priesthood demand that we permit one another to answer to God for his own choices.

Live the Bible

A story is told about the Cherokee chief Yonaguska who opposed the Christian missionaries because he did not trust them. After the Bible was translated into the Cherokee language, he would not allow the Scriptures to be read to his tribe without his approval, which he would not grant until he had personally heard them read. After listening to a few chapters, it is reported that he said, "It seems to be a good book—strange that the white people are not better, after having had it so long." Stranger still that the defenders of the book "are not better."

Much of the rhetoric being broadcast in the name of defending the King James Bible is vitriolic. The tone of writers like Ruckman and Riplinger, and the tactics of distortion of the truth and misrepresentation of those who take an opposing view are not indicative of righteousness. Some have accused good, honorable, and orthodox men of compromise, apostasy, and hypocrisy and then denied them an opportunity to respond by adopting a "bully pulpit" approach to dissemination of those accusations *via* the internet and by the unsolicited mailing of thousands of videotapes. Such a spirit seems more characteristic of the Accuser of the brethren than of the Advocate of the faithful. When those same critics quip, "Count me out of the unity,"[50] we must oblige them.

God did not give us the "sword of the Spirit, which is the Word of God" so we could disembowel one another. Some Bible-believers prefer the Alexandrian Greek text. Others prefer the Majority, or the *Textus Receptus*, or the Eclectic texts. Some Bible-believers prefer the King James English, while others prefer a more recent English translation. We should stand shoulder-to-shoulder, rank-on-rank, preaching the message of the Gospel of Jesus Christ to a lost and dying world. Like Jehoiakim, unregenerate man can ignore and even scorn the Word of God. He can ban and burn the Word of God. But he cannot change it. He may disregard and disobey it, but he will still be judged by it. *The world needs to hear us proclaim with one voice*:

GOD HAS SPOKEN, AND WE ARE RESPONSIBLE TO ACT UPON WHAT HE HAS SAID.

---

[1]William W. Combs, "The Preservation of Scripture," *Detroit Baptist Seminary Journal* (Detroit: Detroit Theological Seminary, Fall 2000), pp. 13-14.

[2]Combs, pp. 37, 39.

[3]Joel Mullenix, *Response to Coalition Critics video* (Pensacola, FL: A Beka Books, 1999).

[4]It is not the purpose of this chapter to enter into a discussion of the interrelationship of God's sovereignty and man's culpability. I merely point out the truth of both—God is in control, and man is responsible for his actions.

[5]Many "KJV Only" advocates make the erroneous claim that Tischendorf found the manuscript in a trash can. For instance, David Sorenson has written, "This Alexandrian manuscript had been in a waste basket ready to be burned by the local monks. Constantine von Tischendorf 'discovered' this ancient manuscript there in 1844" (*Touch Not the Unclean Thing*, [Duluth, MN: Northstar Baptist Ministries, 2001] p. 24. Sorenson's book is identified in footnote 1 on page 2 as "an adaptation of the author's doctor of ministry dissertation received from Pensacola Theological Seminary). However, it seems that what actually happened differs from Dr. Sorenson's description. New Testament scholar John McRay says, "In 1844...Konstantin von Tischendorf, while visiting Saint Catherines' [Greek Orthodox] Monastery at the foot of Mount Sinai, found forty-three leaves of a fourth-century copy of the Old Testament in Greek lying in a wastebasket. Unfortunately, according to one of the monks, two similar baskets full had already been burned. In 1859 Tischendorf returned to the monastery and...[a] monk showed Tischendorf a fourth-century manuscript containing most of the Old Testament and all of the New Testament. This manuscript, which has been dubbed Codex Sinaiticus, is now in the British Museum" *(Archaeology and the New Testament*, [Grand Rapids: Baker Book House, 1991], p. 352). When historical distortion is employed to claim Codex Sinaiticus was found "in a waste basket ready to be burned," (Sorenson) it is an attempt to identify the manuscript as so flawed that it was worthy of destruction. Assuming that the leaves destroyed in 1844 were

from the codex given to Tischendorf in 1859 is mere idle speculation, and claiming that he found the codex in the trash is a falsehood. It is at least as valid to assume that the monks who were willing to destroy valuable manuscripts in order to stay warm had protected this one, sparing it from the flames for an additional fifteen years before being providentially brought to light upon Tischendorf's return.

[6]Erasmus, Ep 844, lines 53-54, May, 1518, cited by Erika Rummel, *Erasmus' Annotations on the New Testament* [Toronto: University of Toronto Press, 1986], pp. 138-139.

[7]Daniel B. Wallace, "Inspiration, Preservation, and New Testament Textual Criticism," *Grace Theological Journal* 12.1 (Winona Lake, IN: Grace Theological Seminary, 1992) p. 32.

[8]Ibid.

[9]*Fideism* is defined as "a mode of philosophical or theological thought according to which knowledge depends upon a fundamental act of faith" (*World Book Dictionary*, Vol. 1, [Chicago: Thorndike-Barnhart], 1989), p. 792. Those who insist on the proverbial "leap into the dark" as the "faith" basis for confidence in the Bible are, by definition, fideists. The Christian faith has never been a blind fideism, but has always relied on both the revelation of God and empirical evidence (i.e., Ex. 3:20-4:9; Mt. 28:6-7; John 20:20, 27, 30-31).

[10]Augustine, *City of God*, chapter 43, as found in *Nicene and Post-Nicene Fathers,* Series I, Vol. 2, in The Master Christian Library, Version 8 (Rio, WI: AGES Software, Inc., 2000), p. 822.

[11]They opposed Erasmus' work from the Greek manuscripts on two grounds: "there was no proof that they were superior to Latin manuscripts, and there was reason to believe that they had been corrupted after the schism to support Greek orthodox doctrine." (Rummel, p. 131).

[12]Those who take the position described usually fail to mention that the translators of the King James used several sources or that the translators chose readings not found in the TR over 190 times. Donald Waite equates the King James Bible and the Textus Receptus when he speaks of "Bible believing Christians—those who hold to the King James Bible and the Textus Receptus" (*Fundamentalist MIS-INFORMATION on Bible Versions*, [Collingswood, NJ: The Bible for Today Press, 2000], p. 25). However, he later reverses himself and admits: "Over 99% of the time the text is Beza's 5th edition (1598)....There are only 190 places where the New Testament Textus Receptus of Beza is not followed, and Dr. Scrivener lists all 190 of those places" (p. 88). His outrage toward those who do not accept his theory of perfect preservation seems a bit overdone if even his perfect exemplars differ at least 1% of the time.

[13]Peter Ruckman, *The Christian's Handbook of Manuscript Evidence* (Pensacola, FL: Bible Baptist Bookstore, 1970), particularly the chapter entitled "Correcting the Greek with the English." Dr. Ruckman concludes a discussion of Acts 19:37 by asserting that "mistakes in the A.V. 1611 are advanced revelation!" (p. 126).

[14]Arlin Horton, "From the President," *PCC Update*, Winter 2001, p. 6.

[15]Without indicating a source, Alister McGrath provides the following quotation from Henry Knighton, who was critical of John Wycliffe's translation of the Bible into the common tongue: "John Wycliffe translated the gospel, which Christ had entrusted to clerics and doctors of the church, so that they might administer it conveniently to the laity, and to lesser people according to the needs of the time and the requirements of their audience, in terms of their hunger of mind. Wycliffe translated it from Latin into the English—not the angelic!—language. As a result, what was previously known only by learned clerics and those of good understanding has become common, and available to the laity—in fact even to women who can read. As a result, the pearls of the gospel have been scattered and spread before swine." (*In the Beginning: The Story of the King James Bible and How It Changed a Nation, a Language, and a Culture* [New York: Doubleday, 2001], p. 20.) Philip Schaff provides a slightly different translation of the same quote in his *History of the Christian Church*, Vol. VI (Grand Rapids: Eerdmans, 1910), p. 343, and gives the source as "Knighton, Chronicle, II. 151 sq."

[16]Philip Schaff says, "The Vatican dogma requires a wholesale slaughter of the intellect and will, and destroys the sense of personal responsibility." He adds a footnote, which reads in part, "Dr. Hodge, of Princeton, says on the Papal theory of Infallibility (*Systematic Theology*, New York, 1872, Vol. I pp. 130, 150): 'There is something simple and grand in this theory. It is wonderfully adapted to the tastes and wants of men. It relieves them of personal responsibility. Every thing is decided for them. Their salvation is secured by merely submitting to be saved by an infallible, sin-pardoning, and grace-imparting Church.'" *The Creeds of Christendom*, vol.3, (New York: Harper, 1877), p. 170.

[17]John A. Broadus concurs with this explanation. He says, "There is no propriety in understanding here a reference to the spiritual life as sustained by God's word, viz., by the Scriptures; the Hebrew phrase and the connection in Deuteronomy quite forbid such an idea...[T]he support of life is not absolutely dependent on ordinary food, but it may be sustained on whatever God shall choose to say, to appoint....To insist on making the passage...apply also to spiritual food, as so many do, is unreasonable, and dishonoring to the Bible, which is not a book of riddles, but given for practical instruction, and must be interpreted on principles of common sense, or it cannot be interpreted at all." (*Commentary on the Gospel of Matthew*, [Philadelphia: American Baptist Publication Society, 1886], p. 64).

[18]Are the TR/KJV Only advocates prepared to insist that Athenasias, Origen, Augustine, etc., were lost because the Bible they used was an Alexandrian text of the New Testament and the Septuagint translation of the Old? I would not endorse every position taken by the North African church fathers, but neither would I challenge the genuineness of their salvation. The orthodox positions on the deity of Christ, the Trinunity of God, and the Canon of Scripture were defined and defended by the church at Alexandria.

[19]Such a proposition would also argue against the infinity of God. Could *every* *one* of an infinite God's words possibly be limited to a finite manuscript?

[20]Combs, p. 40.

[21]*The Translators to the Reader*, preface to 1611 KJV, paragraph 11. The archaic spelling has been retained to contrast the English of 1611 with that found in today's King James Bibles.

[22]Wilber N. Pickering, "An Evaluation of the Contribution of John William Burgon to New Testament Textual Criticism" (Th.M. thesis, Dallas Theological Seminary, 1968), p. 88.

[23]Douglas S. Chinn and Robert C. Newman, "Demystifying the Controversy over the Textus Receptus and the King James Version of the Bible," *Research Report No. 3* (Hatfield, PA: Interdisciplinary Biblical Research Institute, 1980, 1990), p. 6.

[24]Erasmus, *Apologia* Holborn 173:35, Rummel, p. viii.

[25]Erasmus, *Capita contra morosos* 69, Rummel, p. 131.

[26]Erasmus, LB IX 88C-D, Rummel, p. 131.

[27]The earliest comprehensive list of New Testament titles comes from a letter written in AD 367 by Athanasias, bishop of Alexandria, *Festal Letter 39*, paragraphs 3 and 6, as found in *Nicene and Post-Nicene Fathers*, series 2, vol. 4, pp. 1275-1276. Athanasias was the foremost early defender of the deity of Christ and the triunity of God in opposition to the Arian heresy infecting the leadership of the Byzantine church.

[28]A thorough discussion tracing the line of descent of the English Bible is available in *From the Mind of God to the Mind of Man: A Layman's Guide to How We Got Our Bible*, J. B. Williams and R. Shaylor, eds. (Greenville, SC: Ambassador-Emerald Int., 1999).

[29]See Daniel 9:2 for reference to Daniel's having read Jeremiah's prophecy while in Babylon during the first year of the reign of Darius of the Medes.

[30]Evidence from the Dead Sea Scrolls is helpful here. In the various caves, 29 tefillin (phylacteries) and 8 mezuzot (writings attached to doorposts) have been recovered. James VanderKam says, "The scriptural passages in them can vary from

the wording in the traditional (Masoretic) Hebrew text, and at times these variants agree with readings in other ancient versions of the Bible" (*The Dead Sea Scrolls Today*, [Grand Rapids: Eerdmans, 1994], p. 33). It is apparent from the few ancient examples recovered at Qumran that the copying of Scripture, even in short passages for such devout use as in the tefillin or mezuzot, was not done uniformly.

[31]Attested to by the King James translators in the preface, *The Translators to the Reader*: "The translation of the Seuentie dissenteth from the Originall in many places, neither doeth it come neere it, for perspicuitie, grauitie, maiestie; yet which of the Apostles did condemne it? Condemne it? Nay, they vsed it." (par. 12).

[32]Gordon H. Lovik, "KJV Controversy: Textus Receptus, Majority, Text, Eclectic Text—Which?", a paper presented at the National Leadership Conference, Calvary Baptist Church, Lansdale, PA, Feb. 1996, p. 10.

[33]After the Geneva Bible (1599 edition) became the first English Bible to be published without the Apocrypha, the King James translators reinstated the Apocrypha in the version they produced. The Archbishop of Canterbury (1615) established a penalty of one year's imprisonment for anyone caught binding or selling any Bible without the Apocrypha. In 1629 the King finally authorized the publication of a single edition without the Apocrypha. It was not until 1827 that the British and Foreign Bible Society decided, after much debate, to omit the Apocrypha as a matter of course, only including it in occasional special editions. The American Bible Society soon followed their lead.

[34]*The Translators to the Reader*, paragraph 15.

[35]John R. Rice, *Our God-Breathed Book the Bible* (Murfreesboro, TN: Sword of the Lord, 1969), p. 376.

[36]Larry D. Pettegrew, "Historical Overview—The King James Only Position," Chapter 2 in *The Bible Version Debate: The Perspective of Central Baptist Theological Seminary* (Plymouth, MN, 1997), p. 9.

[37]R. A. Torrey, "The Fundamental Doctrines of the Christian Faith," pp. 36-37, cited by McCune, "Doctrinal Non-Issues in Historic Fundamentalism," DBSJ (Detroit: Detroit Theological Seminary, Fall, 1996), p. 174.

[38]Benjamin Keach, *Baptist Catechism* (Sterling, VA: Grace Abounding Ministries, 1977 reprint), p. 21)

[39]John Gill, *A Body of Doctrinal and Practical Divinity*, 1769-70 (Baptist Standard Bearer, reprint of 1839 ed.), p. 12.

[40]Ibid, p. 13.

[41]Charles Haddon Spurgeon, *Metropolitan Tabernacle Pulpit*, Vol. 35, 1889 (London: Banner of Truth Trust, 1970 reprint), p. 257.

[42]John Dagg, *Manual of Theology*, 1857 (Gano Books, 1982 reprint), p. 24.

[43]James M. Gray, "Inspiration of the Bible—Definition, Extent and Proof," *The Fundamentals: A Testimony to the Truth,* Vol. II (Grand Rapids: Baker Book House, 1993 reprint), p. 12.

[44]L. W. Munhall, "Inspiration," *The Fundamentals*, Vol II, p. 45.

[45]John Burgon, *Traditional Text of the Holy Gospels* (London: George Bell and Sons, 1896), p. 7 footnote.

[46]John Burgon, *The Revision Revised* (London, 1883), p. 21.

[47]Gill, p. 13.

[48]Samuel E. Schnaiter, from unpublished thesis God's Providence in the Manuscripts of the New Testament, Ch. 2—"The Inspiration and Preservation of the Text," p. 5.

[49]Chinn and Newman, p. 18.

[50]Dell Johnson, *Response to Coalition Critics video* (Pensacola, FL: A Beka Books, 1999).

BIBLIOGRAPHY

Broadus, John A. *Commentary on the Gospel of Matthew*. Philadelphia: American Baptist Publication Society, 1886.

Burgon, John. *The Revision Revised*. London, 1883.

_____. *Traditional Text of the Holy Gospels*. London: George Bell and Sons, 1896.

Bush, L. Russ and Tom J. Nettles. *Baptists and the Bible: Revised and Expanded*. Nashville: Broadman and Holman, 1999.

Chinn, Douglas S. and Robert C. Newman. "Demystifying the Controversy over the Textus Receptus and the King James Version of the Bible," *Report #3*. Hatfield, PA: Interdisciplinary Biblical Research Institute, 1980, 1990.

Combs, William W. "The Preservation of Scripture," prepublication draft copy written for Detroit Baptist Theological Seminary, 2000.

Dagg, John. *Manual of Theology*. 1857. Gano Books, 1982 reprint.

Gill, John. *A Body of Doctrinal and Practical Divinity*. 1769-70. Baptist Standard Bearer, 1939 reprint.

Gray, James M. "Inspiration of the Bible—Definition, Extent and Proof," *The Fundamentals: A Testimony to the Truth*. Vol. II. Grand Rapids: Baker Book House, 1993 reprint.

Hills, Edward F. *The King James Version Defended*. Des Moines: The Christian Research Press, 1988 reprint of 1956.

Horton, Arlin. "From the President," *PCC Update*. Pensacola, FL: A Beka Books Publications, Winter 2001.

Keach, Benjamin *Baptist Catechism*. Sterling, VA: Grace Abounding Ministries, 1977 reprint.

King James Bible. *The Translators to the Reader*, preface to 1611 reprint. Nashville: Thomas Nelson.

Lovik, Gordon H. "KJV Controversy: Textus Receptus, Majority Text, Eclectic Text—Which?" unpublished paper presented at National Leadership Conference, Lansdale, PA, February, 1996.

McCune, Rolland D. "Doctrinal Non-Issues in Historic Fundamentalism," in *Detroit Baptist Seminary Journal*. Allen Park, MI, Fall 1996.

McGrath, Alister. *In the Beginning: The Story of the King James Bible and How It Changed a Nation, a Language, and a Culture.* New York: Doubleday, 2001.

McRay, John. *Archaeology and the New Testament.* Grand Rapids: Baker Book House, 1991.

Munhall, L. W. "Inspiration," *The Fundamentals: A Testimony to the Truth,* Vol. II. Grand Rapids: Baker Book House, 1993 reprint.

Pensacola Christian College Video Series. "The Bible...Preserved from Satan's Attack," "The Bible...The Text Is the Issue," "The Leaven in Fundamentalism," and "Response to Coalition Critics." Pensacola: A Beka Books, 1996-1999.

Pettegrew, Larry D. "Historical Overview—The King James Only Position." Chapter 2 of *The Bible Version Debate, The Perspective of Central Baptist Theological Seminary,* Michael A. Grisanti, ed. Plymouth, MN: Central Baptist Theological Seminary, 1997.

Pickering, Wilber N. "An Evaluation of the Contribution of John William Burgon to New Testament Textual Criticism." Th.M. thesis, Dallas Theological seminary, 1968.

Rice, John R. *I Am a Fundamentalist.* Murfreesboro, TN: Sword of the Lord Publishers, 1976.

_____. *Our God-Breathed Book the Bible.* Murfreesboro, TN: Sword of the Lord, 1969.

_____. "Some Questions for the King James Fans," *Sword of the Lord,* March 30, 1979.

Ruckman, Peter. *The Christian's Handbook of Manuscript Evidence.* Pensacola, FL: Bible Baptist Bookstore, 1970.

Rummell, Erika. *Erasmus' Annotation on the New Testament.* Toronto: University of Toronto Press, 1986.

Schaff, Philip. *The Creeds of Christendom.* New York: Harper, 1870.

_____. *History of the Christian Church.* Grand Rapids: Eerdmans, 1910.

_____. *Nicene and Post-Nicene Fathers.* Series 1 and 2 in 28 volumes, in The Master Christian Library, Version 5. Albany, OR: AGES Software, 1997.

Schnaiter, Samuel E. "Chapter 2—The Inspiration and Preservation of the Text," *God's Providence in the Manuscripts of the New Testament.* unpublished.

Spurgeon, Charles Haddon *Metropolitan Tabernacle Pulpit*, Vol. 35. 1889,.London: Banner of Truth Trust, 1970 reprint.

Sorenson, David H. *Touch Not the Unclean Thing.* Duluth, MN: Northstar Baptist Ministries, 2001.

Surrett, Charles L. *Which Greek Text? The Debate Among Fundamentalists.* Kings Mountain, NC: Surrett Family Publications, 1999.

VanderKam, James C. *The Dead Sea Scrolls Today.* Grand Rapids: Eerdmans Publishing Company, 1994.

Waite, Donald A. *Fundamentalist Mis-Information on Bible Versions.* Collingswood, NJ: The Bible for Today Press, 2000.

Wallace, Daniel B. "Inspiration, Preservation, and New Testament Textual Criticism," in *Grace Theological Journal,* 1992.

Williams, James B., Ed. *From the Mind of God to the Mind of Man: A Layman's Guide to How We Got Our Bible.* Greenville, SC: Ambassador/Emerald Inter., 1999.

We Have God's Word in Our Hands

Randolph Shaylor

When I think of the statement, "We have God's Word in our hands," I frequently recall my fourth grade teacher in a public school. On the corner of her desk, as in virtually all classrooms of that day, rested a Bible. It was always placed atop any other books on that desk. If a student were to place a paper or a book on that Bible he was sure to encounter a stern reprimand. I do not recall that teacher ever reading from that Bible. (I am sure she must have done so, for I do recall that Bible reading was a daily exercise throughout my school days.) That dear lady physically honored, even "preserved," that Book — as an object. It is important that in our concern for preservation of the Bible that our focus be on something greater than physical possession.

The fact that God's Word has been preserved is irrefutable. That is not an abstract theological statement; it is a historic and practical fact. The Bible exists; we can hold it in our hands. Whether it is in the form of ancient manuscripts, a Biblical language text, a historic version, or a contemporary translation, its content is virtually the same as has been handed down for hundreds, even thousands, of years. It is the differences between translations and the texts that underlie them that have given rise to disagreement between professing Bible believers. In some cases those differences seem insignificant. In others they touch crucial matters and raise questions about the trustworthiness of texts and translations. Christians are confronted by the question, "Can I trust my Bible as the Word of God?"

The Basis of Biblical Doctrine

Within that movement of orthodox evangelical Christianity identified as Fundamentalism there are varied views concerning the preservation of the text of the written Word of God. The terms Fundamentalism and Fundamentalist, contrary to the popular use by the news media and some religious writers, had a specific beginning and specific definition. These developed from a series of booklets published from 1910 to 1915, titled *The Fundamentals: A Testimony to the Truth*, and the coining of the term *Fundamentalist* by Curtis Lee Laws in the July 1, 1920 issue of *The Watchman-Examiner*.[1]

While the matter of how our Bible was transmitted to us should be of concern to all professing Christians, it is most ardently discussed among those who are usually identified with the Fundamentalist movement.[2] The doctrine of plenary verbal inspiration is the cornerstone doctrine of Fundamentalism and of most evangelicals. An acceptable view of the preservation of Scripture must be consistent with that historic Biblical position on inspiration. Without adherence to that definition of how God gave us His Word any view of preservation becomes a meaningless debate.

What we believe must be determined by what the Bible says about itself. Our thinking can be guided by doctrinal statements of churches, the teaching of Bible-believing theologians, the findings of students of manuscripts and texts, the work of copyists and translators, and the preaching and teaching of Fundamentalists. All these help us avoid going astray into some novel or humanly devised view, but the final word must be gleaned from the Scriptures. Earlier chapters have presented the views expressed in the writings and preaching of those who became identified with Fundamentalism and of their predecessors in church history.

The early church concerned itself with recognition of the canon of inspired writings and the doctrinal expression of the teachings of those documents. The focus was more upon refutation of teachings that did not accord with the truth revealed in the extant texts than upon defense of the accuracy of those copies. There appears to be little record of attempts to explain the method of transmission and preservation of the Scripture once questions concerning the canon had been resolved. The existence of a manuscript seems to have been satisfactory evidence of its preservation. On the other hand, there is much evidence of ongoing copying and distribution of the various documents that make up the Biblical canon both in the languages of their original writings and in translated form. Some of the manuscripts available to us today indicate that there was concern for accuracy. Marginal annotations and interlinear recording of variant readings lead us to believe that either the scribe who produced a particular manuscript or others who later emended them recognized variants in earlier copies.

The contributors to this volume believe that God gave His Word inerrantly. They also recognize that His Word will not pass away until all is fulfilled. Those truths are taught in Scripture. God has even told us how He gave that Word. Divinely selected holy men were moved (borne-along) by the Holy Spirit[3] as they recorded God's *words* in written form. For one who accepts the statements of the Bible about itself, the expression of the doctrine of inspiration is simply a matter of presenting the content of those statements in an exegeted and organized fashion. However, expressing a doctrine of how that inspired, inerrant, inscripturated revelation is transmitted to us is more complex.

402

The Importance Of Biblical Preservation

Many doctrinal issues impress the average Christian as dry theological matters better left to theologians and seminary professors. In contrast, discussion of the issue of the preservation of the Scriptures and evaluation of translations has reached into the pews. At first among English speakers and now in other languages, these issues produce emotionally charged reaction. This arises because of two valid concerns—authority and trustworthiness.

The Bible claims, and evangelical and fundamental Christians believe, that the Bible has absolute authority over life and eternal destiny. It is the only source of the absolute moral principles necessary for personal life and the proper function of society. It is the only trustworthy message that explains the existence of evil and deliverance from it. In claiming its source, the Bible, expresses its purpose: *All scripture is given by inspiration of God, and is profitable for doctrine, for reproof, for correction, for instruction in righteousness: That the man of God may be perfect, throughly furnished unto all good works.*[4] For Christians, this authoritative message must be preserved for all ages.

Submission to such authority necessitates complete confidence that we have the Scripture that "God breathed." We must have trustworthy copies of the original language Scriptures and those must be transmitted reliably and translated accurately into the various languages of mankind.

The Purpose of Biblical Preservation

Many manuscript copies of ancient writings have come down to us. These include literary works of the ancients, historical records, even routine business records and notes. Some were purposely preserved; others seem to be primarily the result of natural conditions. The fact that the Scriptures are God's message to humanity is sufficient reason for His Word to be purposely preserved. God's purpose for the Scriptures demands consideration of several factors: distribution of the message; fragility of writing materials; correction of error; availability to successive ages.

After the completion of the inerrant originals that we call *autographa*, or autographs, God entrusted His people with the responsibility of copying and distributing those copies of the autographs. The Acts of the Apostles and the epistles imply that multiple copies of certain epistles were made soon after their composition. We read that, although not a part of inspired Scripture, written instructions were sent to several churches.[5] Paul instructed the Colossian believers to share their epistle with the Laodiceans and the Colossians to read the epistle sent to Laodicea.[6] Making of copies for others was the first step in the continuity of Scripture.

The Word of God endures forever but the writing materials used by those penmen of the Word were perishable. Realizing this, devout copyists made copy after copy of those original writings. Over 5000 ancient manuscript portions of the New Testament have been thus far discovered. In addition, very early translations were made from the original languages into the languages of those to whom God's message was taken. As we examine Biblical language manuscripts we immediately discern that God did not exercise the same supernatural "carrying along" of these copyists that He did for penmen of the original writings. Regardless of the devotion, integrity, skill, and care exercised by those copyists no two copies are identical. We are left with one conclusion: just as He entrusted the proclamation of the gospel to human instrumentality, God entrusted the transmission of His Word to human instruments.

From the earliest centuries, even before the Scriptures were complete, some proclaimed a distorted message. Some were sincere in misunderstanding and open to correction. Others were far less godly in their purposes and sought to turn people from the truth. Church history is replete with error that developed through dependence upon tradition or authoritative leaders. The refutation of error and validation of truth could not be accomplished without the faithful transmission of Truth in written form. Prevention and correction of error necessitates the faithful transmission of God's written Word from one generation to another and from one people to another. It is in this transmission that we depend upon God's providence.[7]

This continuation of God's Word, in spite of the difficulty of making perfect reproductions, is often called "preservation." The term "perpetuity," the quality or condition of being perpetual, lasting forever, might be more fitting. By the very nature of God's eternal being His Word must last forever. The details of how God accomplishes the prevention of the "passing away" of His Word are not explained in His Book. In fact, the Scriptures themselves state that God has not chosen to reveal every facet of truth to us.

> Deut 29:29 The secret things belong unto the LORD our God: but those things which are revealed belong unto us and to our children for ever, that we may do all the words of this law.

> Acts 1:7 And he said unto them, It is not for you to know the times or the seasons, which the Father hath put in his own power.

The fact that God has not revealed the details of His workings does not nullify them. We cannot state authoritatively why God has not revealed precisely how He has preserved His Scripture but we can gain insight from some Old Testament events. A few years ago, interest in finding the remains of Noah's ark became so intense that someone called it "Ark Fever." Even though reports of its existence seemed to have some credibility and intensive efforts were made to locate the ark, to this date, no one has been able to present unquestionable evidence of its current existence. Nevertheless, no Bible believer questions that the Biblical flood and the actual building and use of the ark as described in Scripture took place.

We get a glimpse of His wisdom in not preserving the ark when we read of Israel's worship of "Nehushtan," the brazen serpent that God told Moses to raise up in the wilderness.[8] It outlived its purpose and became an idol. Should archeological evidence of Noah's ark be found, some Christians would likely do the same with its fragments. If the original documents of Scripture were available today they could become objects of worship. In His wisdom, God has not allowed the survival of the original writings but He has allowed the survival of thousands of manuscript copies of portions of the New Testament.[9]

VIEWS OF PRESERVATION OF THE SCRIPTURES

The absence of preserved autographs has led to varied attempts to explain how and where preservation is accomplished. Charles Surrett has suggested four distinct points of view on how the Scriptures have been preserved. We could summarize them this way:

- Those who think that God has not verbally preserved His Word.

- Those who believe that God's words have been preserved in a particular English translation and no other.

- Those who believe that God has preserved the words of the autographa in one particular Hebrew and one particular Greek text.

- Those who believe God's Words are preserved in the multiplicity of manuscripts which must be compared to determine the wording of the originals.[10]

Within these categories there are some variations but these will serve as a helpful basis for consideration of differing views of preservation. Evaluation of these views and determination of which best describes the Biblical teaching requires understanding of several key factors.

A Foundation of Faith

Advocates of perfect preservation in either a particular English Version, one Greek text, or one lineage of texts frequently refer to their position as the "faith" view and to all others as "scientific" or "naturalistic" views.[11]

In reality, any view of preservation demands faith, but there are different kinds of faith. One kind of faith has no objective or rational basis. Far too common is the *fideistic* view: A person just "believes." Such is the circular reasoning of Edward Hills' "logic of faith"

> [H]ow do we know that the Textus Receptus is the true New Testament text? We know this through the logic of faith. Because the Gospel is true, the Bible which contains this Gospel was infallibly inspired by the Holy Spirit....
>
> And how do we know that the King James Version is a faithful translation of the true New Testament text? We know this also through the logic of faith.[12]

In contrast, Biblical faith requires an objective foundation. It is grounded upon the actual teaching of Scripture. Biblical faith demands more than proof texts lifted from their contexts. Truth must be understood by proper exegesis of applicable passages. Thus, proper faith in the preservation of God's Word must rest upon the teachings of the Scriptures themselves not upon our emotional confidence in a familiar, traditional, or preferred translation or text.

The Purpose of the Word Of God

The Bible is more than a religious object to be treasured and reverenced. Across the world biblical manuscripts and Bible versions are on display in museums and libraries. These are nice to view and admire but God has given His Word for other purposes, such as: to produce the belief in the Son of God that brings salvation;[13] to bring joy to the Christian life;[14] to correct error;[15] to equip for service.[16] Having the right text or translation is meaningless if God's purposes are not fulfilled. The elementary school teacher mentioned in the opening paragraph of this chapter had the Word of God in her hands. Far more important is the need to have the Word of God in our hearts and in our lives.

An Understanding of Terminology

Much confusion in the discussion of preservation is produced by misuse or misunderstanding of terminology. Pastors and teachers are often imprecise in their ordinary use of important terms. More precision in our use of terminology will enhance our understanding of this important doctrine of preservation of the Scriptures and help keep our focus on the reason God gave His Word.

The Word of God or the Words of God — Confusion arises when Christians assume that they can have the exact words of God in their language. God's inspiration of His Word was in the languages of Hebrew, Aramaic, and

Greek. He breathed out His *words* in those languages. The purpose of inerrant words was to guarantee an inerrant message. When we have the equivalent words in another language we have God's *Word* but we do not have the actual *words* that He gave. When those translated words accurately convey what was given in the Biblical languages they express the *Word of God* and the truth given by inspiration is present. We can properly call a faithful translation the Word of God.

Inspiration and Preservation — These two truths are closely related but different in their meaning. The English word "inspiration" occurs twice in the King James Version. In Job 8, it translates a Hebrew word (*neshamah*) that in more that twenty other occurrences is translated "breath." The New Testament word *theopneustos* in 2 Timothy 3:16 is God's explanation of how He gave His written Word. It is literally God-breathed. God breathed out His *Word* in His *words,* insuring inerrant recording of His revelation. The word "preservation" does not occur in the English of the KJV but "preserve" is used more than twenty times to translate *chayah*, which most commonly refers to continuation of life. Our English word means to keep from destruction or decay. Thus inspiration has to do with the giving of a message and preservation of the continuity of that message. How that continuity is maintained is the question at hand.

Supernatural or Providential — Inspiration required the supernatural enabling of God as He guided the penmen of Scripture. It was a direct action upon each Scripture writer at a particular moment and with a particular function — the giving of His Word inerrantly. It is distinct from God's providence, which is His constant care over His creation to bring about His purposes. Providence refers to God's activity in the affairs of men without direct supernatural intervention. Inspiration was supernatural, a miracle that is not repeated in the transmission or translation of Scripture. In many discussions of preservation, providential is confused with supernatural. A statement of the doctrine of preservation must not confuse the two.

Textual Criticism — The misunderstanding of this term stems from common misuse of the word "criticism." In its general use, criticism is assumed to refer to negative evaluation or fault finding, whereas its primary meaning actually refers to careful evaluation. In the context of biblical manuscripts, textual criticism refers to the careful study of biblical manuscripts in an effort to determine, insofar as possible, the precise wording of the original documents. It does not mean finding fault with a biblical manuscript. Some who wish to avoid the use of this term speak of "collation"[17] of texts. This may give the erroneous impression that variants can be accommodated by simply combining texts.

Corruption — As related to biblical manuscripts, corruption refers to any changes in wording from the original form. Changes may have occurred accidentally or purposely but in the study of biblical manuscripts corruption does not necessarily imply a malicious intent. When some researchers conclude that manuscripts give evidence of corruption they are simply acknowledging the fact that manuscripts vary one from the other. To students of manuscripts it is obvious that, whereas, there is an extremely high degree of unanimity among biblical MSS, no two are identical.

Version — Commonly, this term refers to an account or description that is different from another account or description. It often carries the connotation of inaccuracy or departure from the truth. This has led some to think of one translation as actually "the" Bible and others as only approximations. However, as applied to Bibles, the meaning of "version" is different. It simply means a translation. Traditionally the English translation of the Bible first published in 1611 is called the Authorized Version or King James Version. Because of confusion about the term some have begun to call it the King James Bible and to call other translations, which they reject, versions.

Textus Receptus — The publication of a Greek New Testament by Bonaventure and Abraham Elzevir in 1633 (or 1634) produced a term that has found its way into almost any discussion of Greek New Testaments. Following the custom of the day, the Elzevirs described their publication in promotional terms. Their statement in Latin described their text as the one in general use, received by all, or *Textus Receptus*—received text. In precise use this term refers only to the Elzevir text but it gained common use for its successors. The preservation debate is often confused by use of *Textus Receptus* to refer to a lineage of manuscripts leading up to the Elzevir publication. In some discussions the term is even applied to Old Testament manuscripts. It is sometimes so loosely applied that readers get the erroneous impression that there was in existence from the time of the apostles a single collection of manuscripts that was copied and recopied in a continuous chain until the late nineteenth century. This loose use of the term creates the idea that texts containing any variant readings are to be rejected. Such a view fails to consider the facts that the several Elzevir editions contained variants and that numerous other published editions that varied from the Elzevirs' preceded them. The 1588-89 and 1598 editions by Theodore Beza utilized by the King James translators are often inaccurately called *Textus Receptus*. The text currently published by the Trinitarian Bible Society as the text underlying the King James Version is actually a reconstruction by F. H. A. Scrivener published in 1894 and 1902.[18]

Corollary—Some truths naturally flow from another. A corollary is a proposition that is inferred immediately from a proven proposition with little or no additional proof necessary. Some passages of Scripture do not specifically state the preservation of the Word of God but *indirectly* teach it as a corollary of a stated truth. Care must be exercised lest corollaries be drawn where none exist. The Scriptures teach their preservation but it is illegitimate to suppose a corollary that preservation is promised for a particular text form or translation.

Fundamentalism and Fundamentalist — As previously noted these terms have specific definitions when properly applied to Christianity. The fundamentals are the doctrines agreed upon as the irreducible absolutes of Christianity. Those doctrines form the basis of fellowship and ecclesiastical cooperation. Every contributor to *The Fundamentals* believed that the inspiration and inerrancy of the original writings of the Scriptures were the foundation from which all other fundamentals derive. Chapter one demonstrates that none of those writers believed that claim could be made for specific manuscripts, a published biblical language text, or a translation. *Fundamentalist* became the identifying label for those who held these foundational doctrines of biblical Christianity. Their successors in the movement evaluated texts and translations on the basis of the doctrine of plenary verbal inspiration. Some Fundamentalists preferred one translation; some preferred another. Most agreed that some translations were unreliable but others were considered trustworthy. Similarly, there were differing views about which text was the most accurate representation of the original manuscripts. Nevertheless, they considered one another to be Fundamentalist brethren. As English translations multiplied in the last half of the twentieth century some writers and preachers have taken a quite different position. They insist that differences over texts and translations demand separation and that only those who hold their view are true Fundamentalists.[19]

Much of the debate about preservation and the emotion that accompanies it can be traced to different understandings of terminology. In order to understand the Bible's transmission and preservation, terminology must be used correctly and understandably.

Correct Interpretation Of Scripture

The Bible's promise of its own preservation must be established by statements in the Scriptures themselves. The Scriptures are replete with passages that speak of the purity, certainty, and perpetuity of Word of God, but they must be understood in the light of sound exegetical principles. Chapter 3, "What the Bible Says About Its Preservation," presents exegesis of several passages that are often cited as proof of perfect preservation of the words of the autographs. Some passages are frequently misapplied; some do not actually state, but imply preservation; others teach preservation indirectly, while some teach preservation more directly.

EVALUATING VIEWS OF PRESERVATION

The importance of preservation demands careful evaluation of each. These evaluations do not seek to impugn the motives or judge the spiritual condition of any who hold them. It is important that believers evaluate the basis of each of the positions. Accusation has been made that those who hold views other than perfect preservation in the Textus Receptus do so because they have not studied the writings that defend the TR only or KJV only view.[20] The contributors to this book have carefully studied the writings and presentations of those who hold various views of preservation and have made a sincere effort to honestly and fairly consider all positions on the issue.

FOUR VIEWS OF PRESERVATION OF THE BIBLE

God's "Words" Have Not Been Preserved

A careful distinction must be made when considering this statement. Surrett exercised great care stating, "[T]here are those who think that the Word of God has not been verbally preserved, at least not in one given text or translation."[21] To those who believe that the Bible is of the Word of God, its very existence is testimony to its preservation. Only those who relegate the Bible to something less than revelation from God could believe that God has not preserved His "Word."

The question is whether God has either supernaturally or providentially preserved the actual words of the autographic copies. To those who, as the authors of this book, believe in plenary verbal inspiration and historical-grammatical interpretation, the words of Scripture are vital to exegesis of its truth.

God's Words Preserved in a Particular English Translation and No Other

This view, as proclaimed by various preachers and writers, takes on a number of aberrations. One extreme, held by a few, insists that the King James Version takes precedent over any Greek text. Greek texts should be corrected to conform to the KJV because the translators had some "advanced revelation."[22] Another extreme view is that the New Age Movenment has corrupted all English translations since the KJV (AV).[23] One of the most extreme views is that one cannot be saved using any translation of the Bible other than the KJV.[24] Some insist that the KJV must be translated into other languages so that all peoples can have the "words of God."

God gave (breathed, inspired) His "words" in the languages of His penmen, Hebrew, Aramaic, and Greek. In translations we may have "equivalent" words but not the "identical" words. That distinction is important. The title of Mickey Carter's book, *Things That Are Different Are Not The Same*,[25] is frequently quoted by those who insist that preservation is in the King James Version alone. In explaining why he believes that the KJV is the preserved Word of God, Carter poses five questions which he summarizes in the sixth, "If God did want us to have the word of God, if He did claim to give it to us, if He did claim to inspire it, if He did promise to preserve it, and if He does have the power to preserve it, then where is the Word of God?"[26] Any Bible believer could answer his first five questions with affirmatives, but doing so does not lead to Carter's final answer, "The King James Version." Such a view presents irresolvable problems. Bibles earlier than the KJV differ from the KJV. Are they not the Word of God? Translations into many other languages preceded English translations. Were they not the Word of God?

More common is the view that the King James Version is God's Word preserved for English speaking people. Such a statement has been incorporated into the doctrinal statements of some churches and ministries.[27] If the Word of God is preserved in one translation for English speakers there must be similar preservation in the other languages of mankind.[28]

Identifying one English translation as the preservation of God's "words" is the Protestant equivalent of the Roman Catholic view of the Latin Vulgate. It relies upon tradition and claims as doctrine something that is not stated in Scripture.

God's Words Preserved in One Particular Hebrew Text and One Particular Greek Text

In the study of New Testament text preservation we must distinguish between the Textus Receptus and the Majority or Byzantine text. Proponents of perfect verbal preservation in one particular published text often equate the two. [29] Further confusion is created by use of the term "Traditional Text" as identical to the TR. Distinction between TR and the Majority Text can be seen in any detailed textual study.

Translations of the Old Testament have generally followed those manuscripts called the Masoretic Text that dates from the work of the masoretes, A.D. 500-1000. Many of those who hold this view do not identify a particular form of the Masoretic Text but D. A. Waite is very specific in his opinion:

> There are two basic texts in existence in Hebrew, the false one, edited by Ben Asher, and the true one, edited by Ben Chayyim. The Ben Asher is exhibited in Rudolf Kittel's BIBLIA HEBRAICA (BHK)

(1937) with all of his suggested footnote changes, as well as in the Stuttgart edition of BIBLIA HEBRAICA (BHS) (1967-77) with all of their suggested footnote changes. The true text of Ben Chayyim on which our KJV is based is also available. It is called the Daniel Bomberg edition or the Second Great Rabbinic Bible (1524-25)....

My personal belief is that the **Traditional Masoretic Hebrew text that underlies the KJV is not only the "closest to the original autographs," but that it is IDENTICAL to those original autographs.** I can't prove that to anybody, but I accept it as a matter of personal faith. I believe we have the very Words that God has preserved through the years. I believe every Word in the Hebrew text is God's Word, preserved because He told us He would preserve it for the next 20,000 to 30,000 years—to a "thousand generations.[30] [bold emphasis added]

Those who hold a one text only position are very specific about the New Testament text. They believe that the "received text" or Textus Receptus is the preserved "Words" of God. The most representative of this view is the statement of Waite:

It is my own personal conviction and belief, after studying this subject since 1971, that the WORDS of the received Greek and Masoretic Hebrew texts that underlie the KING JAMES BIBLE are the very WORDS which God has PRESERVED down through the centuries, being the exact WORDS of the ORIGINALS themselves (italic and capital emphasis Waite's).[31]

Ironically,Waite, the founder and president of the Dean Burgon Society actually goes beyond the Society's published statement. In contrast to his personal "conviction and belief" that the words of the "traditional" texts are the "exact" words of the originals themselves, the published position of the Burgon Society holds that these texts are "closest to the original autographs."

We believe that the Texts which are the closest to the original autographs of the Bible are the Traditional Masoretic Hebrew Text for the Old Testament, and the traditional Greek Text for the New Testament underlying the King James Version (as found in "The Greek Text Underlying The English Authorized Version of 1611").[32]

This widely held view is based on several lines of thought: the belief that the Textus Receptus is based on the best manuscripts (MSS); the assumption that there is a continuous lineage of MSS that can be traced through believers who were theologically orthodox; ecclesiastical recognition of a traditional text; and that it is the same as the majority of manuscripts.[33]

When we call the text found in the majority of the Greek New Testament manuscripts the Traditional Text, we signify that this is the text which has been handed down by the God-guided tradition of the Church from the time of the Apostles unto the present day.[34]

A comparison of the TR with the Majority Text makes obvious the fact that the TR is not identical to the majority of manuscripts. Sturtz, a proponent of the Byzantine text type, recognizes this fact:

> Most textual students of the New Testament would agree that the TR was made from a few medieval Greek manuscripts, mostly Byzantine, of Von Soden's Kx strand. They would further concur that the TR, though it brought the students and translators of the New Testament infinitely closer to the originals than the Latin Vulgate, was far from the pure text of the original autographs. Indeed it was the "text received by all" and therefore used by all. However the principal reason for this was probably the fact that it was the only text available to all.[35]

God's Word Preserved in the Totality of Original Language Manuscripts

Adherents to this view believe that God has providentially preserved His Truth. It was given through penmen who were supernaturally protected from error. In God's providence, multiple copies of those inerrant originals were produced. Of all the extant manuscripts no two have been found identical, indicating that they were not supernaturally produced.[36] Just as understanding of the Scriptures requires diligent study and comparison of Scripture with Scripture, identification of the most accurate representation of the autographs requires diligent study and comparison of all manuscripts. The titles Critical Text (because of the detailed evaluation of manuscripts) and Eclectic Text (because it is derived from a combination of multiple manuscripts) are often applied to this approach. In reality, *all* published texts are both critical and eclectic. Even the TR is based on evaluation of several manuscripts, though admittedly only a small number. For this writer, the situation is more easily understood by thinking of the distinctions as evidence based on the number of MSS containing a reading or evidence based on age of the MSS containing a reading.

Years of study and comparison have led to the development of two basic classifications of preservation of original language manuscripts.[37] The majority of the 5000-plus MSS bear a marked similarity to each other and are assumed to have developed from a common source.[38] These are identified as the Majority Text (MT) type or the Byzantine Text type. The large number is seen as evidence for greater confidence in them. The other view that describes a much smaller number of MSS has been variously called the Alexandrian Text type, the minority text type, the Critical Text (CT) or the Eclectic Text. The belief that the date of the production of these MSS is nearer that of the autographs than those of the Byzantine type promotes confidence that these are more accurate representations of the autographs. More recent printed critical texts give greater consideration to the majority text type than some earlier printed texts. Smallman notes, "The two text families are moving closer to each other as scholars on each side of the 'great divide' take more seriously the witness of the entire range of manuscripts."[39] Few people ever read the introductory matter in Greek New Testaments, but *Novum Testamentum Graece* 26th edition (27th edition now available) contains interesting acknowledgements.

> Neither Codex Vaticanus or Codex Sinaiticus (nor even P75 of two hundred years earlier) can provide a guideline we can normally depend on for determining the text. The age of Westcott-Hort and of Tischendorf is definitely over.[40]

Chapter 6 gives examples of the value of considering readings of three different texts, TR, MT, and CT. Chapter 7 makes a comparison of the differences between printed texts of select New Testament books.

The statement that God's Word is preserved in the totality of manuscripts includes those of both the Majority Text family and the minority text family. In reality there is a greater degree of similarity than differences between the families.

In addition to the original languages MSS, ancient versions (translations) are helpful in determining the accurate reading, especially when an apparent copyist error produces a seeming conflict between parallel passages. Michael Harding in chapter 9 illustrates how ancient translations can be helpful. He points out how the Septuagint can help in harmonizing a seeming discrepancy in Scripture. His conclusion recognizes a problem but expresses the faith of one who believes that God has preserved His Word in the totality of ancient MSS, "I believe the original Hebrew text also reads 'thirty,' even though we do not currently possess a Hebrew manuscript with that reading." Perhaps in God's own time we will be allowed to discover that manuscript. Our confidence in the perfection of the *autographa* is not shaken by incomplete understanding of how and where its wording is preserved.

THE RELATIONSHIP OF THE VIEWS OF PRESERVATION TO FUNDAMENTALISM

The King James Version is a treasured translation. Its contributions to the English language, to the British and American nations, and to concepts of liberty as well as to the spiritual development of English speaking lands around the earth are immeasurable. Two volumes that illustrate this appeared in 2001: *In the Beginning: The Story of the King James Bible and How It Changed a Nation, a Language, and a Culture* by Alister McGrath[41] and *Wide as the Waters: The Story of the English Bible and the Revolution It Inspired* by Benson Bobrick.[42] Prior to the work of Wycliffe and Tyndale the English language was considered barbaric and not worthy of use in education or law and certainly not in Christian worship. The language of the educated and noble was Latin and/or French. In the 250 years following the Wycliffe translation, the English language gained acceptance for use in worship and education.[43] Translations of the Bible, particularly the Geneva and KJV, were major contributors to this. "The King James Bible, along with the works of William Shakespeare, is regularly singled out as one of the most foundational influences on the development of the modern English language."[44] Rather than the KJV literary excellence being derived from the literary quality of the period, it led in the development of that quality.

The King James Version has been the primary English translation for 350 years. Most Fundamentalists use it routinely. The contributors to this book use it in preaching, for memorization and in private study. The fact that it is supplemented by other conservative translations in no way disparages its value. For those who have used it all their lives, there is a strong attachment. They have either learned the meaning of archaic terms or learned to just skip over them. Generations of preachers have supplemented the KJV with Greek texts and study aids to clarify difficult translations. The King James Version is a very important translation, but just a translation, although one of the factors contributing to its longevity is that people forgot that it was a translation.

In contrast, there are many devout, sincere, well-meaning Bible believers who believe that the Scriptures are preserved only in the Textus Receptus and/or the King James Version. Some who hold this view insist that their position is true Fundamentalism, that any other is heresy, and advocates of any other position are apostate. They reason that since the Bible demands separation from apostasy, Fundamentalists must separate from those who do not restrict themselves to the TR and KJV.[45] If that were true the men who were originally designated by that term would have to be separated from Fundamentalism.

415

Chapters 1 and 2 demonstrate, by their own words, the fact that those who were the first to be known as "Fundamentalists," as well as earlier orthodox evangelical Christians, did not restrict themselves to either the KJV or the TR. From the publication of *The Fundamentals* forward, they stressed the fact that inspiration was not claimed for any translation. In their preaching and writing, many utilized translations made from the critical texts such as the English Revised Version and the American Standard Version. Among Bible believers, some did have a strong disagreement about those translations. Most Fundamentalists reacted negatively to the Revised Standard Version but many participated in the translation and publication of the Berkley Version, the New American Standard Bible, and later the New King James Version and projects like the Amplified Bible. Fundamentalists separated from the apostasy of denying the inspiration of the Scriptures, but neither early nor mid-twentieth century Fundamentalists made the use of a conservative "modern" translations or the "critical" text a basis of separation. In reality, it is those who call for separation over this issue and brand use of other translations as heresy who have moved outside the circle of historic Fundamentalism.

Those who recognize that no translation is perfect actually continue the teaching of the those originally called Fundamentalists. Those who believe that the Textus Receptus, the Majority Text, or the Critical Text are not perfectly preserved copies of the autographs but valid efforts to publish an accurate text continue the position of orthodox Christians throughout history.

EVALUATING AND CHOOSING A TRANSLATION

When there is only one, or only one widely used, translation in a particular language, choice of translation does not become issue. Even when revisions offer obvious improvements to translation into a given language, little confusion develops. Proliferation of versions in a particular language makes choice more difficult. Most English-speaking believers are aware of the multiplicity of versions that have been produced in the latter part of the twentieth century. Fewer are aware that there were numerous English translations produced during the sixteenth and seventeenth centuries. In both that period and in the present, professing Christians have disagreed about translations. Some believers have solved this problem by declaring only one translation to be the Word of God. They have relied on some church official or the wisdom of very vocal spokesmen to decree which versions should be used. One goal of this book has been to demonstrate that such a position is neither biblical nor historic Fundamentalism.

Many factors affect Christians' decisions about translations, especially decisions about the best translation(s). Some are valid considerations; others are suspect.

Experience And Emotion

Any true believer has had experience with the Word of God. Scripture tells us that "faith cometh by hearing and hearing by the Word of God." One who has received Jesus Christ as Savior and Lord did so as the Holy Spirit applied God's Word. That Word may have been cited or quoted by one who personally told him the plan of salvation. That experience with God's Word may have come through personal reading of the Bible itself or from some verses printed in a book or tract. That experience may have come as some preacher proclaimed the Word of God. It is natural for a believer to have confidence in the translation that was used by the Spirit of God to bring him to saving faith. As a person regularly reads a particular translation, familiarity, affinity, and confidence for that translation develops. Even when weaknesses of that translation are encountered the reader often simply seeks help from other translations or commentaries but retains an emotional attachment to the familiar version. Experience and emotion are not valid criteria for judging a translation.

History and Tradition

The history of a particular translation should not be minimized. Some translations have enjoyed long and continued use. During the history of a translation, readers become acquainted with its strengths, sometimes with its weaknesses, and become discerning about its use. When acceptance among varied groups of believers has been long and widespread, readers develop a confidence that this version is the Word of God. Theologians, linguists, and translators, as well as average Christians, have opportunity to evaluate a familiar version for accuracy and understandability. Tradition develops around such a long revered translation and history is often accepted as validation of its reliability. Translations that have a long history and tradition are not quickly displaced. Even slight changes in favorite passages "just do not sound right" when read from a different translation. Some other passages lose some impact when the same truth is expressed but not in the familiar words. We expect the 23rd Psalm to contain, "Yea though I walk through the valley of the shadow of death, I will fear no evil.... I will dwell in the house of the Lord forever." Other words, no matter how accurate, just do not "sound like the Word of God." Tradition alone is not a reliable basis for choice, but evaluation that develops throughout the history of a translation can be of great help in decisions about a translation.

Recommendation And Popularity

Preachers, teachers, theologians, commentators, and Christian friends often recommend versions that they find especially helpful. Believers often rely on such recommendations.

Intensive advertising and promotion by Christian booksellers play an important role in the popularity of a particular translation. As I was revising this section, a new catalog from a national book distributor arrived in my mailbox. In addition to twelve pages listing and/or promoting various text and special purpose Bibles, many offered in various translations, two full pages were devoted to different specialized editions of one popular translation. Christians often purchase a particular translation in response to such advertising or on the recommendation of a some friend or bookstore employee.

A version may become widely used because it is recommended by a trusted or popular preacher/teacher or because it is highly advertised. Sometimes such promotion becomes so intense that Bible readers become convinced of the primacy of that version. Criticism of such promotion and advertising may or may not be valid. Pecuniary gain may be the primary interest of some publishers but others may be genuinely convinced of the value of their product. If the recommendation of the pastor, preacher, or teacher is based on valid criteria, it can be helpful.

Purpose and Use

Choice of translation is directly related to purposes: the purpose of the translator(s) and the purpose of the user. Some translations have been produced in an attempt to justify an aberrant doctrinal position. Some have been produced with the goal of supporting the popular thinking of the day. Others have been developed for more legitimate purposes such as the clarification of nuances of meaning expressed in the biblical languages, to take into account the changes in language, or to simplify vocabulary for readers with limited ability.

Some translations are not well fitted for oral reading. An interlinear or an amplified version, while beneficial for preparation of an expositor's sermon or a teacher's lesson, could be very confusing for congregational reading. A very formal equivalency translation, indispensable for the pastor's preparation and the believer's personal study, may not be easily understood in children's church. Those who are just acquiring the English language may have difficulty with a formal or older translation. (In my own congregation some Korean immigrants wrestled with the problem of trying to follow my reading of the King James Version in their Korean-English Bible that is a contemporary version. Similarly, ministering to Russian speaking Jews who are just learning English necessitates an English translation similar to the English they are learning.) A single translation may not fit all uses.

Understandability and Comprehension

Translation involves important factors about spoken languages. Living languages undergo constant change, not only in vocabulary, but also in grammar and syntax. English grammar, or the grammar of any language, is not a set of principles that has been enacted for the creation of the language but an attempt to describe how the speakers of that language use it. Standard English is "standard" because that is the way that careful speakers and writers use the language. Subtle changes are constantly taking place. In our lifetime, things that were once considered sub-standard have become common usage. We are tempted to say that the language has deteriorated, but that may not be true. Some changes may be an improvement; others may just be change.

A Bible translation must be faithful to the Greek and Hebrew text, but it must also be understood by the target audience. We do not really communicate in individual words but in groups of words that function together. A reader may recognize words and even phrases, clauses and sentences, but unless he comprehends the meaning of those words, phrases, sentences, and paragraphs he is not really reading. God inspired words, but He also inspired how those words function together to convey meaning. Our goal is to have a translation that fulfills God's purpose of conveying His meaning to the reader.

Theory and Method of Translation

Translations have generally followed one of two theories, formal (literal) or dynamic (meaning-based) equivalency. James D. Price, a Bible translator as well as a recognized Hebrew authority, reminds us, "A translation is no better than the theory on which it is based. A sound theory produces a sound translation. Yet Bible translators are not agreed on what constitutes 'sound translation theory' for Bible translation."[46] Formal translations attempt to transform from one language to another, retaining the structure of the original language. Dynamic equivalency translations focus on naturalness in the translation.[47]

The historic approach to translation is that of formal equivalency, sometimes called the literal method. Translations that use this approach have some passages that are difficult to understand. It is impossible for a rigidly word-for-word rendering to always convey the meaning of the source language. Differences in language structure, idioms, euphemisms and other linguistic considerations necessitate some flexibility. Even the King James Version, a formal equivalence translation, contains some wordings that might be called

419

"dynamic equivalences." The familiar "God forbid," is the way the 1611 translators expressed an intense negative. The Hebrew and Greek words that mean "God" and "forbid" are not present in the original language texts. Consideration must be given to the linguistics of the receptor language but in doing so accuracy must not be sacrificed. Chapter 8, "The Autographa Yet Speaketh," discusses the problems of maintaining theological accuracy and giving due consideration to linguistics.

Paraphrases, expanded translations, and meaning-based translations attempt to convey meaning without retaining the structure of Greek and Hebrew. Many of the newer translations focus primarily on "naturalness" in the translation. This may increase the understanding of the wording of the translation but may diminish the level of accuracy. When that occurs, the purpose of translation is not accomplished.

We previously described proper translation as expressing the inspired words in equivalent words of the receptor language. Price points out that the goal is not "accuracy or understandability," but "accuracy and understandability."[48] What is needed is not formal equivalence or dynamic equivalence but "complete equivalence."[49] He now believes this theory of translation can be more accurately described as "optimum equivalence" because of the danger of interpreting "complete" as "absolute."[50]

An understanding of the theory of translation is a very important consideration when using a particular translation. This is especially true when using expanded translations, paraphrases, and meaning-based translations.

Accuracy and Reliability

Accuracy and reliability are by far the most important considerations. By accuracy we mean that the translation expresses in the reader's language, as precisely as possible, the meaning of the original language contained in both words and structure. By reliability we mean the translation can be depended upon to be consistently faithful to the original languages. Some translations may be accurate in some portions but not consistently so. This may call into question their trustworthiness as a whole.

WHERE IS THE WORD OF GOD PRESERVED?

The Word of God is preserved. The words that God gave are pure words; they are without error whether they speak of theology, morality, science, history, or the mundane matters of day-to-day life. Because we do not have the actual copies penned by the God-guided "holy men of old" we must rely on the most accurate reproduction of those words that can be discerned. We are thankful that in the providence of God we have been able to locate multiple manuscripts that have been transmitted from original copies. We are also thankful that in His providence He has enabled men to learn the languages that He used and to develop the skills necessary to compare and evaluate copies.

It would be very satisfying if we could point to one manuscript, one group of manuscripts, one translation, or one trail of translations and say this is where God has preserved his Word. But when we consider the fact that God has been pleased to use a multiplicity of manuscripts and translations to reach men with the message of salvation and righteousness we realize that we cannot identify one document or one translation alone as "it."

Whether we believe that the most accurate copies are those that comprise what has been called the Byzantine or Majority Text "family" or those that comprise what has been called the Alexandrian or minority text "family," all exist because at some time they were once a part of someone's Bible. Since no two are identical we must make comparison of the MSS within a family and those from the other family or families. Even the Textus Receptus was developed by making such comparisons. For this reason we believe that the correct reading is found within the totality of manuscripts.

Of course, the average Christian will not become a "textual critic" or fluent in biblical languages. We must resist the tendency to evaluate the accuracy of one translation by another translation even when that translation has been long revered. We can read about the textual base, the translation theory, and the purpose of a given translation. We can learn about the translators: their backgrounds, their theological positions, and their goals in translating. We can utilize language helps that compare the translation with the original languages. We can seek the evaluation of those who hold a sound conservative theological position and have devoted themselves to the study of languages, biblical documents, and the content of God's Word.

Bruce Lackey, known for his support of the King James Version, made this important recognition:

> Any correctly translated scripture, in any version, would be correctly called the inspired Word of God, if it is from uncorrupted texts. Many verses in the Vaticanus (et. al.) are exactly the same as in the Textus Receptus. They are truly God's Word. It is those places where scripture has been changed which are to be rejected. Likewise, John 1:1 reads exactly the same in the King James and The New American Standard Version. We cannot condemn a verse merely on the basis of

the book or manuscript in which it is found. The issue is whether the verse is correct.[51]

Lackey erroneously uses the KJV as his basis of comparison rather than the original language text but correctly recognizes that accurately translated passages should not be condemned. To this we would add this fact: we should not condemn a text or a translation merely on the basis that it is not identical to the Textus Receptus or the King James Version. Neither should we condemn the TR or the KJV because it is not identical to another text or translation. Likewise a particular version should not be condemned due to a poor translation of a particular passage. Some Fundamentalists strongly advocate the TR and the KJV but do not make them a point of contention and separation. They may personally use only the KJV but do not break fellowship with believers who use another conservative translation. The KJV still holds a place of honor and usefulness even among those who utilize other texts and translations.

When we use a faithful conservative translation such as the King James Version, New King James Version, the New American Standard Version, or another version of demonstrated accuracy *we can trust our Bible as the Word of God*. We can be confident that **we have God's Word in our hands**.

---

[1]The origin and use of these terms is widely recognized by writers both within and without the movement. For a detailed discussion see "What is Fundamentalism?" in James Barr, *Fundamentalism* (Philadelphia: Westminster Press, 1977, 1978), pp. 1-10.

[2]For a good brief overview of the definition, development, and current stance of Fundamentalism as a movement see Fred Moritz, *Contending for the Faith*. (Greenville, SC: Bob Jones University Press), 2000.

[3]2 Peter 1:21

[4]2 Timothy 3:16, 17

[5]Acts 15:23

[6]Colossians 4:16

[7]In discussions of the preservation of the Scriptures the distinctions between *inspiration* and *preservation* are often clouded if not confused. *Inspiration* refers to God's direct supernatural giving of the original copies of biblical revelation. Chapter 9 contains a thorough exposition of the primary passages related to inspiration. Preservation refers to God's use of what He has created to bring to pass what He has determined. See the introductory statement, "We Have the Word of God."

[8]Numbers 21:1-9   God punished Israel for speaking against Moses and God by sending "fiery" serpents among them. When many died Israel cried out for deliverance. God instructed Moses to make and raise on a pole a brass serpent. When people looked by faith to it they were healed. Hezekiah destroyed it because the people of Judah had made it an object of worship by burning incense to it (2 Kings 18:4).

[9]Similar statements could be made about the Old Testament writings but the contemporary debate seems to focus on the New Testament.

[10]Charles L. Surrett. *Which Greek Text? The Debate Among Fundamentalists* (Kings Mountain, NC: Surrett Family Publications, 1999) pp. 3, 4.

[11]Cf. David H. Sorenson, "The Double Steam of Biblical Texts" in *Touch Not the Unclean Thing* (Duluth, MN: North Star Baptist Ministries) 2001. Numerous others take a similar position. See Greg Mutch, *Approaches to the Text Issue: Faith, Scientific, or Extremist*, video produced by Pensacola Christian College, 1999.

[12]Edward F. Hills, *The King James Version Defended*, electronic edition, http://www.jesus-is-lord.com/kjvdefen.htm.

[13]John 20:30, 31

[14]1 John 1:4

[15]1 Corinthians 3:1

[16]2 Timothy 3:17

[17]Dictionary definitions of criticism and collation are quite similar. Cf. Meriam-Webster's Collegiate Dictionary, 10th edtion; For Windows (Dallas, TX: Zane Publishing Company. 1995). Gayle Riplinger, who rejects all translations other than the King James Version, in referring to any favorable comparison of manuscripts uses the term "collation" to refer to what others call "textual criticism." Apparently, she invents a distinction that dictionaries do not make. (G. A. Riplinger, *New Age Bible Versions* (Monroe Falls, OH: AV Publications, 1993) p. 468.

[18]*H KAINH ΔIAΘHKH, The New Testament: The Greek Text Underlying the English Authorized Version of 1611* (London: The Trinitarian Bible Society, 1977), preface.

[19]Sorenson, pp. 3-5, describes three characteristics of Fundamentalism as orthodoxy of doctrine, separation from apostasy, and separation from the world. We agree that these three characteristics developed within the movement but we must emphasize the fact that the original focus of Fundamentalism was upon orthodoxy of doctrine and the goal of turning denominations, institutions, and organizations back to orthodoxy. Approaches to separation from apostasy took varied forms and there was no agreed upon criteria for separation from the world. Insistence that use

of any text other than the Textus Receptus or one from the majority text family is a departure from the position of historic Fundamentalism. Sorenson's identification of certain texts and translations with apostasy and demand for separation over them rests upon preference rather than sound exegesis and the history of Fundamentalism. (See Sorenson's chapter "Applying the Principle of Separation to the Textual Issue," pp. 162-184.) Others who hold similar views are included in the bibliography for this chapter. In contrast, Surrett sets forth a much more irenic view (pp. 117).

[20]Sorenson, pp. 11,12.

[21]Surrett, p. 3.

[22]Peter S. Ruckman, *A Christian's Handbook of Manuscript Evidence* (Pensacola, FL: Pensacola Bible Press, 1970), pp. 124, 126, 137.

[23]Riplinger, p. 1. Riplinger's theme has been adopted by many defenders of the primacy of the KJV.

[24]Jack Hyles, *False Bibles: An Enemy of Soul Winning* (Hammond, IN: Hyles Anderson Publishers, 1993) pp. 46, 47. Electronic Edition at http://home.attbi.com/~markharshman1/f_bibles.htm.

[25]Mickey Carter, *Things That Are Different Are Not The Same* (Haines City, FL: Landmark Baptist Press), 1993.

[26]Ibid., p. 76.

[27]Many unfounded, illogical, and erroneous arguments are proposed as proof of the King James Version only view, such as: it is the seventh English translation fulfilling Ps. 12:6 (faulty exegesis); of all English translations only the KJV does not have copyright protection (misunderstanding of copyright law and its earlier forms); the KJV is on a lower reading level any other translation (faulty measurement of reading difficulty level); all great revivals have been produced through the use of the King James Version (inadequate knowledge of church history); the KJV translators were superior in scholarship to and can never be equaled by any other translators. (idolization of 17th century Anglican scholars.)

[28]James Sightler insists that the King James Bible is inspired in the same sense as the autographs and states, "The Lord's ministry in that land of many languages foreshadows the very early translation of the Bible." "The King James Bible Is Inspired," *The Baptist Bible Trumpet*, February, 2003, p. 4.

[29]Surrett, p. 4.

[30]D. A. Waite, *The Four-Fold Superiority Of The King James Version* (Collingswood, NJ: The Bible for Today, 1992) Electronic edition http://www.wayof-life.org.

[31]D. A. Waite, *Defending the King James Bible* (Collingswood, NJ: The Bible For Today Press, 1992), pp. 48-49.

[32]*The Dean Burgon Society's Statement on the Providential Preservation of The Holy Scriptures,* http://www.deanburgonsociety.org.

[33]The TR differs in numerous places from the majority of Byzantine texts. See chapter 4.

[34]Hills, ibid.

[35]Harry A. Sturtz, *The Byzantine Text-Type and New Testament Textual Criticism* (Northville, MI: Biblical Viewpoints Publications, 1984).

[36]Hills, a leading proponent of preservation in the TR recognizes this problem. Hills, ibid.

[37]This is a simplification of a very complex area of study. At various times in the history of textual criticism more and different classifications have been made. The ideas of four distinct text types as proposed by Westcott and Hort and other multi-type classifications have largely been abandoned.

[38]The generally held view that the majority of the extant MSS bear this marked similarity is are based on studies that have been done over generations but as yet are not as complete as desired. Advocates of both the majority/Byzantine/traditional text (Pickering) and the critical text (Aland) recognize the problem. Pickering (advocate of the "traditional" text) cites Aland's (advocate of the "critical text") recognition of this problem: "...the main problem of NT textual criticism lies in the fact that little more than their actual existence is known of most of the manuscripts thus far identified...." [K. Aland, "The Greek New Testament: its Present and Future Editions," *Journal of Biblical Literature*, LXXXVII (1968), pp. 183-184. Quoted in Wilbur Pickering, *The Identity of the New Testament Text*, Nashville: Thomas Nelson Publishers, 1977,1980) p. 149.]

[39]William Smallman, "Printed Greek Texts" in *From the Mind of God to the Mind of Man*, ed. James B. Williams. (Greenville, SC: Ambassador-Emerald International, 1999), p. 182.

[40]Eberhard Nestle, Erwin Nestle, Kurt Aland, et. al. *Novum Testamentum Graece*, 26th edition (Stuttgart: Deutche Bibelstiftung, 1979), p. 43.

[41](New York: Doubleday) 2001.

[42](New York: Simon and Schuster) 2001.

[43]McGrath, pp. 32-36.

[44]McGrath, p. 253.

[45]This is the thesis of David Sorenson. Sorenson, passim.

[46]James D. Price, *Complete Equivalence in Bible Translation* (Nashville: Thomas Nelson Publisher, 1987), p. 5.

[47]Language into which something is being translated.

[48]Price, pp. 5-6.

[49]Price, p. 6.

[50]Arthur Farstad, *The New King James Version in the Great Tradition* (Nashville: Thomas Nelson Publishers, 1989), p. 128. Also e-mail from James D. Price.

[51]Bruce Lackey, "Inspiration and Translation," *O Timothy,* Vol. 9, No. 11, 1992.

BIBLIOGRAPHY

Barr, James. *Fundamentalism*. Philadelphia: Westminster Press, 1977, 1978.

Beacham, Roy E. and Kevin T. Bauder, eds. *One Bible Only?* Grand Rapids: Kregel, 2001.

Beale, David O. *In Pursuit of Purity: American Fundamentalism Since 1850*. Greenville, SC: Unusual Publications, 1986.

Bobrick, Benson. *Wide as the Waters: The Story of the English Bible and the Revolution It Inspired*. New York: Simon and Schuster, 2001.

Bradley, Bill. *Purified Seven Times*. Claysburg, PA: Revival Fires! Publishing, 1998.

Brotzman, Ellis R. *Old Testament Textual Criticism, A Practical Introduction*. Grand Rapids, MI: Baker Books, 1994.

Bruce, F. F. *The Books and the Parchments: Some Chapters on the Transmission of the Bible*. Westwood, NJ: Fleming H. Revell Company, 1963.

_____. *The New Testament Documents*. Grand Rapids: Eerdmans, 1985.

Carter, Mickey. *Things That Are Different Are Not The Same*. Haines City, FL: Landmark Baptist Press, 1993.

Cloud, David. *Myths About Modern Versions*. Oak Harbor, WA: Way of Life Literature, 1999.

Custer, Stewart. *Does Inspiration Demand Inerrancy*. Nutley, NJ: The Craig Press, 1968.

Η ΚΑΙΝΗ ΔΙΑΘΗΚΗ, The New Testament: The Greek Text Underlying the English Authorized Version of 1611. London: The Trinitarian Bible Society, 1977.

Feinberg, Charles L., ed. *The Fundamentals for Today*. Grand Rapids: Kregel, 1958.

Farstad, Arthur L. *The New King James Version in the Great Tradition*. Nashville: Thomas Nelson Publisher, 1989.

Fuller, David Otis, ed. *Which Bible*. Grand Rapids: Grand Rapids International Publications, 1972.

427

Gipp, Samuel C. *The Answer Book.* Shelbyville, TN: Bible and Literature Missionary Foundation, 1989.

Greenlee, Harold. *Introduction to New Testament Criticism.* Grand Rapids: Erdmans, 1964.

Gromaki, Robert G. *Translations on Trial.* Cedarville, OH: Cedarville College, 1996.

_____. *An Understandable History of the Bible.* n. p., 1987.

Hills, Edward F. *The King James Version Defended.* Des Moines: Christian Research Press, 1956. Electronic edition, http://www.jesus-is-lord.com/kjvdefen.htm.

Hodges, Zane, and Arthur Farstad. *The Greek New Testament According to the Majority Text.* Nashville, Thomas Nelson Publishers, 1982.

Hodges, Zane C. "Rationalism and Contemporary New Testament Textual Criticism," *Bibliotheca Sacra,* January 1971.

Hyles, Jack. *False Bibles: An Enemy of Soul Winning.* Hammond, IN: Hyles Anderson Publishers, 1993. Electronic Edition, http://home.attbi.com/~markharshman1/f_bibles.htm.

Hymers, R. L. *Ruckmanism Exposed.* Los Angeles: Fundamentalist Baptist Tabernacle, 1998.

Lackey, Bruce. "Inspiration and Translation," *O Timothy,* Vol. 9, No. 11, 1992.

Lightner, Robert P. *A Biblical Case for Total Inerrancy.* Grand Rapids: Kregel, 1978.

McGrath, Alister. *The Story of the King James Bible and How it Changed a Nation, a Language and a Culture.* New York: Doubleday, 2001.

Metzger, Bruce M. *The Bible in Translation.* Grand Rapids: Baker Academic, 2001.

_____. *The Text of the New Testament: Its Transmission, Corruption, and Restoration.* New York: Oxford, 1968.

Miller, Edward. *A Guide to Textual Criticism of the New Testament.* Collingswood, NJ: The Dean Burgon Society, 1979.

Moorman, Jack. *Forever Settled: A Survey of the Documents and History of the Bible.* Collingswood, NJ: Dean Burgon Society Press, 1999.